D1379676

TRAGIC PLOTS

To my students, who asked the questions

Tragic Plots
A New Reading from Aeschylus to Lorca

Felicity Rosslyn

Studies in European Cultural Transition

Volume Nine

General Editors: Martin Stannard and Greg Walker

Ashgate

Aldershot • Burlington USA• Singapore• Sydney

Published by
Ashgate Publishing Limited
Gower House
Croft Road
Aldershot
Hants GU11 3HR
England

Ashgate Publishing Company
131 Main Street
Burlington
Vermont 05401–5600
USA

Ashgate website: http://www.ashgate.com

British Library Cataloguing-in-Publication data

Rosslyn, Felicity
Tragic Plots: a new reading from Aeschylus to Lorca – (Studies in European
    cultural transition; v. 9)
    1. Tragedy – History and criticism
    I. Title
    809.2'512

Library of Congress Cataloging-in-Publication data

Rosslyn, Felicity, 1950–
    Tragic Plots : a new reading from Aeschylus to Lorca / Felicity Rosslyn.
    p. cm. – (Studies in European cultural transition ; v. 9)
    Includes bibliographical references and index.
    1. Tragedy – History and criticism. I. Title. II. Series.

    PN1892 R67 2000
    809.2'512–dc21   00–063962

ISBN 0 7546 0247 8

Typeset by Pat FitzGerald and printed on acid-free paper
Printed and bound in Great Britain by MPG Books Ltd, Bodmin, Cornwall

Contents

General Editors' Preface   vi
Preface   vii
Acknowledgements   viii

Introduction   1

Part One: Greek Tragedy   7

1   Aeschylus   9

2   Sophocles   32

3   Euripides   54

Part Two: Renaissance Tragedy   95

4   Revenge and the Machiavel   97

5   Shakespeare   120

Part Three: Modern Tragedy   171

6   Ibsen and Strindberg   173

7   Lorca   196

Part Four: Conclusion   215

8   Tragedy and the Historical Moment   217

Bibliography   242

Index   246

General Editors' Preface

The European dimension of research in the humanities has come into sharp focus over recent years, producing scholarship which ranges across disciplines and national boundaries. Until now there has been no major channel for such work. This series aims to provide one, and to unite the fields of cultural studies and traditional scholarship. It will publish the most exciting new writing in areas such as European history and literature, art history, archaeology, language and translation studies, political, cultural and gay studies, music, psychology, sociology and philosophy. The emphasis will be explicitly European and interdisciplinary, concentrating attention on the relativity of cultural perspectives, with a particular interest in issues of cultural transition.

Martin Stannard
Greg Walker
University of Leicester

Preface

This book was set in motion over twenty years ago when, as a fledgling teacher, I was invited to lecture on 'The Tragic Play'. How to define this genre has preoccupied me ever since, and many friends and colleagues have helped me clarify the views expressed here. I thank them all, for their sense of the importance of the subject and for the time they gave to reading various drafts of the book. In particular, I am grateful for the early responses of Tess Cosslett, Lee Horsley and A.E. Sharpe, and for the comments of Gordon Campbell, Nieves Díaz, P.E. Easterling, D. Gervais, W.F.T. Myers, Jan Parker, Mark Rawlinson, Roger Warren and Blair Worden on subsequent versions. G.F. Parker read the final draft with the kind of critical sympathy authors dream of.

My greatest debt as a critic is owed to the late H.A. Mason, who taught me how to think about Greek drama and Shakespeare in the same language. He also helped me understand how differently tragic dilemmas look from the male and female point of view. He would have disagreed with many of my conclusions, but I hope he would have assented to my search for the 'truly human' position somewhere between the two. The University of Leicester allowed me to set up my own tragedy course, and gave me study leave on several occasions to write this book. Working for the Cambridge Tripos 'tragedy paper' first helped me frame the subject, so I am also very grateful to Jean Gooder for inviting me to return and try out my ideas on her students. I would not have discovered Lorca without the prompting of her seminars.

A strong influence on the direction of the argument of the book has been the dismemberment of former Yugoslavia in the 1990s. The resurgence of ethnicity there and its effect on the structures of civilization gave me direct insight into the fascination and danger of blood ties, particularly in Sarajevo, where I taught and had many friends. I am all the more indebted to those who listened to the argument of the book and reinforced its emphasis on civility and the law with their own stories, Jasna Levinger, Zvonko Radeljković, Rada Šević, and the late, courageous, Ana Radin.

My greatest personal debt is inevitably to my husband, Piotr Kuhiwczak, and to my children, Lidia and Adam. Parents often add 'without whom this book would have been finished faster', but in my case it would have been a completely different book: what I have learnt from watching them both grow up is inscribed on every page. My husband, meanwhile, not only continued to bring home the bacon, but to cook it. He put democratic justice into domestic life and demonstrated that androgyny is a goal that can be approached from either direction.

F.R.
Leicester, January 2000

Acknowledgments

I am grateful to the following for permission to reproduce copyright material:

The heirs of Federico García Lorca for extracts from *Bodas de sangre*, *Yerma*, and *La casa de Bernarda Alba* by Federico García Lorca from *Obras completas* (Galaxia Gutenberg, 1996 edn) © Herederos de Federico García Lorca.

Translation of *Bodas de sangre* and *Yerma* by Gwynne Edwards © Gwynne Edwards and Herederos de Federico García Lorca.

Translation of *La casa de Bernarda Alba* and *Yerma* by Michael Dewell and Carmen Zapata © Michael Dewell, Carmen Zapata, and Herederos de Federico García Lorca. All rights reserved.

Oxford University Press, for extracts from: *Henrik Ibsen: Four Major Plays* © 1961 by James McFarlane; *Sophocles: Three Tragedies*, © 1962 by Oxford University Press; Chekhov, *The Cherry Orchard*, © 1964 by Ronald Hingley; and for permission to reprint material in Chapter 6 which was published as 'Lorca and Greek Tragedy' in *Cambridge Quarterly*, 29 (2000), 215–36, © by Felicity Rosslyn.

Random House, for extracts from *Medea* © 1944 John Lane, The Bodley Head.

The University of Chicago Press, for extracts from: *The Bacchae*, © 1959 by The University of Chicago Press; *Hippolytus*, © 1942 by The University of Chicago Press; *The Oresteia*, © 1953 by The University of Chicago Press.

Introduction

Drama is the most collaborative of all literary experiences. The audience and the drama are two sides of the same event, and the audience can withdraw its cooperation at any time. It is this that gives theatre its electric charge, even in these days of state subsidies and well-behaved audiences. An event takes place which anyone in the auditorium is free to interfere with; and the fact that almost no one ever does makes the theatre the location of something quite rare, a contract to undergo an intimate experience in company. And because no one knows who else is making the contract at the same time – who else is sitting there, who is standing on stage – we may discover we cannot know by ourselves: what we have in common with these others that makes us all laugh or cry at the same time.

If this is true of any kind of play it is most strikingly true of tragedy. The playwright who offers to keep us sitting still, contributing our full attention to his potentially harrowing theatrical experience, must feel that he knows something we all, in some sense, need to know. We are collaborating with him as he dwells on the most disturbing of all questions: what is the worst that can happen to us, being human? The tragic dramatist takes advantage of the social contract that brings us together in his theatre to take us down beneath our daily preoccupations; we pass through distractions to the truth we need, in the spirit of Matthew Arnold's pointed distinction:

> Below the surface-stream, shallow and light,
> Of what we *say* we feel – below the stream
> As light, of what we *think* we feel – there flows
> With noiseless current strong, obscure and deep,
> The central stream of what we feel indeed.[1]

In this book I attempt to trace the 'central stream' of feeling in tragic dramas across time and cultural barriers. If it is true that tragedies are the outcome of an unusual collaboration between the audience and the dramatist, it ought to be possible to analyse what both sides are implicitly saying: what the audience needs to have expressed, and what the artist does to meet that need. The novelty of this approach is in assuming that the plays themselves are the evidence, if we look at them hard enough; that the plots themselves tell us which problems the audience is most preoccupied with. But we have to be alive to the difference between what they *say* they are about, what they *think* they are about, and what we sense they really *are* about, because the playwright may be as unclear about his real motive for writing as is his audience. 'Authenticity' and 'truth' are two of the most slippery words in the language, and when 'life and death' are thrown in for good measure we are in an area of profound psychological ambivalence. The prestige of tragedy and the emotions associated with it are so great that it is easy to take the

---

[1]   'Below the Surface-Stream', *The Poetical Works of Matthew Arnold* (London: Oxford University Press, 1942), p. 483.

desire to write tragedy for tragedy itself, both for writers and audiences. In this book I assume that tragedies that cut deeply and accurately into the human condition are actually quite rare, and get written under quite specific cultural circumstances. What those circumstances are becomes clearer as we journey farther from the Greek theatre towards our own. Most of the rest of the time the appetite for watching tragedy does not disappear – far from it; but it has to satisfy itself with borrowed examples. Every society cannot generate the dramas it wants.

What are the tokens of well-founded tragedy? D.H. Lawrence says that 'tragedy is a great big kick at misery' and tragic drama at its best is emotionally unambivalent. The emotions are felt and known for what they are; and however painful that is, there is a kind of security inherent in the experience. 'This is how bad it gets; this is what we never knew', leads to the thought, 'so now we *do* know'. One of the things that comes out of real tragedy is an odd sense of comfort, which follows from having tested the limits of what can be borne. Aristotle famously said that tragedy generates pity and fear to bring about the *katharsis* of these emotions; and though the exact meaning of *katharsis* has been much debated, there are innumerable voices supporting the idea that we leave a tragedy in a calmer emotional state than the one we arrived in. We know more precisely than we did what we are really afraid of; and we are much less afraid of our fear, which turns out to have been a large part of the problem. Just as depression is not really grief, but a fear of grief, so ambivalent anxiety is a sub-tragic emotion. A well-based fear is much less frightening, because it incorporates valid experience and tells us what to avoid. It teaches us to use our fear, in George Eliot's sharp phrase, 'as a safeguard'.

It follows from this that the best-founded tragedies convince us immediately that they are about the world as we know it. They are the opposite of fantasy: indeed, the collaborative nature of theatre makes it impractical for them to be anything else, because everyone in the audience must find something of themselves in the play before they will support the performance. And so it is less surprising that tragic plays are so often centred on families, the one social configuration on which we are all experts, and circle endlessly round the problems that, because of the trajectory of human life, no one entirely escapes. We are born from the cooperation of two people, and fight our way to physical and mental freedom – only to find that the only physical immortality available to us lies in cooperation with someone of different gender, from a different gene pool, and in the production of a new body, just as determined to win its physical and mental freedom from us.

In this stressful trajectory of individuality and merging, creativity and isolation, we are torn between the irreconcilable demands that Greek drama personifies as Apollo and Dionysus. Apollo, the god of reason, would have us rational, individuated, firmly outlined in our personal skin – but his offer of consciousness comes at a cost: 'knowing' displaces the experience of 'being'.

Dionysus, the god of passion, would have us be the thing itself, fluid, creative, at one with life's own processes – but at the price of knowing anything about it. If it were up to Dionysus, there would be no tragic plays; but if it were up to Apollo there would be no experience to put in them. In Greek drama these gods actually appear on stage and argue for their respective rights and powers. But if we look carefully at later dramas, we find the tug of war still going on – not so much in deference to the Greeks, as in response to the facts of life itself. For there is a good case for saying that man is tragic because he is an animal with self-consciousness, and is therefore strung eternally between two worlds. As Fulke Greville put it in the seventeenth century, when 'reason' and 'passion' were the names of the antagonists,

> Oh wearisome condition of humanity!
> Born under one law, to another bound:
> Vainly begot, and yet forbidden vanity,
> Created sick, commanded to be sound:
> What meaneth nature by these divers laws?
> Passion and reason, self-division cause . . .[2]

That self-division is what tragic plays most often dramatize: and the essence of the tragedy is not that humanity would be better off with one or the other, but to be truly human we need both.

Perhaps we can see in this light why the tragic plot that has the best claim to be archetypal is one about a young man, his mother, and his dead father. If we take the vote of the ages, this is the story which has mesmerized most audiences, in the most disparate languages and settings and under the largest number of titles: the *Oresteia*, *Oedipus*, *Hamlet*, *Ghosts*, to name only those dealt with here. It is a family story, we notice, in the highest degree. There is one son, and his mother; the father only exists as a ghost or a memory. The simplicity of this cast list cuts through to all sorts of family issues from which each playwright will take the particular elements he needs for his plot. But among the most obvious ones are the mother–son connection in the absence of the father (will it become disastrously sexual, or inhibitingly maternal?), and the ghostly father–son connection in the presence of the mother (will it be the son's only route to his identity, or his utter ruin?). Above all, the son's predicament on the verge of maturity, unable to live for himself until he has dealt with the different threats posed by his father and his mother, speaks for the central problem of tragedy, the problem of individuation.

As we probe tragic dramas for their deepest concerns across the ages, this is the inescapable issue: the shock of finding oneself alone, with an Apollonian consciousness registering every psychological tremor, and yet entangled in a past

---

[2]   Fulke Greville, 'Chorus Sacerdotum' from *Mustapha* (1633), 1–6, in *Selected Writings of Fulke Greville*, ed. Joan Rees (London: Athlone Press, 1973), p. 138.

of someone else's creation. To be born is to be born of the Dionysiac union of two parents, and the first conscious discovery of the son is that physical individuation is only the beginning of the process. There is a mental journey to be made, also; and the hero reaches out for his kingdom only to find that he must deal with his parents' unfinished business first. This is the particular value of revenge plots, which turn on righting the wrongs of the past: 'what freedom does anyone have to live in the present?' they ask, and 'can an individual life make sense by itself?' Above all, the question seems to phrase itself most sharply for male protagonists, as if the process of individuation for the male were harder, more richly perilous than for the female of the species. It is true that all the plays under discussion were written by men and may therefore represent a kind of special pleading; but the correlation between these plots and the findings of developmental psychology makes it worth heeding their repetitive claim that being male is intrinsically difficult, an achievement against long odds.

One of the key problems for the male, at its most obvious in the Oedipus plot, is of course women. All men are 'born of woman', complains Strindberg, but 'no woman is born of man'.[3] This seems too obvious for comment, but tragic plays insist we engage with what follows, for both sides. Is there a sense in which the mother and her centrality must be repudiated by the son, if he is to survive in maturity? – and conversely, a danger that women may pervert the power to give life into the power to take it away? Dr Johnson dryly remarks that 'Nature has given women so much power that the law has very wisely given them little',[4] and if we consider women in tragedy as merely disempowered by an oppressive patriarchy, we miss the underlying assumption that women are overwhelmingly powerful already. One way of reading the *Oresteia* would be that it shows the founding principle of civilization to be the right of a son to kill his mother (under very specific circumstances, of course, and with the gods attending); and *Oedipus* could be said to show the worst that might happen when he does not. The son makes a long detour through a delusory life of civilized achievement, only to find himself back in his mother's bed, exactly where he began. Other Greek plots, as we shall see, freely posit the possibility of a mother killing her sons to take them away from their father, or dismembering an adored child in a temporary state of Dionysiac frenzy. However we respond to these acts, we are forced to see that from the hero's perspective the power of the mother is awesome, and older than his own. And even when a woman is viewed as a marriage partner rather than a mother, it is her connections with the irrational, with Dionysiac animality and passion that is at the forefront of the drama. If gender is another central concern in tragedy, it has to be because women give birth, and men do not. The hero must cooperate

---

    [3]   August Strindberg, *The Father*, in *The Father, Miss Julie and The Ghost Sonata*, trans. Michael Meyer (London: Methuen, 1976), p. 47.
    [4]   Samuel Johnson, letter to Dr Taylor, in *Boswell's Life of Doctor Johnson*, ed. G.B. Hill (Oxford: Clarendon Press, 1887), vol. 5, p. 226, n. 2.

with such a creature if he wishes for offspring; but tragic plays are full of his ambivalence, and his desire to deny that he too was born of a Dionsyiac union.

The third archetypal concern of tragedy which is implicit in the Oedipal plot is with what lies beyond the family, the city. In Greek dramas this is literally the city-state, the *polis*, whose novel structure released the extraordinary energy of fifth-century Athens. But it need be nothing more specific than what lies beyond the confinement of the home and the valley, as it is in Ibsen. Just as the princes and kings of tragedy are not literally royal, but souls endowed with royalty, not unlike ourselves, so their cities and kingdoms translate psychologically into the world they hope to inherit when they are ready. And tragic plots turn again and again on what it takes to 'be ready', and point again and again at the traps lying at the feet of the hero, if not in the shape of his mother or his wife, then in the shape of his own divided nature – Dionysiac by origin, but Apollonian in its self-consciousness. In *Oedipus*, *Hamlet* and *Ghosts*, the hero does not make it. Oedipus thinks he has, of course, and that he is king of Thebes, the husband of his wife and the father of his children. But the plot unravels to show that he has never crossed the generational barrier that makes these achievements possible: instead he is his mother's husband and his children's sibling, unfit to live in the city he governed. Hamlet spends the time he should be avenging his father and claiming Denmark in destroying any prospect of marriage with Ophelia and trying to call a halt to his mother's sexual activity. In *Ghosts* the young artist's life is ending almost before it has begun, wrecked by his father's bequest of syphilis, and menaced by the prospect of unending nursing of his mindless body from his loving mother.

Clearly tragic plays are obsessed by the difficulty for the youthful hero of standing forth to claim his kingdom. From the *Oresteia* however, we can learn something more. Because the play is a trilogy it has time to explore Orestes' problem in a wider context, and alone among our tragedies it proposes an optimistic outcome. What if the mother is actually killed, and the youth stands free of blood ties, with a bloody sword in his hand? Athens will offer him a home, and the goddess Athena will offer to protect him: because after families come wider society and the bonds of citizenship, founded not on the uniqueness of blood ties, but on equality before the law. Mothers give birth to sons in the flesh; but civic ties give birth to grown-up human beings, no longer entangled in the past but free to live and choose in the present. Aeschylus was confident about this, as we shall see, because his audience had recently made the same transition; and though few later playwrights have shared his optimism, the paradigm of a journey away from blood to law, from ethnicity to citizenship or from the home to the city remains central to tragic plots.

The wide recurrence of the issues we have been sketching, individuation, gender and the state, makes it possible to guess at an answer to one of the most puzzling questions in tragic drama – why the plays get written when they do.

Particular societies seem to produce them in large numbers; but plenty is followed by drought, or plays that seem to have lost the secret, and take refuge in parody or over-sophistication. We can guess from the central concerns we have been tracing that when tragedies cut deepest and most accurately it is because they are responding to a contemporary disruption – a social reorganization profound enough to shake the individual into heightened self-consciousness and draw all his old relations into question. Political emancipation is the archetypal disruption of this kind, which invites each citizen to renounce time-honoured patterns of behaviour and belief in favour of a dangerously new kind of self-definition. Excitement is one face of this opportunity and guilt is the other; because the assertion of selfhood and its value carries with it the dread of offending against old pieties. And so long as these feelings are fresh and powerful, tragic drama is the 'collaborative experience' in which the population and the playwright meditate on their inner lives. But no crisis of this kind continues for long: the feelings become familiar, the conundrum loses its compelling interest, and so the great periods of drama are followed by more conventional ones, in which the tragedy of the human predicament is somehow taken for granted. What was a discovery has become a commonplace; what was true theatre becomes theatrical ritual. The argument of what follows is that tragedy depends on profound disturbances, like the invention of democracy in Athens, and its many varied reinventions since. But this is not only a historical enquiry; for the stress of individuation, and the endless negotiations between the claims of the family and the world beyond, are the lot of every thinking individual. Insofar as we must all grow up, we are all Athenians, and the Athenian diagnosis of our ambivalence towards this demand is eternally fresh.

PART ONE

Greek Tragedy

Chapter 1

Aeschylus

Greek tragedy, scholars are increasingly willing to grant, is not an accidental accompaniment to democracy, but in some sense what democracy needed to help it function. The drama seems to show 'a social body carrying out quite publicly the maintenance and development of its mental infrastructure', as one classicist has recently phrased it; and 'the mental underpinning of such a daring society can certainly have been no simple matter'.[1] Before scrutinizing the plays themselves for what they tell us about this from the inside, we may note some of the external features of the situation, which might help explain the extraordinary level of creativity reached by the Greeks of the fifth century BCE. Who were the playwrights and the audience, and what was their democracy like?

All our plays were written by Athenians, for Athenians. There were many other city-states (*poleis*) in what we loosely term 'Greece', but Athens was the only site of what at the time seemed a radical and dangerous political experiment – the sharing of power (*kratos*) among the people (*demos*). Athens had arrived at this point after trying the more usual forms of government, rule by a small elite (oligarchy) and rule by one strong leader (tyranny). But in 507 an inspired reform was instituted to distribute power to individual Athenians and encourage them to define themselves, not as members of a family, class or clan, but as citizens with equal rights before the law. The energy and intelligence thus mobilized from the population as a whole (though citizenship, of course, was an entirely male affair – the *polis* did not acknowledge women or slaves) helped create the Athens that beat back the Persian empire at Marathon (490) and began to acquire power over the Greek world as a whole. Our plays date from the optimistic high point of the Athenian experiment, when Persia had just been defeated, through the decades of expansion that followed, and end with the disastrous close of the Peloponnesian War which Athens lost to Sparta (431–404).

'Citizenship' and 'the democratic vote' are not terms to make the pulse beat faster now, but that is because the power an individual wields in the modern state is largely talismanic. If a state can be compared to a ship, the modern version has a small, highly trained crew, but carries innumerable passengers. The *polis*-ship of Athens, however, had, apart from the non-citizens, only sailors.[2] All its decisions were taken by majority vote. The decision-making body was the Assembly, which every citizen had the right to attend, and when the debate began with the formula, 'Who wishes to speak?', his voice and vote were the equal of every other. The Athenian was both amateur and professional: if he voted for a

---

[1]   Christian Meier, *The Political Art of Greek Tragedy*, trans. Andrew Webber (Cambridge: Polity Press, 1993), p. 4.

[2]   Ibid., p. 36.

law, he might well find himself on the first jury that had to apply it, and if he supported a belligerent foreign policy, he might be part of the army that had to carry it through. Democratic power meant democratic responsibility, and utilizing an individual vote meant living with the consequences; the *polis* was so small that political life was a kind of theatre, in which men took their key decisions in full view of one another.

But the *polis* also supported the real theatre – paid for by the public purse, and organized with great solemnity. The tragedians and actors were citizens, not low-caste professionals as in most theatres subsequently: men who in their other lives fought Athenian wars and held public offices. The plays of three writers survive, though there were many more: they are Aeschylus (525/4–456 BCE), Sophocles (*c*.496–406 BCE) and Euripides (*c*.485–406 BCE), and they presented their plays to the assembled citizens as part of the great annual festival of the Great Dionysia. The structure of this event shows how far the Greek sense of theatre was from an entertainment: the festival began with a great procession, animal sacrifices and choral singing, and then, on three subsequent days, the three invited tragedians would stage a tragic trilogy (or three separate plays) and a comedy. The setting was a huge amphitheatre holding perhaps 16,000 people, whose attention was funnelled down towards a small, distant stage on which four actors and a chorus spoke metrical verse through naturalistic masks. The relative rank of the playwrights' work would then be determined by ten judges, chosen by lot from the city as a whole.

The subject matter of these tragedies is to all appearances traditional: they tell stories about gods (like the god presiding over the festival, Dionysus) or mythical heroes like Hercules or Prometheus or characters from the Trojan War. On closer scrutiny, however, their apparent conventionality is only the starting point: the Athenian audience is invited to watch a familiar story being treated in a new way, and the challenge issued by the playwright is to see what new perspectives follow from each change of emphasis. There are, for instance, numerous versions of the Oedipus story, beginning with the one narrated in the *Odyssey*, in which the hero's mother hangs herself, but he continues to be king after the revelation about his birth. When Sophocles dramatizes the story, he makes Oedipus blind himself in remorse; while Euripides conceives of the blinding as being done by the servants, which quite alters its meaning. (We wish we knew what happened in Aeschylus' version of Oedipus, too, but this is completely lost.) In the same way, there are at least three versions of how Orestes and Electra punish their mother for murdering their father: the *Oresteia* of Aeschylus, which concentrates on Orestes' point of view, Sophocles', which concentrates on Electra's, and the sharply realistic play by Euripides, which seems to be a satirical comment on both. The traditionalism of the plots is best understood as a kind of shorthand, by which the playwright quickly focuses the audience on a complex situation, and teases out the implications that concern him.

One other issue needs to be glanced at before we turn to the plays. This is the status of the Greek gods, in whose name the plays are performed, and who themselves often figure in the drama. We are not well adjusted to polytheism as inheritors (however passive) of a monotheistic tradition; but to the Greek mind 'theology' did not mean truth, dogma or moral teaching but simply stories (*logoi*) about the gods (*theoi*). The fact that the gods were viewed as having human shape meant that the sense in which they were really the embodiment of human qualities was an open secret, from Homer onwards. Not everyone trod the sceptical path, but even the most conventional believer allowed playwrights the freedom to represent the gods (within recognizable limits) in the way that suited them. So the god Apollo, traditionally associated with the sun, enlightenment, reason and poetry, is represented by Aeschylus as a young god with some things still to learn, by Sophocles as the unquestioned voice of age-old authority, and by Euripides as a callous automaton, all without ceasing to be Apollo. The gods are part of the Athenian vocabulary, and they make it possible to discuss immense issues in a small compass – as when Aphrodite, goddess of love, and Artemis, goddess of chastity, contemptuously repudiate one another in their tug-of-war over the beautiful youth, Hippolytus; or Apollo in his radiant youth and rationality confronts the oldest and most irrational goddesses, the Furies, in the first trilogy we shall examine, the *Oresteia*.

The *Oresteia* (458 BCE)

This play dates from the most confident period of Athenian democracy and we cannot doubt that it is a play about Athens. It begins in the mistily heroic past, with the arrival home of Agamemnon after the Trojan War, but it ends in the city of Athens itself. The question the play poses is one only the city can resolve, and the solution requires the involvement of the city's guardian goddess Athena and its familiar institutions. To feel the audacity of this we might imagine a version of *Hamlet* where the hero travels to the English court and has his problems somehow alleviated by Elizabeth I and English law. Clearly, Aeschylus is not working at a level of simple realism, but supplying his city with a founding myth about its origins; in this complex and thick-textured trilogy he is showing the momentous decisions that went into creating the life contemporary Athenians enjoy. What also emerges is the delicacy of the balancing act that both he and his audience must practise to keep it going.

To emphasize how deeply Athenian the *Oresteia* is, however, risks implying that it is less than universal. The materials are certainly local, but the implications Aeschylus uncovers have resonance for any society moving out of tribalism; and because the experiment is so new he can analyse what is at stake with revelatory clarity. (It may not be irrelevant that Aeschylus himself fought at Marathon: he has in himself the multifaceted energy and sense of living at a turning point that marks Athenian culture as a whole.) Thus the story he takes for his plot is, as we have noted, the Oedipal one that has some claim to be the *ur*plot of tragedy. But unlike his successors, Aeschylus conceives of the fundamental family drama as only making sense inside society as a whole: beyond the family threshold is the *polis*. This is what his audience of citizens knows for themselves: that although everyone is born inside a family, to grow to full maturity it is necessary to leave it. We are born in blood and darkness, says Aeschylus, but our true humanity develops in the light of reason, with the freedom to act as citizens, not sons. The dilemma the trilogy sets out to answer is how to do justice to the primacy of the dark, our Dionysiac origins in a mother's body, while journeying always towards the light: the realm of consciousness that belongs to Apollo.

Aeschylus carefully shapes the story of Agamemnon's homecoming from the Trojan War to illuminate why this dilemma is so painful – why there is so much to say on both sides. The story was familiar to his audience from the *Odyssey* (Book 3), where Agamemnon is said to have wearily returned by sea to his own country, only to be treacherously slain at a feast by his wife's secret lover, Aegisthus. Eight years later his son Orestes returned from exile and 'killed the snake that killed his father. / He gave his hateful mother and her soft man / a tomb together'.[3] For Homer there was no problem: justice was done for a villainous crime. But Aeschylus complicates things by giving Clytaemnestra a motive for destroying her husband. He borrows from a story that puts Agamemnon in a more ambiguous light: before he sailed to Troy, Agamemnon's fleet was becalmed and for the sake of a wind he sacrificed his and Clytaemnestra's daughter, Iphigenia. In Aeschylus' version, the murder of Agamemnon is now carried out by Clytaemnestra, who has waited ten long years for her opportunity. Thus the first play of the trilogy, the *Agamemnon*, pits the warrior king against the mother, and brings male and female values into the sharpest conflict. In the second play, the *Libation Bearers*, the conflict is expressed in the confrontation of Orestes with his guilty mother, and the tug-of-war between all the reasons for punishing her and for letting her go; and in the last play, the *Eumenides*, the conflict is expressed in the open debate between Apollo, who defends Orestes, and the Furies of Clytaemnestra, who want to eat him alive. The wonderful comprehensiveness of the trilogy comes from these parallel structures, which represent the struggle as happening at the same time at a family level, a psychological level, and a political level. It is also implied that somehow they are linked; and if a solution can be found at one level, it will yield a clue to all three – liberating not only Orestes, but Athens, and ourselves, from a dilemma in which there is a perplexing amount of truth on both sides.

---

[3]   *The Odyssey of Homer*, trans. Robert Fitzgerald (New York: Doubleday, 1961, repr. 1963), p. 44.

The trilogy is so dense and dramatic that teasing out its full meaning would demand a book-length study. Here we must confine ourselves to the main lines of argument implied in each of these three confrontations, beginning with the *Agamemnon*. Aeschylus shows Agamemnon arriving home triumphantly at the end of ten years' war. We watch him enter on a chariot (with part of his royal booty, a new concubine, beside him) and we hear him salute his city and the 'just gods'[4] who helped him to victory. He is immovably secure that Troy's punishment was deserved, and therefore its defeat is the end of the matter: 'For their mad outrage of a queen we raped their city – we were right' (F 133). Whatever horrors were perpetrated in that act of punishment, it is clear that he does not intend to think about them, and anything that preceded the war – like the sacrifice of Iphigenia – has entirely slid from view. His task now is to pick up the reins of government in Argos, nurturing whatever is healthy in the state, and taking the surgeon's knife to what is not.

This portrait of heroic self-sufficiency, simple to the point of stupidity, is brilliantly contrasted with that of Clytaemnestra, silently waiting onstage. It does not occur to Agamemnon that others can also define what is healthy and unhealthy and perform surgical operations, or that the hero of Troy might appear to his wife a mere infanticide. But the ten intervening years have hardened Clytaemnestra into a child-avenger, and whatever respect she once felt for her husband has been consumed by maternal fury. When he lifted the sacrificial knife to his own child, he ripped the family structure apart, and when she looks at the hero in his chariot she sees only a body to be disposed of physically, as she has already disposed of him mentally. With fathomless irony, she expresses her relief at finally having him home, and what she says of his role as her lord and master sounds so properly in his ears, he does not question that he is all these things to her:

> . . . the watchdog of the fold and hall;
> the stay that keeps the ship alive; the post to grip
> groundward the towering roof; a father's single child;
> land seen by sailors after all their hope was gone.[5]

This is how a subordinate wife should sound; but Clytaemnestra's real relation to Agamemnon is expressed in another way, in an invitation to walk triumphantly into the palace on purple tapestries and express his *hubris* openly before the city. Agamemnon instinctively shrinks from such self-assertion (it is the sort of thing Asian kings do, not Greeks) but because he does not grasp the contemptuous subtext of her action, he does not exert himself to resist. 'I tell you, as a man, not god, to reverence me' (L 925), he says, modestly; but she makes it seem an act of

---

4   *The Oresteia*, trans. Robert Fagles (Viking, 1975, repr. Harmondsworth: Penguin, 1985), p. 133. Hereafter F and line number.
5   *Oresteia*, trans. Richmond Lattimore, *The Complete Greek Tragedies* (Chicago: University of Chicago Press, 1953), vol. 1, p. 62. Hereafter L. This translation will be quoted wherever it gives a clearer sense of the Greek.

graciousness to give in ('Oh yield! The power is yours. Give way of your free will'; L 943). He allows himself to be persuaded, and utters the pious hope that he will not pay for this act of self-assertion, especially if he takes his sandals off first:

> Since you must have it – here, let someone with all speed
> take off these sandals, slaves for my feet to tread upon.
> And as I crush these garments stained from the rich sea
> let no god's eyes of hatred strike me from afar.
> Great the extravagance, and great the shame I feel
> to spoil such treasure and such silver's worth of webs. (L 944–9)

It might seem impossible to improve on the myopia of this, but his next injunction is that Clytaemnestra take good care of his new Trojan concubine, Cassandra:

> So much for all this. Take this stranger girl within
> now, and be kind ...
> Gift of the host to me, and flower exquisite
> from all my many treasures, she attends me here. (L 950–1, 954–5)

This is the ending Agamemnon promised himself for the ten years at Troy, as he re-enters his palace in triumph: his city and his wife just as he left them, and he himself enriched with fame and booty.

Aeschylus' sense of the mutual misunderstanding between this husband and wife has certain parallels with Rebecca West's lively formulation of the characteristic failings of men and women in general. Her diagnosis has resonance for gender roles in numberless tragic plots:

> The word 'idiot' comes from a Greek root meaning private person. Idiocy
> is the female defect: intent on their private lives, women follow their fate
> through a darkness as deep as that cast by malformed cells in the brain. It
> is no worse than the male defect, which is lunacy: they are so obsessed by
> public affairs that they see the world as by moonlight, which shows the
> outlines of every object but not the details indicative of their nature.[6]

Agamemnon's 'lunacy', his reliance on the heroic outline of his situation rather than its real nature, is beautifully evinced by his treading on the tapestries. He knows it is hubristic, but he does it anyway, uttering the futile prayer that his deed should have no consequences. In the same way, he assumes that he is still married to a loyal wife, though he has slaughtered one of the children that bound them together, and brought a concubine home into the bargain. Most fundamental of all, he has razed the altars of Troy and annihilated its inhabitants: the brilliantly coloured path on which he treads is also a trail of blood, and it leads him into a palace that will soon be a slaughterhouse.

---

[6]   Rebecca West, *Black Lamb and Grey Falcon* (New York: Viking Press, 1941) vol. i, p. 3.

But Clytaemnestra's 'idiocy' is evident in her scheming, too, clever as she is. 'Intent on her private life', she has slipped into a female position that cannot locate the father anywhere on its map; he may once have had a function, but the significance of it is quite forgotten. She does not remember that Iphigenia was Agamemnon's daughter as well as her own, or that he was the head of a becalmed and mutinous army when he made his fatal decision. She has arrogated to herself the roles of judge and executioner, and the energy of her speeches indicates how absolutely she knows herself to be in the right. She takes treacherous advantage of the warrior's first bath in his own palace – the final moment of disarming in the security of home – to entangle him shamefully in a robe; and her description of his death represents it as a glorious sacrifice to Zeus. The shower of blood is as welcome as spring rain:

> That he might not escape nor beat aside his death,
> as fishermen cast their huge circling nets, I spread
> deadly abundance of rich robes, and caught him fast.
> I struck him twice. In two great cries of agony
> he buckled at the knees and fell. When he was down
> I struck him the third blow, in thanks and reverence
> to Zeus the lord of dead men underneath the ground.
> Thus he went down, and the life struggled out of him;
> and as he died he spattered me with the dark red
> and violent driven rain of bitter savored blood
> to make me glad, as gardens stand among the showers
> of God in glory at the birthtime of the buds. (L 1381–92)

The 'idiotic' extent to which she makes up the laws, and takes the boundaries of her own concerns as the boundaries of what is significant, shows in her ability to ignore the great crime she herself has committed against Agamemnon. While he was absent she took Aegisthus as a lover and allowed him to usurp power in Argos. Because this was her own act, she ignores it: there is only one traitor in their marriage, and that is Agamemnon. Even if we take her at her own estimation, as a passionately loyal mother, there remains a deep flaw in her argument; for she has two other children living, and she has degraded Electra into a household slave and sent Orestes into exile. She has suppressed the rights of both for the sake of her liaison with Aegisthus, and ceased to be a real mother to either – and yet it is in the name of motherhood that she justifies her revenge, conceived as an absolute blood tie formed in the womb.

The climactic moment of this play shows Clytaemnestra presenting Agamemnon's bleeding corpse to the elders of Argos and glorying in her act. Her justification is that there was no law in Argos to protect her tie with Iphigenia, and the elders would never have held Agamemnon to account for what he did:

> Yet look upon this dead man; you would not cross him once
> when with no thought more than as if a beast had died,

when his ranged pastures swarmed with the deep fleece of flocks,
he slaughtered like a victim his own child, my pain
grown into love, to charm away the winds of Thrace.
Were you not bound to hunt him then clear of this soil
for the guilt stained upon him? (L 1414–20)

Because there was no justice among men, Clytaemnestra has turned herself into
her child's avenging Fury. Like these ancient earth goddesses, she had defined the
flesh as the supreme reality, and taken the equation between blood and life in a
literal spirit. She gave blood and life to Iphigenia, through the agony of childbirth
no man will ever know ('my pain grown into love'). Agamemnon took them away
– and she is taking them back again from him, rejoicing in the justice of it like
swelling buds in springtime.

What is the tragic conflict Aeschylus is exposing here, as Clytaemnestra
stands victorious over her husband's body? One way of putting it would be that
men and women are so unlike each other that marriage is too frail a structure to
hold them together for long. The value of setting this conflict in the context of the
Trojan War becomes clear: for that whole ten-year disaster was set off by Paris's
abduction of Helen from Menelaus. The entire Greek army was assembled to
rectify that outrage to hospitality and marrriage, and now the victor who
annihilated Troy has returned home to find that he is no longer married, either.
The marriage of Agamemnon was dissolved at the moment Iphigenia was lifted
to the altar, and deliberately buried when Clytaemnestra took Aegisthus to her
hearth. There will be revenge for this, too, of course – Orestes will return as his
father's Fury – but this only underlines how deep is the disturbance caused by
broken faith, and how unstable are arrangements based on human promises. The
defencelessness of marriage seems to be central to this story.

It seems worth meditating on the fragility of the marriage tie, because the rest
of the trilogy asks in various ways, which is more important and fundamental,
marriage or motherhood? And the final answer is given by the goddess Athena,
when she votes to set Orestes free of the charge of matricide: that the law must
protect marriage rather than motherhood. This decision has caused such critical
scandal that it is important to dwell on the train of thought by which Aeschylus
finally arrives at this solution; and the stress he lays here on the defencelessness
of marriage is central to his logic. For marriage, it appears, is only words and a
promise, guaranteed by nothing more reliable than will and memory. The parties
to it are of different sex, history and preoccupations, and they are easily tempted
to forget that they voluntarily bonded at all. The importance of marriage,
genetically and socially, is that it lifts each individual out of his or her gene pool
to mate with what is irredeemably 'other'. But the risk is that each party may
cease to believe in the reality of the foreign body, as Clytaemnestra does here.

The key factor, in Aeschylus' account, is the difference between male and
female values. Clytaemnestra and Agamemnon feel no shame at what they are

doing – both assertively justify themselves – but neither can hope to convince the other. Agamemnon returns as a war hero, but to his wife, an infanticide. Clytaemnestra kills him as her daughter's loyal avenger, but to him, as a traitor and adulteress. What is dividing them is perhaps best defined as a question of honour. Both consider they have it; but they are clearly defining it in different ways.

For Agamemnon, honour is the quality central to the heroic life, the core of a man's self-definition and the arbiter of his behaviour. Honour is what the Greeks won back at Troy when they recovered Helen; and honour was the bitter obligation forcing Agamemnon to sacrifice Iphigenia – for a wind, for the troops, for the avoidance of shameful failure. Honour could thus be defined as part of the 'lunacy' ascribed to the male by Rebecca West, for in the course of pursuing its moonlit outline an endless train of bloody acts was committed. But we cannot entirely share Clytaemnestra's contempt for this invisible quantity, because the play also encourages us to feel the value of such invisible ties. When Paris abducted Helen he was the guest of Menelaus, enjoying the sacred privilege of hospitality under a foreign roof. When he violated it, he violated the whole code of forbearance on which civilized life reposes – a bond protected by Zeus himself. This code is fundamental to civilization because without it, no one can leave the safety of his own hearth for anyone else's; it encapsulates our ability to trust others beyond the tribe, and to inhabit a world larger than the stockade. This code is suggestively parallel to the bond of marriage, in that it depends on trust and is guaranteed by nothing in nature; and its very fragility, perhaps, is what requires the concern of the greatest of the gods. Agamemnon's definition of honour, then, cannot be simply discounted in the spirit of female pacifism ('war is a game men play for their own ends'); Zeus's involvement is a reminder that an honour code is what raises any community above tribalism.

Honour for Clytaemnestra, however, is something a woman dispenses with – or, more precisely, something she defines for herself. True honour is the sacrifice of it: the determination to put loved ones first, before the mumbo-jumbo of codes and values. A woman, caught between her duties as wife and mother, keeps her grip on the real: the real body of a child, with real blood in its veins. And the logic of this is underwritten by biology, for it is no mere metaphor that Iphigenia is flesh of Clytaemnestra's flesh; unlike the bonds of hospitality and marriage, this is a bond guaranteed by nature. She can indeed say that Agamemnon has slain their marriage, since the child was the one place where he and she were incontestably united. But what is nonetheless 'idiotic' in Clytaemnestra's version of honour is her presumption that biological motherhood outweighs all other considerations – her own disloyalty to her marriage, and her failure to nurture her other children. What is alarmingly regressive in all this is her obsession, not only with blood, but with spilt blood, the dead rather than the living; and she drains Iphigenia's share from the corpse of Agamemnon in just the literal spirit that her

Furies will one day seek Orestes' blood, in exchange for hers. The rapture she feels over Agamemnon's body is as sadistic and literal-minded as any they express, and like them, she is inhumanly lacking in doubt. She has completed her own revenge, and what follows after is no concern of hers – though her achievement is only one more turn of the wheel in the unending torment of her family.

The conflict as Aeschylus shapes it in this first play, then, is that men and women differ so radically in their values that marriage between them is only the temporary reconciliation of opposites. Lunacy, says the woman, of her husband's reliance on honour and transcendental codes of value in the public sphere. Idiocy, says the husband, of his wife's obsession with private life, her equation of what is real with what is tangible and close in blood. It is not that either is wrong, Aeschylus implies, but that the way in which both are right cannot yet find adequate expression. Clytaemnestra, for instance, surely has grounds for her rage at the fact that there is no law to fit Agamemnon's infanticide, so that Argos simply accepts him home with contaminated hands. But simply to drain from him the blood he owes Iphigenia is no real answer, merely a private satisfaction. Agamemnon, meanwhile, could plead that in his role as commander which forced him into the sacrifice, he was going about the business of Zeus himself – enforcing the sanctity of the marriage bond, and the bond of hospitality, on the oath-breaker Paris. He was defending the world of private values by public means; true, he did it grossly and came home swollen with conceit, but Clytaemnestra's sadistic complacency is no more attractive. Each of them has a grasp of an essential truth, it seems, but no way of accommodating their partner's.

Thus far the tragedy shows the clashing of two incompatible worlds of value. But before we move on to the next definition of this conflict, in the confrontation of Clytaemnestra with Orestes, it is perhaps worth noting that there is a significant imbalance between the kinds of truth each side is trying to protect. The male perception is transcendental (in the literal sense of existing beyond the world of matter), and hence not producible as evidence. But the truth the female argument protects is material and undeniable, located in the realm of blood and bodies. There is a deep vulnerability in this imbalance, for both men and women, Aeschylus implies, because the male must rely on insubstantial words, not things – while the female, dazzled by the substantiality of things, may have no value for words.

In the second play, the *Libation Bearers*, the grown-up Orestes returns from exile and is reunited with Electra at Agamemnon's grave. Together they work themselves into a state of mind in which the long-dreamt-of vengeance can take place, and Orestes tricks his way into the palace. There he confronts Clytaemnestra with a sword in his hand, and their dialogue takes us to the heart of the male–female conflict again, in a fascinating variant of the collision between Agamemnon and Clytaemnestra. Before we analyse their exchange, however, it may be worth lingering for a moment on why this configuration is the archetypal one of mother and son. (Sophocles, as we shall see, puts Electra at the centre of the story, to quite different effect.) Why does 'son' translate so naturally into 'tragic hero'?

At the start of the play we meet Electra with a chorus of slaves – enslaved women from some other war – sent by Clytaemnestra to pour libations on Agamemnon's grave. They wail for their utter powerlessness: the slaves have been beaten out of the palace, and tear their own clothes in a frenzied lamentation for the dead king and for themselves; Electra is transfixed by the horror of the murder, when she 'stood apart, dishonoured, nothing worth, / in the dark corner, as you would kennel a vicious dog' (L 446–7). The contrast with Orestes emerges strongly from this opening: a hero has the power in his own arm to rectify a wrong. But women cannot hope to change anything – they are sub-heroic because they are not free to act. Lacking the strength to defend themselves, they can only show tenacity in suffering; and endless suffering makes them slaves in emotion, as well as status. Electra and the slave women hunger for retribution, to pay back their enemies in a strict application of the *lex talionis* ('an eye for an eye and a tooth for a tooth'). They dream of inflicting pain as gleefully as Clytaemnestra herself. Electra prays wildly,

> May Zeus, from all his shoulder's strength,
> pound down his fist upon them,
> ohay, smash their heads.
> Let the land once more believe.
> There has been wrong done. I ask for right.
> Hear me, Earth. Hear me, grandeurs of Darkness. (L 394–9)

The chorus, with unnerving excitement, anticipates fresh bloodshed in an endless sequence:

> It is but law that when the red drops have been spilled
> opon the ground they cry aloud for fresh
> blood. For the death act calls out on Fury
> to bring out of those who were slain before
> new ruin on ruin accomplished. (L 400–4)

This is contrasted with the attitude of Orestes, who joins them in their prayers round the grave. His sense of the task has none of the women's gusto, and he promises himself no savage gratifications in carrying it out. The fact that he is strong enough to kill his mother means that it is the dilemma itself that preoccupies him; he is confused and bewildered, and can only look to Zeus for an answer:

> Hear me, you lordships of the world below.
> Behold in assembled power, curses come from the dead,
> behold the last of the sons of Atreus, foundering

> lost, without future, cast
> from house and right. O god, where shall we turn? (L 405–9)

Because he is strong enough to act, he also anticipates the consequences of his deed and and fears having to live with them: it is this combination of freedom to act and acceptance of responsibility that defines the heroic position.

The other thing we may note about Orestes before the climactic scene is that his revenge is motivated at a theological level too: the oracle of Apollo ordered him to return home and re-establish Agamemnon's honour by killing Clytaemnestra and Aegisthus. He is threatened with 'sicknesses, ulcers that ride upon the flesh . . . and with wild teeth eat away the natural tissue' (L 279–81) if he fails in his task. It is not until the last play that we understand why Apollo should care so much about Agamemnon's honour; but the involvement of a god in Orestes' destiny, and his own need to find security in a god's will rather than his own, marks an important shift in the cycle of revenge.

Orestes and his faithful companion Pylades trick their way into the palace by pretending to have news for Clytaemnestra and Aegisthus – of Orestes' death in exile. They take Aegisthus unawares, and kill him. Clytaemnestra rushes to the scene and there Orestes confronts her, over her lover's corpse. She understands what he intends to do to her, and her immediate response is to play the strongest card she holds: she shows him her breast:

> Hold, my son. Oh take pity, child, before this breast
> where many a time, a drowsing baby, you would feed
> and with soft gums sucked in the milk that made you strong.
> (L 896–8)

She appeals to the literal, bodily truth of their relationship: it is this breast and no other that nurtured Orestes, and if this is not sacrosanct, what can be? The breast is the primal experience of generosity (the mother's body is drained to make the baby grow) and of reciprocity, too: what is so valuable and so lovingly given stirs the first tenderness and concern in the child. Orestes shows how she has checkmated him in turning to his friend without giving her an answer: 'What shall I do, Pylades? Be shamed to kill my mother?' (L 899). And his friend opens his lips for the one and only time in the play, giving his utterance an oracular force:

> What then becomes hereafter of the oracles
> declared by Loxias at Pytho? What of sworn oaths?
> Count all men hateful to you rather than the gods. (L 900–2)

At this stage there is nothing to hold on to but the fact of Apollo's will. Thus prompted, Orestes prepares to kill his mother over her lover's corpse.

Clytaemnestra does not give up: she forces Orestes to know what profound sanctities he is betraying and how terrible the price will be. She argues generically, for her inviolability as a mother: he owes her care in her old age for the care she once took of him, he overestimates her crimes and forgets Agamemnon's, and above all, he forgets how fearful are the Furies roused by matricide: 'Your mother's curse, like dogs, will drag you down' (L 924). Orestes struggles in the midst of this to articulate something else, his sense of her as an individual, who failed him as a mother and forfeited the privilege of protection by her own actions. She betrayed a husband at war, and then disposed of him as an unwanted witness: 'You bore me and threw me away, to a hard life' (L 913). She accuses Orestes of matricide, but does not see how entirely his deed is the consequence of hers ('It will be you who kill yourself. It will not be I'; L 923). Above all, though the murder of a mother cannot be right, the murder of a husband cannot go unavenged. The deeds go together: 'You killed, and it was wrong. Now suffer wrong' (L 930). In this immovable dilemma Clytaemnestra hears her sentence; Orestes takes her offstage to carry it out. What she says about a mother's Furies is immediately vindicated, however: when Orestes returns onstage with bloody hands, his brain is already reeling with terror. The black-robed goddesses with snaky hair are hunting him down: 'They are clear, / and real, and here; the bloodhounds of my mother's hate' (L 1053–4).

If we pause here to ask what is familiar and what is new about the male–female conflict of the *Libation Bearers*, one new element seems to be a nascent appetite for justice on Orestes' side. He does not murder Clytaemnestra in the spirit she murdered Agamemnon, of a literal exchange of blood for blood and body for body. Justice requires her death, but he does not delude himself that the deed is 'right'. It feels in every way wrong; it is only because Apollo's oracle says it must be done that Orestes can steel himself to do it at the climax. And the immediate entry of Clytaemnestra's Furies proves that, just as she claimed, matricide is a crime so primal that the oldest earth goddesses exist to avenge it. Aeschylus is moving towards an argument framed, not in terms of characters, but of basic principles – the opposition between the primary claim of motherhood and the abstract claims of justice and reason, defended by Apollo.

What is familiar in this conflict is that the dilemma Aeschylus dramatizes is genuine. It is not just the appearance of a clash, but the emergence of two vital and irreconcilable truths. Both Clytaemnestra and Orestes have committed unthinkable crimes, the murder of a husband and the murder of a mother; and both claim to have acted in protection of an 'absolute' value, motherhood on the one hand, and male honour on the other. Central to the problem here, as we are beginning to understand, is that the first position is literal: the woman literally gives her body to create a child. The second is transcendental, if the word can be used without philosophical overtones: the husband creates a marriage on the basis of a promise, and the marriage becomes the key location of his public self, his honour. The existence of the Furies is a reminder, if we needed reminding, that motherhood is indeed the root of human life: if this is not sacred, nothing can be. But if marriage and husbands are not sacrosanct in their turn (as Apollo will argue) there can be no mutuality of trust, and therefore no expression of it in children.

The clash between these positions should not, realistically, exist at all; for common sense tells us that all children are born in families and then make families of their own. All human life depends both upon blood, and upon promises; but the heart of the dilemma is that it does not depend on them in the same way. A body deprived of blood is simply and literally dead. But a body deprived of its trust is annihilated in a different way – in its sense of its own reality, and the value of being human. This may explain why the god who takes it on himself to interfere in Orestes' destiny is a male god, and the newest of the Olympians. Apollo stands for something recent, as it were, in human evolution, the realm of consciousness in which values are generated. And he is male, because this is the realm in which masculinity does its work: at a remove from literal childbirth, but life-giving in another sense – because transcendental values give life its meaning. This can be corroborated even from Rebecca West's definition of the characteristic male vice as 'lunacy' and female as 'idiocy'. For the masculine ability to see 'the outlines of every object but not the details indicative of their nature' is also the power of abstraction that Orestes shares with Apollo, and which enables them to conceive of justice while recoiling from blood. Female idiocy, the rootedness in family and blood ties, is shown in different ways by Clytaemnestra, Electra and the Furies; and while it is founded in a great truth, that life itself precedes values, it has the inherent defect of resisting transcendence. If it were left to the female agents in the play, the blood cyle could not be brought to an end.

In the third play of the trilogy, the *Eumenides*, Aeschylus finally brings both the Furies and Apollo on stage to assert their rights. He handles them with startling theological freedom, and implies as ever that each side has a genuine case to make, but may not be making it in the right way. Apollo is handsome and rational, of course, and the Furies are ugly and passionate; but both enjoy manifesting intransigence and abuse one another, and the audience is invited to draw its own conclusions from all they say and do. They are not a diversion from the issues at the human level, but the clearest embodiment of them; and the difficulty of reconciling the truths they protect shows in the way nothing can be resolved until a third goddess appears – the spirit of Athens itself, Athena.

The play shows Orestes taking refuge in Apollo's shrine at Delphi. Here he can, technically, be cleansed of blood guilt by the god who accepts responsibility for his deed – but nothing shakes off his pursuers. The blood of a mother is indelible, and the Furies surround him even as he makes the ritual supplication. The only solution for Orestes, says Apollo, is something new that lies in faraway Athens: 'There we shall find those who will judge this case, and words / to say that will have magic in their figures' (L 81–2). Thus Aeschylus hints at the coming exchange of the *lex talionis* for trial by jury, and the 'magic' power of words to make judgment civilized in the world his Athenian audience lives in. For Orestes, none of this is intelligible as yet: all he knows is that his flight must continue, but that Apollo will protect him as he goes. The god feels as he does about the loathsome, black-clad, foul-breathed goddesses who have trapped him. Apollo, who protects male honour and the value of oaths, hates their obsession with blood ties (to them, the murder of Agamemnon was no crime, because it did not entail 'the shedding of kindred blood'; L 212). The Furies, 'gray and aged children', belong to a regressive old order with which the radiant Olympians can have nothing to do: 'they hold the evil darkness of the Pit below' (L 72) and their hunger for blood fits them only for places where justice is a pretext for sadism. Throat-cutting, torture and castration are their kind of pleasures and Apollo scourges their shabby filthiness out of his shining temple: 'Out then, you flock of goats without a herdsman' (L 196).

The Furies stubbornly set off again to trail Orestes to Athens. They sing a refrain of complacent, primal power which justifies Apollo's shudder:

> Men's illusions in their pride under the sky melt
> down, and are diminished into the ground, gone
> before the onset of our black robes, pulsing
> of our vindictive feet against them
>
> For with a long leap from high
> above and dead drop of weight
> I bring foot's force crashing down
> to cut the legs from under even
> the runner, and spill him to ruin. (L 368–76)

What exists beyond the world of blood is an 'illusion' to be melted down. Theirs is a primeval privilege that no young god is going to rob them of. But at the same time we glimpse the truth of their assertion that they are the primal defenders of justice. Their sternness is what underpins a world of order and righteousness, and the fear they generate is indispensable. Unloved and unvalued they may be in the new Olympian order, but their compensation is their own pride in their vital work:

> All holds. For we are strong and skilled;
> we have authority; we hold
> memory of evil; we are stern
> nor can men's pleadings bend us . . .
> Is there a man who does not fear
> this, does not shrink to hear
> how my place has been ordained,
> granted and given by destiny
> and god, absolute? Privilege
> primeval yet is mine, nor am I without place
> though it be underneath the ground
> and in no sunlight and in gloom that I must stand. (L 381–4, 389–96)

Orestes arrives at the Acropolis and prays to Athena's statue there, which brings the goddess promptly to enquire what is needed. She addresses them all equally politely, the matricide, the god and alarming goddesses 'like no seed ever begotten' (L 410), because in a place of justice there must be no prejudgement, as she says. And in the calm atmosphere she brings with her, Apollo and the Furies agree to lay Orestes' case before her, though each is convinced there can be only one result. Athena proposes that a case as serious as this, and as potentially dangerous to Athens, should not be decided by a goddess or any single party, but by a joint decision of citizens. She will establish a court for manslaughter in her city to endure for all time: 'they shall swear to make no judgment that is not / just, and make clear where in this action the truth lies' (L 488–9). She chooses twelve of the 'finest of her citizens' for jurors, and with careful legality asks the prosecution first to outline their case.

What is the Furies' accusation? Matricide, they say, in a word: Orestes severed the closest of blood bonds, while Clytaemnestra killed a man of different blood. She has paid with her death, while he has yet to pay. Since he does not deny the murder, the case is clear. Apollo then addresses the jury in defence of Orestes, and makes a series of points of increasing tendentiousness. He begins with the fact that avenging Agamemnon was Zeus's will, but he does not rest his case on this. (The authority of Zeus is not 'admissible evidence' in the legal atmosphere Aeschylus is creating, though it gives a foretaste of the conclusion.) His next line of defence is the nature of Clytaemnestra's crime: it was the murder of a high-born man, a ruler, finally home from a campaign in which 'he had done / better than worse, in the eyes of a fair judge' (L 631–2). The plea here is for the status of man's work: authority and order, secured by physical strength – a plea underwritten by Zeus, who gave Agamemnon the sceptre he wielded in Argos. But above all, the murder was an act of unparalleled feminine treachery. Clytaemnestra caught 'the lord of the host of ships' at his one moment of vulnerability, at the edge of the bath: 'in the blind and complex toils' of a robe she 'tangled her man, and chopped him down' (L 634–5). By describing the crime thus emotionally, Apollo intends to sting the male jury into an automatic male response.

His last and most unexpected point, however, is a blunt rebuttal of the Furies' obsession with mothers: looked at properly, a mother is not a parent at all. 'The parent is he who mounts', the active father, he says. The mother merely takes care of the child he deposits with her – she is 'nurse of the new-planted seed / that grows' (L 658–60).[7] So far from being central to the whole arrangement, she is 'a

---

[7]   This is our first encounter with what Vernant has nicely dubbed 'the dream of a purely paternal heredity' in Greek drama (J.-P. Vernant, *Myth and Thought among the Greeks* (London: Routledge & Kegan Paul, 1983), p. 134). See the discussion of Jason and Hippolytus in Chap. 3, below. The argument was certainly current in this form in Athens, and many Greeks denied that the womb had power to engender, since ovulation was not understood (Ruth Padel, *In and Out of the Mind* (Princeton and Oxford: Princeton University Press, 1992), pp. 106–9).

stranger [who] preserves a stranger's seed' (L 661). And to demonstrate the truth of the proposition that there can be fathers without mothers, Apollo points across the courtroom to Athena:

> . . . There she stands,
> the living witness, daughter of Olympian Zeus,
> she who was never fostered in the dark of the womb
> yet such a child as no goddess could bring to birth. (L 663–6)

This startling reversal is the most open revelation of the nature of male rationality in the play. This is what consciousness can do: by force of abstraction deny the female roots of being, and convert pregnancy into the incubation of seedlings. Even the substantiality of marriage is dismissed by this vision: the woman is 'like a stranger' to her husband, providing him with a temporary service. What is real in this arrangement is his seed, which carries the embryo already inside it.

Even this special pleading, however, is capped by Apollo's appeal to Athena as evidence, the daughter who leapt fully formed out of Zeus's forehead. This is a stroke which raises complicated issues: from one point of view it only exposes the impossibility of what Apollo claims, for nothing could mark the difference between gods and men more dramatically than such a hygienic and simple method of parturition. Whatever may be possible on Olympus, birth without blood and pain is not known on earth. But if we view her novel birth symbolically, we can see that Athena's leaping forth from her father's forehead makes her a mental conception, in the fullest sense of that term. She is, we may say, Zeus's best idea; and because ideas are neither male nor female, she is necessarily androgynous, partaking of the divinest, most Zeus-like elements of both men and women. She has female form, but she wears male armour; she has a female grip on realities, but she is free to act in the world of men. For the first time we can hope that the male–female divisions which haunt this trilogy are less insoluble than they seem: Athena is the arbiter who understands both sides, but sees farther than they do.

Athena addresses the jury before the votes are cast, and we see how naturally she enters into Apollo's concern for justice on the one hand, and the Furies' respect for terror on the other. The Hill of Ares on which they are all standing is henceforth to be consecrated to justice. The cycle of blood revenge is at an end; blood crimes will be judged by a jury of citizens in a court whose name is familiar to the Athenian audience, the Areopagus. But the forces that will support institutional justice are still the ancient ones the Furies so value, 'the reverence of citizens' and 'their fear' (L 690–1). Athena speaks in the Furies' own vein when she urges her citizens to sustain a middle way between anarchy and tyranny in their city, using active fear as the safeguard of their democracy:

> No anarchy, no rule of a single master. Thus
> I advise my citizens to govern and to grace,
> and not to cast fear utterly from your city. What

> man who fears nothing at all is ever righteous? Such
> be your just terrors, and you may deserve and have
> salvation for your citadel, your land's defence,
> such as is nowhere else found among men. (L 696–702)

She shares the Furies' respect for terror, but she has a more formalized location for it than they do – in the key institution of her city, the law-court, and thus inside the mind of each self-conscious citizen. For the suggestion that only this can safeguard democratic Athens from the danger of anarchy on the one side, and tyranny on the other, is politically deeply acute. Anarchy results from the breakdown of inner monitors, while tyranny results from delegating to an external figure the responsibility for discipline that properly belongs in each individual. The precondition of true freedom is to internalize terror, in the positive sense of 'conscience', inside each citizen: their '*just* terrors' may create a social harmony 'such as is nowhere else found among men'.

It is only when Athena has shown how fully she grasps the basic wisdom of the Furies that she also demonstrates the allegiance Apollo was assuming, to the shining pantheon of Olympos and to her father Zeus. As the Athenian jury place their ballots in the urn she says that should the votes be equally divided, she will render final judgment herself:

> This is a ballot for Orestes I shall cast.
> There is no mother anywhere who gave me birth,
> and, but for marriage, I am always for the male
> with all my heart, and strongly on my father's side.
> So, in a case where the wife has killed her husband, lord
> of the house, her death shall not mean most to me. And if
> the other votes are even, then Orestes wins. (L 735–41)

The votes are counted, and they fall equally on both sides of the argument. Athena's judgment becomes decisive: she tips the balance to protect the male, as she promised, and Orestes finally goes free of the charge of blood. He gratefully promises Athens eternal friendship as he returns to claim his kingdom – and the Furies are left onstage hissing malice and terrorist reprisal.

How should we interpret the two elements here, of human judgement and divine? The decision of the jury would imply that ordinary human judgement cannot actually solve Orestes' dilemma: when the jurors assess whether Clytaemnestra or Orestes has committed the greater crime, they find that 'marriage or motherhood' is not a proposition with an answer, if the human race depends equally on both. But the verdict of a jury is nonetheless a significant advance on blood revenge: for these are voices detached from kinship, considering a dilemma for which they have deliberately assumed responsibility, in a clear-headed spirit Apollo approves of. The jurors are, so to speak, sociable strangers to Orestes. The allure of kinship does not confuse them, but neither does Apollo's transcendentalism: half of them would exonerate him, but half consider him eternally polluted. This is not yet a resolution, then, but it is a demonstration of the process Athena is placing so much reliance upon. The jury of Athenians, and by extension the city as a whole, is taking to its bosom external terrors and building conscious judgements on the basis of them. A less healthy city would simply expel Orestes and give him up to the Furies, gaining nothing from the extraordinary opportunity he represents. Athens has chosen to harbour the matricide and internalize his meaning.

What can be said of Athena's own vote, however, releasing Orestes on the grounds that 'no mother anywhere gave [her] birth'? This is the key moment of the resolution, and numerous critics who admire the rest of the play have denounced it as a mere trick of mythology, a *dea ex machina* for an insoluble dilemma. It is, clearly, a speech that could only be made by a goddess. No human being can say the same, and the half of the jury that voted against Orestes evidently agreed: there is no way around the primacy of the mother, in whose body the child's body is made, and with whom the root of all piety begins. But the other half of the jury was still more aware that what happens beyond birth, beyond blood ties, is also in need of protection. This is the right to individuate from the mother and to mature in the realm of consciousness. The blunt facts of birth must be repressed to make possible the long journey towards the realm of conscious choice, where marriages are made – the supreme act of human individuation.

Athena, born from her father's forehead, derives from this realm of consciousness too. Her critics would insist that she is only a concept, impossible in biology; but this can be admitted without sacrificing the more important point, that it is precisely in the realm of conceptions that she offers to work. It is not human bodies she aims to give birth to, but citizens; and citizenship is transcendental, involving assent to impalpable things. It makes connections where no bonds exist, between stranger and stranger, between Orestes and Athens, and even, by the end of the play, between Athens and the Furies. It cannot begin without bodies, and therefore maternal bonds are basic to its construction. But it cannot function until the dazzling, bewildering primacy of motherhood is screened from view; for blood bonds lead naturally to tribalism, where belonging is a matter of genetic connection only. To construct a society where the rights of all are respected, whatever their genetic distance, takes the most refined effort of human consciousness.

The *Oresteia* sets out to praise the achievement of human consciousness we call the 'sense of law'; and it is all the more persuasive because Aeschylus so genuinely admits that rationality has its defects. Apollo has the immaturity and extremism of the *arriviste*: he is so determined to detach his protégé from the Furies that he cannot admit the reality of their powers, and he is as irrationally hostile to the earth goddesses as they are to him. His fantasy of motherhood is a bloodless incubation period, and his dream of legality is simply to banish the Furies. Rationality like his is on the verge of deracination; it does not have the saving quality of Athena's, which freely accepts the relationship of the dark to the light. Athena's judgment in favour of Orestes, however, shows the astonishing leap that rational consciousness can make at its best. This is the deliberate effort to counterbalance the glamour of the blood tie with the weight of law. As goddess of the city, she sets the precedent of protecting what will not otherwise be protected; and she inaugurates a civil state where citizens are bonded by their common submission to the laws. If this seems artificial, Aeschlyus might well respond that it is. But it cannot be said to be unrealistic – for he is also reminding his Athenian audience of the downgrading of clan ties by law that recently took place in the history of their own flourishing democracy. They are living testimonies to the possibility of what he is describing.

The depth of Aeschylus' understanding shows in his awareness that the decision about Orestes has only settled half the dilemma. The Furies are still hissing and seething onstage, frantic with baffled rage. They trusted Athena to do them justice, and they feel mocked, cheapened, abandoned; since their primal power has been overridden, it will now convert to a root-and-branch revenge:

> Gods of the younger generation, you have ridden down
> the laws of the elder time, torn them out of my hands.
> I, disinherited, suffering, heavy with anger
> shall let loose on the land
> the vindictive poison
> dripping deadly out of my heart upon the ground;
> this from itself shall breed
> cancer, the leafless, the barren
> to strike, for the right, their low lands
> and drag its smear of mortal infection on the ground. (L 778–87)

The whole of Athens will become their victim, since they have no single body to drain the blood from (the very point, of course, of trial by jury); and Athena's city will become a blighted wilderness. The true wisdom of the goddess shows in the way she responds to the hunger for justice that energizes this language, rather than the threats they make. She calmly reminds them that the trial did not humiliate them, because half the votes were theirs; and she knows as well as they do that the trial is not truly over until a place has been found for the truth they represent. As before, it is a formalized and precise location she offers them – not cast out from civilization but enthroned at the centre of it, beneath her city:

> In complete honesty I promise you a place
> of your own, deep hidden under ground that is yours by right
> where you shall sit on shining chairs beneath the hearth
> to accept devotions offered by your citizens. (L 804–7)

This is the instinct of a supremely healthy consciousness, without the defensiveness of Apollo's: to affirm its relation to what is 'deep hidden underground' and offer the Furies shining thrones in a place of darkness. Athena is not placating these frantic forces but uttering the simple truth when she says,

I will bear your angers. You are elder born than I
and in that you are wiser far than I. Yet still
Zeus gave me too intelligence not to be despised. (L 848–50)

The Furies are wiser because they have a grasp of the beginnings of things: earth, blood, darkness, the origins of life that Apollo could not bear to look at. Impossible to convince them that life does not precede values, or that fear is not the origin of virtue: their implacability has a vital function.

But Zeus has made Athena wise also, wise enough to admit the connection between blood-thinking and thinking, guilt and goodness. Her 'sweet' voice of persuasion does not convert the Furies because it is diplomatic, but because she is speaking so reverentially of the value of the things that come out of the dark. She sees the Furies as they see themselves, as the beginning of fruitfulness. They are at the roots of the richness of physical life, and of the harmony of conscious life, too. They create human beings, and so ultimately law-loving citizens also. And as the significance of Athena's offer dawns on them, they warm more and more to the thought of new honours:

Fur. Lady Athene, what is this place you say is mine?
Ath. A place free of all grief and pain. Take it for yours.
Fur. If I do take it, shall I have some definite powers?
Ath. No household shall be prosperous without your will.
Fur. You will do this? You will really let me be so strong?
Ath. So we shall straighten the lives of all who worship us.
Fur. You guarantee such honour for the rest of time?
Ath. I have no need to promise what I can not do.
Fur. I think you will have your way with me. My hate is going.
(L 892–900)

This deference from the conscious mind to the unconscious is the 'spell' that converts the *Erinyes* (Furies) to the Eumenides (well-wishers, *eu-menides*). The power of the Furies is not contained by frustrating it, but by according it honour and giving it a place of its own.

The trilogy ends with the Eumenides putting their own spell upon Athens, with a glorious promise of fruitfulness, fertility and peace:

Let there blow no wind that wrecks the trees.
I pronounce words of grace.
Nor blaze of heat blind the blossoms of grown plants, nor
cross the circles of its right
place. Let no barren deadly sickness creep and kill.
Flocks fatten. Earth be kind
to them, with double fold of fruit
in time appointed for its yielding. Secret child
of earth, her hidden wealth, bestow
blessing and surprise of gods . . .

> Death of manhood cut down
> before its prime I forbid:
> girls' grace and glory find
> men to live life with them.
> Grant, you who have the power. (L 938–48, 956–60)

Singing this comprehensive prayer, the Eumenides are led offstage, as honorary Athenians – or, more precisely, *metics*, 'guests of the state' (L 1011): the status given in contemporary Athens to foreigners allowed to share some of the rights of native citizens. This conclusion underlines the multilayered meaning of the entire trilogy, which has been at the same time psychological, evolutionary, and political. For the Athens of this period showed its superior sanity (so Pericles claimed) by its lack of xenophobia towards foreigners, and welcomed its *metics* in an annual procession, which the closing procession of this play much resembles. The work of Zeus, which is identified as caring for the guest-stranger, is fulfilled in this welcome accorded to Athena's terrible guests; and by a paradox that the trilogy has at last made intelligible, the Furies are shown to be central to the health of Athens.

Not every critic has accepted this harmonization as final, and feminists in particular have been inclined to take the Furies' place underground as a mark of degradation. But if we follow the logic of the symbolism, the offer of a permanent home in the earth of Athens is an open admission of the primacy of female power. The burden of the play is that the Furies cannot in their nature be defeated – and indeed, that unless they are genuinely honoured, life is blighted at its root. Johnson's trenchant perception that 'nature has given women so much power that the law has very wisely given them little' is more wisely phrased by Aeschylus: since nature has given women so much power, it is the ultimate test of civilization to know how to manage it. And the burden of Athena's role in the play is that only a graceful acknowledgement of the bloody roots of culture and consciousness can keep these things vitally alive. The sense in which the Furies come first, then, is not in question: they are what they say they are, the oldest and wisest powers.

But if they come first, what comes next? The feminist reading does not confront this question, but a tragedian in a self-conscious new democracy is vividly aware of it. What comes next is what distinguishes an Athenian from a Spartan or a Persian: the perilous journey away from blood bonds (mother, the home, the clan) to individuation, and the award of that individual portion of responsible power called the vote. This individual, aware of his roots but not entangled in them, is also capable of contracting a marriage – the ultimate guest–friendship bond, where one person consciously commits himself to another, who does not resemble him in face, gender or genetic origin.

It is because his treatment of the evolution of Athenian justice illuminates these other subjects – why marriage is the test of maturity, why individuation is so hard, and why the sexes so mistrust one another – that this early tragedy of

Aeschylus seems so wonderfully comprehensive. Even more interestingly, perhaps, he explains how the law comes to be anti-female at its very inception, and why it is abstract, bloodless and indifferent to persons. It is all these things because it is the one place where creatures born in blood attempt to see beyond blood, and where the life of conscious responsibility is lived by creatures of flesh.

Chapter 2

Sophocles

The *Oresteia* supplies the parameters of later Greek tragedy. Other dramatists may take up particular elements of Aeschylus' plot, and handle them differently; but if we probe beneath the surface, the conflict remains the one he so lucidly laid bare. As Hegel noticed long ago,

> Its essence is not very extensive. The chief conflict treated most beautifully by Sophocles, with Aeschylus as his predecessor, is that between the state, i.e. ethical life in its *spiritual* universality, and the family, i.e. *natural* ethical life. These are the clearest powers that are presented in tragedy, because the full reality of ethical existence consists in harmony between these two spheres and in absence of discord between what an agent has actually to do in one and what he has to do in the other.[1]

The Greek term for the family ethos is *oikos* and that for the state is *polis*, and the tension between them is dramatized again and again by Sophocles, most famously in the *Antigone*.

But if Sophocles and Aeschylus have a grasp on the same forms and materials, the meaning they fashion out of them is unexpectedly different. It is tempting to assume that the ancient Greeks agreed with one another by nature, and thought 'Greek' thoughts; but since the openly provocative Euripides was a contemporary of Sophocles' too, it is clear that drama was actually the arena for vigorous debate and mutual contradiction. If we look carefully at the arguments implied by Sophocles' plots, we seem to be told that the journey Aeschylus was inviting us to make has been cancelled – and that nothing disperses the original smell of blood.

Certainly Sophocles is a different kind of playwright. Unlike Aeschylus, he does not think in trilogies; on the evidence of what survives, at least, he writes single plays on major subjects, and leaves loose ends dangling where he must. Powerful head-on conflicts are the life of his plots, rather than temporary incompatibilities looking for a reconciliation; and the free movement between the human and the divine that is so exhilarating in the *Oresteia* is not a Sophoclean mode. It would not be true to say that the gods are never seen on stage in Sophocles – Athena sets the action going in the *Ajax* – but in the plays we shall consider here there is a strong feeling that the gods' significance is in proportion to their invisibility. Their presence makes itself felt in oracles, or in thunder; their authority is absolute and their *numen* profound, but they never take on individual qualities and quarrel in public view. This reticence, which makes Sophocles quite

---

[1]   G.W.F. Hegel, *Aesthetics*, trans. T.M. Knox (Oxford: Clarendon Press, 1975), vol. 2, p. 1213.

unlike his two contemporaries, makes him paradoxically more recognizable to modern eyes: there is a kind of Christian decorum to it that seems 'religious'. But considered technically, in terms of stagecraft, the gods' invisibility has a direct impact on his argument. Sophocles' plots are not kinetic, like those of Aeschylus, showing evolution among both gods and men: they are revelatory, rather, of truths that cannot change.

The novelty of viewing Sophocles as the conscious antagonist of Aeschylus might make more sense if we began with an analysis of some key elements of the *Electra*, which by common consent is a difficult play to reconcile with the *Oresteia*. In this play Sophocles handles the material of the *Libation Bearers* as if it were self-contained: Electra and Orestes avenge themselves successfully on Aegisthus and Clytaemnestra, and no Furies arrive to prolong the issue. Classicists have never been able to decide whether the Furies are missing because Sophocles does not believe in their necessity, or because they are so obviously due to burst onstage that we must mentally supply them (the Sophoclean 'irony'). But in other ways, too, Sophocles shows that a single play cannot do the work of a trilogy – and perhaps that he has a quite different aim in mind from his predecessor.

Electra (?418 BCE)

To tell this revenge story as if it were Electra's, Sophocles resorts to an open stratagem: he shows Orestes returning, and then removes him from view on the pretext of making a libation at his father's tomb. The brother and sister are not reunited until the play is almost over; meanwhile Electra dominates the stage, and vividly shows us what it means to live in the shadow of an unrevenged crime. She weeps passionately all night, and speaks bitterness all day; we see her tottering under the burden of remembering what everyone else has forgotten. She calls on all the gods of the underworld without distinction – Hades, Persephone, Hermes, Ara and the Furies – to avenge her wicked mother's acts of murder and adultery, and she is savagely certain that there is only one fit punishment for these crimes. The issue that so preoccupied Aeschylus, of how blood revenge against a mother might call for vengeance in its turn, does not raise its head; the agony Electra is enduring is only the long drawn-out wait for the just executioner.

To set her fidelity and obsessiveness in the strongest light, Sophocles shows her spurning her would-be comforters. The chorus of attendants beg her to have faith in Zeus and Time; Electra passionately insists on her hopeless state, bereft of strength, enslaved, unmarried and childless. Even her brother's long-distance promises are delusive, she says in despair: 'He longs to be here, but not enough to come!'[2] Her chafing anger bursts out against her two sisters (brought into the

---

[2]   Sophocles, *Three Tragedies* [*Antigone, Oedipus the King, Electra*], trans. H.D.F. Kitto (London: Oxford University Press, 1962), *Electra*, p. 106. Hereafter K.

myth from a faint reference in Homer), who have adapted to their new circumstances and would have her do the same. One sister warns her that there is a plan to imprison her in a dungeon where she 'will never see the sun again', but Electra's contemptuous response is to embrace her fate, the darker the better: 'At least / I shall be out of the sight of all of you' (K 388).

Certain notes of criticism are sounded about this fierce heroine. The sympathetic but dubious attendants say she is 'consuming her own life' (K 149), and to hostile Clytaemnestra she is a kind of palace vampire, 'draining me of life' (K 778). But from the lonely prominence she enjoys in the play we deduce that what is ugly in all this loyal tenaciousness cannot be otherwise. This is what remembering means: sacrificing the future, because the will to live itself connives with those who would deny the truth of the past.

The key scene of confrontation in this play is inevitably between Electra and Clytaemnestra, rather than mother and son. Not only are the dramatis personae different, but the balance of the argument, too: this Clytaemnestra mixes a stout defence of her past actions with much shallow ingenuity. If Agamemnon had to sacrifice a child, surely a son of Menelaus and Helen's, who started the war, would have made a better victim – or was Agamemnon so unnatural as to prefer his brother's children to his own? she enquires. The monster deserved to die, and if Iphigenia could testify she would certainly agree. Electra's arguments in rebuttal tumble over one another: Agamemnon was guiltless and the real fault lay with Artemis (Sophocles here follows a different myth Aeschylus had rejected); he sacrificed Iphigenia 'in anguish, and after long refusal' (K 566–7). But this in any case is only Clytaemnestra's excuse: justice was not the motive, Aegisthus was. If Electra is 'unfilial, disloyal, shameless, impudent' as charged, she is only following her mother's example. This Clytaemnestra is indeed a creature of startling wickedness: we are told that she did not merely chop off Agamemnon's limbs but wiped the bloody sword on his hair, and that she celebrates the murder every month with a feast. The dilemma is not how to punish such a mother without incurring her Furies (these are only mentioned in passing, and on Agamemnon's side of the argument) but how to get access to plant the necessary blow.

Because the issue of punishment is no more complicated than this (and the actual deed of vengeance will take no more than a hundred lines at the end of the play), Sophocles sustains the drama with new material that sets Electra's psychology in the strongest light. She is drawn in, unwittingly, to the stratagem Orestes and his old tutor invent to get access to the palace, and has to listen to an agonizingly detailed description of how her brother met his end in a chariot race at Delphi. She receives from a disguised Orestes the urn that contains his pretended ashes and cradles it in anguish. Her bitterness is absolute: it should have been her sisterly hands that prepared his body for the funeral fire, not those of a stranger. She was more his nurse than his nurse was, and more his mother than Clytaemnestra; and now the lovely boy who called her 'nurse' and 'sister' is gone, and all that remains is ashes and a shade. Since both he and Agamemnon are dead, she yearns to join them below in nothingness; she is nothing, now, herself. And she pleads to share as entirely with Orestes in death as she did in life. Only burial in the same grave could alleviate the agony of separation.

Orestes finally reveals himself when it is safe to do so, and her rapture on being reunited is unrestrained and tumultuous in proportion. Then the play hastens to its conclusion, in which Electra is still kept in the forefront of the action. Orestes takes Clytaemnestra unawares and leads her offstage for the climactic blow: and as we imagine the deed being done, what we see onstage is Electra urging him forwards, so that it is her hatred that seems to supply the energy of his unseen actions: 'strike her again, if you have strength enough!' (K 1393). As Orestes comes back to dispatch Aegisthus, she again takes the lead: Aegisthus begs for reprieve, 'a little time, / to speak', but Electra cuts him off with the most vindictive lines of the play:

> No, by the gods, Orestes! No
> Long speech from him! No, not a single word!
> He's face to face with death; there's nothing gained
> In gaining time. Kill him at once! And when
> You've killed him, throw the body out of sight,
> And let him have the funeral he deserves.
> Animals shall eat him! Nothing less than this
> Will compensate for all that he has done. (K 1458–65)

This, aside from a terse remark of Orestes, to the effect that if there were more capital punishment, there would be fewer villains, is where the *Electra* comes to an end.

What is unmistakable in this portrait is that Sophocles is showing the heroic aspect of the qualities Aeschylus associated with the unconverted Furies. Like them, Electra never wavers, never forgets; if the future must be sacrificed out of loyalty to the past, let it be so. She contemplates going into the dark with stubborn indifference (the threatened dungeon, or her brother's grave) – for what is unbearable is to live in daylight without justice. But justice here is defined as the *lex talionis*, the shedding of blood for blood. 'Those who were killed of old now / Drink in return the blood of those who killed them' says the Chorus at the close (K 1387–8), and so the play ends with no advance on the logic that Electra used in denouncing Clytaemnestra: it is a joy to punish where punishment is so richly deserved. Another familiar element is Electra's passionate attachment to her brother – her bodily cradling of his ashes, and her sense that she belongs with him under the earth. Blood bonds make up the whole of her sisterly reality. Impossible to think of this Electra contracting a marriage or having children; her self-repression is part of her greatness.

The silence at the end of the play thus leaves us with a fundamental puzzle. Is Sophocles actually intending to unmask Electra and show us, by her vindictive rapture, what the true consequences of vengeance are? Is it possible to deduce a whole reading of the play from what is *not* said?[3] Or must we take the play at face value, and see it as a heroic account of the Furies' world-view, as embodied in a sister? This reading is not without difficulty, either, since the real logic of the Furies would leave Orestes indelibly polluted by maternal blood.[4] In addition to this, Clytaemnestra and Aegisthus have had children of their own, and Orestes must be as proper an object of their vengeance as Aegisthus was of his. What should we conclude?

Perhaps these puzzles cannot be solved in the framework of the play itself. If we put the *Electra* in the context of the earlier *Antigone*, however, we may find firmer grounds for judgement – for what is immediately striking is how much overlap there is between the two heroines and the scenes Sophocles constructs for them. The *Antigone*, however, famously represents two sides of the argument, in playing off the *oikos*-centred concerns of the heroine with the *polis* concerns of Creon, king of Thebes.

Antigone (441 BCE)

The plot turns on the proper burial of the corpse of Antigone's brother Polyneices. He and his brother Eteocles have fought each other to death over the inheritance of Thebes, and Creon, the new king, has decreed two different fates for their corpses: honoured burial for Eteocles, who defended the city, and disgraceful exposure for Polyneices, who attacked it. The issues are thus made visible in two dead bodies. Which should matter more to human beings, politics or heaven? Which has the higher claim, family feeling or the stability of the state? Creon is Polyneices' uncle as well as king of Thebes, but it would be weakness, he says, to let that cloud his judgement. The *polis* comes first, and loyalty to its friends. The ship of state must be kept watertight, in the long-term interest of everyone on board.

Antigone's position is equally clear from the moment she enters, having heard Creon's proclamation. It is the culmination of a train of agonies: from Oedipus'

---

[3]   George Thomson thinks we are expected to supply the Aeschylean context throughout (*Aeschylus and Athens: A Study in the Social Origins of Drama* (London: Lawrence & Wishart, 1941, repr. 1973), p. 336) and C.P. Segal reads the play as an ironic exposure of vengeance (*Tragedy and Civilization: An Interpretation of Sophocles* (Cambridge, Mass.: Harvard University Press, 1981), p. 249).

[4]   Brian Vickers accuses Sophocles of 'sweeping awkward issues under the carpet ... he ignores the problems of human law, social law, and divine approval of human destructiveness' (*Towards Greek Tragedy: Drama, Myth, Society* (London and New York: Longman, 1973, corr. edn 1979), pp. 572–3). Jebb was long ago amazed at a plot that took matricide as a well-deserved punishment and left Orestes unpolluted: 'I do not know any adequate solution of this difficulty' (*The Electra of Sophocles*, ed. R.C. Jebb (Cambridge: Cambridge University Press, 1908), p. xxxii).

incest to her brothers' fratricide, her family has known every calamity but this. The remedy, however, is heroically simple: to bury her brother's body at whatever risk to herself, since the gods require it, and her own feelings demand it. The dead are dead much longer than the living are living. Her loyalty is to eternal values, even if that means joining her brother among the dead; she will nonetheless please those it most matters to please.

We recognize the colliding spheres of Apollo and the Furies again. Creon, like Apollo, lives in the light of day and sees a clear distinction between what supports the *polis* (friendship) and what undermines it (treachery). Since it is the *polis* that creates meaningful alliances out of chaos, and gives friendship its basis, the *polis* is decisive – and bodies, even dead ones, take their value from their relationship to it. Antigone's values, however, are those of the Furies, and her position coincides in many ways with Electra's: she must remember, when everyone else is forgetting, and be loyal to old truths even at the sacrifice of her own future. Human beings may live briefly in the light, but the darkness of earth embraces them before and after; this, not the light, is the fundamental reality. Antigone offers to go into the dark, the living tomb Creon prepares for her, because the rest of her *oikos* is already there – Oedipus, Jocasta, Polyneices and Eteocles. Blood bonds are the ultimate tie, and her planned marriage to Creon's son Haemon does not weigh significantly in the balance. The weight of the real is found in the earth, in blood, and the unchanging laws of the gods, which the law-making of the *polis* can never displace.

As in the court scene of the *Eumenides*, it is a genuine dilemma being outlined here. When Creon speaks about the *polis* and friendships, he invokes those values we called masculine and transcendental – the sphere in which one man may decide to attack the *polis*, another to defend it, and both accept to be defined by that choice. But Antigone's world is female, and the reality she grasps is that the city's attacker has become a dead body, a thing of earth that deserves burial on general, not specific grounds. Do bodies come before cities, or cities before bodies? The dilemma is intractable because, posed in these terms, the questions do not intersect. When Aeschylus contemplated a parallel dilemma, however, he did two things: he exposed the inadequacies of each argument when taken to extremes; and introduced an androgynous third term, Athena. Something similar happens in this play, but to suggestively different effect.

Sophocles certainly complicates the issue outlined above by showing how weak Creon is, even as he insists on political stability. No sooner has he outlined his policy than a reluctant guard appears, with the news that someone has performed the traitor's funeral rites. Creon promptly justifies the guard's reluctance: he scents a conspiracy ('wagging of heads in secret', K 291), accuses the guard himself of accepting a bribe ('of all vile things . . . none is so vile as money', K 294–5), and promises to hang him if no other criminal is found. These are the responses of a tyrant, whose only concept of stability is the conformity of the city to his single will. When Antigone is brought forward as the culprit he is particularly stung to find she is a woman ('Now she would be the man, not I, if she / Defeated me and did not pay for it', K 474–5); and in a fine illustration of arbitrary justice, he resolves to punish Ismene into the bargain. In all this, Creon exposes the Apollonian weakness of his strength to the point of parody. Whatever truth there is in his defence of the polis, it is undermined by his egotism; and though he ostensibly places impersonal values above family ties, he interprets justice in the most partial spirit.

Is Sophocles' portrait of Antigone equally sceptical? This is the key question, for her behaviour is certainly painted as extreme. From the moment of the proclamation she is ready to pay the ultimate penalty, provided it leads to her brother's grave: 'If I have to die for this pure crime, / I am content, for I shall rest beside him' (K 72–3). It is left for Ismene to feel the horror of the dilemma, but from the unheroic position of female timidity: 'I yield to those who have authority', she says (K 67). When Ismene will not join her, Antigone contemptuously invites her sister to denounce her to Creon instead. Indeed, she will hate her if she does not. Like Electra, Antigone revels in her isolation and is equally intemperate in love and in hatred: 'Let me be, / Me and my folly! I will face the danger / That so dismays you' (K 95–7). When Ismene later begs to be allowed to share her punishment, Antigone fiercely refuses; and it is altogether much less clear than might be expected that she would choose a different fate if she could. The thought of lying in her brother's grave has a kind of rapture (no one else could be so near and so dear); and though she laments her doom pitifully when the time of punishment comes, she gives her ultimate reasons with a clarity that has cooled the goodwill of a thousand commentators. The speech is quite unexpected:

> Yet what I did, the wise will all approve.
> For had I lost a son, or lost a husband,
> Never would I have ventured such an act
> Against the city's will. And wherefore so?
> My husband dead, I might have found another;
> Another son from him, if I had lost
> A son. But since my mother and my father
> Have both gone to the grave, there can be none
> Henceforth that I can ever call my brother.
> It was for this I paid you such an honour,
> Dear Polyneices, and in Creon's eyes
> Thus wantonly and gravely have offended. (K 878–89)

To say in all sincerity that she would not have made this sacrifice for a son or husband puts Antigone far outside the orbit of Western thinking, still saturated as it is in Christian values. But it does not clash with the assumptions of the Furies: husbands and sons from their point of view are renewable resources (marriage, after all, is only a breath, a promise) – but a brother is something weightier, an irreplaceable reality. Since their mother Jocasta is dead, there can be no more brothers: and so a brother takes priority. Antigone puts her blood bond with Polyneices before any bond she might make in the future, because she distinguishes as clearly as the Furies between the world of matter and a merely hypothetical marriage. Brothers are real; husbands are, relatively speaking, shadows: 'my husband dead, I might have found another'. They result from a contract that can be made, broken, and made again.

Is this portrait of a heroine who cannot live for the future as critical as that of Creon? It is the same question we encountered with Electra, though this is a heroine who strikes us as much fresher to her heroic challenge, a less brooding and morbid character altogether. Nonetheless, Sophocles has anticipated a number of the same effects: the heroine spurning the milk-and-water nature of a sister, running headlong towards her punishment, and finding her consolation in unity with her brother, rather than a husband (to the point where she greets the dark tomb as her bridal chamber). Critics have been divided about the reservations that might be implicit in this; but it is hard to avoid the conclusion that Sophocles is deeply moved by a heroine so attached to the 'real', and so reckless in self-sacrifice. Antigone and Electra evoke all the power of his artistic sympathy, while his male protagonists are sketchy like Orestes, or sardonically handled like Creon; although the claims of the city and of the family pose a genuine dilemma, it is Antigone's side of the argument which is overwhelming in its effect on us.

The impression that Sophocles does not give equal credit to both sides of the dilemma is reinforced by his introduction of the Athena-like mediator, Haemon. He is wonderfully placed to understand both sides of the argument: he is Creon's son, but betrothed to Antigone, tied by blood in one direction and by conscious choice in the other. His arguments are immensely tactful, the spirit of persuasion embodied. It is his love for his father that forces him to report that the city itself is united in Antigone's favour; and it is for Creon's true credit, he says, that he urges him to retract his sentence on her. When Creon explodes that he himself is the *polis*, Haemon's riposte is unanswerable: only if the *polis* is a desert. And when Creon says that Haemon's plea is only for his beloved, Haemon answers with a wisdom worthy of Athena, 'And me, and you – and [for] the gods below' (K 735). We glimpse the argument of the *Eumenides* again: the world of light owes homage to the world of dark, and it must never be forgotten which of them has priority.

In terms of the plot, however, Haemon's plea is ineffective. Creon will hear no arguments from a woman's pawn, and the next thing we hear of Haemon is his death. When Creon finally comes to release Antigone, he finds his son embracing her dead body. Haemon attempts to kill his father, then falls on his sword, and dies with Antigone's corpse in his arms. His intervention is not, after all, what brings Creon to repentance: that role goes rather to Teiresias, and the medium of conviction in this play is not language (Athena's 'magic words' of persuasion) but divination. Teiresias is driven to confront the king by evidence that the *polis* is sickening along with Creon's state of mind: the dogs and birds that gorged themselves on the body of Polyneices are now polluting the shrines and altars of the gods. For Creon's great crime, Teiresias foresees a precise punishment, corpse for corpse. He has arrogated rights that belonged neither to him nor even the Olympians, but to the ancient gods down below:

> Because you have thrust down within the earth
> One who should walk upon it, and have lodged
> A living soul dishonourably in a tomb;
> And impiously have kept upon the earth
> Unburied and unblest one who belongs
> Neither to you nor to the upper gods
> But to the gods below . . .
> Therefore the gods arouse against you
> Their sure avengers. (K 1031–7, 1038–9)

These are the Furies, whose payment will be extracted, as ever, in literal form. For when Creon – after his usual worries about money and fraud – has finally given in to Teiresias, and has arrived too late to save Antigone, he not only fails to save Haemon from suicide, but returns to the palace to find his queen has killed herself. She died with a curse on her lips for the husband who destroyed her son. Two bodies pay for two bodies: in this terrible equation, Creon is reduced to less than nothing. He begs to be led away, out of men's sight; death is all he can wish for.

Whatever is said, then, about the reality of Creon's dilemma, the plot's hammer blows are reserved for him. He is the one who spoke big words in his pride, and whom the gods teach wisdom the hardest way. Antigone, it may be said, pays for her intransigence too; but she goes to her tomb accepting the judgment of the gods, and we cannot doubt that it is in her favour – indeed, that she gets her last wish, that her punishers be punished. What is problematic in this is the number of questions raised by the play which it does not quite answer: for instance, whether the *polis* is an achievement in itself, and whether its new values, generated by consciousness, can be coordinated with the old, which are rooted in earth. The satiric handling of Creon implies that consciousness leads automatically away from wisdom, towards a deracinated arrogance that the gods will punish for the fatuity it is. It is true that Thebes itself has the wisdom to side with Antigone; but Creon's is the voice that defends the values of the *polis*.

Oedipus (*c.*429 BCE)

If it is true that Sophocles' theme is the danger of deracination, the arrogance of rationality, then the Oedipus plot is a wonderful vehicle for such a philosophy.

The play opens with a tableau in which the hero stands before his plague-stricken people. He is the embodiment of kingliness, of heroic individuation; and as his suffering 'children' fling themselves on his support he says, 'my heart is heavy with / The city's pain, my own, and yours together' (K 61–3). He is the father of his people, 'wise above all other men to read / Life's riddles' (K 33–4); and he alone will know what to do.

The responsibility and power Oedipus exudes are stressed because of course this opening is ironic: nothing is as it appears. The myth was so familiar that Sophocles could rely on his audience's foreknowledge, as we see from numerous strokes of dramatic irony in the phrasing. And so this tableau carries an extraordinary message: 'Here is what full individuation looks like – and it is all a delusion.' This father of the city, bonded in loving and responsible citizenship, is actually too bonded by primal blood ties to live in a city at all. This man of intellect, solver of life's riddles, is himself the answer to the riddle of the plague. And the one who offers so intellectually to restore the city to health, is its physical pollution embodied.

A plot that turns upon unwitting incest is also profoundly demonstrative of the theme of unavailing rationalism. For incest is the crime Oedipus most consciously intends not to commit, and it is the steps he takes to avoid it which bring it about: he flees the parents he thinks are his as soon as he hears the disastrous oracle. This central idea is also expressed in the tight plot structure, by which each step Oedipus takes towards the light only leads him deeper into the dark. Each attempt at control reveals more of Oedipus' real powerlessness: it is because of his attempt to fix some intelligible blame on Creon that his wife Jocasta is brought onstage, and Oedipus hears for the first time that Laius was killed 'where three roads meet'. It is because he is determined to rid himself finally of fear that Oedipus tells the old prophecy to the Corinthian messenger, and hears what is meant to comfort him, that Polybus and Merope were not his real parents. The plot is a series of tripwires over which not only Oedipus, but Jocasta, and even the messenger fall. The only characters inside the plot who know enough to try and halt its unravelling are Teiresias, and the shepherd who witnessed Laius' killing. And their testimonies are wrung out of them by force, in spite of their attempts at control.

Above all, the nature of incest tells the same essential story: for incest is the impulse that subverts rationality, maturation and the *polis* at a stroke. The play itself is not 'about' incest in any detailed sense, admittedly; it has been usefully remarked that if Oedipus were truly Oedipal, his fixations would be on the parents he thought were his, Polybus and Merope. The incest Oedipus commits is as abstract as possible, and there is nothing in his scenes with Jocasta to suggest a bond other than a connubial one. Perhaps because of the depth of the taboo that he is handling, Sophocles is very careful in his treatment; Oedipus is like the man who dreams he has committed a crime, only to wake and find he has. But

Sophocles seems to be as aware as Freud of the interplay between primal allure and primal destructiveness in the bond between sons and mothers. When the oracle is weighing heavily on Oedipus' mind, he makes Jocasta brace him by saying, 'How many men in their dreams have married their mother!' (ll. 981–2). Jocasta thinks she is revealing male fantasies for what they are; but the play, with the darkest irony, shows the fantasy to be the truth.

Perhaps we should pause here, and ask what exactly it is that makes mother–son incest the primal taboo in civilization. Psychoanalysis suggests that in the kinetic development of the individual away from its parents, incest is a short-circuiting of the necessary energy. The sexual vitality that should propel the child into autonomy and bonds of its own choosing, merely knits the child more firmly into its original blood bonds. Individuation is indefinitely postponed; and the state is left with no role to play in ushering the child towards maturity. Indeed, from the incestuous family's point of view, the outside world is the enemy, for it represents the challenge to individual development that incest precludes. This applies to all forms of incest; but the reasons mother–son incest might be viewed as the most disastrously regressive were famously articulated by Freud, with the help of this play. In the sense that every boy is born into a sexual triangle, in which his love for his mother makes him the rival of his father, male identity is built on a basis of fear and renunciation. Fear of incest and parricide are two sides of the same coin: the father is superfluous to requirements and in the boy's imagination easily removed, though not without terror of the consequences. But the mother, desired and forbidden, generates still deeper terrors, because it is only by resisting identification with her that the boy can construct his own, distinctly male, identity. If he re-enacts sexually the primary bond, he returns all too literally to the womb.[5]

A play which turns so dramatically on the unavailing power of rationality and human will creates certain difficulties when it comes to the justice of the hero's fate. First-time readers often feel indignant on Oedipus' behalf: 'The gods did it to him – it wasn't his fault!' Classicists have spent much ink dispelling the

---

[5]   Freud thought that this 'secret meaning' in the play was what distracted the original audience from what was obviously immoral in the play's overt meaning: 'It is surprising that Sophocles' tragedy does not call forth indignant remonstrance from its audience ... For at bottom it is an immoral play; it sets aside the individual's responsibility to social law, and displays divine forces ordaining the crime and rendering powerless the moral instincts of the human being which would guard him against the crime. [In the hands of 'the critical Euripides' it would probably have been an 'accusation'] but with the reverent Sophocles there is no question of such an intention; the pious subtlety which declares it the highest morality to bow to the will of the gods, even when they ordain a crime, helps him out of the difficulty. I do not believe that this moral is one of the virtues of the drama, but neither does it detract from its effect; it leaves the hearer indifferent; he does not react to this, but to the secret meaning and content of the myth itself.' *Introductory Lectures on Psychoanalysis* (1929), trans. Joan Rivière (London: George Allen & Unwin, 1970), p. 270.

assumptions behind such thinking: for instance, the fact that an oracle foretells an event does not compel it to happen, it merely shows foresight. And the fact that Oedipus is not intentionally at fault does not erase the crime: witness the pollution in Thebes. But beyond these corrective views we may acknowledge real difficulties in responding to such a tight-lipped masterpiece of plotting. If the gods are not to blame, why does Oedipus, blinded, cry, 'It was Apollo, friends, Apollo. / He decreed that I should suffer what I suffer' (K 1276–7)? And if Oedipus did everything he could to avoid making the oracle come true, in what sense is he at fault? The very brilliance of the plot compounds the sense that Oedipus had no choice: the less his will is involved, the greater the role necessarily ascribed to 'fate'.

Numerous efforts have been made to involve Oedipus in his own fate by imputing faults to him. These have ranged from the silly ('He should have taken a vow not to marry an older woman'), to the more plausible accusation of *hubris*: he is too hasty and violent in pursuit of his goal, and it is his own overconfidence that undoes him. A classic instance would be the moment at which he provokes Teiresias into speech, in spite of the seer's determination:

> Teir. I'll say no more, and you, if you so choose
>   May rage and bluster on without restraint.
> Oed.   Restraint? Then I'll show none! I'll tell you all
>   That I can see in you: I do believe
>   This crime was planned and carried out by you,
>   All but the killing; and were you not blind
>   I'd say your hand alone had done the murder.
> Teir. So? Then I tell you this: submit yourself
>   To that decree that you have made; from now
>   Address no word to these men nor to me:
>   *You* are the man whose crimes pollute our city. (K 336–46)

Oedipus is clearly possessed by his rage, and his wild accusations show all the symptoms of a *tyrannos* abusing his power. But it is surely one thing to say this violence is wrong, and another to say that the play shows Oedipus being punished for it. The punishment shown is for a much greater crime, committed long before; and there is nothing in the drama to associate it specifically with *hubris*. (Perhaps a case could be made for the connection between his hasty temper and the violent attack on Laius, but it is not one pointed up by Sophocles. Laius has a hasty temper too.)

The earlier *Antigone*, however, supplies a context which makes this scene easier to interpret. This seems to be another instance of Sophocles repeating his significant effects, and the collision here is already familiar in two versions: as Creon's attack on the reluctant guard (*Ant.* 289–326), and his encounter with Teiresias (1033–63). Here, again with Teiresias, the blindness of the old prophet only causes Oedipus a moment's hesitation: the crime was 'planned and carried out' by him, with an assistant, doubtless, for the killing (K 340–1). Creon, too, was tyrannically quick to scent a conspiracy and pinned instant blame on impossible candidates. The fact that he was not punished in *Antigone* for tyrannical hastiness, but for his desecration of two human bodies, confirms our impression that *hubris* is not Oedipus' crime in itself: his overinterpretation of the evidence here is a symptom, not a cause.

But a symptom of what? Here again, Creon is the model for Oedipus: when wholly crushed by his discoveries at the end of *Antigone*, he acknowledges himself at last for what he is, 'a rash, misguided man, / Whose blindness has killed a wife and a son' (K 1281–2). The man of power has become less than nothing, a wreck to be hidden from men's eyes. Without willing it, he has killed those whom he loved most: this fearful destiny is beyond bearing, he moans. This is the *anagnorisis*, recognition, that Aristotle thought the key to tragic effect. For Oedipus this recognition is wrought to a higher pitch, out of yet more dreadful discoveries. He becomes exactly what Teiresias foretold he would:

> Listen – since you have taunted me with blindness!
> You have your sight, and yet you cannot see
> Where, nor with whom, you live, nor in what horror.
> Your parents – do you know them? or that you
> Are enemy to your kin, alive or dead?
> And that a father's and a mother's curse
> Shall join to drive you headlong out of Thebes
> And change the light that now you see to darkness?
> Your cries of agony, where will they not reach?
> Where on Cithaeron will they not re-echo?
> When you have learned what meant the marriage-song
> Which bore you to an evil haven here
> After so fair a voyage? And you are blind
> To other horrors, which shall make you one
> With your own children. Therefore, heap your scorn
> On Creon and on me, for no man living
> Will meet a doom more terrible than yours. (K 403–19)

When Oedipus emerges self-blinded from the palace six hundred lines later, he 'sees' what blind Teiresias saw – that all his knowledge was ignorance, and all his light mere darkness.

If we return to the question, what it was his *hubris* was a symptom of, the answer would seem to be – of the arrogance inherent in thinking at all. The plot shows every lucid perception of Oedipus' merely to hasten the onset of darkness, just as his intelligent answer to the riddle of the Sphinx was the very thing that made him Jocasta's husband. The truth is that he does not even know who his parents are: there could be no more fundamental way of implying that he knows nothing worth knowing. We are reminded of the key effect of the opening scene: a comprehensive irony has enveloped Oedipus from the first, and Sophocles has never allowed us to lose sight of the fact that his individuation, wisdom and freedom are all equally delusive. The play underlines the inherent lunacy of rationalism, which sees 'the outlines of every object but not the details indicative of their nature'.

The view of Sophocles that takes him as the conscious opponent of Aeschylus may seem more justifiable now, for the play's anti-rationalist logic is familiar. Although the Furies are notably missing from the argument, the way the plot functions is not unlike their awful implacability, and it concludes in a way that justifies their derision at the whole idea of transcendence. We recall the terms in which they vaunted their power over Orestes, and anyone else who might try to slip out of the noose of blood bonds: the world beyond is an illusion of man's pride, which it is their job to melt down. With a 'long leap from high / above and dead drop of weight' they 'cut the legs from under even / the runner, and spill him to ruin' (*Eum.* L 372–6). In the same way, this plot trips up and crushes Oedipus. Sophocles here defends the primal authority of the earth goddesses, much as he did in the *Electra* and *Antigone*. He responds to their weight and grandeur, and ignores what Aeschylus imputed to them, titanic complacency and blood-snuffing regression.

Another way of putting the paradox of *Oedipus* is that it implies that Apollo and the Furies protect the same truths. The portrayal of deities in drama is of course a matter for each playwright, and Sophocles is not bound to follow Aeschylus' characterization of either. But the handling of deities in any play needs to be clear and significant, and here, the presentation of Apollo only through his oracles, and the absent-but-omnipresent nature of the Furies, creates a puzzle. Is there no deity in Sophocles to protect the city, the life of the mind, the human achievement of consciousness and transcendence? Certainly these are not the sphere of his Apollo, and it is not Apollo whom Sophocles intends to undermine through his revelation of the weakness of rationality. He remains at the centre of the play, though invisible, the god of unchanging and unchangeable truth and the linchpin of the system of piety. If his oracles are not valid, nothing else holds, says the chorus with a shudder:

> No longer shall Apollo's shrine,
> The holy centre of the Earth, receive my worship;
> No, nor his seat at Abae, not
> The temple of Olympian Zeus,
> If what the god foretold does not come to pass.
> Mighty Zeus – if so I should address Thee –
> O great Ruler of all things, look on this!
> Now are thy oracles falling into contempt, and men
> Deny Apollo's power.
> Worship of the gods is passing away. (K 864–73)

The terror of the collapse of religion envisioned by this chorus is far greater than the terror that – in accordance with the oracle – Oedipus has killed his father and

married his mother. In this context, Oedipus' crimes are a kind of relief: they are
as they were said to be; the gods do exist.

If it is true that Sophocles finds the Furies more weighty than squalid, more
profound than regressive, we can understand the interplay here between his
stagecraft and his philosophy. As we began by noting, Sophoclean plots are not
kinetic and evolutionary as the *Oresteia* is, but revelatory: the old truths still
pertain. A god like Apollo cannot therefore be shown as having something to
learn, and the Furies cannot undergo a conversion, either. Thus far, his argument
with Aeschylus may seem only a matter of religious style; but Sophocles' respect
for the unconverted Furies has important consequences at the level of meaning,
too. For his attitude to Oedipus' crime of incest at the end of the play is more
ambiguous than might be expected. It is, of course, a thing of horror; but it is not
only that – it is part of what makes Oedipus a hero too. This is how Oedipus
confronts the chorus at the end of the play, when they are astonished that he has
not committed suicide, but has chosen to blind himself instead. He raves as he
describes his unspeakable crimes:

> O you three ways, that in a hidden glen
> Do meet: you narrow branching roads within
> The forest – you, through my own hands, did drink
> My father's blood, that was my own. – Ah! do you
> Remember what you saw me do? And what
> I did again in Thebes? You marriages!
> You did beget me: then, having begotten,
> Bore the same crop again, and brought to light
> Commingled blood of fathers, brothers, sons,
> Brides, mothers, wives; all that there can be
> Among the human kind most horrible!
>   But that which it is foul to do, it is
> Not fair to speak of. Quick as you can, I beg,
> Banish me, hide me, slay me! (K 1337–49)

There could be no more dramatic account of the terrible ambiguities spawned by
incest. The blood of Laius that Oedipus shed was his own; he has been his
mother's husband, and brother to his own sons and daughters, while Jocasta's
blood has circulated between them as if they all made one undifferentiated body.
Because it intermingles the generations, incest arrests the flow of time, just as it
arrests the development of individuals. It creates the world the Furies would
choose to inhabit, where all is stasis and only blood creates realities. And to full
humanity it is a blight, the very plague of infertility that infests Thebes, which
only the expulsion of Oedipus can remove.
But what is unexpected about the litany of horrors Oedipus recites is that he
seems to grow in stature as he speaks. Even as he acknowledges himself an
abomination he strikes the note of command, and finishes his speech with
authority:

> ... throw me forth
> Into the sea, where I may sink from view.
> I pray you, deign to touch one so afflicted,
> And do not fear: there is no man alive
> Can bear this load of evil but myself. (K 1350–4)

The merest contact with him should be as lethal as the original plague, but he exempts himself: 'deign to touch one so afflicted, / And do not fear'. He is polluted, but somehow not polluting. His contact with the darkest realms of experience has marked him out: 'no man alive / Can bear this ... but myself', and he has become a kind of seer, like Teiresias, destined for an unprecedented purpose:

> My home must be the mountains – on Cithaeron,
> which, while they lived, my parents chose to be
> My tomb: they wished to slay me; now they shall.
> For this I know: sickness can never kill me,
> Nor any other evil; I was not saved
> That day from death, except for some strange doom. (K 1390–5)

The last line points forward to the story Sophocles tells in *Oedipus at Colonus*, where indeed it emerges that his unique crimes and sufferings have converted Oedipus into something else: a source of strange power, and benefit for any city that will harbour him.

In the same way, there is a paradoxical innocence in the way Oedipus now reaches out to his daughters for the last time. This infinitely pathetic scene of farewell depends on our not registering their changed relations (and, perhaps, on the absence of Polyneices and Eteocles, the brother-sons of Oedipus, who would certainly darken the tone):

> Where are you, children? Where? O come to me!
> Come, let me clasp you with a brother's arms,
> These hands, which helped your father's eyes, once bright,
> To look upon you as they see you now –
> Your father who, not seeing, nor enquiring,
> Gave you for mother her who bore himself.
> See you I cannot; but I weep for you,
> For the unhappiness that must be yours,
> And for the bitter life that you must lead. (K 1416–25)

In a sense, 'I *must not* clasp you with a brother's arms' would be still more pathetic, and truer to the situation; but Sophocles maintains a paradoxical view of Oedipus which makes his last agonized half-line – 'Do not take them away from me!' – the climax of paternal pathos. Perhaps this is the same paradox by which he maintains the awesomeness of the Furies in spite of their squalor, and the greatness of Antigone, in spite of regression: in his understanding, the incest-entangled Oedipus stands at the very heart of fatherhood.

Oedipus at Colonus (?406 BCE)

This play, which takes the aged Oedipus to his death in Athens, cannot be viewed as a direct sequel: it was written some thirty years later, and Creon and Oedipus differ in some important aspects in this incarnation. Creon, for example, is a hypocritical villain, and Oedipus announces his innocence at every point. But the fact that Sophocles at the end of his career is imagining an end to the indelible pollution of parricide and incest, and showing under what circumstances it may become a blessing, makes this plot highly suggestive.

Even more suggestive is the location at which this conversion takes place: Colonus is a grove sacred to the Eumenides, a mile outside Athens. The plot shows a wise and diplomatic Theseus extending Athenian citizenship and protection to Oedipus here. At the end of the play, summoned by the thunder of Zeus, Oedipus disappears into the grove to become a 'friend underground' to Athens; he promises to protect her against hostile Thebes into futurity. This combination of motifs is so reminiscent of the *Oresteia* – the conversion of a thing of terror into blessing, the city's enlightened welcome of a polluted outsider, the use of a location sacred to the Eumenides themselves – that we cannot doubt Sophocles is still working over Aeschylean materials, and bringing those ideas to his own conclusion. *Oedipus at Colonus* is his final answer to the *Oresteia*.

But his answer, as might be deduced from the previous plays, is deeply conservative: it is not confrontation between new and old gods that will make the difference, or 'magic words' of enlightenment, but a mystery centred on blood that cannot be explained. Oedipus has become an awesome being, intransigent, wrathful and in touch with the deepest sources of knowledge. At the climax of the play, he is summoned by thunder and taken into the gods' protection; and the messenger who returns can only say that a miracle has occurred, and if anyone does not believe it he will not exert himself to persuade them. Nothing could be less Aeschylean: instead of a debate, there is a miraculous disappearance. Much commentary on this play has been coloured since the last century by Christian sympathy, but at least one puzzled scholar has asked, 'Is it too much to say that Oedipus earns his status as a chthonian [earth] power by acting like the unpersuaded Furies of the *Oresteia*?'[6] In the light of the other plays, the answer is hard to avoid: Sophocles is asserting for one last time the primacy of the Furies' world-view.

This may also be why the play's central emphasis goes on family feeling, and the reciprocal bonds between family members. True family feeling is what is shown by Antigone and Ismene. They have looked after their decayed father for years, while Polyneices and Eteocles have been selfishly preoccupied with their own status (the plot of this play lies between the time of Oedipus' self-blinding

⁶ R.P. Winnington-Ingram, *Sophocles: An Interpretation* (Cambridge: Cambridge University Press, 1980), p. 275.

and the struggle of his sons for Thebes, before the *Antigone*). The key effect of the opening is the contrast between the daughters and sons, and their father's love for the first and hostility to the second. Antigone has been her father's faithful nurse and guide, wandering the land in poverty, as hungry and barefoot as he is; and she has found even these hardships sweet, because of the nature of father–daughter love. But the white-haired Oedipus we see her leading across stage feels a fathomless bitterness towards Polyneices and Eteocles. His daughters have been the real men, he asserts, while his absent sons have been like the ignominious Egyptians who let their womenfolk do all the work. They are not sons at all, but strangers to him. When they had the choice they chose their own power rather than their father's rights, and instead of saving him from exile, they squabbled over the throne. (Sophocles implies that Oedipus was not expelled from Thebes immediately, after all, but remained there until a sudden decision was made to cast him out. This helps motivate Oedipus' rage at Polyneices, for not preventing it.) His response is to curse them, with a comprehensive savagery: neither will win the battle for Thebes, because they will kill each other with their own blood-bonded hands. Curses are Oedipus' only weapon, but he launches them from the bottom of his heart, to teach the piety and respect that are owed to parents. And as we know from the *Antigone*, they are terribly effective.

The seeming weakness of Oedipus, then, hides a titanic power; and the play underlines it by showing him in confrontation with Polyneices, who has come to persuade him to return to Thebes. Polyneices has a long, rhetorical plea for assistance which invokes, one by one, the whole range of male realities that the myopic Furies would leave out of account in their world-view. He begins by saying that his younger brother Eteocles has deposed him, appealing to seniority and legality; that he has made an alliance with Argos, and brought seven allied armies to attack Thebes, an Agamemnon-style argument, appealing to oaths and the obligations of leadership; and then, for good measure, he moves into the style of an epic catalogue and describes with appropriate epic details just what this means. Not only Amphiaraus – but Tydeus – and Eteoclus – and Hippomedon – and Capaneus – and Pathenopaeus – and lastly himself, are all camped outside Thebes to punish the usurper and return the throne to Polyneices (and, he is careful to add, to Oedipus). The one thing needful is the support of Oedipus himself. And to this appeal from the public world of arms and allegiances Oedipus answers simply as an embittered father to an unfilial son: 'Never!'

In his relations with his sons, then, it is no exaggeration to say that Oedipus shows the wrath and intransigence that Aeschylus associated with the Furies. For Sophocles it seems justified by the nature of parenthood: the word Oedipus uses for this is like 'planting' (*phuteusantes*, l. 1377) and the son who does not feel what is owed to his planter, the origin of his life, is cast out from the nexus of all human sanctities. At the apogee of his rage, Oedipus denies that these sons are his own – overtopping even the Furies in his literal-mindedness, for where there is no family love he will acknowledge no kinship. But the other side of this emotion is shown in his relation with his daughters, which glows with mutuality. As at the end of the *Oedipus*, Sophocles seems to show no anxiety about the incestuous origin of this intensity. It is portrayed as supremely valuable, and the climactic scenes of pathos are those where the blind, white-haired father is forcibly parted from his nurses, who not only function as his eyes, but often as his legs, arms and voice as well.

In the first of these scenes, Sophocles creates an episode in which a hypocritical Creon abducts Antigone and Ismene. Theseus quickly halts the violence and brings the daughters back, and the scene that follows is reminiscent of Electra's agony over Orestes' urn. The rapture of the reunion for the daughters and their father is close to anguish: they cling together like a single body that has been surgically divided. Blind Oedipus reaches out frantically for his darlings, the props of his old age, and now he can feel them again he would be happy to die: 'press close to me, child[ren], / Be rooted in your father's arms; rest now from the cruel separation.'[7]

The second scene comes when the agonizing division is made by impending death. When thunder summons Oedipus away, the girls cling to his knees and beat their breasts in despair. Then, as the messenger reports it,

> He put his arms around them, and said to them:
> 'Children, this day your father is gone from you.
> All that was mine is gone. You shall no longer
> Bear the burden of taking care of me –
> I know it was hard, my children, and yet one word
> Frees us of all the weight and pain of life:
> That word is love. Never shall you have more
> From any man than you have had from me.
> And now you must spend the rest of life without me.'
>
> That was the way of it. They clung together
> And wept, all three. (FF, pp. 161–2)

The pathetic element here is that, for all the horror of the past, Oedipus and his daughters shared true happiness between them. It is not possible, in this way of thinking, to be too dear to one's dearest; 'love' is the little word that makes the heaviest burdens light, and Antigone and Ismene will never have 'more / From any man' than they have had from Oedipus. There can be no husbands for girls who have been so loved; but they have had paternal love without precedent.

Oedipus makes a promise to Theseus, his 'most cherished friend', that 'you and this your land and all / Your people may be blessed', in exchange for being allowed to die in an unknown location nearby. Theseus may follow him there but never disclose it to another, until he comes to die himself; and thus the secret will

---

7 *The Oedipus Cycle*, trans. Dudley Fitts and Robert Fitzgerald (New York: Harcourt, Brace & World, 1939, repr. 1971), p. 140. Hereafter FF.

become an other-worldly support to Athens for ever: 'If you obey, this will count more for you / Than many shields and many neighbours' spears. / These things are mysteries, not to be explained' (FF, pp. 158–9). He then disappears in a way the messenger cannot understand; he only knows that Theseus himself shaded his eyes as it happened, and Oedipus passed over the threshold of the merely human:

> We turned around – and nowhere saw that man,
> But only the king, his hands before his face,
> Shading his eyes as if from something fearful,
> Awesome and unendurable to see.
> Then very quickly we saw him do reverence
> To Earth and to the powers of the air,
> With one address to both.
>
> But in what manner
> Oedipus perished, no one of mortal men
> Could tell but Theseus. It was not lightning,
> Bearing its fire from Zeus, that took him off;
> No hurricane was blowing.
> But some attendant from the train of Heaven
> Came for him; or else the underworld
> Opened in love the unlit door of earth.
> For he was taken without lamentation,
> Illness or suffering; indeed his end
> Was wonderful if mortal's ever was. (FF, pp. 162–3)

This is the point at which the messenger comments that anyone who is not persuaded by this, he would not want to persuade; and Jebb remarks, 'To the ancient Greek, who enjoyed discussion, there was something peculiarly impressive in declining it.'[8] Sophocles has brought us to the limits of human understanding; the rest is faith.

The stress Sophocles lays here on what cannot be understood returns us to an earlier way of thinking which Aeschylus does not share, indeed repudiates: the conviction that sanctity is the other face of pollution. Orestes comes polluted to Athens, as Oedipus does, but he is not sacred in himself or capable of bestowing sanctity. What deserves to be called sacred is the evolution of a new process to contain him, with the law above ground and the conscience-generating Eumenides below. But Oedipus' blood pollution is what makes him sacred, in and of itself. It is not that he has transformed its nature by the length of his suffering, or even that he has internalized his guilt – he now says that his self-blinding was too harsh a punishment. He protests that he is innocent, and suffered his deeds rather than acting them. We have to imagine him not the weak old man he appears, but a chosen vessel in which an alchemical–religious reaction has taken

---

[8]   *The Oedipus Coloneus*, ed. R. C. Jebb, in *Sophocles: The Plays and Fragments*, 2 (Cambridge: Cambridge University Press 1900), p. 256, 1663 n.

place. By the gods' desire, his body has become the location of forces greater than itself. He is valuable because he is the thing he is, the only man to have murdered his own father, and made the forbidden journey back to his mother's womb.

Sophocles is reinstituting a paradox that Christianity later embraced about blood sacrifice, which may be why it seems familiar: that the gods confer gifts in exchange for suffering and death. The analyst of Indo-European languages, Emile Benveniste, comments on the two-faced nature of the sacred, as in the Latin *sacer*, 'consecrated to god and affected with an ineradicable pollution, august and accursed'. He scrutinizes the term 'sacrifice' in a way that may shed light on the play's ending:

> How does it come about that 'sacrifice' although it properly means 'to make sacred' (cf. *sacrificium*) actually means 'to put to death'? . . . Sacrifice takes place so that the profane world can communicate with the divine world through the priest and by means of the rites. To make the animal 'sacred', it must be cut off from the world of the living, it has to cross the threshold which separates these two universes; this is the point of putting it to death.[9]

Is Oedipus a go-between in this sense, a sacrificial communication between worlds, whose blood-soaked pollution is the most valuable thing about him?

There are two last points to be made at the end of this fascinating debate between Sophocles and his great predecessor. One is that the plots of these plays have some significant loose ends which Aeschylus might have noticed: Orestes kills his mother but in some inexplicable way avoids her Furies, and Oedipus is polluted but declares himself unpolluting. In this last play, the curse that Oedipus lays on his hated sons is exactly what brings about the death of his best-loved daughter, not long after. There is no evidence that Sophocles wanted us to be aware of this dark irony, but it has profound implications for the 'heroic' status of Oedipus' rage, from the Aeschylean point of view, as it ricochets down the generations of his family. The more central problem is that the unreserved praise of family bonds is not cross-cut with any consideration of outward-turning love and marriage: new marriages are never contracted in Sophocles, although they are the precondition for creating new families.

Another way of phrasing the difficulty set up by this revision of Aeschylus is that it would be very hard to deduce from the plays of Sophocles how Athens itself had come into existence. It is not that he ignores the *polis*, for he is evidently admonishing it about its foundations: let it never forget the blood bonds that create bodies, or the terrors that create awe. But although that is similar to the meaning Aeschylus conveys, the net effect is different. There is no forward-pointing logic to Sophocles' plots, as there is to the *Oresteia*. What is so

---

9   Emile Benveniste, *Indo-European Language and Society*, trans. Elizabeth Palmer (London: Faber, 1973), pp. 452–3.

remarkable about the *Eumenides* is its free admission that the Furies have the monopoly of the real that they say they do; and therefore the next question has to be: what now? How do we move from blood-thinking to disinterestedness, and from fear to goodness? Sophocles brings us to the first stage, to the admission that the Furies are as central to civilized life as to primitive. But he is so compelled by this truth that he does not move the argument forward – closer to himself, and to Athens. For the audience at his plays is made up of citizens, bonded by law even more than by blood; and the art he uses to communicate with them is, in the last analysis, Apollonian, an abstract system of signs. But nothing in the plays hints at how the hunger for law and abstraction can come to such visibly good ends.

Chapter 3

Euripides

Euripides perhaps represents what Sophocles was most afraid of: although only ten years or so younger he breathes the air of sceptical rationalism, and acknowledges no mysteries that the mind cannot probe. We know that he moved among the intellectual 'sophists' and probably therefore knew and debated with Socrates. Certainly he is proof of the astonishing swiftness of mental emancipation that came with democracy. This shows in his provocative representations of the gods (he considers the cult of Apollo at Delphi an immoral and reactionary institution, and so represents him with sarcastic detachment) but equally in his use of myth and language. The myths are reworked to the point of parody and the language his characters speak, although it can rise to poetry too, is intellectually clear and often verges on everyday speech. When Euripidean characters argue, they cut into each others' lines with a rapidity that Aristophanes called 'chatter' (*lalia*), and when they present their case we often have the sense of listening to public speech-making in the *agora*.

The Athens Euripides is addressing has also changed in important ways. The *Oresteia* (458 BCE) dates from the first flowering of democratic confidence, when the consequences of individuation at a psychological and political level were first laid bare. But all Euripides' major works date from the period of democratic collapse inaugurated by the start of the Peloponnesian war (431 BCE) when it was too late to praise the achievement of the *polis*, or to admire the nature of the new kind of man it produced. The *polis* was the place where, increasingly, men's power over words gave a glossy surface to irrationality, and democratic debate simply led to good arguments being ousted by bad. Demagogues learnt to sway the mob, and men rushed to obey their worst instincts as war-panic and plague swept through the city. Euripides' deepest and most rational preoccupation is with the irrational in man.

His plays are very various, and some have no contemporary reference at all, but his version of Orestes' story is shot through with political meaning and is highly characteristic of his sceptical position. By the time of the two plays Euripides writes about Orestes' vengeance Athens has been at war for twenty years. Peace has been rejected, even when within reach, and Athens has grown hardened to sacrifices, reprisals and revenge. If the story of Clytaemnestra, Orestes and Electra is still germane it is because the *polis* itself is caught up in the blood cycle, and Euripides' theme is now the human cost. The plays suggest no political structure, no new Areopagus, by which the law of revenge can be modified into something civilized; but they return again and again to images of pure suffering and mad waste.

Electra (?413 BCE)

It seems likely (though not certain, since the dating of this play is conjectural) that this *Electra* was written after Sophocles produced his (in ?418). The two plays are evidently part of a debate, and the Euripidean play implicitly makes a lively critique of Sophocles' manner and assumptions, with some broadly comic references to the *Libation Bearers* as well. The point which chiefly occupies Euripides and colours the whole play is that when revenge is stripped of its heroic dignity it has none of its own. Nothing in this play is palliated by mythic grandeur: Electra is first seen carrying a water jar, and Euripides represents her as married in degradation to a peasant farmer. (To add to the provocative realism, he insists on the moral worth of the farmer, as opposed to all the aristocrats in the cast: the farmer is one of 'nature's gentlemen'[1] and has left Electra untouched from genuine respect to her and her family.) Orestes is first seen skulking near the peasant hut with one eye on the border in case of escape; and his reunion with Electra is not delayed by his need to visit the grave, as in Sophocles, but more realistic considerations. Electra was too young when they parted to recognize him even when they do meet, and when an old servant finds the tokens Orestes left at the tomb – the same lock of hair and print of his boots that in the *Libation Bearers* brought final conviction – Electra rejects them with a rationalist disgust that reads momentarily like a scene from Aristophanes. How could a man's lock (unkempt, virile) resemble a girl's well-combed hair? And how could the rocky ground retain a boot print – which, if it were her brother's, would be bigger in any case? When the old servant feebly mentions the possibility of baby clothes, Electra's scorn overflows: 'How could a growing boy still wear that cloth / unless his shirt and tunic lengthened with his legs?' (V 543–4). The parodic tone does not subside until the servant recognizes Orestes from a scar over his eye, and the brother and sister, after the briefest embrace, set about plotting the murders to come.

Aegisthus and Clytaemnestra are represented in a similarly unheroic mode. We hear that Aegisthus almost beat Orestes to death as a child, before the affectionate old servant spirited him away, and that his fear of Electra's ability to bear sons would have made him kill her too, if Clytaemnestra had not intervened. Packing her off to a degraded marriage is his compromise, and meanwhile he leaps up and down on Agamemnon's grave in his drunken fits, and pelts it with stones, defying Orestes to stop him. Clytaemnestra is as disloyal to his bed as he is to hers, and leads a life of Asiatic luxury in the palace. She is waited on by numberless slave girls, while Agamemnon's unwashed blood still festers on the floor. No grounds of special consideration are given for this degraded couple, except that they, too, are human beings; and their killing, by contrast with

---

[1]   Euripides, Electra, trans. Emily Townsend Vermeule, in *Euripides, The Complete Greek Tragedies*, ed. David Grene and Richmond Lattimore, 5 (Chicago: University of Chicago Press, 1959), vol. 5, p. 19. Hereafter V.

Sophocles' treatment, is rendered in detail, so that we see exactly what it means to rob a body of life. Aegisthus is at a sacrifice, slaughtering a bull and looking into its viscera, when Orestes strikes home. (Aegisthus may be a drunkard and blasphemer, but Euripides does not blacken him in his death: this is one of his pious days, and he has welcomed Orestes as a guest.) As the messenger relays it to Electra,

> Aegisthus heaped the soft parts, then
> sorted them out. But while his head was bent above them,
> your brother stretched up, balanced on the balls of his feet,
> and smashed a blow to his spine. The vertebrae of his back
> broke. Head down, his whole body convulsed, he gasped
> to breathe, writhed with a high scream, and died in his blood. (V 838–43)

It is typical of Euripides that we feel the full weight of the blow ('balanced on the balls of his feet') and hear what it does to vertebrae. Meanwhile, Electra has sent a message to Clytaemnestra that she has just had a baby son, and her mother promptly arrives in a chariot. Their mutual recriminations are strongly reminiscent of Sophocles' scene, but with interesting variations. Sophocles made Clytaemnestra wonder why Menelaus could not spare a child in Iphigenia's place. Euripides' Clytaemnestra more pointedly uncovers the double standard upheld by patriarchal custom: *she* had to sacrifice a daughter for Helen's lust but, she asks with a startling twist of argument,

> If Menelaus had been raped from home on the sly,
> should I have had to kill Orestes so my sister's
> husband could be rescued? You think your father would
> have borne it? He would have killed me. (V 1041–4)

And when it comes to adultery, wasn't it Agamemnon who brought Cassandra home from Troy and expected Clytaemnestra to bear it, 'two brides being stabled in a single stall'? (V 1034). She is willing to admit that 'women are fools for sex, deny it I shall not' (V 1035) – 'But then the dirty gossip puts us in the spotlight; / the guilty ones, the men, are never blamed at all' (V 1039–40). Electra in return reminds her how she was checking her hairdo in the mirror the same day Agamemnon left for Troy, and how she was the only Greek wife who rejoiced in Trojan victories. And Iphigenia aside, why did it follow that Clytaemnestra should exile Orestes and enslave Electra, Agamemnon's legal heirs – if not because her lover came first? If Orestes should avenge himself on Clytaemnestra, it would be precisely as just as her murder of Agamemnon.

To our surprise, Clytaemnestra takes these reproaches mildly. Electra has always loved her father most, which is quite understandable; 'I am not so happy / either, child, with what I have done or with myself' (V 1105–6). In this thoughtful and far from triumphant mood (Euripides by no means wants us to see her as a demon), Clytaemnestra walks into the house to perform a childbirth sacrifice for her daughter – and becomes a sacrifice herself. Orestes comes back onstage in horror to tell us how:

> Or. You saw her agony, how she threw aside her dress,
> how she was showing her breast there in the midst of death?
>   My god, how she bent to earth
> the legs which I was born through? and her hair – I touched it –
> Cho. I know, I understand; you have come
> through grinding torment hearing her cry
>   so hurt, your own mother.
> Or. She cracked into a scream then, she stretched up her hand
> toward my face: 'My son! Oh, be pitiful my son!'
> She clung to my face,
>   suspended, hanging; my arm dropped with the sword –
> Cho. Unhappy woman – how could your eyes
> bear to watch her blood as she fought
>   for her breath and died there?
> Or. I snatched a fold of my cloak to hood my eyes, and, blind,
>   took the sword and sacrificed
> my mother – sank steel to her neck. (V 1206–22)

This scene reads like Euripides' riposte to the tight-lipped version of Clytaemnestra's slaughter in Sophocles, in which she is despatched after a single plea for mercy. This Clytaemnestra appeals to the sanctity of the maternal breast – the same unanswerable move she makes in the *Oresteia*. And for an awesome glimpse of where the Furies come from, Orestes sees the legs that kneel to him as 'the legs which I was born through'. The same posture brings her lovely, fragile hair within reach ('her hair – I touched it') and makes her his suppliant, touching his cheek and imploring him in a voice that has nothing mythic about it: 'My son! Oh, be pitiful my son!' The only way this Orestes can fulfil the oracle is with his cloak before his eyes – the same cloak he and Electra later use to wrap the body, in agonized remorse.

There can be no satisfactory conclusion to a play which shows revenge in such a close-up focus, and so Euripides ends with our first experience of a *deus ex machina*: the sudden appearance of a god to tie up the ends. He brings on the twin Dioscuri to announce the fate that Apollo and Zeus have decreed for everyone concerned. Electra can marry Pylades and go home with him to Phocis. Her first husband, the farmer, should be richly compensated; meanwhile, Orestes must go to Athens and submit his case to the Areopagus, where Apollo will support him and he will stand trial for murder. The consequences will be more or less the same as in the *Oresteia*, but these now sound quite uninteresting and notional; Athena is missing and all the implications she brought with her. The foundation myth has clearly lost its meaning for Euripides:

> But the voting-pebbles will be cast equal and save you,
> you shall not die by the verdict: Loxias [Apollo] will take
> all blame on himself for having asked your mother's death,
> and so for the rest of time this law shall be established:
> *When votes are equal the accused must have acquittal.*
> The dreadful goddesses, shaken in grief for this,
> shall go down in a crack of earth beside the Hill
> to keep a dark and august oracle for men. (V 1265–75)

Euripides is not entirely uninterested in myths, however: he allows the Dioscuri to make dubious noises about Apollo's involvement:

> As for Phoebus, Phoebus – yet he is my lord,
> silence. He knows the truth but his oracles were lies. (V 1245–6)

On this unhelpful note, Electra and Orestes part in anguish, and the Furies arrive to speed us on to the next play. They are Clytaemnestra's 'hounds', 'serpent-fisted and blackened of flesh, offering the fruit of terrible pain' (V 1345–6); and their arrival is one last token of Euripides' resistance to Sophocles' interpretation of the myth. Not only are Aegisthus and Clytaemnestra human beings whose murder is squalid and blasphemous however justified – but the matricide has precisely the consequences it always had. Orestes goes mad.

Orestes (408 BCE)

A few years later Euripides takes up the story again and opens his play with the most dramatic representation of what that means. Orestes is still in Argos a week after the funeral, too sick to move on, fasting, unwashed and intermittently psychotic. As Electra describes him,

> Orestes, wasted with a fierce disease,
> Lies where he fell, here on this pitiful fevered bed,
> His mother's blood like a charioteer wielding the whip
> Of insanity – for I will not name those Powers whose terror
> Ravages him, the 'Kindly Goddesses' [Eumenides]. Today
> Is the sixth day since fire consumed and purified
> Our mother's murdered body; all this time no food
> Has passed his lips; he has not washed; he lies huddled
> Under his cloak, and in short periods of relief
> He knows himself, and weeps; then suddenly, like a colt
> Throwing off the yoke, he leaps from bed and rages round.[2]

---

[2]   Euripides, *Orestes and Other Plays*, trans. Philip Vellacott (Harmondsworth: Penguin, 1972), pp. 301–2. Hereafter Ve.

For the visible Furies of Aeschylus' staging, Euripides substitutes the psychological experience and the language of metaphor. 'His mother's blood' in Orestes is 'wielding the whip / Of insanity', like a charioteer; he in his madness is like the whipped and frenzied horses. When Orestes is questioned by Menelaus – 'What agonies? What is the disease that ravages you?' – he knows very well that his disease is internal: 'Conscience. I recognize the horror of what I did' (Ve 395–6; *synesis*, cognizance). In this dazzling portrait of mental agony, Euripides goes so far as to make the confused Orestes wrestle with Electra, who seems to him another Fury, and shoot his bow at his invisible enemies.

In creating the internal landscape of what Aeschylus represented externally, Euripides is inaugurating one of the most potent motifs in tragic drama: the sickness of the son who cannot deny the primacy of his relationship to his mother. We are two millennia away from Hamlet's whirling words and suit of inky black, but Orestes is unmistakably suffering from the same disease. And Euripides, like Shakespeare, does not conceive of any solution to his problem in terms of political structures or social evolution: the hero suffers his problem as an individual, though he inherited it from a past he did not create. Euripides makes his victim live through no mythological solution but a standard fifth-century reaction to blood crime. Orestes is isolated by the community and condemned to death by stoning. The isolation is to prevent the contagion spreading, and death by stoning is to prevent any of his executioners from being polluted by direct contact.[3]

Euripides is also inaugurating here the tradition by which the hero who has our sympathy is at loggerheads with the law. The law, which in Aeschylus was uniquely able to purify the stink of blood and put an end to tribalism, has lost its novelty and idealism; for Euripides the law is one more human institution with human flaws, and it is hopelessly inadequate to a case as difficult as Orestes'. In fact, it creates a parody of justice, and makes Orestes into an 'outlaw' in spite of himself. He cannot perform the cleansing rites for blood pollution because no house in Argos is open to him; and the only alternative to the death penalty imposed on him by his fellow Argives would be immediate suicide – a more acceptable solution because it would save everyone else from risking pollution by contact. Euripides' ambivalence about the law shows in the speech he puts in the mouth of Tyndareus, Clytaemnestra's father. Tyndareus wants Orestes condemned, and his position is that Orestes should have had proper recourse to the law in the first place:

> When Agamemnon gasped his life out, with his skull
> Split by my daughter's weapon – an outrageous act
> Which I'll never defend – his duty was to take
> Lawful proceedings, prosecute for murder, and
> Expel his mother from the palace. In that way
> From his misfortune he would have won a name for wise

---

3   Vickers, *Towards Greek Tragedy*, p. 575.

> Behaviour, would have preserved both law and piety.
> But now, his life bears the same curse his mother bore. (Ve 497–504)

Tyndareus is apparently a good Athenian; he continues, 'I'll back the law with all my power, / To check this bestial, bloodthirsty rage [of revenge], which still / Destroys our cities' (Ve 523–5), but his argument has the frustrating quality of excessive reasonableness that Apollo's arguments with the Furies had. (It is also quite compatible with suborning someone else to argue for Orestes' stoning at the public trial, it turns out.) The law Tyndareus is arguing for is quite incapable of meeting the true facts of the situation – Orestes was a child when Clytaemnestra killed his father, and she and Aegisthus have been 'the law' in Argos ever since. This is the legal lunacy that responds to the outlines of a problem, but not the details of its real nature.

When Orestes argues with Tyndareus, he recapitulates most of the familiar points from the trial scene in Aeschylus, though without mythological support. He admits that he is polluted insofar as he killed his mother, but in that he avenged his father, he is guiltless. Fathers matter more, because the father is the real parent of a child, while the mother is 'a field sown with another's seed' (Ve 551) – and in any case, Clytaemnestra was an adulteress who 'indulged in lecherous and unlawful intercourse / In a lover's bed' (Ve 556–7). Euripides is not particularly interested in these arguments, but he homes in on the implications of the terrible moment when Clytaemnestra bared her breasts to her son in both the *Libation Bearers* and his own *Electra*. The nub of the issue is that the primal claim of motherhood can undo every patriarchal structure. No husband will ever feel safe in bed with his wife again, if Orestes' duty of vengeance is not conceded now:

> As for your demand
> That I be stoned to death, my answer is that I
> Am a benefactor of all Hellas. For if wives
> Grow bold enough to kill their husbands, and then fly
> For refuge to their children, snaring their soft hearts
> With bared breasts, husband-murder will become a sport,
> Excused by any trifle. What you loudly call
> My 'crime' at least has made that ploy improbable. (Ve 564–71)

What indeed guarantees the safety of husbands, if the mother's breast is an absolute value? Euripides has found his way back to an Aeschylean theme, however unexpectedly. What in Nature protects the marriage tie, as motherhood is protected?

But at the same time, Euripides marks an absolute distinction from his predecessor by making Orestes place the blame squarely where it belongs – with the god who gave him the order:

> Look at Apollo:
> There from his shrine at the earth's centre he dispenses
> Words of pure truth; what he commands, that we obey –

> I killed my mother in obedience to him!
> Call him polluted, then; stone him to death! The sin
> Is his, not mine. What ought I to have done? (Ve 591–6)

This is the fifth sarcastic reference to Apollo in the play, and the suggestion of actually stoning an immortal deity reveals anthropomorphic religion as a lost cause for Euripides. If Apollo means nothing except a servile habit of thought, he cannot represent a necessary polarity in tragedy between the claims of reason and passion, law and blood. Euripides is deeply alive to these conflicts, but Apollo is not part of his vocabulary for expressing them.

In the same spirit of scepticism, Euripides represents the *polis* in all its practical weakness. It is not the place where men are reborn as citizens, newly released into the full enjoyment of their conscious powers. It is simply where men's worst passions wear a cloak of rationality. The *agora* is doubly disgusting, because irrationality loves the opportunities provided by democratic procedure – as Euripides shows at Orestes' public trial, where good decisions are immediately overridden by bad. His scathing view of his fellow-citizens shines forth in every line: first Talthybius speaks (Agamemnon's herald and a toady by profession), praising Agamemnon ambiguously and keeping one eye anxiously on Aegisthus' old friends; then Diomedes argues rationally for a sentence of banishment. But the good effects of Diomedes are lost in a gross, blustering speech by a vulgar orator put up to the job by Tyndareus, who insists that nothing but stoning to death will do. The kind of man democracy was meant to empower, a courageous and sensible 'manual labourer – the sole backbone of the land' (Ve 920), argues cogently that Orestes should be honoured for protecting fathers, and that if he is not, no one will take the risk of going off to battle and leaving their wives behind ever again. Honest judges agree; but they are too few. Even when Orestes speaks out and makes plain the fact that patriarchy itself is what is at risk, the argument does not turn in his favour:

> In your defence, no less than in my father's cause,
> I killed my mother. For if wives may kill husbands
> And not be guilty, you had all best lose no time,
> But die today, before your wives make slaves of you.
>
> ... If you now kill me
> The law is void; the sooner a man dies the better,
> Since wives lack but encouragement, not enterprise. (Ve 934–8, 941–2)

Even this clear appeal to their most intimate interests does not affect the mood of the assembly: the vulgar orator who argued for stoning carries the day.

Euripides has now pulled the knot as tight as he can. Orestes is hopelessly polluted and the *polis* will only tolerate him dead; there is nothing more to be done with this material, and so he abandons the issue of justice for Orestes altogether (to be settled in a few dull lines at the end), and turns the play in a new direction. Euripides announces the theme which energizes his greatest plays: that bad laws produce outlaws. Excessive vengefulness is the by-product of despair; and he shows his helpless victims, Orestes and Electra, becoming startlingly vindictive. They have lost any hope of justice, human or divine, and so they take the one recourse available other than complete submission – they become as savage as their predicament dictates. Euripides essentially portrays in human form the dynamic that Aeschylus dramatized between the Furies and Apollo: that a baffled hunger for justice will express itself in infuriated destructiveness, and those who feel themselves most abused will abuse with interest.

The turning point comes when Pylades makes common cause with Orestes and Electra. He makes the exhilarating suggestion that, since all three of them are about to die anyway, they should 'ensure a share of suffering for Menelaus' before they go, because he has failed to support them as family loyalty dictated (Ve 1099). 'Let's kill Helen – and send Menelaus raving mad' is his plan (Ve 1105). Since Helen is inside the palace with effete Phrygians in attendance, 'chaps who polish her mirrors and set out her scents' (Ve 1112), this will be no hard task for such desperadoes. And vengeance will be intensely sweet, in the familiar mode of the Furies. As Orestes says,

> Since I am now at my last gasp in any case,
> I want to hurt my enemies before I die,
> To pay back those who have betrayed me in their own coin,
> And hear them howling who brought misery on me. (Ve 1163–6)

Electra chimes in with an improvement: if they take a hostage against the vengeance of Menelaus, they have the chance of not only enjoying their revenge but escaping too. Hermione, his daughter, is the perfect weapon against her father; the main thing is to show no mercy:

> Tell him you'll kill Hermione. You must draw your sword
> And hold it tight against her throat. If Menelaus,
> With Helen's body lying in blood before his eyes,
> Will promise you your life to save Hermione's,
> Then hand her over to her father; but if he
> Attempts to kill you in his uncontrollable rage,
> Then cut Hermione's throat. (Ve 1193–9)

Everything turns out neatly as planned. We see Electra onstage urging the murder of Helen offstage, in a dreadful reminiscence of Sophocles' Electra: 'Kill, stab, destroy her, both of you! / Aim your swords – in! – in! / Two hungry blades flashing in your hands! / Kill her!' (Ve 1302–4). Then we hear the rest of the story, in broken 'foreign' idiom, from the sole Phrygian slave who has escaped the carnage. As always, it is the physical facts of murder Euripides wants us to face:

> Like mountain boars they stand facing a woman;
> And they say, 'You shall die, you're going to die,

And your death will be due to your treacherous husband,
Who in the Assembly of Argos
Betrayed his brother's son to death.'
Then Helen screamed aloud,
'What shall I do?' she screamed.
Her white arms beat upon her breast, her hands
Battered her head with pitiful blows.
Then she try to escape;
Her gold sandals clattered as she ran.
Orestes in his hunting-boots darted at her;
He twist his fingers in her hair;
He bent her neck down to her left shoulder;
He held his black sword ready
To drive into her throat. (Ve 1460–72)

The height of pathos is reached with the contrast between the murderer's boots and Helen's clattering gold sandals. The sacrificial victim is left helpless on the floor in her own blood.

The exhilaration of flouting mythological expectations spills over now into a scene of wild comedy. The panicky Phrygian slave is pursued and caught by Orestes, and swaps grovelling cross-talk with the sardonic man of power: *Or.* 'You weren't shouting to Menelaus to come to the rescue, were you, now?' *Ph.* 'No! I shouted, Come and help Orestes! – You're the better man' (Ve 1510–11). Nothing can stop Orestes in this state, and in something of the same spirit, Euripides winds his plot up to a climax that has the headlong momentum of a farce, yet is made out of entirely tragic materials. Menelaus beats at the palace doors in the hope of saving Hermione, while Orestes holds a sword to her throat on the battlements and trades insults with her father. The question of whose hands are more polluted, and whether Orestes was right to be loyal to his father, makes a brief appearance among the taunts:

Men. My hands are clean.
                          Or. Your heart's corrupt.
Men. What man would speak to you?
                          Or. Every man who loves his father.
Men. What of one who respects his mother?
                          Or. A lucky man! (Ve 1604–6)

But there is no question of meditating on the old paradoxes: Euripides is simply stoking the blaze, and the whole plot is about to go up in flames, literally, since Orestes' last weapon against Menelaus is to make a bonfire of the palace and everyone in it ('Electra! now's the moment! Set this house on fire!' Ve 1618).

At this crisis, when Orestes has pushed the logic of being an outlaw to its catastrophic conclusion – and Euripides has coerced the myth as far as it could conceivably go, without falling into absurdity – the only possible ending is supplied by another *deus ex machina*. Apollo himself appears, as a kind of theological marionette, to wrench the plot back on to its familiar course. There is no pretence that his decisions are anything but outrageous in the circumstances; but they are traditional. Orestes must stand trial at Athens, where 'gods shall dispute your case, and cast / Most righteous votes; and you shall leave their court absolved' (Ve 1650–2). (Euripides shows even less interest in the details than in the *Electra*.) Then he must marry Hermione, even if at the moment he has his sword to her throat. Pylades will marry Electra and be very happy; poor Menelaus can go back and reign in Sparta; and Apollo himself will settle the awkward business of Orestes' relation to Argos, since the murder was instigated by him (no explanation supplied). The big surprise in all this is that Helen is not dead after all: Apollo snatched her away from the scene of carnage. She has been enthroned in heaven as a star for sailors, next to her brothers Castor and Pollux. And if we want to understand the gods' plan beyond this, Euripides gives Apollo a chilling explanation:

> . . . Helen's beauty was to the gods their instrument,
> For setting Greeks and Trojans face to face in war
> And multiplying deaths, to purge the bloated earth
> Of its superfluous welter of mortality. (Ve 1639–42)

So that plan at least was a success: the world is less burdened with superfluous humanity.

Euripides writes very like a modern, as has often been said; and his objections to religion are familiar from the nineteenth century – rational disgust for superstition, an awareness of its political uses, and a contempt for those who identify god with their own purposes (as Zeus was confidently invoked to help murder Helen, *Or.* 1242). If Aeschylus could be said to think 'in' gods and Sophocles keeps gods above the sphere of thought, Euripides is trying something quite new: thinking without gods at all. But the plots of the *Electra* and *Orestes* show what technical difficulties this involves him in, what gaps of logic and jumps of tone; and the refusal is not wholehearted because the gods are required to end plots which cannot otherwise come to a conclusion. They are actually the precondition of his experiments, and show the artist in the paradoxical light of creating entities for the sole purpose of denying their meaning.

In plays where Euripides is less hampered by conscious scepticism, however, he finds a deeper tone for expressing his key theme – the way irrationality bursts through individual natures. The old debate between the Furies and Apollo, blood and the law, may be a dead letter to him, but he is passionately alive to it as an internal experience: the way each conscious organism must negotiate between its animal and intellectual impulses to find its happiness. Although his stage representations of Apollo are parodic, he is never less than serious in his representation of the realm of conscious, individuated life that Apollo protects, and its constant invasion by irrational passions that energize the body – of which the chief is love. When Euripides is profoundly invested in his representations of deity, it is usually in the deities who represent passion. This is the force in human affairs he is himself in awe of; and which he sometimes represents as Aphrodite, and sometimes as Dionysus.

Because of this, his plays are full of vivid portraits of women who are shown to embody the Dionysiac challenge to the hero. The male stands forth with all his powers – strength, virility, law, and language – and confronts a powerful woman who by her very nature reminds him of his body, and his origin in a woman's body. His angry heroes make some of the most bitterly misogynistic speeches in drama as a result; and his heroines make some of the most intelligent feminist answers. Euripides can see both sides of the question with great clarity, as he shows in allowing Clytaemnestra to challenge the double standards of patriarchy over Iphigenia. But to put the challenge of Dionysus to rationality in the clearest light, he returns again and again to plots in which women defeat men, not through their cunning, but through being what they biologically are: mothers as well as women, creatures of nature as well as of civilization. In three of his greatest plays he shows mothers as being the death of their sons, through hate (*Medea*), through love (*Hippolytus*), and worst of all, without any conscious intention (*The Bacchae*). Euripides thus considers Orestes' tragedy from the opposite angle. If the son is *not* somehow allowed to kill his mother, what then? Are those who give life, by definition strong enough to take it away again?

Medea (431 BCE)

Just as he demythologizes Orestes and Electra, Euripides detaches Medea from her spectacular mythic past and gives her the voice of a contemporary Athenian woman. In this guise she unveils the truth that 'of all living, thinking creatures, women are the most miserable' (ll. 230–1). The traditional details are assumed in the plot – that she is a barbarian sorceress from the Black Sea, that she helped Jason take the Golden Fleece from her father, whom she held back from pursuing them by strewing pieces of her murdered brother on the waters – but as Euripides portrays her she is no barbarian, but a woman who is, or wants to be, a good wife and mother. She has taken every step a woman can to attach her husband to her, and for love of him she has renounced family, country and all sources of safety. It is Jason who is now casting off the connection: he is reneging on his promise by taking a new wife, the daughter of the king sheltering them in Corinth. And what that means for Medea is graphically described by her old nurse:

> She lies without food and gives herself up to suffering,
> Wasting away every moment of the day in tears.
> So it has gone since she knew herself slighted by him.
> Not stirring an eye, not moving her face from the ground,

No more than either a rock or surging sea water
She listens when she is given friendly advice.
Except that sometimes she twists back her white neck and
Moans to herself, calling out on her father's name,
And her land, and her home betrayed when she came away with
A man who is now determined to dishonor her.[4]

This is not a temporary feminine collapse, but a growing anger dreadfully flavoured with gall. The dishonour she is overwhelmed by is something only a woman can know: the annihilation of her selfhood in a world where her status hung entirely on another. Medea without Jason is an un-person, with no acknowledged place in the state, and no family to return to. It is not that she is naturally a barbarian, a wild outlaw, but that he is making her into one. Her choice was the Apollonian one, of reliance on contracts and promises. Loving Jason unreservedly, Medea took the heroic step of gathering her life's meaning into a single commitment. Therefore in one step he has been able to rob her of everything:

It has broken my heart. I am finished. I let go
All my life's joy. My friends, I only want to die.
It was everything to me to think well of one man,
And he, my own husband, has turned out wholly vile. (W 226–9)

In *Medea* Euripides explores the same problem that so preoccupies Aeschylus, that marriage, the supreme act of conscious choice, is protected by nothing in nature. It evaporates with a word; it has no location in the world, no visible manifestation – save in the children it produces, a fact Medea will seize on with terrible precision.

Her famous speech to the chorus of Corinthian women uncovers the predicament of women everywhere, as they are both controlled and unsupported by the law. The marriage bond makes two individuals share one destiny; and the outcome is unlikely to be happy for the woman. She is a rational being prevented from exercising choice:

Of all things which are living and can form a judgment
We women are the most unfortunate creatures.
Firstly, with an excess of wealth it is required
For us to buy a husband and take for our bodies
A master; for not to take one is even worse.
And now the question is serious whether we take
A good or bad one; for there is no easy escape
For a woman, nor can she say no to her marrriage. (W 230–7)

---

[4]   *Medea*, trans. Rex Warner, in Euripides, *The Complete Greek Tragedies*, ed. David Grene and Richmond Lattimore, 1 (Chicago: University of Chicago Press, 1955, repr. 1967), pp. 59–60. Hereafter W.

It takes a dowry to make her acceptable, and in exchange she acquires an absolute master over her body. She must instantly develop a sixth sense to please him, having given up everything familiar at home for his unknown world:

> She arrives among new modes of behavior and manners,
> And needs prophetic power, unless she has learned at home,
> How best to manage him who shares the bed with her.
> And if we work out all this well and carefully,
> And the husband lives with us and lightly bears his yoke,
> Then life is enviable. If not, I'd rather die.
> A man, when he's tired of the company in his home,
> Goes out of the house and puts an end to his boredom
> And turns to a friend or companion of his own age.
> But we are forced to keep our eyes on one alone. (W 238–47)

If the husband feels happy with his half of the yoke, marriage can be enviable – if not, 'I'd rather die'. For a man is not expected to make his whole world out of marriage; he can find it in a host of chosen relations. But the woman has the duty of making her whole happiness out of a single bond. Medea knows, of course, what safety and protection the patriarchal contract offers women in exchange for confinement, but she has a credible answer to it:

> What they say of us is that we have a peaceful time
> Living at home, while they do the fighting in war.
> How wrong they are! I would very much rather stand
> Three times in the front of battle than bear one child. (W 248–51)

In nature's battle formation women stand foremost, and undergo trials men cannot imagine – not imposed from without, by duty, but imposed from within, by the nature of their bodies. In all these ways, Medea says to the chorus, women suffer as intelligent creatures denied the freedom intelligence craves. Theirs is a life of struggle; but her own predicament as a foreigner is uniquely wretched:

> Yet what applies to me does not apply to you.
> You have a country. Your family home is here.
> You enjoy life and the company of your friends.
> But I am deserted, a refugee, thought nothing of
> By my husband – something he won in a foreign land.
> I have no mother nor brother, nor any relation
> With whom I can take refuge in this sea of woe. (W 252–8)

Euripides shows how the secret alliance of women is formed. When robbed of the support of family, marriage or law, Medea has no other recourse but the solidarity of her own sex:

> This much then is the service I would beg from you:
> If I can find the means or devise any scheme
> To pay my husband back for what he has done to me –

> Him and his father-in-law and the girl who married him –
> Just to keep silent. For in other ways a woman
> Is full of fear, defenseless, dreads the sight of cold
> Steel; but, when once she is wronged in the matter of love,
> No other soul can hold so many thoughts of blood. (W 259–66)

The Corinthian women immediately understand her: 'This will I promise. You are in the right, Medea, / In paying your husband back' (W 267–8). There is a thought-provoking analogy here with that other group of wronged women, the Furies, and the way that the Apollonian imagination readily sees women as multiple, rather than individual entities, 'a flock of goats without a herdsman'. And Medea, like a Fury, already knows that her revenge cannot stop short of blood: she has been wronged in her marriage, which was the sole location of family, marriage and law to her. Now there can be no constraints on her at all.

Thus Euripides brings us to his main point in a few hundred lines: Medea is made into an outlaw by the law itself. She has taken the very journey patriarchal law requires, away from family and homeland to a life based on a legal contract – and the contract has been rescinded. More humiliating still, she has slipped from an individual freely creating her own destiny (the one who actually made Jason's mythic feats possible), to a generic creature, 'all woman', obsessed with revenge. As an older wife cast off for a younger one, she is trapped by the fate of a woman whose value in society depends on her usefulness as a conduit for another's fertility and power. But in the admirably even-handed treatment Euripides gives her, she remains able to comment on her predicament to the last, and she sees better than anyone what it means to slide from what she was, to what she must become.

Jason, on the other hand, is represented as magnificently obtuse. He is another version of Agamemnon, so secure in his patriarchal power that he overrides Medea's emotions and walks confidently into the trap she lays for him. Like Tyndareus, he knows the law (which allows him to divorce a foreigner), and ignores the misfit between the law and the human reality beneath. And like Apollo insulting the Furies in the *Eumenides*, he sees the outline of the problem of Medea's resentment but not the details of its terrible nature. Euripides brings Jason onstage to debate with Medea in full rhetorical confidence. He has heard that Creon, king of Corinth, intends to exile her for fear of reprisals, and complacently points out how her rage is only making things worse, for her and their two boys. He stokes the flames with self-conscious rectitude: he wants to make 'some provision . . . so that you and the children may not be penniless or in need of anything in exile' (W 461–2). When Medea bitterly recapitulates what he really owes her, from the Golden Fleece to these offspring, he makes the most insulting excuse of all – that it was not Medea who was responsible for his triumph at Colchis but Aphrodite:

> Since you insist on building up your kindness to me,
> My view is that Cypris was alone responsible
> Of men and gods for the preserving of my life.
> You are clever enough – but really I need not enter
> Into the story of how it was love's inescapable
> Power that compelled you to keep my person safe. (W 526–31)

Jason regrets that he must be so disobliging, but far from being the agent of her destiny, Medea has been a mere pawn in a transaction between himself and Olympus. In any case, she has already had her reward, which is to live under Greek law and be famous:

> But on this question of saving me, I can prove
> You have certainly got from me more than you gave.
> Firstly, instead of living among barbarians,
> You inhabit a Greek land and understand our ways,
> How to live by law instead of the sweet will of force.
> And all the Greeks considered you a clever woman.
> You were honored for it; while, if you were living at
> The ends of the earth, nobody would have heard of you. (W 534–41)

This kind of rationality gives reason a bad name: Medea should have felt sufficiently honoured to live under Greek law, even though it did not operate to protect her, and to enjoy the sunshine of fame, even while being unprecedently betrayed. He even asks her to assent to his strategy, since she must agree that nothing could be luckier for an exile than the chance of marrying the king's daughter. It is not that he is tired of her ('the point that seems to upset you', W 555), but it is a way of securing all their futures – his, the children's, and even Medea's own, if she had been more sensible. If she had not brought exile on herself and the children by cursing the king, they could all have carried on living in Colchis, with the new children of the royal marriage living happily side by side with their brothers. But women are so irrational. And Jason takes this masculine train of thought to its logical conclusion: life would really be easier without them:

> . . . Do you think this a bad plan?
> You wouldn't if the love question hadn't upset you.
> But you women have got into such a state of mind
> That, if your life at night is good, you think you have
> Everything; but, if in that quarter things go wrong,
> You will consider your best and truest interests
> Most hateful. It would have been better far for men
> To have got their children in some other way, and women
> Not to have existed. Then life would have been good. (W 567–75)

Thus logic takes wing from the earth and becomes pure wishfulness: let babies come *allothen*, 'some other way'. It is women who always seem to be the problem, women who compromise male rationality; the hero's head is transcendently clear but his feet are being sucked into the primal mire. This 'dream of a purely paternal heredity'[5] reverberates back to Aeschylus' Apollo and throughout Greek tragedy; it is articulated most passionately by Hippolytus in our next play, when he recoils from Phaedra's passion into a desperate fantasy of women-free reproduction. And here, Euripides sardonically gives Apollonian logic free rein: if humanity consisted of men alone, there would be no problem. Jason rests his case.

When Medea is reproached for 'calling down wicked curses on the king's family' she embraces her new identity in as many words: 'A curse, that is what I am become to your house too' (W 608). Like the Furies, however, she carries the power of creativity and destructiveness in equal measure, and she can bless when she chooses. She strikes a bargain with Aegeus, King of Athens, as she prepares her escape route for after the planned catastrophe. She will cure his infertility in exchange for his protection in 'the town and fortress of Pallas' (W 771). This is the third invocation of the hospitality of Athens to Furies we have encountered, a third version of the interplay between danger and blessing:

> . . . Receive me in your land and at your very hearth.
> So may your love, with God's help, lead to the bearing
> Of children, and so may you yourself die happy.
> You do not know what a chance you have come on here.
> I will end your childlessness, and I will make you able
> To beget children. The drugs I know can do this. (W 713–18)

The drugs are a reminder of the mythic Medea's reputation for witchcraft. But because Euripides so resolutely interprets her psychology in human terms, we can also see her gift of fertility as part of her natural power as a woman and mother. As such, Medea stands at the centre of life's secrets; so that, when she turns her mind to death, her success is correspondingly complete.

Euripides chooses the most appalling of the various stories of Medea's revenge. In another version she murders Creon and flees, leaving her children behind her, who are then killed by the Corinthians. It seems to be Euripides' own invention to have Jason's princess first consumed by the fire that bursts out of a poisoned robe and crown, which Medea has sent to the bride as gifts – and to have Creon consumed in his turn, as he embraces the corpse in futile tenderness. Then he shows that, having annihilated Jason's marriage and hopes of future progeny, Medea still has one more task to perform: to annihilate their own marriage, and its physical embodiment in their children. Only then will she have brought Jason to the desired point of nothingness – the point at which he will say, while gratifyingly still alive: 'O woman, you have destroyed me!' (W 1310).

Her murder of their two sons is so shocking that it might seem paradoxical to claim that Euripides does not want to demonize Medea. But the play stays close

---

5   See Chap. 1, n. 7.

to her point of view for as long as possible, and shows us her predicament as she sees it herself. And at the end Euripides, remarkably, allows her to triumph over Jason, and to escape to Athens in an airborne chariot drawn by dragons – as dramatic a demonstration of flying free of the consequences as could be imagined. This is, in fact, another of the endings which does not solve the problem proposed, and which Aristotle singles out as a particularly glaring abuse of *ex machina* solutions. (*Poetics*, Chap. 15). But Euripides is not committed to unpicking knots; the energy of his drama depends on tying them as tight as possible, and here he shows Medea as a loving mother who raises her hand against her children only with the utmost reluctance and heartache. By this he opens up a more frightening vista – the possibility that motherhood is a deadly state in itself, so fraught with power that even love cannot prevail against it.

Medea says goodbye to her children in a long speech full of agonized second thoughts. She laments that she will never see them married, and that they will never give her in return the precious office of care in old age: 'What was the purpose, children, for which I reared you? / For all my travail and wearing myself away? / They were sterile, those pains I had in the bearing of you' (W 1029–31). Their bright eyes and sweet smiles temporarily make her break down and resolve to take them with her: 'Why should I hurt their father with the pain / They feel, and suffer twice as much of pain myself?' (W 1046–7). But it is a duty to avenge herself on Jason, and to stop short of what is possible is weakness; she steels her resolve, and then takes her last farewell of her sons in an ecstasy of mother love. The passage conveys better than any other in tragedy the physical exquisiteness and moral charm of children:

> Come, children, give
> Me your hands, give your mother your hands to kiss them.
> Oh the dear hands, and O how dear are these lips to me,
> And the generous eyes and the bearing of my children!
> I wish you happiness, but not here in this world.
> What is here your father took. Oh how good to hold you!
> How delicate the skin, how sweet the breath of children!
> Go, go! I am no longer able, no longer
> To look upon you. I am overcome by sorrow. (W 1069–77)

The rapture of a mother admiring the lovely bodies she has brought to birth goes along with the ominous reservation, 'I wish you happiness, but not here in this world. / What is here your father took.' The world as Medea sees it is the whole world, theirs and hers, and Jason has ruined it. To clasp the children to her and take them right out of it is a maternal impulse – all the more natural because they are so deserving. This overweening maternalism is one side of the coin, the other side of which is fury. Medea 'knows' that what she plans is unspeakable, but her rancour overrides everything:

> I know indeed what evil I intend to do,
> But stronger than all my afterthoughts is my fury,
> Fury that brings upon mortals the greatest evils. (W 1078–80)

In the grip of this fury she will plead with herself to forget how dear the children are to her, as mothers in tragedy normally plead with bloodstained men with swords:

> Oh, arm yourself in steel, my heart! Do not hang back
> From doing this fearful and necessary wrong. (W 1242–3)

And then the cries of the children are finally heard offstage: 'What can I do and how escape my mother's hands?' (W 1273). Euripides returns, as ever, to the physical realities of murder. These children are not babies, but neither are they big enough to defend themselves against a grown woman. And their voices are not audible to a mother who is 'repossessing' their bodies, as if birth were a process that could be reversed.

Medea's triumph over Jason is then to taunt him with these bodies from the height and safety of her chariot, as he rages in impotent, maddened disbelief. She has succeeded in making him taste what she tasted, the status of an un-person who would sooner be dead. Utterly deracinated, without posterity and with no hope of any, he can fully measure how wishful was his fantasy that men should get children without the help of women. He awakens from his Apollonian trance of rationality in an agony of desire for physical connection. At last his sons' bodies are as real to him as to her:

Jas.	Oh, children I loved!
Med.	I loved them, you did not.
Jas.	You loved them, and killed them.
Med.	To make you feel pain.
Jas.	Oh, wretch that I am, how I long
	To kiss the dear lips of my children!
Med.	Now you would speak to them, now you would kiss them.
	Then you rejected them.
Jas.	Let me, I beg you,
	Touch my boys' delicate flesh.
Med.	I will not. Your words are all wasted. (W 1397–1404)

It is the perfection of her maternal power that she can deny him access to their bodies even in death, and leave him raging to Zeus that he ever begot them.

Hippolytus (428 BCE)

In this play Euripides returns to linger on the paradox of Medea's admission, 'I know indeed what evil I intend to do, / But stronger than all my afterthoughts is my fury.' He seems to have Socrates' famous teaching on his mind, that it is sufficient to know the good to want to do it – that 'virtue is knowledge'. At the height of her misery Phaedra returns Socrates an answer: that 'there are many who know virtue. / We know the good, we apprehend it clearly. But we can't bring it to achievement.'⁶ The play explores the way both she and Hippolytus passionately pursue virtue, to their mutual destruction; and it lays the blame squarely on the goddess of love, Aphrodite.

In Hippolytus Euripides creates a hero at the age Greek culture found the male most attractive – early manhood, the stage of hunting exploits with dogs and horses, with women entirely out of the picture. Hippolytus has a shuddering aversion to Aphrodite and strides past her altars without acknowledgement: the 'God of nocturnal prowess is not my God', (G 106) he says. Physical prowess should be virginal, athletic; Hippolytus worships Artemis, the chaste huntress, and brings her offerings of newly picked flowers from an uncut meadow:

> My Goddess Mistress, I bring you ready woven
> this garland. It was I that plucked and wove it,
> plucked it for you in your inviolate Meadow.
> No shepherd dares to feed his flock within it:
> no reaper plies a busy scythe within it:
> only the bees in springtime haunt the inviolate Meadow.
> Its gardener is the spirit Reverence who
> refreshes it with water from the river.
> Not those who by instruction have profited
> to learn, but in whose very soul the seed
> of Chastity toward all things alike
> nature has deeply rooted, they alone
> may gather flowers there! the wicked may not. (G 73–81)

In the self-conscious virtue of this speech, its youthful extremism, Euripides is already uncovering the charm and paradox of Hippolytus' stage of life – that it is only a stage, and must necessarily give way to something else. Only a goddess like Artemis can be chaste as an unchanging condition, pursued to the limit. She can be as pure as an 'inviolate meadow' without *hubris*, and rejoice all year long in the companionship of her chosen mortal (she and Hippolytus hunt with hounds together, to the point of depopulating the area of wild animals). But the perfection of purity that can be attained by a human being has a date attached – just like the bloom of the flowers that Hippolytus has woven into his garland. The intensity of his commitment to Artemis is generated precisely by the ephemerality of his youth; and the aggression he shows towards Aphrodite is a presentiment of what is lying in wait for him – marriage, and the merging of his selfhood in union with another.

---

⁶ *Hippolytus*, trans. David Grene, in Euripides, *The Complete Greek Tragedies*, ed. David Grene and Richmond Lattimore, 1 (Chicago: University of Chicago Press, 1955, repr. 1967), pp. 179–80. Hereafter G. Line numbers refer to the Greek text.

There is a shadow of a younger Jason in this portrait, the male who suspects that contact with women will always be compromising, a kind of contamination. And Euripides shows how far this dream of purity is from the facts of life by opening the play with a speech from Aphrodite in person. The spectacle we are about to witness is her necessary revenge; she is not a goddess to be bypassed and stinted of honour. Nothing that lives under the sun is not under her rule, and certainly not Hippolytus:

> I am called the Goddess Cypris:
> I am mighty among men and they honor me by many names.
> All those that live and see the light of sun
> from Atlas' Pillars to the tide of Pontus
> are mine to rule.
> Such as worship my power in all humility,
> I exalt in honor.
> But those whose pride is stiff-necked against me
> I lay by the heels. (G 1–8)

Her punishment for Hippolytus has already begun. She has made his stepmother Phaedra fall in love with him; and although Phaedra is wasting away without breathing a word, Aphrodite will make sure the whole story comes out in front of Theseus. The incensed father will condemn his son to death, 'this son that is hateful to me' – and Phaedra must die too. This is unfortunate, but 'her suffering does not weigh in the scale so much / that I should let my enemies go untouched / escaping payment' (G 48–50).

There is an echo of Medea here, and of the offended pride that steeled her to her cruel decision: Euripides does not mind showing the gods to be similarly vindictive. But his intention is not merely parodic, for a goddess who 'rules all those that live and see the light of sun' might well express her power in these knock-down terms. This tone and her power are much the same thing: she is the principle of life itself, the obligation to love, merge and multiply. She is a reminder that whatever is not life is death, and she is not to be gainsaid. The play shows her plan unstoppably unrolling, and the interest of the intervening scenes is the experience of passion from the characters' point of view – the shock Aphrodite represents to human values and self-control.

In Phaedra Euripides opens up the paradox he located in Medea: the conflict inside the woman who wants to be civilized and views the 'natural' in her nature much as a man might do. But Medea's struggle was quickly renounced; in this play, the encroachment of passion on Phaedra is played out in slow motion, and the battle is not lost until her last speech. She does not reach out hungrily for the gratification of her desires (Euripides had tried this cruder conception in an unsuccessful earlier play, the lost *Hippolytos Kalyptomenos*). Just the opposite: she feels all the charm of Hippolytus' untamed chastity and his way of life. She fantasizes about drinking spring water in an inviolate meadow of her own, where she might be safe from the torment of her wants ('If I could only lie beneath the poplars, / in the tufted meadow and find my rest there! G 210–11). She could wish to be Hippolytus herself, able to direct her energy outward in an ecstasy of power, mastering the outer wildness, instead of suffering the wildness within:

> Bring me to the mountains! . . . where the huntsman's pack
> trails spotted stags and hangs upon their heels.
> God, how I long to set the hounds on, shouting!
> And poise the Thessalian javelin drawing it back –
> here where my fair hair hangs above the ear –
> I would hold in my hand a spear with a steel point. (G 215, 216–22)

This yearning for an a-sexual freedom contrasts poignantly with Phaedra's real condition. The man may ride away from the *oikos* (as Hippolytus does, and Theseus has) but the woman is confined to it on penalty of dishonour. Phaedra's passion is so forbidden that she can do nothing but seal her lips, both against the words that would betray it and the food that would prolong it. For she is herself what she abhors: her body and mind want two opposing things, and if she does not actively seek death, she is assenting to dishonour.

The play treats stepmother–stepson incest as if it were absolute. It seems to combine two sources of horror: displacing the father in the marital bed, and the abuse of the (step)mother's access to a young male. (Hippolytus' own mother is of course Hippolyta the Amazon.) It may be that this plot is as close as Euripides can come to the radioactive topic of mother–son incest; at any rate, he handles the topic even in this guise as the breaching of a profound taboo, and there is no question that Phaedra is right, at the start of the play, to have chosen to die. If her terrible secret nonetheless comes out, to destroy her and Hippolytus together, it is through the agency of someone else: Euripides uses the Nurse here to keep Phaedra's role as sympathetic as possible. Just as Phaedra is no animal, she is no weakling; although the Nurse acts like the agent of her secret desire, she is not actually that, but someone with a right to implore Phaedra to save herself, because she loves her mistress so much (too much for her own good, she herself suspects). It is her suppliant plea that compels Phaedra to speak; and it is because she has bonds of obligation to others that Phaedra cannot die in silence as she intends. But all she technically does is to admit to the Nurse that Hippolytus is the man, and accept some mysterious 'charms' to assuage her love. The decision to speak to Hippolytus is the Nurse's own.

The savage tirade the Nurse elicits from him in response is also at the extremity of passion – of unbridled misogyny. Hippolytus recoils from the 'tainted', loathsome mess that women get men into. He calls aloud to Zeus: couldn't a god have thought of something better? Like Jason, Hippolytus yearns for a clean and rational form of all-male reproduction – a kind of banking:

> Women! This coin which men find counterfeit!
> Why, why, Lord Zeus, did you put them in the world,
> in the light of the sun? If you were so determined
> to breed the race of man, the source of it
> should not have been women. Men might have dedicated
> in your own temples images of gold,
> silver, or weight of bronze, and thus have bought
> the seed of progeny, . . . to each been given
> his worth in sons according to the assessment
> of his gift's value. So we might have lived
> in houses free of the taint of women's presence. (G 616–24)

And he runs through a catalogue of the husband's woes in marriage that is much in agreement with Medea's speech on the wrongs of women – but viewed, now, from the other side of the fence. Women are so inherently valueless that fathers must pay husbands to take them away; then the deluded husband must impoverish himself for the useless, extravagant creature. The depth of this grievance (not actually very credible in Hippolytus' inexperienced character) suggests a kind of sexual parallel – the husband being 'drained' of what 'enriches' the woman:

> But now, to bring this plague into our homes
> we drain the fortunes of our homes. In this,
> we have a proof how great a curse is woman.
> For the father who begets her, rears her up,
> must add a dowry gift to pack her off
> And he again that takes the cursed creature
> rejoices and enriches his heart's jewel
> with dear adornment, beauty heaped on vileness.
> With lovely clothes the poor wretch tricks her out
> spending the wealth that underprops his house. (G 625–33)

If a wife is clever, so much the worse, from the male point of view:

> That husband has the easiest life whose wife
> is a mere nothingness, a simple fool,
> uselessly sitting by the fireside.
> I hate a clever woman – God forbid
> that I should ever have a wife at home
> with more than woman's wits! Lust breeds mischief
> in the clever ones. The limits of their minds
> deny the stupid lecherous delights.
> We should not suffer servants to approach them,
> but give them as companions voiceless beasts,
> dumb . . . but with teeth, that they might not converse,
> and hear another voice in answer.
> But now at home the mistress plots the mischief,
> And the maid carries it abroad. (G 638–50)

Hippolytus would not be content just to chain women to the hearth. Only by keeping company with dumb animals could they be prevented from making their lust known outside. Sexual voraciousness is their overriding characteristic, a truth incapable of exaggeration, as he insists in his staggering finale:

> I'll hate you women, hate and hate and hate you,
> and never have enough of hating ...
> > > > Some
> say that I talk of this eternally,
> yes, but eternal, too, is woman's wickedness.
> Either let someone teach them to be chaste
> or suffer me to trample on them forever. [Exit] (G 664–8)

He rushes off to find water to purify his ears of the 'filth' the Nurse has poured into them.

Euripides is showing how, in spite of Socrates, virtue can be the death of the hero. At the level of the gods, it was Hippolytus' unwise contempt for Aphrodite that set the plot in motion; and at the human level it is the extremism of this speech that seals his fate. Phaedra cannot suppose that anyone so full of abhorrence will keep her secret – although, when the time comes, Hippolytus does keep honourably silent before Theseus. She resolves to hang herself to escape the shame, but she intends to teach him a lesson as she goes. From the depths of her bitterness she will make him 'share in this my mortal sickness / and learn of chastity in moderation' (G 730–1). She leaves a message to incriminate him with Theseus, which has the desired outcome. And as Hippolytus sadly sums up their disastrous relations after her death, and shortly before his own, it *is* possible to be virtuous to excess:

> Virtuous she was in deed, although not virtuous:
> I that have virtue used it to my ruin. (G 1034–5)

The root of the Greek word means 'having a sound mind' (*sos* + *phren*, adj. *sophron*) and its meaning extends over 'purity, chastity' to 'self-control, moderation'. Hence the paradoxes here: Phaedra can be said to have been *sophron* (virtuous) in killing herself though not *sophron* (chaste); and Hippolytus can say that he was *sophron* (chaste) but not *sophron* (moderate) as he needed to be.[7]

The case of Hippolytus is less complex and suggestive, however, than the case of Phaedra, and this is perhaps why the plot has subsequently been given her name and been treated as her tragedy in later versions. With Phaedra, Euripides lingers on the deeper agony of a nature divided against itself, and the horrified consciousness of invasion by a blunt, demanding, omnipotent deity. The finest scenes of the play tell us about the experience of involuntary love and the way it

---

7   Christopher Gill, 'The Articulation of the Self in the *Hippolytus*' in Anton Powell (ed.), *Euripides, Women, and Sexuality* (London and New York: Routledge, 1990), p. 81.

distorts the mind – beginning with the Nurse's response, when she first discovers
Phaedra's secret. She is initially horrified and would sooner be dead than live
with this knowledge. She rushes offstage saying, 'Cypris [Aphrodite], you are no
God. / You are something stronger than God if that can be' (G 359–60). But when
she comes back, her love for Phaedra has taught her to come to terms with the
situation. The gods have hardly set mortals a good example in their love affairs;
and honour after all is only a word. 'What you want / is not fine words, but the
man! Come let's be done' (G 490–1). The unmistakable depth of her original
revulsion makes her new tone all the more meaningful: this is how Aphrodite
makes people talk, as if they have had a moral lobotomy. The Nurse now argues
for a human latitude, and a willingness to slide: 'We should not in the conduct of
our lives / be too exacting' (G 467).

This capitulation puts Phaedra's heroic resistance to Aphrodite in a strong
light. She blames the Nurse for abusing the power of language and making words
palliate a terrible evil. Using oratory to bad ends is what destroys the *polis* and
the home (Euripides is clearly thinking of debates in the Athenian *agora* again);
and the fact that her advice is welcome does not make it right for Phaedra:

> This is the deadly thing which devastates
> well-ordered cities and the homes of men –
> that's it, this art of oversubtle words.
> It's not the words ringing delight in the ear
> that one should speak, but those that have the power
> to save their hearer's honorable name. (G 486–9)

But to maintain her name, as she has recognized from the beginning of the play,
she must stop breathing; by remaining alive she prolongs her dishonour, to which
her body has consented if not her mind. The fact that she *is* still alive, and capable
of wishing, gives the Nurse a handle on Phaedra she is quick to use:

> *Nur.*   'The deed' is better if it saves your life:
>   than your 'good name' in which you die exulting.
> *Pha.*   For God's sake, do not press me any further!
>   What you say is true, but terrible!
>   My very soul is subdued by my love
>   and if you plead the cause of wrong so well
>   I shall fall into the abyss
>   from which I now am flying. (G 501–6)

Phaedra's dilemma goes back all the way to the *Agamemnon*: the conflict
between the claims of honour and of life itself. But unlike Clytaemnestra and the
Nurse, for whom honour is a mere expense of breath, Phaedra has internalized the
definition of honour as something greater than oneself, and worth the sacrifice of
life if necessary. She wants to leave behind an honourable 'name'; but her body
does not want the same thing. In any conflict between the two the need to live and
love will have the upper hand, because the need for honour is transcendental, and

lives in the realm of consciousness; but love is rooted in the body, which eats and breathes and seeks another body to join. This is what it means to be invaded by imperious, tyrannical Aphrodite; and this is why she says,

> Many a time in night's long empty spaces
> I have pondered on the causes of a life's shipwreck.
> I think our lives are worse than the mind's quality
> would warrant. There are many who know virtue.
> We know the good, we apprehend it clearly.
> But we can't bring it to achievement. (G 375–81)

'Knowing the good' is one thing, achieving it in a world of passions is another. But so long as Phaedra speaks like this, we cannot call her dishonourable. She is noble in her ability to look straight at her own contamination and give it its proper name; it is not until the Nurse has broken her secret to Hippolytus that her tone collapses and she sounds less than a heroine, heaping furious blame on the Nurse and ignoring the love of her mistress that made her act:

> This is fine service you have rendered me,
> corrupted, damned seducer of your friends!
> May Zeus, the father of my fathers' line,
> blot you out utterly, raze you from the world
> with thunderbolts! Did I not see your purpose,
> did I not say to you, 'Breathe not a word of this'
> which now overwhelms me with shame? But you,
> you did not hold back. And therefore I must die
> and die dishonored. (G 682–8)

It is only now that Phaedra falls as low as her passion – in pursuit of the public name that she fears she has lost for ever. To protect her reputation after her death she will dishonour Hippolytus by a terrible lie. This is the first fling of savagery in her nature, the first point at which she is truly dishonoured; and by the sharpest irony, it is only to re-establish her public name that she does it.

As Artemis explains to Theseus at the end, Hippolytus was perfectly guiltless of what he was accused of, and Phaedra was innocent in her own way too. She most unwillingly lost the battle with the invasive passion of Aphrodite:

> I have come here for this – to show you that your son's heart
> was always just, so just that for his good name
> he endured to die. I will show you, too,
> the frenzied love that seized your wife, or I may call it,
> a noble innocence. For that most hated Goddess,
> hated by all of us whose joy is virginity,
> drove her with love's sharp prickings to desire
> your son. She tried to overcome her love
> with the mind's power, but at last against her will
> she fell by the nurse's stratagems. (G 1298–1306)

The two protagonists have both been victims in their different ways; if there is anyone to blame, the play seems to say, it is 'that most hated Goddess', Aphrodite.

Bacchae (405 BCE)

In this late play, staged only after his death, Euripides brings the paradox of humanity's dual nature into the boldest focus and differentiates unforgettably between male and female ways of experiencing it. *Medea* showed how a woman might be precipitated into madness, and *Hippolytus* how a woman might consciously prolong the fight against wrongdoing, before capitulating at the last. But in the *Bacchae*, the mother, Agave, is acting in a trance, and only wakes to consciousness after committing the same irreparable crime as Medea, the murder of her son. Euripides in this play seems to be asking as radically as possible: if women are closer to Nature than men, what terrible powers does this give them, at what personal price? And where does this leave men? The fact that Pentheus has his head torn off by his own mother suggests his answer. The power of the mother is staggeringly great, and inexpressively primitive; what Medea did with a sword, Agave can do with her bare hands.

Pentheus' predicament similarly takes those of Jason and Hippolytus to an extreme. If Jason's troubles begin with ignoring Medea's reality, and Hippolytus dies of trying to avoid all connection with the female, what kills Pentheus is the attempt to assert his masculine values against the marauding, footloose Bacchants that threaten his city. The action of the play is his attempt to drag their Dionysiac energy back inside the walls and repress it; and when the frustrated energy finally erupts, it takes Pentheus with it. The hero of consciousness and law, defender of his city, is torn into bloody pieces, and the Bacchants play ball with them.

The boldness and centrality of this play, which everyone feels, come from Euripides' decision to embody Dionysus on stage and pit him openly against the male hero. In representing Dionysus as a character he finishes the thought he began in Aphrodite: if there is a god who rules the whole realm of nature, with its law of reproduction and death, that god must be as terrible as beautiful. Aphrodite is only represented in her opening speech (and by proxy, in the tone of voice of the Nurse) and the brutality of her power is taken for granted in the play without discussion. But Dionysus elicits from Euripides all his dramatic skill. Here is a god so paradoxical that no contradiction need be mitigated in representing him – a god so ambiguous that he can house Euripides' mistrust and creative energy at their highest pitch. For Dionysus has the advantage over Aphrodite that he springs from the natural world, and puts human sexuality back in its natural context. In the resonant description of E.R. Dodds,

> To the Greeks of the classical age Dionysus was not solely, or even mainly,
> the god of wine. Plutarch tells us as much, confirming it with a quotation

from Pindar, and the god's cult titles confirm it also: he is *Dendrites* or *Endendros*, the Power in the tree; he is *Anthios* the blossom-bringer, *Karpios* the fruit-bringer, *Fleus* or *Fleos*, the abundance of life. His domain is, in Plutarch's words, the whole of the *hygra phusis* – not only the liquid fire in the grape, but the sap thrusting in a young tree, the blood pounding in the veins of a young animal, all the mysterious and uncontrollable tides that ebb and flow in the life of nature.[8]

Dionysus reveals the truth underlying the whole effortful and exhausting construction of the *polis*, about which Euripides has been so piercingly sceptical: man is an animal, and whatever part words and reason play in his construction, Nature provides the key to the rest.

A play about the pre-eminence of nature and the frailty of the *polis* might be a recapitulation of Sophocles' argument in the *Oedipus* plays, which seemed so conservative in their implications. It is also notable that, like Oedipus, Agave commits her crime against her will: she too wakes out of a nightmare to discover that it was real. But this is another case where the meaning of a play depends more on the author's way of handling the subject matter than on its apparent content. Euripides the radical is unmistakably present in his readiness to put the god of nature on stage, where he must explain his decisions and stand by his actions like everyone else.

What Dionysus explains (much like Aphrodite in the *Hippolytus*) is that he is far too great a god to be ignored, even though he is a new arrival in Greece. He will not tolerate failure to acknowledge his divinity; and what has brought him to Thebes, temporarily disguised as the leader of his own cult, is that the new king, Pentheus, and his mother and sisters, are all denying that he is a god. He has already avenged himself on the women for their stubborn resistance by putting them in a state of Dionysiac possession, so they are dancing wildly on the mountains; and now he will test the young king to see if he will persist in his blasphemy. Thus far the exposition has been mechanical, and offers little insight into Dionysus beyond the deadpan tone he takes, which is reminiscent of Aphrodite's in its non-human confidence. For the god, it is all a matter of honour; respect is owed, and respect must be paid.

But the superiority of Dionysus to Aphrodite for the purposes of the play becomes clear in the speeches of the chorus, the group of genuine Bacchants who have followed him to Thebes from Asia. These women praise him for an experience no other Olympian deity can offer: self-loss in the group experience of his presence, the sense he gives his worshippers of actually sharing in his power. This ecstasy of belonging puts the god's need for honour on a different footing, for in an important sense he only exists while he is being worshipped:

---

[8]   In Euripides, *Bacchae*, ed. E.R. Dodds (Oxford: Oxford University Press, 1944, repr. 1960), pp. xi–xii.

–Blessèd is he who hallows his life in the worship of god,
  he whom the spirit of god possesseth, who is one
  with those who belong to the holy body of god.[9]

This experience of the group will be central to the play, and strikes a novel chord in tragedy, where the only groups we have known have been choruses of the powerless (women, slaves, old men) who affect the drama, if at all, by being mute. Euripides is planning to explore the strength that comes from being a conduit for group energy, when inhibiting self-awareness has been abolished. And this opening chorus already hints at the double-sided nature of what Dodds calls 'the easy power which is the especial gift of Dionysus',[10] that it transmutes equally easily into destructiveness. The power shows at its sweetest and most miraculous in

–With milk the earth flows! It flows with wine!
  It runs with the nectar of bees! (A 143–4)

But this god who is so inward with nature shares nature's lack of any moral sense:

–He is sweet upon the mountains. He drops to the earth
  from the running packs.
  He wears the holy fawn-skin. He hunts the wild goat
    and kills it.
  He delights in the raw flesh.
  He runs to the mountains of Phrygia, to the mountains
    of Lydia he runs!
  He is Bromius who leads us! *Evohé!* (A 135–42)

It is a token of how seriously Euripides takes Dionysus that the note of exaltation in this chorus, its easy embrace of the miraculous, is not put in a satirical light by the rest of the play. The earth does flow with milk and honey for the Bacchants, we will hear, and when the dancing bands of women are filled with the power of the god, their terrible strength enables them to uproot trees to 'delight in the raw flesh' of their victim. When they revel,

. . . the beasts and all the mountain
  seemed wild with divinity. And when they ran,
  everything ran with them. (A 726–7)

The astonishing locution by which everything else on the mountain becomes suffused with Bacchic energy at the same time is ratified by the drama. Although this is only a messenger's speech, it describes the true extent and nature of the god.

---

[9]   *The Bacchae*, trans. William Arrowsmith, in Euripides, *The Complete Greek Tragedies*, ed. David Grene and Richmond Lattimore, 5 (Chicago: University of Chicago Press, 1959, repr. 1975), p. 158. Hereafter A. Line numbers refer to the Greek text.

[10]   *Bacchae*, ed. Dodds, p. 74 (ll. 65–7 n.).

Because Dionysus is the *hygra phusis*, the flowing power of life itself, the contrast he makes with the constructed meanings of civilization is poignant in the extreme. In three central scenes, Euripides confronts Dionysus with Pentheus, and shows in dazzling detail how the apparent power of the *polis* melts to nothing beside the real power of Nature. Indeed, the more civilization asserts its strength the more it subverts itself.

In the first confrontation, Pentheus thinks he has captured the 'effeminate stranger' who 'infects our women' by making them disorderly Bacchants (A 354). For him, dancing in the god's train implies sexual promiscuity too, though he has been assured by Tiresias that women who are naturally chaste remain so in these rites (A 314–16). But Pentheus is in a state of mind parallel to that of Hippolytus in his last tirade: once they have got loose from male authority, women sink naturally to the lowest levels of bestiality, and what is drawing them to the dance on the mountain is the hope of initiation by a 'charlatan magician' into 'filthy mysteries' (A 234, 260). This insistence that what Dionysus releases is only women's sexual energy at its most animalistic will turn out to be the crack in Pentheus' male armour, the half-hopeful suspicion that will lure him to his death. And his prurience shows already in the mingled fascination and disgust at the stranger himself, who strikes Pentheus as disturbingly effeminate, but alluring ('at least to women', he hastily adds):

> . . . So,
> you are attractive, stranger, at least to women –
> which explains, I think, your presence here in Thebes.
> Your curls are long. You do not wrestle, I take it.
> And what fair skin you have – you must take care of it –
> no daylight complexion; no, it comes from the night
> when you hunt Aphrodite with your beauty. (A 453–9)

The intimacy of attention here bodes ill for Pentheus: Euripides captures the magnetic tension between the assertive masculinity of the young king, shorn, tanned and hardened by exercise, and the fluid softness of a body that represents all he must renounce to stay the way he is. The unequal struggle between the two (the audience knows that the stranger is the god himself) gives a special irony to Pentheus' sarcasms and aggression. They represent civilization's attempt to answer back to nature, and we are mesmerized by their hubris, and their futility.

What Pentheus thinks he has on his side is rationalism, Greek civilization, and the military strength to make these prevail. Rationalism prevents him from being taken in by a new god: when Dionysus says he is the son of Zeus, Pentheus says sarcastically, 'You have some local Zeus / who spawns new gods?' (A 466–7). And a god of 'mysteries' who requires 'initiation' into his rites is particularly dubious: 'Tell me the benefits / that those who know your mysteries enjoy' (A 472–3). And as a Greek, to be told that the new worship is spreading abroad cuts no ice with him:

Dio.   Foreigners everywhere now dance for Dionysus.
Pen.   They are more ignorant than Greeks.
Dio.   In this matter
they are not. Customs differ. (A 482–4)

Euripides is exposing the rationalism which is really irrationality in disguise. Pentheus cannot be diverted from what he thinks he knows, and the menacing honesty of the stranger is wasted on him, though Dionysus gives him all the information he needs. This stupidity at the level of thinking is not very different from his aggression at the level of action. Both are *hubris* in the strict sense of the term, 'violence against a god'. And as the young king settles the disturbance by sending Dionysus off to be chained in the palace without his thyrsus and shorn of his curls, the Asian Bacchants beat their drums in agony at this act of sacrilege. The young king's last and most Greek remark is that these superfluous women should be sold as slaves, or put to work at the loom. Their frantic chorus expresses what such aggressive masculinity feels like from the other side of the Dionysiac divide:

> With fury, with fury, he rages,
> Pentheus, son of Echion,
> born of the breed of Earth,
> spawned by the dragon, whelped by Earth!
> Inhuman, a rabid beast,
> a giant in wildness raging,
> storming, defying the children of heaven.
> He has threatened me with bonds
> though my body is bound to god . . .
> Descend from Olympus, lord!
> Come, whirl your wand of gold
> and quell with death this beast of blood
> whose violence abuses man and god
>   outrageously. (A 538–46, 553–5)

If Pentheus could only register it, there is already enough indication here of the power that will rip him to pieces. The energy of these women is severed from consciousness, and to them it is not a metaphor that he is 'a rabid beast, / a giant in wildness raging'. That is how they experience him, and their fear and horror are proportionate to his monstrosity. In their state of Bacchic fusion they do not differentiate between moral and physical realities, and analysis gives way to overwhelming conviction – which can be as wrong at one level as it is right at another. Just as they are right to call on the power of the god, but cannot see that he is already present, so they are wrong to think of Pentheus as a mad beast, though it is true he is committing *hubris*. It is only the verdict of Dionysus on Pentheus that has truth at all levels:

> You do not know
> the limits of your strength. You do not know
> what you do. You do not know who you are. (A 506)

When Pentheus returns for the second confrontation scene he has had ample opportunity to learn the limits of his strength – he has failed to chain the god and the palace has been shaken to pieces by an earthquake – but he is still resisting the truth. His attempt to shackle Dionysus has only revealed that what he is doing is wrestling with something else, an animal power far greater than himself. As the god describes it to the anxious chorus:

> He seemed to think that he was chaining me but never once
> so much as touched my hands. He fed on his desires.
> Inside the stable he intended as my jail, instead of me,
> he found a bull and tried to rope its knees and hooves.
> He was panting desperately, biting his lips with his teeth,
> his whole body drenched with sweat, while I sat nearby,
> quietly watching. (A 616–22)

The god's quiet ease and relaxation is deliberately contrasted with Pentheus' sweat and misplaced labour. Pentheus is still insisting on what he thinks he knows, even though he cannot distinguish the bull from the stranger – having begun, in this sense, to enter into the confused state of the Asian Bacchants. And he is still trusting in fortifications ('I shall order every gate in every tower / to be bolted tight' A 653) when there is no palace left to fortify.

At this crisis the messenger arrives from Cithaeron with the key speech of revelation (and warning) that represents Pentheus' last chance to acknowledge the truth. This is the speech that, as noted above, ratifies the miraculous powers of Dionysus without irony: it is Euripides' most dazzling representation of this double-natured god, who aptly calls himself 'most terrible, and yet most gentle, to mankind' (A 861). Here Euripides seems to be supplying an element missing from his portrait of Aphrodite: love's gentle benignity, its creativity, the fertility that makes it so central to human life. Now that his subject is not a monstrous sexual passion but 'all the mysterious and uncontrollable tides that ebb and flow in the life of nature', Euripides can lend his imagination to nature as a blessing. And the messenger's speech is a unique attempt in tragedy to do justice to the original state of nature, as Bacchants might recreate it on a mountain far from the *polis*. What the messenger unwillingly testifies to is paradisal, a natural order without organization, a harmony without law:

> About that hour
> when the sun lets loose its light to warm the earth,
> our grazing herds of cows had just begun to climb
> the path along the mountain ridge. Suddenly
> I saw three companies of dancing women,
> one led by Autonoë, the second captained

> by your mother Agave, while Ino led the third.
> There they lay in the deep sleep of exhaustion,
> some resting on boughs of fir, others sleeping
> where they fell, here and there among the oak leaves –
> but all modestly and soberly, not, as you think,
> drunk with wine, nor wandering, led astray
> by the music of the flute, to hunt their Aphrodite
> through the woods. (A 677–88)

The women are neither drunk nor promiscuous. But their new closeness to nature is hinted at in their deep sleep and the way they lie scattered among the oak leaves. If they are still inherently modest, the quality is unconscious, innate.

> But your mother heard the lowing
> of our horned herds, and springing to her feet,
> gave a great cry to waken them from sleep.
> And they too, rubbing the bloom of soft sleep
> from their eyes, rose up lightly and straight –
> a lovely sight to see: all as one,
> the old women and the young and the unmarried girls.
> First they let their hair fall loose, down
> over their shoulders, and those whose straps had slipped
> fastened their skins of fawn with writhing snakes
> that licked their cheeks. Breasts swollen with milk,
> new mothers who had left their babies behind at home
> nestled gazelles and young wolves in their arms,
> suckling them. Then they crowned their hair with leaves,
> ivy and oak and flowering bryony. (A 689–703)

The unity of the group, the way Dionysiac energy flows simultaneously through each body, shows in the response to Agave's cry: they rise 'all as one' in a miraculous motion. A Bacchant's preparation for the day is nature's variant on the dressing ritual: putting the hair down, not up, and tying fawnskin tunics with snakes that harmlessly lick the women's cheeks. And the harmony between these women and the world of animal nature is confirmed by their ability to suckle the young of other species, however shy or fierce ('gazelles and young wolves'). The *hygra phusis*, the flow of liquid nature, passes through and between them all. And finally it is shown gushing towards them from the earth itself:

> One woman
> struck her thyrsus against a rock and a fountain
> of cool water came bubbling up. Another drove
> her fennel in the ground, and where it struck the earth,
> at the touch of god, a spring of wine poured out.
> Those who wanted milk scratched at the soil
> with bare fingers and the white milk came welling up.
> Pure honey spurted, streaming, from their wands.

> If you had been there and seen these wonders for yourself,
> you would have gone down on your knees and prayed
> to the god you now deny. (A 704–14)

The earth yields its blessings freely to the Dionysiac touch. Here is the Athenian version of Eden, where the earth feeds its creatures as naturally as the Bacchants feed the wolves. Nature is revealed as a joyful exchange of wine and water, milk and honey, and the great god who energizes this exchange should bring Pentheus, like the messenger, to his knees.

Euripides here is clearly approaching the central question: if women are closer to nature than men, what terrible powers does this give them, and at what personal cost? The play takes it for granted that women are more open to Dionysiac experience than men, and that Dionysus himself has female qualities – visible in the soft, accessible, fluid body that so repels Pentheus. Here, on wild Cithaeron, the god can return women to the matrix of mother earth: their conscious, constructed selves are lost in a group unity that brings them to their feet in a single movement, and their bodies become conduits for energy – the energy of the god in the dance, and the fertility of nature that wells up through their milky breasts. The bliss of this state is that it is orderly, but not organized. It is not what the women wanted (they were as willing to slander the god as Pentheus), but what they found in themselves. What is terrible about it, however, is precisely the result of its involuntary origin. Dionysus bypasses the conscious mind, and his trance cannot be monitored by a separate self. The individual is flooded by an infinitely greater power, which cannot be held back, or stopped, any more than a mother can require her milk not to flow. And the personal cost to Agave, the play will show, is fearful.

But men are her fellow-sufferers. If they are not as close to nature as women, they are not outside it, either, and the play shows them transfixed by the spectacle of nature in women without understanding the danger of their own relation. These women are in Eden only until jolted out of it by male interference:

> We cowherds and shepherds
> gathered in small groups, wondering and arguing
> among ourselves at these fantastic things,
> the awful miracles those women did.
> But then a city fellow with the knack of words
> rose to his feet and said: 'All you who live
> upon the pastures of the mountain, what do you say?
> Shall we earn a little favor with King Pentheus
> by hunting his mother Agave out of the revels?'
>
>   . . . It happened, however,
> that Agave ran near the ambush where I lay
> concealed. Leaping up, I tried to seize her,
> but she gave a cry: 'Hounds who run with me,

men are hunting us down! Follow, follow me!
Use your wands for weapons.'
                                        At this we fled
and barely missed being torn to pieces by the women.
Unarmed, they swooped down upon the herds of cattle
grazing there on the green of the meadow. And then
you could have seen a single woman with bare hands
tear a fat calf, still bellowing with fright,
in two, while others clawed the heifers to pieces.
There were ribs and cloven hooves scattered everywhere,
and scraps smeared with blood hung from the fir trees. (A 714–21,
    728–42)

The simple herdsmen might have been content to marvel at the women, but they are seduced by 'a city fellow with the knack of words' whose consciousness, like that of Pentheus, is walled in against conviction. The connection of 'city' and 'words' is damning, as so often in Euripides: the safety of the city has merely made the citizen arrogant, and his words trivial and deracinated. His advice is lethal: it tips the women in their trance over the border from unselfconscious bliss into blind panic. Now the power that flows through them is purely destructive, and their women's hands all share in the limitless power of the group. Feeling themselves to be hunted, they become hunters (E 732), swift as a flock of birds (E 748) and as terrible as an invading army (E 752) – more so, indeed, because they cannot tell the difference between a herd of animals and a human settlement. They sweep like a flood into the villages in the foothills; and men once again engage them in a futile battle of weapons, spears against ivy wands:

Like invaders they swooped on Hysiae
and on Erythrae in the foothills of Cithaeron.
Everything in sight they pillaged and destroyed.
They snatched the children from their homes. And when
they piled their plunder on their backs, it stayed in place,
untied. Nothing, neither bronze nor iron,
fell to the dark earth. Flames flickered
in their curls and did not burn them. Then the villagers,
furious at what the women did, took to arms.
And *there*, sire, was something terrible to see.
For the men's spears were pointed and sharp, and yet
drew no blood, whereas the wands the women threw
inflicted wounds. And then the men *ran*,
routed by women! Some god, I say, was with them.
The Bacchae then returned where they had started,
by the springs the god had made, and washed their hands
while the snakes licked away the drops of blood
that dabbled their cheeks. (A 751–68)

All the fortifications of masculinity – settlements, weapons, rationality itself – are swept away by the Dionysiac flood. In their undifferentiated group frenzy the women are invulnerable to personal hurt: flames cannot touch them, and the plunder stays on their backs as if magnetized. The 'pointed and sharp' spears of the men can do no harm, but their own ivy wands draw blood: inanimate metal has no power against the vitality of living weapons, which draw their strength from the unstoppable growth of nature itself. The messenger has seen Hippolytus' worst nightmare embodied, the women of the city running loose in an unmediated relation with Nature; and he has seen the effect on the men with disbelief: 'the men *ran*, / routed by women!'

As if sensing that even this testimony will not be enough, the messenger caps his speech with some last words of persuasion, by which Euripides underlines the sense in which men are part of nature, too. And the greatest blessings they enjoy are the gifts of Dionysus:

> Whoever this god may be,
> sire, welcome him to Thebes. For he is great
> in many other ways as well. It was he,
> or so they say, who gave to mortal men
> the gift of lovely wine by which our suffering
> is stopped. And if there is no god of wine,
> there is no love, no Aphrodite either,
> nor other pleasure left to men. (A 769–74)

Dionysus is behind whatever releases us from the strain of being an individuated self – love, wine, pleasure of all kinds. He is the welcome loosener of the tie between body and consciousness, and when this is not taken to the Bacchant extreme, it is equally the secret of our fusion with another in love, and of our release from bodily pain ('wine . . . by which our suffering is stopped'). The god puts all human bodies back where they belong, in the great system of flow and interchange that is nature.

But in his savage response, Pentheus only displays the horror consciousness may feel – particularly male consciousness – at the human body it is tied to:

> You there. Go down quickly to the Electran gates
> and order out all heavy-armored infantry;
> call up the fastest troops among our cavalry,
> the mobile squadrons and the archers. We march
> against the Bacchae! Affairs are out of hand
> when we tamely endure such conduct in our women. (A 780–6)

Although he has just been told that weapons are ineffective against the Bacchants, Pentheus can only think of deploying the heavy infantry. Although every attempt he has made to 'get a grip' on the situation has merely given Dionysus a better grip on him, he still plans to solve the crisis by marching the women back to Thebes.

This obsession with the women's freedom, so similar to that of Hippolytus, allows Euripides to suggest how differently men and women experience their human duality. Both sexes have bodies and consciousness, both sexes belong to nature and to the *polis*. But because the *hygra phusis* flows more visibly through women, as the milk in their breasts and the growing children in their wombs, the man is more mesmerized by nature in women than by nature as a whole. Insofar as he is individuated and conscious, he is holding at bay the undifferentiated, unconscious life he once was – in the womb, united with his mother. And the accompanying terror of regression is displayed in the young king's frantic invocation of military force: so long as the women are under lock and key, he feels, the threat can be contained. It is not his city walls he really means to fortify, but the walls of his male psyche. And in this context we can appreciate the new development Euripides adds to the familiar story of Pentheus and the Bacchants – that it is his own mother whom he must restrain above all, and who thus becomes his murderer.[11]

The sense in which Pentheus' fight with the women is a battle inside himself is dazzlingly exposed by the sudden reversal that follows his rejection of the messenger's advice. Pentheus has had his last chance, and the god now takes a different tack. As he calls for his armour, Dionysus makes an irresistible offer:

> Dio.   *Wait*!
>   Would you like to *see* their revels on the mountain?
> Pen.   I would pay a great sum to see that sight.
> Dio.   Why are you so passionately curious?
> Pen.   Of course
>   I'd be sorry to see them drunk –
> Dio.   But for all your sorrow,
>   you'd like very much to see them?
> Pen.   Yes, very much.
>   I could crouch beneath the fir trees, out of sight. (A 810–16)

Pentheus' unhesitating response to an opportunity to be prurient – and the thin veil of social decorum he drapes over it ('Of course / I'd be sorry to see them drunk') – show how his militaristic resistance to his fears has merely increased their power over him. The flow of vitality in him is stagnant but it nonetheless exerts a massive force against the dam: he is suddenly desperate to see the sight he has forbidden himself, and he anticipates it in the most lascivious terms ('I can see them already, there among the bushes, / mating like birds, caught in the toils of love', A 957–8).

The catch, says Dionysus, who understands his enemy very well, is that he must disguise himself as a Bacchant to evade detection: he will need a dress, fawnskin, wig and snood, and a thyrsus in his hand. All Pentheus' male pride revolts ('I would die of shame') but now his unconscious excitement cannot be

---

[11]   T.B.L. Webster, *The Tragedies of Euripides* (London: Methuen, 1967) p. 269.

contained and, with the proviso that he will be taken secretly through the back streets of Thebes, he goes offstage to be dressed. 'Now', says Dionysus as he leaves, with bottomless irony,

> He shall come to know
> Dionysus, son of Zeus, consummate god,
> most terrible, and yet most gentle, to mankind. (A 859–61)

Pentheus is poised to know Dionysus from the inside of his Dionysiac trance, and also to know that the stranger has been Dionysus throughout. But most of all he is about to learn the god's dual nature, gentle to those who give him admission and terrible to those who block him out.

When Pentheus returns for the third of the confrontation scenes that make up the centre of the play, he is in a state of parody feminity, as grotesque in its relation to actual womanhood as his prurient imaginings were in relation to the real Bacchants. But this, Euripides implies, is what happens when masculinity keeps femininity at bay for so long. Now Pentheus yearns to be told that he looks just like his mother and sister, and he stands happily submissive as Dionysus tucks a curl back in his snood loosened by his head-tossing. This transvestite Pentheus frets anxiously about his hemline and his girdle; but he also has delusions of power. He is uncertain whether he sees one sun or two, and whether the god has become a bull. But most of all he feels like a conduit for unspeakable energy: 'Could I lift Cithaeron up, do you think? / Shoulder the cliffs, Bacchae and all?' (A 945–6). In this intoxicated state he no longer seeks to be hidden, but to be paraded 'through the very heart of Thebes' (A 961). The struggle between the *polis* and Dionysus that has underlain the whole play now resolves itself in his delusions to a matter of his individual daring ('I, alone of all this city, dare to go', A 962). And his eager misprisions cut across the god's ambiguous promises with dreadful irony:

Dio.	You and you alone will suffer for your city.
	A great ordeal awaits you. But you are worthy
	of your fate. I shall lead you safely there;
	someone else shall bring you back.
Pen.	Yes, my mother.
Dio.	An example to all men.
Pen.	It is for that I go.
Dio.	You will be carried home –
Pen.	O luxury!
Dio.	cradled in your mother's arms.
Pen.	You will spoil me.
Dio.	I *mean* to spoil you.
Pen.	I go to my reward.
Dio.	You are an extraordinary young man, and you go
	to an extraordinary experience. You shall win
	a glory towering to heaven and usurping
	god's. (A 963–72)

In confirming that 'you and you alone will suffer for your city', Dionysus underlines the identification between the city and Pentheus, and the sense in which the city itself has been at war with the god from the first. Pentheus is embarking on 'a great ordeal' – and somehow he already anticipates that the climax of this will not be his bringing his mother back in triumph, but being brought *by* her, 'an example to all men' (a hero, as he understands it, a ghastly warning, as Dionysus knows). There is a chilling ambiguity to 'you will be carried home [i.e., as a trophy]', which Pentheus understands as the luxury of being brought down in a litter. But the consummate touch of the god's persuasion is the addition, 'in your mother's arms'. This is the forbidden place of regression, the last taboo for the grown male, as desirable as forbidden; and it is the mark of how completely Pentheus has renounced the struggle to be male that he accepts with a happy simper: 'You will spoil me.' This, indeed, is the god's intention; and Pentheus can go forth, confident that he is an 'extraordinary young man' destined for 'an extraordinary experience'.

It is Pentheus' personal servant who returns to tell us the upshot. Pentheus found the Bacchants singing and playing in their calm, Edenic state. Disappointed of his expectations, he asked the 'stranger' for a better view; so a great fir was miraculously bent over for him and he was placed on the very top, where the Bacchants could see him as well as he now saw them. The god then shouted aloud to the women to take vengeance on the unbeliever; and with their terrible strength the women uprooted the tree, fell on their victim, and ripped him limb from limb, his mother the foremost. His whole body was stripped of flesh and the women played ball with the scraps. Agave impaled his head on her thyrsus, taking it for a mountain lion's, and is now bringing it back to Thebes in triumph to boast how well a woman can hunt.

The most harrowing part of this agonizing recital is the face-to-face encounter between the son and his mother with Pentheus, now awake from his transvestite trance, touching his mother's cheek in formal supplication:

> . . . But snatching off his wig and snood
> so she would recognize his face, he touched her cheeks,
> screaming, *'No, no, Mother! I am Pentheus,*
> *your own son, the child you bore to Echion!*
> *Pity me, spare me, Mother! I have done a wrong*
> *but do not kill your own son for my offense.'*
> But she was foaming at the mouth, and her crazed eyes
> rolling with frenzy. She was mad, stark mad,
> possessed by Bacchus. Ignoring his cries of pity,
> she seized his left arm at the wrist; then, planting
> her foot upon his chest, she pulled. (A 1115–27)

The gulf between Pentheus' act of supplication and Agave's response is absolute. The supplicant gesture he uses is for Greeks a reminder of the victim's 'human rights' – the same gesture the Nurse made to Phaedra – and anyone who ignores it sinks beneath the level of true humanity. But Agave has already been sundered from her humanity. To her, Pentheus is a hunter's problem in dismemberment only, and she cannot pull off his arm till she has her foot on his chest. His appeal to her as a mother marks the hopeless distance between them: the most tender and specific of connections is ineffective to an unseeing Bacchant, and though he gives her his name, relationship and lineage (*'I am Pentheus, / your own son, the child you bore to Echion!'*) he cannot elicit her recognition. A member of the Dionysiac band, a conduit through whom all the power of the god is flowing, may hear the words, but her mind cannot process them. Not even his statement of the crime she is about to commit can make her understand: *'I have done a wrong, / but do not kill your own son for my offense.'*

The ripping apart of Pentheus may be viewed as the far end of the debate we have been tracing all the way from the *Oresteia*. Just as the trial scene there pitted Orestes against the Furies of his mother (who also looked forward to reducing him to blood and rags), and the future of the *polis* rested on the outcome, so this play shows Thebes failing to find some way of containing the frenzy of the Bacchants, and Pentheus paying the price, for lack of an Athena to negotiate a solution. Pentheus is in the human predicament of Orestes (he is less strong than his mother's Furies, less rooted in Nature) but even more strikingly, he is in the same aggressive state as Apollo, seeking no compromise with the Furies and horrified by their claims. Euripides is as clear as Aeschylus about the fact that maleness of this Apollonian kind provokes its own *nemesis*, and if the *polis* is to survive it must find an acknowledged home for Dionysus, just as the Eumenides have been lodged under Athens by Athena.

Another indication that Euripides is still thinking about the issues raised by the *Oresteia* is his inclusion of Agave's tragedy alongside that of Pentheus. It would have been easy to end the play with his murder and the veiled presumption that Hippolytus was right: women are animals who happen to have the power of speech, and who should never be let out of doors without a male keeper. But Euripides, like Aeschylus, is sure that women are creatures of reason who belong inside the city – all the more so if they have close ties with nature. For their female power comes at terrible cost to themselves as well as men, and where will they learn restraint if not there? His picture of Agave's return to consciousness in Thebes shows in slow motion her inevitable journey from Nature to Culture, from group to individual. This conversion of a triumphant Bacchant into a bloodstained mother is Euripides' most careful account of the moment of tragic recognition (*anagnorisis*) – and it underlines a fact central to our study, that tragedy depends on consciousness.

As Cadmus says, looking at his still-intoxicated daughter, she could be happy for ever if she could only stay unaware:

> When you realize the horror you have done,
> you shall suffer terribly. But if with luck
> your present madness lasts until you die,
> you will seem to have, not having, happiness. (A 1259–62)

But Agave is already uneasy at his lack of enthusiasm for her bloody trophy ('Is there something wrong? A 1263) and the 'flurry' inside her is subsiding. She begins to see the sky more clearly and, 'I feel as though – / My mind were somehow – changing', she says (A 1269–70). When he asks what she holds in her hands she answers insecurely, 'A lion's head – or so the hunters told me' (A 1278). Cadmus finally brings her to the point of knowledge:

> *Cad.*   Look directly at it. Just a quick glance.
> *Ag.*   What is it? What am I holding in my hands?
> *Cad.*   Look more closely still. Study it carefully.
> *Ag.*   *No!* O gods, I see the greatest grief there is. (A 1279–82)

When at last she *sees* – 'the greatest grief there is' – we understand why the verb occurs so often in the last scenes of tragic plays. For mere seeing is nothing (even as a Bacchant, Agave had the use of her eyes); but true seeing is knowing, and being the complete conscious person who sees and knows. 'Now, now I see', says Agave; 'Dionysus has destroyed us all' (A 1296).

Part Two

Renaissance Tragedy

Chapter 4

Revenge and the Machiavel

If this account of family resemblances in Greek plots carries conviction, it raises the interesting possibility of tracing parallels in later tragedies too. Do the other great periods of tragic drama reveal the same preoccupations? But to find a group of comparable dramas we have to leap two millennia, to the Renaissance. This raises questions about the conditions for tragedy we might briefly explore. Why, in the history of literature, is tragedy so intermittent?

The answer may lie in the brevity of the Athenian achievement itself: once the surprise of the democratic experiment has subsided, the conditions of fear and insight are no longer acute enough to generate such serious drama. Euripides himself mixes tragedy with comedy in awkward proportions as his career goes on, and often seems to administer shocks to the audience to retain their wandering attention. Although new theatres were built everywhere across the Greek world after his death (and the 'classics' of the fifth century were repeatedly revived), the creative tragic period was acknowledged to be over by the end of the Peloponnesian war (404). Scholars know the names of more than 60 dramatists who continued to write, ransacking mythology for myths no one had yet used (the story of Leda, of Adonis), but although these plays were performed, not one of them has survived. The energy of Greek drama seems to have gone into the social problems of the New Comedy, and its intellectual content into philosophy (the process we can see beginning in the debate about virtue in the *Hippolytus*). Plato writes a great monologue in which his hero Socrates drinks hemlock for the sake of Athenian law – but he does so in prose.

Powerful tragic theatre is always likely to be a transitory phenomenon. The period for which any writer senses he has his audience's full attention is inevitably brief, and the insight he has to share is always perishable. More common is what we mostly find in history, theatres without tragedy (as in the long drought since Shakespeare) and tragedies without theatres (many emerging nations have made the Athenian journey from tribalism to the law, but few have left plays behind them). Seneca, in the first century AD, is a paradoxical variant of the problem: everyone acknowledges his importance in literary history, but no one can quite bear to call his nine plays tragedies in the full sense of the term. The plays all have Greek models, but they are rhetorical pieces for recitation, not performance, so they escape the discipline of what can credibly be acted out in front of a wide public. Their 'events' all occur at the level of language, at which level the message sent is deeply ambivalent: the Silver Latin is as neatly fitted as carpentry, and gives sententious solidity to an emotional undertow on the verge of hysteria. Seneca's Oedipus, for instance, fears the worst from the very beginning, and the atmosphere never lightens; portents abound, the sacrificial wine turns to blood, and a foetus is found in an unmated heifer, which then writhes back into life and jumps off the altar. When Oedipus punishes himself, he scrabbles in the cavities of his eyes and pulls out the remaining shreds of flesh. The narrative is all gothic clutter and pain, a way of cauterizing the sensibility rather than eliciting thought.

Seneca's plays suggest that it is possible to retell the Greek plots without creating either drama or tragic emotion; and the fact that he writes under a tyranny suggests one more factor in the rarity of tragic drama. The subject matter of Greek drama, we began by saying, is in some sense the by-product of democracy; and although the conclusion should not be drawn too narrowly, it is hard to deny that the drama of any period reflects its politics. In the sense that politics are the effective result of power relations and are acted out in front of an audience, indeed, they are themselves a sort of drama. This is why Plato in the *Laws* seems to say that his ideal state will have no use for playwrights – because their work would only be a shadow of what is already being achieved in everyday life. He would turn them away, he says, in these words:

> Respected visitors, we are ourselves authors of a tragedy, and that the finest and best we know how to make. In fact, our whole polity has been constructed as a dramatization of a noble and perfect life; that is what we hold to be in truth the most real of tragedies. Thus you are poets, and we also are poets in the same style, rival artists and rival actors, and that in the finest of all dramas, one which indeed can be produced only by a code of true law – or at least that is our faith.[1]

This vision of civic life as a 'dramatization' (*mimesis*) of the best existence, underpinned by 'true law', is unmistakably related to the debate in Athenian drama; even though the dramatists say in their various voices how hard it is to make law so well loved.

If democracy reveres law with good reason, it is not surprising that it produces dramas which probe so deeply into the human mind and passions, the eternal obstacles to legality. And by the same token, there can be little genuine speculation in corrupt tyrannies like that of Nero, where law is despaired of and public life is a matter of Stoic impassivity, until the day the fatal letter arrives (Nero invited Seneca to commit suicide in AD 65). Seneca's plays have one explanation for all their griefs: Fate, which explains everything and nothing, but sonorously fills the mouth: *Fatis agimur; cedite fatis*, as the chorus tells Oedipus (l. 980, 'the Fates rule us, yield to them'); *quid ratio possit?* asks Phaedra helplessly (l. 184, 'what use is reason?').

In this context, the body of Renaissance drama written under Elizabeth I and James I raises interesting new questions. What kind of tragic drama gets written under monarchies, and why is the Renaissance ripe for the re-emergence of the

---

[1]   Plato, *The Laws*, trans. A.E. Taylor (London: Dent, 1934), p. 203.

genre? What questions is it trying to answer, and how coherently does it frame them? This period's preoccupation with revenge plots and the figure of the Machiavel are very suggestive.

Thomas Kyd, *The Spanish Tragedy* (1592)

It is striking that here, right at the beginning of the renewed tradition, is another play about revenge. Clearly the topic does not go away: for Kyd, as for Aeschylus, the quickest way of suggesting what destabilizes society and sends heroes mad is to describe a crime against family feeling – and the desperate search for reparation that follows. The debate is going on at court, as well as in the theatre, as we can see from Bacon's famous aphorism, 'Revenge is a kind of wild justice.' Bacon's metaphor suggests that the passion for revenge is inherent in family ties themselves, and the hunger for it bears the same relation to civic justice as a wild crop bears to a cultivated one. It is a beginning, he acknowledges, just as the Furies themselves were guardians of primitive justice; but it must not be allowed to develop on its own terms or it will choke the growth of justice itself – as the aphorism continues, 'which the more man's nature runs to, the more ought law to weed it out'.[2]

But when we pick up Kyd's play we are reminded how indirect was the part Greek culture played in the rebirth of tragedy. The works of Seneca stand firmly between Athens and the Elizabethans: their *Agamemnon*, *Oedipus*, *Phaedra* and *Medea* are his, as 'Englished' from the 1560s onwards. Refracted through Seneca, the Greek plots arrive cluttered with sensational elements – tortures, ghosts, madness and underworld excitements. Kyd's hero, Hieronymo, even carries a copy of Seneca's plays – which at pertinent places he quotes, in Latin, to validate the play's claim to tragedy, should the audience be in any doubt. Revenge comes on stage with a speaking role, and promises justice with heavy sententiousness: 'The sickle comes not till the corn be ripe. / Be still' (II.vi.9–10).[3]

But this naive device is all Kyd can supply to give his play dignity. There is no serious consideration of the problems revenge poses, the way one man's revenge is another generation's injustice; and after Greek drama it is startling to find how easily the subject collapses into the tit-for-tat exchange of pain, with the presumption that every audience enjoys the sight of someone else's distress. The play ends with a ghost anticipating the punishment of all his recently deceased enemies in Hell. Indeed, he asks to be allowed to allot them their tortures:

---

[2]   *The Essays of Francis Bacon*, ed. Samuel Harvey Reynolds (Oxford: Clarendon Press, 1890), p. 34.
[3]   Thomas Kyd, *The Spanish Tragedy*, ed. J.R. Mulryne (London and New York: A. & C. Black and W.W. Norton, 1970, repr. 1989), p. 47.

> Let loose poor Tityus from the vulture's gripe,
> And let Don Cyprian supply his room;
> Place Don Lorenzo on Ixion's wheel,
> And let the lover's endless pains surcease –
> Juno forgets old wrath, and grants him ease;
> Hang Balthazar about Chimaera's neck,
> And let him there bewail his bloody love,
> Repining at our joys that are above . . . (IV.v.31–8)

And Revenge sets about the job with unapologetic relish:

> Then haste we down to meet thy friends and foes:
> To place thy friends in ease, the rest in woes.
> For here, though death hath end their misery,
> I'll there begin their endless tragedy. (45–8)

The elaborate sadism of the punishments, however, seems less genuine than Kyd's pleasure in displaying the Renaissance learning painfully acquired in the schoolroom (from *Aeneid VI*). His closing use of the term 'tragedy' to mean something like 'unnatural pain' shows how debased is the understanding derived from Seneca; and at every turn of the plot, his one recourse is to stimulate a strong reaction by whatever means. A quick survey of the stage directions is indicative: *'They hang him in the arbour'* (II.iv.53); *'Shoots the dog'* (III.iii.32); *'Stab him, Stab herself'* [*sic*] (IV.iv.67); *'He bites out his tongue'* (IV.iv.191). The familiar occasions of tragic emotion are to be glimpsed amidst the havoc, as Hieronymo grieves over a handkerchief soaked in his dead son's blood, or Isabella commits suicide by stabbing 'the hapless breast that gave [her dead son] suck' (IV.ii.38) – but none of the enormous events that take place yields sufficient meaning for the play to rest on, and the plot terminates in a pile of corpses, from mere exhaustion. It is noteworthy, though, that the avengers are as dead as everyone else: although Kyd sympathizes with wronged Hieronymo, he does not contemplate the possibility of a happy revenge.

Ineffectual as this play is in itself, it offers a number of pointers to the re-emergence of tragedy. One is that, authorized by Seneca, the drama offers a home to the deepest and most primitive emotion. The relation of private revenge to public law is a profound intellectual issue, but it does not have to eventuate in profoundly intelligent plays: it is enough to bring the audience into the area of the difficulty, to have their total attention. What Kyd offers his audience here is the thrilling gratification of blood spilt for blood. As Hieronymo says to the king, standing over the corpses of his enemies,

> . . . Here behold this bloody handkercher,
> Which at Horatio's death I weeping dipped
> Within the river of his bleeding wounds:
> It as propitious, see I have reserved,
> And never hath it left my bloody heart,

Soliciting remembrance of my vow
With these, O these accursed murderers:
Which now performed, my heart is satisfied. (IV.iv.122–9)

This Senecan morality leaves us stranded somewhere at the level of Clytaemnestra and the Furies. It belongs to the mind-set that is so dazzled by the primacy of blood, it cannot look beyond it to the abstract issue of how 'wild' justice can be cultivated and improved; and so it remains bound to the wheel by which revenge propagates itself and the victim becomes victimizer in his turn. Nonetheless, precisely because the problem is so insoluble and so exciting, each play leads to a new one: the public appetite for revenge plots is insatiable.

Another point that emerges is how difficult it is to canvass revenge as an issue in a Christian context. Kyd knows, like all the revenge playwrights who follow him, that vengeance is a pagan impulse forbidden by God. Hieronymo is made to quote the precise text: '*Vindicta mihi!*' (III.xiii.1) – 'Vengeance is mine; I will repay, saith the Lord' (Rom. 12: 19). But the plot does nothing to give this admonition weight, and in the speech where Hieronymo reminds himself of it, he immediately contradicts himself with a vengeful line from Seneca that puts the play back on course: 'strike, and strike home, where wrong is offered thee' (III.xiii.7). The fact that Hieronymo himself dies at the end seems to be the moral sop to Cerberus by which Kyd acknowledges that revenge, however justified, is also a crime. But between this tardy admission, and the biblical quotation, there is no attempt to construct the missing logic, either in Christian or Classical terms.

How can the victim not become victimizer in his turn? St Paul could have supplied Kyd with one answer: 'Vengeance is mine . . .' is followed with the excellent psychological insight, 'therefore if thine enemy hunger, feed him; if he thirst, give him drink: for in so doing thou shalt heap coals of fire on his head' (Rom. 12: 20). But this Christian way of arresting the wheel is no more investigated in the play than the Classical one, of taking the issue to a jury of fellow-citizens. (Hieronymo does have a temporary hope of being given justice by a good king, but wicked persons at court prevent him from being heard.) The characteristic attitude to revenge in this play, which Kyd bequeathes to the whole revenge tradition, is that there is really no alternative – and so the exciting, disturbing spectacle must go on.

The Christian aspect of this play that makes the clearest break with the classical past is its differentiation of characters into two camps, the 'good' and the 'bad'. This seems to be what hampers Kyd in his analysis of revenge as a phenomenon: for the revenger is good insofar as he suffers unjustly, but bad insofar as he pre-empts God's vengeance, and the paradox cannot be untangled in the terms available. Issues of goodness and badness lower the discussion to a level that makes us sharply aware of the intelligence built into Athenian drama, with its emphasis on *hamartia* and *nemesis*. There, the questions were all about what actions people took, on what presuppositions, leading to what inevitable consequences; heroes and heroines were not good or bad, but a complex mixture of reason and passion, which led them to make dangerous mistakes about themselves and the world around them.

But Christianity introduces two new assumptions which put questions of responsibility and guilt on a quite different footing. One is that virtue lies in the heart, and in deciding someone's responsibility for their actions it is vital to take account of their *intention*. (Thus, good people may accidentally do bad things, but they may nevertheless be essentially innocent.) This undoes the strict classical connection between an agent and his act – as Oedipus was still polluted by his blood crimes, even when no one knew he had committed them. The other unclassical novelty Christianity brings with it is a proscription of knowledge. It is not that knowledge is not enough (a position shared by all the Athenian dramatists) – but that it is not meant for humanity. The Christian virtues, as propagated by the Church, are acceptance, obedience, submission; it was by eating the fruit of the Tree of Knowledge, expressly forbidden by her Maker, that Eve brought about the Fall.

The orthodox position that to think for oneself is somehow to encroach on God's prerogative may explain the new character who appears in *The Spanish Tragedy* and preys on the mind of all subsequent dramatists – the 'Machiavel'. In the camp of the bad, he is by far the most wicked: he is characterized by his elaborate plots, his ability to act a part, his manipulation of others and his impenetrable secrecy, so that no one knows who he 'really' is. (Because of the historical Machiavelli, however, he is usually recognizable by his Italian name; he may even speak snatches of Italian, like Kyd's Lorenzo, who rejoices in the fact that no one else knows what he is up to: '*E quel che voglio io, nessun lo sa*', III.iv.87) If we look closely at this character, however, and consider the elements of his wickedness impartially, another way of viewing him would be as the 'new man' of the Renaissance who, like Machiavelli, has thrown off the world-view he grew up with and will not pretend otherwise. (The full modernity of *The Prince* is felt in such casual propositions as, 'putting aside, then, all the imaginary things that are said about princes and getting down to the truth . . . '.)[4] The Machiavel feels himself isolated from others by his heightened self-consciousness; he compensates by using his brain without any reference to authority and flaunting the results. The frisson he stimulates in the audience comes from their orthodox sense that free thought is inherently impious. And the odium he incurs, as a self-enclosed element in society using others to further his own ends, comes from the alarm those still embedded in the matrix of blood bonds and unquestioned arrangements of feudal reciprocity must feel at anyone acclimatized to the colder air of full individuation. The Machiavel has cut the bonds binding him in fellowship to the rest of humanity; it is not his heart that moves him, but his head.

---

4   Niccolò Machiavelli, *The Prince*, trans. Robert M. Adams (2nd edn, New York and London: Norton, 1992), pp. 42–3.

Perhaps this is why 'bond' is a key word in the plays of this period, as has long been recognized; and issues of knowledge and submission to authority have a centrality to Renaissance plots that is quite foreign to Athenian, or indeed Senecan ones. The taboo on knowledge brings with it the converse temptation of 'daring to know' which, it is not surprising to find, the playwrights handle with unresolved ambivalence – at once the most inflammatory, exciting and weakly analysed of all their plot motifs.

One last point about the new elements in Renaissance tragedy is essentially political, but not unrelated to the prominence given the Machiavel. This is the fact that the plays are written inside a monarchy, and often posit a good ruler (like Kyd's king) at the heart of the elaborate system of reciprocal love and duty, who would rectify all injustice if the plot would only allow him. In other plots the good king is dead (like old Hamlet), which is itself the tragedy; but either way, these plots suggest how deeply internalized in the psychology of the period is the hope of social justice from a king acting in quasi-paternal authority. (In *Macbeth*, which in some ways is the climax of the revenge tradition, the worst of all Machiavels is pitted against the best of all kings, Duncan – though by this stage Shakespeare has outgrown the original conception, as I argue below.)

Because monarchy is a quasi-familial relationship it is strongly resistant to analysis. We see this from the difference between the level of political *nous* in Shakespeare's Roman plays, where he analyses the power relations of a republic with forensic skill, and that of the history plays, where the urgent problems raised by monarchical weakness (*Richard II*) and usurping strength (*Henry IV*) are all forgotten in the context of a more successful monarch (*Henry V*). The psychology of monarchy at its purest is heard in Prince Henry's cry at King John's deathbed: 'What surety of the world, what hope, what stay, / When this was now a king and now is clay?' (*King John* 5.7.68–9). The king, like the sun, is the ongoing life and warmth of the world. He alone makes it habitable; and his mortality reveals it as a sterile promontory of flux and pessimism.

The childlike poignancy of this brings an awkward element into tragic plots, which tend to treat kings as if they were made of different earth, and as if their subjects need not carry full responsibility for the burden of public justice. If we think back to Greek tragedy, it is striking how it takes for granted the way personal issues become political issues and vice versa; with Aristotle, it says that man is a political animal, because he lives in a *polis*. And the special value of a democratic atmosphere for tragic drama is that the lack of any higher authority, and the possession of an individual vote, makes every Athenian a king to himself. There are no fathers to shelter their sons and rectify injustice in the world, and only the powerless choruses ever turn to their kings with such a hope; solutions are to be found by more sophisticated means. But in this respect Renaissance tragedies remain a-political. The backdrop to their world-view is the hope – eternally disappointed – of finding safety in another's authority.

Christopher Marlowe, *The Jew of Malta* (*c*.1590)

Marlowe is a striking example of pagan/Christian ambivalence, for his plots are typically centred on a character whom he deplores but shows in a quasi-heroic light for most of the play – until the approach of Act V returns the drama to orthodoxy. In an early play like *Tamburlaine the Great* (*c*.1587), he gratifies his heterodoxy by taking a barbarian hero from Scythia whose *hubris* never reaches its *nemesis*, in spite of rivers of blood, the use of captured kings as footstools, and the slaughter of four suppliant virgins. The excitement of this propels Marlowe through five more 'high astounding' acts in *Tamburlaine the Great Part II*, where the hero harnesses conquered kings to his chariot and burns the Koran as a personal taunt to Mahomet, before succumbing to a 'distemper' – and dies, not regretting his crimes so much as the few parts of the world he has yet to annexe ('And shall I die, and this unconquered?', V.iii.151).[5] The timing of Tamburlaine's illness seems to indicate that Mahomet has had enough; but Marlowe, ambivalent to the end, makes little of the implied *nemesis*. Because Tamburlaine is entirely outside the Christian world, he supplies his author with a fine opportunity for scoffing at Christian morals from a distance (Christian kings break oaths made to Mohammedans, to Mohammedan astonishment) but his exoticism also prevents Marlowe from seriously considering the issues he raises, which are dispersed in rhetorical euphoria: 'Is it not passing brave to be a king, / And ride in triumph through Persepolis?' (II.v.53–4).

It is in *The Jew of Malta* that Marlowe comes closer to the issues, though they are still framed in a plot that says opposite things simultaneously. Just as Kyd's play was introduced by Revenge in person, *The Jew of Malta* has a prologue spoken by the ghost of Machiavelli himself, which raises the topics of Christianity, forbidden knowledge, and the ambivalent allure of the Machiavel, much as we have been considering them. The famous ghost introduces himself with disdain: 'To some perhaps my name is odious', he says, but 'I weigh not men, and therefore not men's words' (*Prol.* 5–8):

> Admir'd I am of those that hate me most.
> Though some speak openly against my books,
> Yet will they read me, and thereby attain
> To Peter's chair; and, when they cast me off,
> Are poison'd by my climbing followers.
> I count religion but a childish toy,
> And hold there is no sin but ignorance.
> Birds of the air will tell of murders past.
> I am asham'd to hear such fooleries!
> Many will talk of title to a crown:

---

[5]   *The Complete Plays and Poems of Christopher Marlowe*, ed. E.D. Pendry (London and Rutland, Vt.: Dent, 1976, repr. 1997), p. 119.

> What right had Caesar to the empery?
> Might first made kings, and laws were then most sure
> When, like the Draco's, they were writ in blood. (9–21)

Wearing the mask of Machiavelli, Marlowe is able to say publicly things that would not otherwise be tolerated in a Christian state. Even those who pretend to hate Machiavelli's 'policy' are fascinated by it ('Admir'd I am of those that hate me most') and his skills are what puts a Pope on St Peter's chair (before he is 'poison'd by my climbing followers'). Denigration of the papacy is not perhaps a problem in a Protestant state, but what follows is one of the 'horrible blasphemies' for which Marlowe was notorious: 'I count religion but a childish toy, / And hold there is no sin but ignorance.' Religion is a 'childish toy', designed (as he is reported as saying) 'to keep men in awe'.[6] In affirming that 'there is no sin but ignorance' it is striking how accurately Marlowe echoes the Greek position that virtue is not the point, but knowledge – or rather, that virtue *is* knowledge, in a world where the primary human obligation is to understand the way the world works, so as not to commit *hamartia* unwittingly.

But the next lines go beyond even the Athenian world-view: 'Birds of the air will tell of murders past. / I am ashamed to hear such fooleries!' Leaving the precise details of bird-lore aside, what the Machiavel repudiates is the entire presumption that blood crimes have their consequences. It is only a matter of secrecy and security – security achieved by force and maintained by Draconian laws. When all 'Titles' to crowns and claims to 'divine right' are stripped of their pretensions, they come down to the same brute fact: 'Might first made kings'.

Perhaps Marlowe himself could not have said for certain how much he meant of this: one of the useful things about employing a dramatic mask is that an author does not need to know. He may use the opportunity to display in public the ambivalence he cannot settle in private – or he may simply enjoy shocking others. But in either case, a playwright is responsible for binding his play into a coherent whole, on penalty of draining the meaning from even the strongest parts; and when we read on, we find that the issues so provocatively canvassed here are not pursued. Marlowe defies Christian assumptions with less and less energy, until his exhilaratingly clear-thinking hero declines into pantomime wickedness and is finally boiled in oil – an orthodox sacrifice to piety.

It is worth noting, however, that Marlowe makes the Machiavel inside his play a Jew (the forerunner of Shakespeare's Shylock), whose one redeeming characteristic is his love of his daughter. Otherwise Barabas acknowledges no ties at all – and finally to blacken him, Marlowe makes him turn against her too.

---

6   See the record of Marlowe's pub-talk (the 'Baines Note'): 'That the first beginning of religion was only to keep men in awe' and 'Christ was a bastard and his mother dishonest.' He also expresses a partiality for Barabbas, whose name he borrows for the Jew of Malta: 'That Christ deserved better to die than Barabbas and that the Jews made a good choice' (*Complete Plays and Poems*, p. 513).

When Abigail uncovers her father's plots and converts to Christianity, he renounces his paternity in the course of a few lines and poisons her, along with all the nuns in her nunnery – a level of pantomime evil from which the play never recovers. Nonetheless, we can trace under the grotesque exaggerations of the plot the outline of the Renaissance case against the Jew, that he is a creature unnaturally exempt from human bonds – except the legal bond of usury, of course, on which, like Shylock, he will insist to the death. Barabas is not even loyal to his fellow Jews, or his ingenious partner in infamy, the Turkish slave Ithamore. Being outside society, the Jew takes all the privileges of isolation.

Because he belongs to an international religion, however, he also sees the scope and scale of the world in a quite foreign light. Barabas sends Spanish oil to Italy and Greek wine to the Middle East; his treasure ships ply between Malta and Alexandria, and he gloats over the world's richness in rhetoric that often sounds like Tamburlaine's. In this sense he has quasi-heroic status – but to the extent that he personally owes nothing to his city or state, he is also shown as capable of any treachery: Barabas is 'of' Malta, but not in the least Maltese, and in the course of the plot he sells Malta to the Turks, is made its Governor, and attempts to sell the Turks back to the Maltese, before being unmasked.

In Barabas's happy gloating over his accumulating wealth we glimpse Marlowe's appreciation of the mental freedom and wide horizons brought by embryonic capitalism, with the underlying awareness that this level of individuation and pursuit of worldly ends is the very definition of 'wickedness':

> These are the blessings promis'd to the Jews,
> And herein was old Abram's happiness:
> What more may heaven do for earthly man
> Than thus to pour out plenty in their laps,
> Ripping the bowels of the earth for them,
> Making the sea their servant, and the winds
> To drive their substance with successful blasts?
> Who hateth me but for my happiness?
> Or who is honour'd now but for his wealth?
> Rather had I, a Jew, be hated thus,
> Than pitied in a Christian poverty;
> For I can see no fruits in all their faith,
> But malice, falsehood, and excessive pride. (I.i.107–19)

Beneath the satiric inflation of this we can feel Marlowe's ambivalent appreciation of the Jewish clarity (which is Machiavellian, and modern) that so fearlessly makes the world yield its riches ('Ripping the bowels of the earth') and brings status ineluctably with it ('who is honour'd now but for his wealth?'). Marlowe does not pretend that the Christians are any differently made, only more hypocritical and less successful: one of the genuinely funny scenes in the play is when two friars compete to attract Barabas and his wealth to their different religious houses, and end up in a fist fight. ('O good Barabas, come to our house!

... Their laws are strict ... They wear no shirts, and they go barefoot too',
IV.1.80, 85, 87.)

But this admission that money is a secularizing force on all sides does not take away the fact that it undoes the proper bonds between man and man, and replaces them with mysterious, intangible links of 'credit'. It also raises Jews to unique positions inside each state, to which, like Barabas, they do and do not belong; as he lists them,

> There's Kirriah Jairim, the great Jew of Greece,
> Obed in Bairseth, Nones in Portugal,
> Myself in Malta, some in Italy,
> Many in France and wealthy every one;
> Ay, wealthier far than any Christian. (126–30)

There is a nervous apprehension in all this that the Jews are living in a world organization which anti-Semitism will call 'the International Conspiracy', but which we now recognize as modernity: a world of organized capital, financial risk and international banking. (We may also notice in passing that in *The Merchant of Venice* Shakespeare does not represent Shylock as a merchant at all, but as a mere usurer who makes coins 'breed' in an unnatural way. The merchant Antonio, meanwhile, is represented as having no commercial passions whatever: his goods circulate the globe so that he can lend money at nil interest or give all he has to his friends. Shakespeare's insistence on Antonio's impossibly unmercantile psychology may suggest the contamination implicit in understanding how money works; perhaps he was even more uncomfortable on this point than Marlowe.)

But the interesting questions Barabas raises about modernity are lost to view as the play develops, and by half-way through the Jew has been demonized. To boil him in oil is clearly no solution, and indeed, one of the characteristics of early Renaissance plays, as we are discovering, is the difficulty they have in pursuing any subject coherently by means of the plot. Stage events are too easily foisted in to please public taste – Barabas becomes a scapegoat for public unease, as does Shylock, and boiling him is presumably quite acceptable – and the public appetite for horrors and rhetoric means that the most serious acts cannot be seriously treated. Murders are so frequent and grotesque that they only raise the technical problem of how the playwright will surprise us next. Religion also adds to the lack of clarity, particularly the Christian claim to be a universal truth. For there can be no question of equal treatment for Judaism and Islam in the public theatre, even where they are admitted to be potent forces.

The Greeks, we realize, were fortunate in the plasticity of their theology, their lack of a holy Book. There is no argument in their plays about orthodoxy of belief, but only about openness to the gods' reality: when Pentheus tries to say that only barbarians worship Dionysus, he is promptly told that they are wiser than the Greeks. But the fact that Barabas is a Jew clearly means that Marlowe need not take him too seriously, even though he expresses some of Marlowe's own best thoughts; just as the exoticism of Tamburlaine, his exploits off the Christian map, mean Marlowe can glamorize his bloodiness and insatiability without more than a faint gesture at their consequences. In neither case does he push his thoughts to a conclusion: Jews and Moslems are somehow different.

Doctor Faustus (c.1593)

Does the story of a scholar who learns to fear his books bring Marlowe closer to a subject he can deal with coherently? *Doctor Faustus* is the one play which we might legitimately suppose to overlap with Marlowe's real anxieties – not least, that there is a price to be paid for putting Christianity in the same intellectual frame as Aristotle and Justinian. But, as every reader finds, it is an exceptionally uneven text, in which only the opening and closing scenes sound like Marlowe. The laboured clowning that fills up the centre of the play may be his, but it has been ascribed to at least three other hands, and new material was certainly added after Marlowe's death.[7] Therefore, although the subject seems promising, we must deduce that this is another play where Marlowe cannot quite complete what he begins.

Perhaps the heart of the problem is that Faustus is not another Machiavel, though at first glance he might seem to be – and his problems are not really Marlowe's, in spite of appearances. When Faustus runs through the contents of his library and finally dismisses them in favour of his books of magic, the implied morality is purely orthodox. This scene has been called 'an inventory of the Renaissance mind',[8] but we may be more struck by how it evades the key issues that were pressing on Marlowe. Faustus is not captivated by classical learning or pagan morality: he is bored by its seeming limitations. He is shown dismissing Aristotle's *Analytics* (two works on the nature of proof in argument) as if they stood for his whole philosophy, and saying that Galen would be worth studying, were Faustus himself not already so knowledgeable about medicine that he has saved 'whole cities' from the plague.[9] Justinian's account of Roman Law, the *Institutes*, deals with petty details of legacies – mere 'external trash' for 'mercenary drudges'; and Jerome's Bible is repellent for its gloomy doctrines, which Faustus smartly ridicules:

---

[7]   Thomas Nashe has been credited with the character of Wagner and the scenes I.ii and iv, and the comic actor John Adams with the clowning routines. The 'B' text of 1616 has 'new Additions' by Samuel Rowley and William Byrd (*Doctor Faustus*, ed. Roma Gill (London: A. & C. Black, and New York: W.W. Norton, 1968, repr. 1991), intro., pp. xiii–xv).

[8]   Harry Levin, *The Overreacher: A Study of Christopher Marlowe* (Cambridge, Mass.: Harvard University Press, 1952, repr. 1964), p. 113.

[9]   *Complete Plays and Poems*, p. 276.

> Jerome's Bible! Faustus, view it well.
> *Stipendium peccati mors est.* Ha! *Stipendium, etc.,*
> 'The reward of sin is death'. That's hard.
> *Si pecasse negamus, fallimur, et nulla est in nobis veritas.*
> 'If we say that we have no sin
> We deceive ourselves, and there is no truth in us.'
> Why then, belike, we must sin,
> And so consequently die.
> Ay, we must die, an everlasting death.
> What doctrine call you this? *Che sera, sera.*
> 'What will be, shall be.' Divinity, adieu! (I.i.38–48)

The keynote struck in all this is Faustus' vaulting ambition, his impatience with studies that satisfy everyone else. His rejection of the Bible is clearly the acme of this, and it prepares us directly for his fall. As has often been noted, his damaging quotation is actually only half the relevant verse, so his impatience in reading is part of his problem: the wages of sin is death – but 'the gift of God is eternal life through Jesus Christ our Lord' (Rom. 6: 23). Faustus' annoyance at being caught up in the consequences of the Fall, and his contempt for the logic of predestination ('What will be, shall be'), are clearly meant to prepare us for his next leap, his aspiration to be a demi-god himself:

> These metaphysics of magicians
> And necromantic books are heavenly;
> Lines, circles, scenes, letters and characters:
> > . . . Emperors and kings
> Are but obeyed in their several provinces,
> Nor can they raise the wind or rend the clouds.
> But his dominion that exceeds in this
> Stretcheth as far as doth the mind of man:
> A sound magician is a demi-god. (I.i.49–51, 57–62)

We cannot expect that Faustus will be anything but damned after this.

But (to state the obvious) Marlowe's own problem is not the temptation of becoming a necromancer, but of reading the Bible with a scholar's cold eye and seeing it shorn of its protective aura. One of the most telling of his opinions recorded in the 'Baines Note' is that 'all the new testament is filthily written' (meaning, presumably, that anyone trained in classical Greek finds it wanting stylistically); and that 'if he were put to write a new religion, he would undertake both a more excellent and admirable method'[10] (that is, Christianity is one invented system among many, and could easily be improved upon). It is not so much that Marlowe should have rewritten the *Faustbook* to bring Faustus' predicament up to date (with the New Testament of Erasmus and Machiavelli perhaps on the bookshelf), but that the original conception is so profoundly

---

[10] Ibid., p. 513.

medieval, it offers him nothing to engage with. Once Marlowe embraces Faust as a hero, he has to accept the simple definition of evil and the muddle of folk demonology that go along with him. More awkwardly still for his stagecraft, he has to accept the reality of magic and demonstrate it for all to see. If he avoided writing the scenes in which Faustus enjoys his magic powers (touring Europe in a chariot drawn by dragons and boxing a Pope's ears), we need not be surprised.

But unsatisfactory as the play is as a whole, no one ever forgets the last speech in which Faustus recognizes the approach of damnation. The intensity of the poetry tells us that Marlowe is in earnest here, whatever his daylight views on the doctrine expounded. It is not difficult to believe that the price of his conscious atheism was corrosive fear in other moods, and Faustus' choked panic on hearing the clock striking his last hour, half-hour, and minute, is feelingly realized. Here we have one tragic element fully present: the consciousness of having done a deed whose consequences must now be acknowledged. Faustus' terror at the 'heavy wrath' of his Father is expressed in the desperately childlike need to hide; and he yearns for his corporeal self to disperse in a kind of *sparagmos* that takes the dismemberment of Pentheus to a frantic new level:

> Mountains and hills, come, come, and fall on me,
> And hide me from the heavy wrath of God.
> No, no!
> Then will I headlong run into the earth.
> Earth, gape! O no, it will not harbour me.
> You stars that reign'd at my nativity,
> Whose influence hath allotted death and hell,
> Now draw up Faustus like a foggy mist
> Into the entrails of yon labouring cloud,
> That when you vomit forth into the air
> My limbs may issue from your smoky mouths,
> So that my soul may but ascend to heaven. (V.ii.153–64)

The Christian doctrine that makes God the author of the universe gives a twist to Faustus' despair unimaginable to a Greek: the earth itself will not 'harbour' him, and the only kindness he can look for is from the (presumably pagan) stars, who might exhale him like a 'foggy mist'. Faustus' agony stems not only from his possession of a body but from the immortality of his soul. His most precious attribute will become the essence of his torment:

> No end is limited to damned souls.
> Why wert thou not a creature wanting soul?
> Or why is this immortal that thou hast?
> Ah, Pythagoras' *metempsychosis*, were that true
> This soul should fly from me, and I be chang'd
> Unto some brutish beast. All beasts are happy,
> For when they die

> Their souls are soon dissolv'd in elements,
> But mine must live still to be plagu'd in hell.
> Cursed be the parents that engend'red me!
> No, Faustus, curse thyself, curse Lucifer,
> That hath depriv'd thee of the joys of heaven.
>   *The clock striketh twelve.* (V.ii.172–83)

We can trace the outline of genuinely classical tragic issues here, in Faustus' awareness that tragedy is possible because man is more than an animal, a creature of consciousness (or Christian soul); and in his *anagnorisis*, his recognition of the consequences of his own actions. When he is tempted to evade responsibility, he corrects himself: 'Cursed be the parents that engend'red me!/ No, Faustus, curse thyself.' Faustus finally acknowledges that he is the agent of his own undoing – though not without diabolical assistance: 'Curse Lucifer,/ That hath depriv'd thee of the joys of heaven.'

Aside from this, however, the end could not be less classical, in its emotionality and lack of analysis. We are watching an absolute punishment, for an absolute sin; and its compelling power may return us to the last context in which we were capable of such emotion, to childhood, when we confronted enraged patriarchy in all our weakness and wished, from the bottom of our hearts, that we were not guilty as charged. What is so unclassical in this denouement is that error is shown as leading to punishment, but not to anything else. That is, the consequences of error are not themselves the problem (as Pentheus' arrogance goads Dionysus to revenge, or Jason's goads Medea): the disobedience itself takes precedence. Hence perhaps the tendency of the tragic hero to seem infantilized by the Christian context: it is not for him to act and know, but to submit to God's knowledge, which alone is perfect. And hence, too, the mixture of fear and relief with which we may regard Faustus' 'hellish fall': it is true that he is damned, but God is still our Father, and we are making private vows to be very good in future.

The centrality of the issue of obedience here may also shed some light on Marlowe's obsession with 'overreaching'. However often he deplores it, it is the subject he cannot leave alone, and his plays give enormous scope to the delicious emotions the spectacle arouses. Perhaps it is the very authoritarianism of this God that makes Marlowe feel aspiration is always in some sense legitimate (although, of course, 'wrong'). But from our point of view, he pays a heavy price for his tug-of-war with orthodoxy: for he does not have the mental energy to pursue the question beyond its exhilarating 'wickedness'. When Tamburlaine has conquered half the world, the plot terminates in exhaustion, without confronting the true monstrosity of a man who mistakes himself for a god. When Barabas and Faustus overstep their boundaries, the punishment meted out to them is not bound up in the consequences of their own actions (as, for instance, Faustus might have found that being a demi-god costs him too much in terms of human love and society, and a kiss from Helen was not adequate compensation) – but arrives as a climactic punishment to terminate their career. This interplay between aspiration and submission seems to be the Renaissance legacy from Christianity: a see-saw of ambivalent discomfort.

William Shakespeare, *Hamlet* (*c.*1600)

As we take a survey of the plays which inaugurated the great period of tragic theatre, it may seem odd to separate *Hamlet* from the rest of Shakespeare's achievement discussed in the next chapter. But it may also be refreshing to view it in the context in which it was seen by its original audience – as a new Revenge play built on the foundations of *The Spanish Tragedy*, by the author of *Romeo and Juliet* and *Titus Andronicus* (the latter a 'Most Lamentable Roman Tragedy' of Senecan bloodiness). If we do view it in such a context, we may be struck by how many of the famous 'problems' associated with the play could actually be the by-products of Shakespeare's attempt to reanimate the crude conventions of Revenge drama. It has been usefully speculated that Shakespeare's theatrical brief was to make the old play 'life-like' for an audience that had outgrown Kyd's wooden stagecraft,[11] and this would certainly explain the amount of conscious theatrical reference in the play (the players' pastiche of the old Marlovian rhetoric and up-to-date theatre talk) and the self-conscious modernity of Hamlet's theatrical taste – his emphasis on naturalism in both speech and movement.

It might also explain the mixed messages sent by other revisions: if we are unsure whether Hamlet's madness is real or feigned – or both, and when exactly they merge into one another – this could well be the effect of Shakespeare's dazzling rewriting of Hieronymo's role. Hieronymo 'cloaks' himself in feigned 'simplicity' because that is one of the things revengers do to put their enemies off the scent (III.xiii.29–33). But the pretence of madness also acts as a kind of lightning conductor for his revenger's melancholy: we see him in wild antics like ripping valuable money bonds with his teeth and skipping offstage, pursued by the angry losers ('Tush, no; run after, catch me if you can' he calls, with Hamlet-like facetiousness, 132). Kyd's characterization is too superficial for questions of pretence or reality to be worth raising; what is clear is that the audience is moved by the tragical spectacle of madness among 'great ones', and the more madness

---

[11] William Empson, in *Hamlet*, ed. C. Hoy (New York and London: W.W. Norton, 1963), p. 291.

he supplies the better. (Kyd's bereaved mother, Isabella, also runs pathetically mad in a mode that Shakespeare will improve into Ophelia's, talking of children's toys and herbs.) Shakespeare brings wonderful verisimilitude to what Kyd left in embryo, but the inconsequentiality of the underlying conception cannot be mended in this way.

Perhaps more importantly, if we get no clear sense of whether or not Hamlet is a Revenger, it may be because the subtle revisions of his psychology leave him stranded in a Revenge plot to which he is no longer suited. Much ink has been spilt on why he is such an ineffectual agent, but the very proliferation of theories suggests that there is no obvious solution. If we approach the Revenge issue as another problem of revision, however, it may well be another element of the play where an improvement in one direction creates problems in another. The more sensitive, intelligent and 'life-like' Hamlet becomes, the less he can share Hieronymo's Senecan world-view, in which blood is its own satisfaction, and the less soluble is the contradiction between the duty of revenge and its forbidden status. The whole issue of revenge begins to cry out for modernization; and Shakespeare seems to temporize by giving Hamlet intermittently 'bloody' thoughts, and then excusing their non-implementation by new turns of the plot, until his hero finally does kill the usurper, by means of a poisoned rapier intended for himself. There is a strong impression that Hamlet is sheltered throughout from the real question revenge plots raise, of how the victim can avoid becoming a victimizer in his turn, and that Shakespeare's energy is being devoted to something quite different – to dramatizing how such a predicament feels from the inside: 'O cursèd spite, / That ever I was born to set it right!'[12]

If we take an even longer perspective on Shakespeare's experiment and view it through Greek spectacles, we can perhaps see its key characteristics more clearly. He could be said to have the materials of the *Oresteia* in front of him, transposed to Denmark: Claudius is the usurper Aegisthus, Gertrude the treacherous Clytaemnestra, Denmark is the suffering state, and Hamlet is the young prince returned from exile to purify the past. But to notice the parallels is only to feel the difference: Hamlet's career does not remind us in the least of Orestes' because the issues so clearly canvassed in the *Oresteia* are half-muffled by his lack of action. Instead, we have prolonged thoughts about action – and a climactic last scene with four killings. Nor is Gertrude very like Clytaemnestra: although Hamlet confronts his mother's breast like Orestes, there is no question of his seeing her as the main goal of his revenge, still less of becoming her executioner. His focus is on Claudius – which leaves Gertrude apparently innocent of the crimes going on in Denmark (Hamlet has to tell her that his father was murdered, 3.4.28–9). Her crime is 'Frailty', and Hamlet's only 'deed' in

---

[12] *William Shakespeare: The Complete Works*, ed. Stanley Wells and Gary Taylor (Oxford; Clarendon Press, 1988, repr. 1997), p. 663. All subsequent Shakespeare references are to this edition.

relation to his mother's breast is to reanimate her widow's loyalty to her dead husband, instil disgust at Claudius' 'reechy kisses', and make it impossible for her to go back to his bed.

Gertrude's character seems to belong to a chivalric convention by which women can be sexually weak, but not actively bad (if we think forward to Lady Macbeth, we can feel the difference) – so the plot leaves her as a moral simpleton who can be reclaimed for virtue by her Confessor-son. It reserves moral self-awareness for Claudius, the usurper. His monologue about the difficulty of penitence and his distance from true remorse is the one sustained analysis of moral issues in the play (3.3.36–72) – but it is not supplemented, as it might have been in Aeschylus, by another from Hamlet, after he has done the deed of killing his stepfather and begun to live with the consequences. The Revenge tradition reserves its energy for the fascinating means of killing (poisoned chalices, accidentally exchanged rapiers), not for the analysis of the disequilibrium revenge produces. And if Hamlet dies along with Claudius, the question of the future need hardly arise.

Through Greek spectacles, then, the play offers a less focused version of familiar materials. There has been usurpation, treachery to the marriage bond, and displacement of an heir. But from the Aristotelian point of view we are given endings rather than intelligible resolutions: if 'the denouement . . . should arise out of the plot itself, and not depend on a stage-artifice'[13] we need more than the arrival of Fortinbras to bring the play to a close. On the subject of human bonds, too, *Hamlet* is particularly unforthcoming: if the *Oresteia* shows how family bonds, and particularly the bond between mother and son, can be transmuted into civic ones that also nurture and sustain, then the young prince's career seems almost perverse. The play shows him making no new bonds, and cutting off the tenderest and most promising bond he has, with Ophelia. If he has any ties, they are of the most hampering kind: with his dead father and living mother. His only other sustained connection in the play is with Horatio – a young man with no ties or obligations of his own, whose outstanding characteristic (as a consequence, perhaps) is integrity. This relationship solves nothing, of course; but it is more consoling than anything else Hamlet has.

To describe what the play does not do, however, is to ignore what it so obviously does: represent the suffering self-consciousness of a young avenger. The less Shakespeare can do with the Revenge plot at the level of action, the more brilliantly he invests in Hamlet's consciousness of his predicament. He writes monologues of astonishing length and frequency in which Hamlet expresses a self-consciousness marooned in time, blighted within and without, travelling helplessly in circles. No classical play could use so many words to say so little, relative to the plot; but we cannot doubt that this, in some sense, is what the play is 'about':

---

[13]   *The Poetics* 15, in *The Complete Works of Aristotle*, trans. Jonathan Barnes (Princeton: Princeton University Press, 1984), vol. 2, p. 2327.

Yet I,

A dull and muddy-mettled rascal, peak
Like John-a-dreams, unpregnant of my cause,
And can say nothing – no, not for a king
Upon whose property and most dear life
A damned defeat was made. Am I a coward?
Who calls me villain, breaks my pate across,
Plucks off my beard and blows it in my face,
Tweaks me by th' nose, gives me the lie i'th'throat
As deep as to the lungs? Who does me this?
Ha? 'Swounds, I should take it; for it cannot be
But I am pigeon-livered and lack gall
To make oppression bitter, or ere this
I should 'a' fatted all the region kites
With this slave's offal. Bloody, bawdy villain!
Remorseless, treacherous, lecherous, kindless villain!
O, vengeance! –
Why, what an ass am I? Ay, sure, this is most brave,
That I, the son of a dear father murderèd,
Prompted to my revenge by heaven and hell,
Must, like a whore, unpack my heart with words,
And fall a-cursing like a very drab,
A scullion! Fie upon't, foh! – (2.2.568–90)

Hamlet plays Hamlet here – being taunted as a coward, as a ranting Revenger from Kyd, and as a humiliated ironist. It is tempting, but probably erroneous, to isolate this last as his 'real' voice. (The next decision he makes is to stage the play-within-the-play, which he makes with a conventional Revenger's confidence: 'the play's the thing / Wherein I'll catch the conscience of the King', 606–7.) What is more notable is the fluidity of movement between all his voices, the swift interplay between inner and outer, and the astonishing variety of linguistic resources Shakespeare brings to the task.[14] But if there is no 'authenticity' here, the question arises no less sharply: who is Hamlet? And perhaps more importantly: what is a self?

The fascination of these monologues has filled a library of commentary, as readers have been forced to become collaborators, and supply a character to fit the words. So much linguistic vivacity, operating in the vacuum of the plot, has proved irresistible. But the undeniable importance of Hamlet as a phenomenon may return us to our opening question, why the Renaissance should have seen the rebirth of tragic drama after two millennia. The mental solitude of Hamlet may be part of the answer: melancholic, detached from human bonds and cast out of

---

[14] There are more first-time usages of words in this play than in any other of Shakespeare's (over 600), many of them new to English; the play is a watershed linguistically, as well as generically (*Hamlet*, ed. G.R. Hibbard (Oxford and New York: Oxford University Press, 1987), pp. 30–1).

society as he is, he represents perhaps another facet of the modernity we found in the Machiavel. Unlike the Machiavel he has wronged no one – rather, he has been severely wronged; but the net effect is not so different, as he nurses his self-consciousness on the edge of the stage and comments with bitter precision on the world around him. He has fallen out of the old world of unquestioned bonds and reciprocal pieties, and woken up in the bracing, but cold atmosphere of individuation, as one of the 'new men' his contemporary John Donne describes:

> 'Tis all in peeces, all cohaerance gone;
> All just supply, and all Relation:
> Prince, Subject, Father, Sonne, are things forgot.
> For every man alone thinkes he hath got
> To be a Phoenix . . .[15]

The world of the play shows 'all Relation gone': what remains is the shocked consciousness of an individual.

But this is not all that makes the play so remarkable, for what the consciousness of a young male discovers is that the primary relation of 'Sonne' remains, to a hampering degree. If there is a classical parallel to *Hamlet*, it is not the *Oresteia*, but *Oedipus*, as has often been noted. There is a resemblance at the level of plot, in that both plays subsist by a kind of nightmare logic, and the heroes find themselves 'guilty' of something they have not wittingly 'done'. But the more striking parallel is that each hero reaches out for public self-definition, only to find himself entangled in the maternal bond. Oedipus, of course, has solved the Sphinx's riddle and lived as a king before he discovers he has never truly left his mother. Hamlet's defining moves are still all to come, and it is much of the pathos of the play that they never do: we can only imagine what a prince he might have been, 'th'expectancy and rose of the fair state' (3.1.155). But although what Hamlet *does* hardly justifies his status as a tragic hero, what he *says* is deeply significant. The great difference between Athenian and Renaissance stagecraft is the extent to which the hero's inner world takes precedence over the outer; and Hamlet's obsession with sexuality, particularly women's, and with death, to which it is mysteriously connected, colours the whole play.

Nobody misses the leap of energy and purpose in the quality of Hamlet's scene with Gertrude (even if they conclude, with T.S. Eliot, that 'his mother is not an adequate equivalent for [his disgust; it] envelops and exceeds her').[16] Although the Revenge plot says that Hamlet here is 'reclaiming' his mother for chaste widowhood, what tumbles out of Hamlet's mouth is a frenzied denunciation of

---

[15]   John Donne, 'An Anatomie of the World' (1612), ll. 213–17, in *The Epithalamions, Anniversaries and Epicedes*, ed. W. Milgate (Oxford: Clarendon Press, 1978), p. 28.

[16]   *Hamlet*, ed. Hoy, p. 183.

maternal sexuality. Here is another hero discovering that he has never truly left his mother:

> What devil was't
> That thus hath cozened you at hood-man blind?
> [Eyes without feeling, feeling without sight,
> Ears without hands or eyes, smelling sans all,
> Or but a sickly part of one true sense
> Could not so mope.]
> O shame, where is thy blush? Rebellious hell,
> If thou canst mutine in a matron's bones,
> To flaming youth let virtue be as wax
> And melt in her own fire. Proclaim no shame
> When the compulsive ardor gives the charge,
> Since frost itself as actively doth burn,
> And reason panders will.

> *Qu.* O Hamlet, speak no more!
> Thou turn'st mine eyes into my very soul,
> And there I see such black and grainèd spots
> As will not leave their tinct.

> *Ham.* Nay, but to live
> In the rank sweat of an enseamèd bed,
> Stewed in corruption, honeying and making love
> Over the nasty sty –   (3.4.70–84)[17]

Even when we have taken account of the technically incestuous nature of Gertrude's remarriage, and Hamlet's plan 'to speak daggers to her, but use none' (3.2.385), there is an overplus of energy here. Hamlet's imaginative pertinacity is astonishing ('eyes . . . ears . . . smelling sans all', 'in the rank sweat of an enseamèd bed') – as is Gertrude's docility (her ready horror at the 'black spots' in her soul, and her willingness to let him remain her 'sweet' Hamlet, 86). We only have to imagine how Clytaemnestra might have answered Orestes' speculations on her love life to feel the Elizabethan quality of this: how deeply the Church's general abhorrence of female sexuality feeds Hamlet's specific revulsion, and allows him to tell his own mother how to repress her vice of sleeping with Claudius while he remains as apparently unimplicated as a Father-Confessor.

There is a similar leap of energy in Hamlet's exchanges with Ophelia, who is even more obviously 'not an adequate equivalent' for the feelings discharged. He wounds her with stabbing innuendoes, gratuitous insults and quite open obscenities. His excuse is his 'antic disposition', but he does not sound mad as he interprets *The Murder of Gonzago* for her, and makes one nasty thrust after another:

---

[17]   Quarto lines my addition, *The Complete Works*, p. 689.

> *Ham.* This is one Lucianus, nephew to the king.
> *Oph.* You are as good as a chorus, my lord.
> *Ham.* I could interpret between you and your love if I could see the puppets dallying.
> *Oph.* You are keen, my lord, you are keen.
> *Ham.* It would cost you a groaning to take off mind edge.
> *Oph.* Still better, and worse.
> *Ham.* So you mis-take your husbands. (3.2.232–9)

We have to seek for the sources of such 'whirling' wit outside Ophelia (though in a play with a less chivalric attitude to women, the interplay between her meekly unresisting victimhood and his cruelty might be its own explanation). Hamlet's themes in relation to her are always the same: female frailty, the 'trap' of beauty that masks decay and horror, the 'breeding of sinners' and the inevitability of death. He seems to treat her, in the words of the famous sonnet on lust, as 'a swallowed bait / On purpose laid to make the taker mad' (129.7–8). But Hamlet will refuse the bait, and in defiance of human nature, he will not join the life cycle that leads through sexuality to death ('I say we shall have no more marriages', 3.1.150).

It is not a great step from here to the world of *Oedipus*, psychologically speaking, if we think of the price Oedipus paid for his return to the womb – the blighting plague in Thebes, the terrible mingling and confusion of generations, and the arrest of time in a family where sexual activity does not lead outwards. *Hamlet* is full of responses that are weakly explained in terms of plot, but have a compelling underground coherence; and the connection between the hero's recoil from sex and his fascination with death, the trail that leads him from his mother's closet to speculations in a graveyard, has an undeniable logic to it. The more vividly Hamlet apprehends sex as the gateway to death (or the 'breeding' of more 'sinners' like himself) the more he represses it in his mother and Ophelia. And the more vehemently he cuts himself off from the processes of life the more aware he is that nothing but the meaninglessness of death remains.

We cannot call perhaps call *Hamlet* tragic, when the hero has no defining deed, and hence no error and no reckoning to make; but its self-consciousness on the threshold is immensely familiar, as the hero imagines all he might be and might do, without taking any steps towards self-definition. There is a helplessness about this hero which has softened criticism towards him, from Gertrude to the twentieth century; and perhaps he can be said to expose the central dilemma of tragedy, even if he cannot help us analyse it. For in his finely wrought Apollonian self-consciousness he testifies again to the horror of the Dionysiac, the mind's recoil from the body's processes. The underground logic of the play climaxes in the graveyard with Yorick's skull, even if the revenge plot pretends otherwise. And what Hamlet has to say is that sexuality leads to death, and dead bodies turn to mud:

> Alas, poor Yorick. I knew him, Horatio – a fellow of infinite jest, of most excellent fancy. He hath borne me on his back a thousand times; and now, how abhorred my imagination is! My gorge rises at it. Here hung those lips that I have kissed I know not how oft. Where be your gibes now, your gambols, your songs, your flashes of merriment that were wont to set the table on a roar? Not one now to mock your own grinning? Quite chop-fallen? Now get you to my lady's chamber and tell her, let her paint an inch thick, to this favour she must come. Make her laugh at that. Prithee, Horatio, tell me one thing.
>
> *Hor.* What's that, my lord?
>
> *Ham.* Dost thou think Alexander looked o' this fashion i'th' earth?
>
> *Hor.* E'en so.
>
> *Ham.* And smelt so? Pah! [*He throws the skull down*]
>
> *Hor.* E'en so, my lord.
>
> *Ham.* To what base uses we may return, Horatio! Why may not imagination trace the noble dust of Alexander till a find it stopping a bung-hole? ... Alexander died, Alexander was buried, Alexander returneth to dust; the dust is earth, of earth we make loam; and why of that loam whereto he was converted might they not stop a beer-barrel? (5.1.180–200, 204–7)

Hamlet's sickened fascination with Yorick's skull, and the swift connection with female beauty ('get you to my lady's chamber'), give the impression of a hysteria barely contained. If he details so carefully how Alexander's dust might come to stop a beer barrel, it is not to improve the joke but because, try as he might, he cannot convey the depth of his revulsion. Hamlet speaks as a superfine consciousness, which has fought off the Dionysiac temptation of self-loss in erotic identification with another. But defend himself as he may, here is one form of mingling he will not avoid: with the undifferentiated earth, where Alexander and Yorick melted away before him. Nature, who is not witty, will have the last word; and the Apollonian consciousness is aghast.

Chapter 5

Shakespeare

With Shakespeare's mature plays we come to the most interesting of all possible comparisons with Greek tragic plots. Is the overlap in subject between Aeschylus, Sophocles and Euripides not only a formal resemblance, but a mark of what makes tragedy essentially 'tragic'? If so, we would expect Shakespeare to have located parallel issues, however differently he treats them; and it is the aim of what follows to make out a case for his gradual uncovering of the same tragic essentials by taking *Othello*, *Lear*, *Macbeth* and *Coriolanus* in sequence of composition. Jacobean London is not experimenting with democratic reform (though it cannot be irrelevant that within 50 years it saw the ultimate political drama, the execution of Charles I, and the victory of a republican psychology) but nonetheless, as we have seen, there is a strong sense of living at a turning point in the definition of a human being. Shakespeare's tragedies convey that the 'new man', prised out of the cocoon of religious and social pieties, finds himself painfully alone under the stars.

Othello (c.1604)

After *Hamlet*, we cannot help but be struck by the clarity of the plot of this play, and Shakespeare's firm handling of it. In *Hamlet* the theme emerged more by accident than design; but the fact that *Othello* begins boldly with a 'mixed marriage' is clearly central to the conception. Shakespeare is reanimating the Greek sense of the role played by free choice and oaths in adulthood, and the way they seal the dignity of a life lived beyond blood ties. He could not make it plainer than by making Othello black and Desdemona white: the rest of their world mutters about 'sooty bosoms' and 'delicate youth' unnaturally seduced (1.2.71–6), but Othello and Desdemona glory in their free choice. 'I saw Othello's visage in his mind' (1.3.252), she says. 'She had eyes and chose me' (3.3.193) affirms Othello, who has 'confined' himself in marriage against his own expectation, from pure love:

> But that I love the gentle Desdemona,
> I would not my unhousèd free condition
> Put into circumscription and confine
> For the seas' worth. (1.2.25–8)

Before everything goes wrong, Shakespeare lends this couple the unqualified tenderness of the truly well matched, united in body and spirit. When Othello ushers his new wife offstage to consummate their marriage there is nothing to foresee save the purest intimacy and sexual happiness:

>   . . . Come, my dear love,
> The purchase made, the fruits are to ensue.
> That profit's yet to come 'tween me and you.
> Good night.' (2.3.8–11)

The fact that the hero gets from here to a quite different, but similarly passionate, intimacy with Iago in one easy bound, testifies to Shakespeare's wonderful grasp of the vulnerability of oaths. When Othello binds himself to Iago only one act later, it is in a revival of the tremendous oaths of the Revenge tradition – though here there is nothing but a mad dream to avenge; and Iago kneels as submissively to pledge his service as if it were a marriage:

> *Oth.*   [*He kneels*] Now, by yon marble heaven,
>   In the due reverence of a sacred vow
>   I here engage my words.
> *Iago*   Do not rise yet.
>   [*Iago kneels*]
>   Witness you ever-burning lights above,
>   You elements that clip us round about,
>   Witness that here Iago doth give up
>   The execution of his wit, hands, heart,
>   To wronged Othello's service. Let him command,
>   And to obey shall be in me remorse,
>   What bloody business ever.
>   [*They rise*]
> *Oth.*   I greet thy love,
>   Not with vain thanks, but with acceptance bounteous,
>   And will upon the instant put thee to't. (3.3.463–74)

The grotesqueness of this transition from a male–female unity, to an 'all-male league' in which womanhood is the enemy, is so insisted upon that we cannot doubt Shakespeare has on his mind another classical theme: the difference between men and women. Though marriage may make a harmony from that difference, it breaks down to jangling discord at the slightest strain.

Shakespeare also builds the plot catastrophe on classic ground: it is the question of Desdemona's relation to sexuality and nature that Iago raises to wreck Othello's trust in her, the question Euripides would have framed as her relation to Dionysus. Out of the torment of his new vision of Desdemona, Othello is transformed from a paragon of controlled energy to a rigid parody of a revenger beneath a 'marble' heaven, his 'icy current' of will all flowing in one direction. He becomes a Tamburlaine of rhetoric and moral stupidity; 'like to the Pontic Sea', he boasts,

>   Whose icy current and compulsive course
>   Ne'er knows retiring ebb, but keeps due on
>   To the Propontic and the Hellespont. (3.3.457–9)

The psychological credibility of this, and the free grotesquerie of Shakespeare's handling of Othello – falling in fits, mumbling obscenities, and savagely striking Desdemona – may remind us of the dramatic reversal Euripides effects with Pentheus' nature in the *Bacchae*. Pentheus is another hero whose problems with woman and nature lead to a psychological collapse, and just as Euripides found that the best way to explore his subject was to present it as a wrestling match between Pentheus and Dionysus, the one apparently so powerful, and the other apparently so powerless, so Shakespeare gives us Othello and Iago, whose human strengths and weaknesses are shown to fit together as part of the same jigsaw. Othello is the great general, Iago the mere 'Ancient' passed over for promotion; but Iago knows he has got the upper hand when, like Dionysus, he has so 'possessed' Othello that he agrees to be a humiliated eavesdropper on scenes not meant for him; and exchanges his own heroic idiom for Iago's gross vocabulary: 'Goats and monkeys!' (4.1.265).

Initially, however, Othello might seem the Dionysiac character: he has the happiest combination of unconscious power with self-conscious control. He has the quiet but absolute authority of Dionysus over his Venetian audience in Act I; and in Act II, when we see him in his military guise, it is not uncomfortably worn like defensive armour. Leadership is natural to him, and he modulates easily from martial grandeur to kissing his wife, from the language of power to the language of feeling. When the Turkish fleet is dispersed he orders a dual celebration, of the victory and his marriage; a Dionysiac release that, but for Iago's plots and Cassio's weak head, would only show him more the leader ('It is Othello's pleasure . . . that . . . every man put himself into triumph; some to dance, some to make bonfires', 2.2.1–5). His integration of the natural and the acquired, of physical magnificence and mental command, gives him a compelling power over the State of Venice itself, as much as over his soldiers: he is truly 'the noble Moor whom our full senate / Call all-in-all sufficient' (4.1.266–7).

Iago's nature, by contrast, is not a harmony of opposites but something simpler and uglier that may remind us of Pentheus. Like the young king, he exposes the rigidity of masculinity in his relentless hostility to women, his preference for male company at any price. Here too is the endless dirty-mindedness that sees sexual appetite as degradation, particularly in women. As Iago ripostes to Roderigo's remark about Desdemona, 'She's full of most blessed condition' – 'Blest fig's end! The wine she drinks is made of grapes. If she had been blessed, she would never have loved the Moor' (2.1.249–53). The particular rightness of Shakespeare's matching him with Othello derives from the sense in which Othello is rich in everything Iago lacks, and what is open in Othello is fiercely closed in Iago. But Iago is also clearly the Renaissance Machiavel, who delights in his doubleness ('I am not what I am', 1.1.65) and allows no human bonds to restrain him (he will kill his wife Emilia for testifying against him, 5.2.243). His is not a character that can break down in interesting ways. Indeed,

Iago's climactic line is the ultimate in Machiavellian self-enclosure: 'From this time forth I never will speak word' (5.2.310). It is not out of Iago that Shakespeare makes his tragedy, but out of Othello, that magnificent achievement of both culture and nature that turns out to be so vulnerable to collapse.

Why should it be so? Shakespeare's answer again has a classical familiarity: it is because of Othello's honour. Once he has lost that, he has lost everything, and it is a short step from the happiest integration ('My soul hath her content so absolute . . .', 2.1.192) to degradation of the most humiliating kind ('I had rather be a toad . . .', 3.3.274). Shakespeare's representation of honour is of course profoundly coloured by the chivalric tradition, not least in the presumption that sexual honour is at the heart of it (so that Desdemona's honour is synonymous with chastity) – but the outlines of the subject would still be recognizable to Agamemnon. For 'honour' is man's constructed self in the world, the name he makes for himself: a mere breath in essence, yet a transcendent way of creating oneself, inside and outside of time. All the elaborate debate in the play about Reputation is there to fix this truth. Iago, of course, thinks honour a social farce; but Cassio, after being cashiered by Othello, knows better:

> *Cass.* Reputation, reputation, reputation – O, I ha' lost my reputation, I
> ha' lost the immortal part of myself, and what remains is bestial!
> My reputation, Iago, my reputation.
>
> *Iago* As I am an honest man I thought you had received some bodily
> wound. There is more sense in that than in reputation. Reputation
> is an idle and most false imposition, oft got without merit and lost
> without deserving. You have lost no reputation at all unless you
> repute yourself such a loser. (2.3.256–65)

For Iago, reputation is one man's word against another's, and his ability to manage other people's public reputations for most of the play shows how much truth there is in this. But there is a higher truth about honour that is out of his grasp: Cassio feels he has lost 'the immortal part of [him]self', and 'what remains is bestial'. His reputation was the value attaching to the name of Cassio, which he gloried in having created, and which it was his life's work to live up to; the body without the name is merely animal.

Since Shakespeare insists so strongly on this theme, perhaps we should understand the centrality of honour to the chivalric life as a kind of second birth, which plays a role equivalent to the birth of the citizen in the *Oresteia*. The first birth is all a physical business, with mother, spilt blood, and the Furies round the cradle. The second takes place much later, when the child has reached the age of autonomy, and can choose who to be and what to do by the light of Apollonian day. This is the point at which the child becomes an Iago or a Cassio: and we see why Cassio's choice is properly called 'heroic', for the hero submits all his actions to public judgement, where Iago hides from view, accepting no one else's judgement and not even admitting that he can be known.

What is true of Cassio is even more true of Othello: he has been creating his name from a boy of seven, in a sequence of 'disastrous chances', 'moving accidents' and 'hair-breadth scapes', not excepting a period of enslavement (surely a unique qualification among tragic heroes, 1.3.131–41). All this, with his subsequent valuation by the Venetian state, adds up to such a magnificent re-creation of his original selfhood that the story of it was enough to woo Desdemona and make the Duke say, 'I think this tale would win my daughter, too' (170). When we are trying to understand how this paragon of both nature and culture ends up striking Desdemona in front of the Venetian ambassador, we need to measure the vertiginous risk Othello took in pinning his self-definition to Desdemona's love. As he phrases it himself, in the midst of his jealous anguish,

> But there where I have garnered up my heart,
> Where either I must live or bear no life,
> The fountain from the which my current runs
> Or else dries up – to be discarded thence,
> Or keep it as a cistern for foul toads
> To knot and gender in! (4.2.59–64)

His gift of himself to Desdemona was a 'garnering up', a harvest of all he had been, and his life was to have flowed out from their union as a clear current from a fountain. When that 'flow' has become stagnant, a place for the propagation of toads, there is no knowing what mischief may follow: for the Othello who was being created no longer exists.

There is an interesting parallel here with another of Euripides' plots, though it might not be evident at first glance. The only other tragic character who has pinned so much to a single promise, leaving country, kin and childhood so desperately far behind her, is Medea. Shakespeare's alertness to the role played by free choice and oaths in adulthood has helped him create a similar tragic crux in the plot: a 'barbarian' arriving in civilization has placed absolute confidence on a civilized promise – only to be told that he has been duped. Othello's frenzy and moral collapse have much in common with Medea's at the start of the play, when she is lying prostrate, groaning and hardening herself for an atrocious revenge. As we noted then, 'the dishonour [Medea] is overwhelmed by is something only a woman can know: the annihilation of her selfhood in a world where her status hung entirely on another. Medea without Jason is an un-person, with no acknowledged place in the state, and no family to return to. It is not that she is naturally a barbarian, a wild outlaw, but that he is making her into one' (p. 66 above).

Perhaps in the context of *Othello* the assumption that this is an experience only a woman can have needs qualification: for a black man may share a female vulnerability about his place in the world, and the grounds on which he is tolerated. Certainly Iago does all he can to make Othello recognize himself as a complete outsider. Euripides is positing the hardest case, of someone whose legal as well as emotional position hangs on a promise; and Shakespeare finds something radically parallel in Othello's position in Venice.

But Shakespeare's wronged barbarian is nevertheless male, and in the Renaissance atmosphere of the story it is clear that Shakespeare could never make the leap of imagination Euripides makes, in showing a woman capable of vengefulness in proportion to her wrongs. Desdemona is made of different materials. She shields Othello to the last, even claiming that she killed herself. And the betrayal is hypothetical, in any case: it is not that Othello has been wronged, as Medea was so emphatically wronged by Jason, but only that he thinks he has. (One is to suppose that heroines *never* commit adultery.) These hesitations produce a plot that lacks the analytic energy of Euripides', but has a kind of nightmare sequentiality to it. Out of dread that his trust may be misplaced, Othello tumbles into the certainty that it has been; and from a few whispers and a dropped handkerchief there comes Desdemona's cold corpse, and his own beside it.

These chivalric assumptions go along with another, still more formative, which is related to Christianity's proscription of knowledge: that only bad characters are self-conscious and 'knowing', like Iago. Good characters, like Othello and Desdemona, are purely, unconsciously, themselves (and therefore may 'as tenderly be led by th' nose / As asses are', 1.3.393–4). Perhaps this is the reason we feel Shakespeare has a classical subject, in the relation of a hero to his honour, but pursues it in a quite unclassical spirit. For the nightmare 'realism' of Iago is counterpointed by an atmosphere of poignant idealism, which keeps the psychology of Desdemona in particular out of clear focus. Again and again the play returns to the psychology of chivalry and the connection between goodness and lack of awareness. This, indeed, is what enables Iago to hold the reins of the plot: Cassio, Desdemona and Othello are simply too good to imagine what it is Iago is doing; their 'free and open natures' forbid them to suspect it. But instead of probing the logic that makes 'asses' of his finest characters, Shakespeare contents himself with reiterating how perfectly they live up to their own code – even while his plot shows that it is this that kills them.[1]

The unclassical part of this honour code is that it is made to guarantee the unity of the inner and outer man or woman. We know that Iago is evil when he says 'I am not what I am'; we know that the 'freedom', 'liberality' and 'openness' associated with Othello, Cassio and Desdemona are theirs all through. Iago expatiates on a version of human psychology that sounds much more credible than this, in that it allows welcome and unwelcome thoughts to mix in the mind and consciousness to choose between them. But then, he is a Machiavel:

---

[1]   The fact that Shakespeare has already anatomized chivalry in *Troilus and Cressida* (c.1602) and shown Troilus tortured by the ugly discrepancy between his code and reality, does not seem to affect this play. Perhaps Shakespeare cannot yet negotiate these thoughts in tragic mode; they belong to satire.

> Utter my thoughts? Why, say they are vile and false,
> As where's that palace whereinto foul things
> Sometimes intrude not? Who has that breast so pure
> But some uncleanly apprehensions
> Keep leets and law-days, and in sessions sit
> With meditations lawful? (3.3.141–6)

'Where's that palace?' challenges Iago; and the play says, initially, that it is the bosom of Othello. And after that has been infested by 'uncleanly apprehensions', there is still Desdemona's heart 'whereinto foul things intrude not'. The mere attempt to think of herself as a whore leaves her torpid – 'Faith, half asleep' (4.2.101); this is an idea she has no word for, no concept ('Am I that name, Iago? ... Such as she said my lord did say I was.' 4.2.121–3). Sooner than develop into a new Desdemona who can understand contamination and bar the door, she goes to bed in her shroud.

With the heroine's dreamlike passivity, and impenetrable goodness, the play slips into a realm of fantasy that evades the questions that it promised to answer. The Desdemona of Act I had judgement and made choices; she heard Othello's story and wished that 'heaven had made *her* such a man' (1.3.162, my italics). Most strikingly, she withstood her father's authority with an unanswerable appeal to the facts of nature:

> My life and education both do learn me
> How to respect you. You are the lord of duty,
> I am hitherto your daughter. But here's my husband,
> And so much duty as my mother showed
> To you, preferring you before her father,
> So much I challenge that I may profess
> Due to the Moor my lord. (1.3.182–8)

Writing in this vein, Shakespeare was within reach of the Euripidean sense that women too have their defining acts of selfhood, and the intelligence to think and speak for themselves. This Desdemona also insists on following Othello to war instead of being a sheltered housewife ('a moth of peace', as she puts it, 1.3.256). But from the moment Othello turns on her, her role collapses into bewildered passivity, and it becomes clear how much her characterization has in common with Ophelia's. Without going mad, she too sings and sleepwalks her way to the end of the plot, and the interesting questions associated with her female individuation dissolve away in pathos.

The chivalric view of women, in short, cannot keep up the level of realism required to analyse Desdemona's predicament. Even Iago's wife and Cassio's whore are protected by it: Emilia talks about paying husbands back in their own coin, but we know that she does not take her own advice, and Bianca is a model of loyalty. But if Shakespeare cannot transfer into the tragic mode what he knows about Rosalinds and Violas in the comic mode, he is less hampered in his handling of Othello. Here, as we noted above, his vision is astonishingly clear;

and though he may not be asking himself as openly as in the *Bacchae* what it is that turns Dionysus from the 'most gentle' to the 'most terrible' power, the process he traces of the collapse of civilized constraint is appallingly credible. Just as Pentheus was too perturbed by the Bacchants' relation to nature to question his own, so Shakespeare sees with classical precision that Othello fails to be concerned with his own relation to nature, while he is obsessively concerned with Desdemona's. 'Nature' is the key word in Othello's exchanges with Iago; and it is a vertiginous concept in relation to women, for if it does not mean something wonderful ('natural perfection'), it means something beyond redemption ('natural depravity').

Iago brings Othello to the edge of the abyss by insinuating that Desdemona's innocence is not what it seems. Adultery is standard among Venetian wives, and she has already acted a double part, as Othello knows – 'She did deceive her father, marrying you' (3.3.210). But what tips Othello over is this:

> *Oth.*   I do not think but Desdemona's honest.
> *Iago*   Long live she so, and long live you to think so!
> *Oth.*   And yet how nature, erring from itself –
> *Iago*   Ay, there's the point; as, to be bold with you,
>   Not to affect many proposèd matches
>   Of her own clime, complexion, and degree,
>   Whereto we see in all things nature tends.
>   Foh, one may smell in such a will most rank,
>   Foul disproportions, thoughts unnatural! (3.3.230–8)

Iago's malicious obscenity picks on Desdemona's very choice of Othello as the proof of her unnatural appetite. Her dazzlingly free decision in the teeth of race, country and paternal authority, the very act that demonstrated how equal she was to Othello, is converted into proof of her 'rank will'. And Othello cannot resent the slur to her or even the insult to himself, because his thoughts are apparently running along these lines: 'I cannot think Desdemona dishonest: everything about her announces that she is perfect – perfect as nature is. And yet . . . nature does err from itself – and so may Desdemona.' Iago is only gleefully embroidering this same perception: 'What better proof, than that she wanted you? Even animal nature cleaves to its own kind.'

The thought on which Othello slips into the abyss is that women and nature are the same thing, and there are no better guarantees for the one than the other. This opens the way for Iago to use 'nature' in the wholly unredeemed sense suggested by the dregs of chivalric sublimation – as the knotting and engendering of toads, which lurks at the back of Othello's mind as much as Iago's. From here, Othello is as lost as he supposes Desdemona to be, and the whole elaborate heroic structure that was 'Othello' collapses. For men *have* values, but woman *is* a value, the chief value man has. Without his faith, Othello's 'occupation' is indeed 'gone':

> I had been happy if the general camp,
> Pioneers and all, had tasted her sweet body,
> So I had nothing known. O, now for ever
> Farewell the tranquil mind, farewell content,
> Farewell the plumèd troops and the big wars
> That makes ambition virtue! O, farewell,
> Farewell the neighing steed, and the shrill trump,
> The spirit-stirring drum, th'ear-piercing fife,
> The royal banner, and all quality,
> Pride, pomp and circumstance of glorious war!
> And O, you mortal engines whose rude throats
> Th'immortal Jove's dread clamours counterfeit,
> Farewell! Othello's occupation's gone. (3.3.350–62)

The interplay of self-pity and self-dramatization here is unsparingly observed. The heroic integration of Othello's quiet rebuke to Cassio – 'How comes, it, Michael, you are thus forgot?' (2.3.181) – has already fallen apart. What we have instead are the lesser components of heroism, absurdly out of balance: the pleasure of self-approval (the 'tranquil mind'), the validation of ambition ('the big wars / That makes ambition virtue'), the excitement of martial music ('spirit-stirring drum . . . ear-piercing fife') and the rapture of setting off cannon ('you mortal engines . . . Th'immortal Jove's dread clamours counterfeit'). There is a repellent childishness about all this that is underlined by his choice of the word 'occupation': war here is seen as an ego-supporting pastime, severed from all regard of service, or fear of bloodshed. It is the wounded male speaking, and the thought which triggers this elaborate 'farewell' to his past is the most childlike of all: that anyone in the camp would have been welcome to Desdemona's 'sweet body', provided Othello had not known. Inauthenticity can go no farther.

It is only a short step from here to his physical collapse, and the mad fit that is the apogee of his frenzy – though, in Othello's own logic, his passion is 'Nature's' proof that he has good reason for it:

> *Oth.*   Nature would not invest herself in such shadowing passion without
>   some instruction. It is not words that shakes me thus. Pish! Noses,
>   ears, and lips! Is't possible? Confess? Handkerchief? O devil!
>   [*He falls down in a trance*]
> *Iago*   Work on; my medicine works. (4.1.38–43)

There is a Greek clarity here to the interplay between Iago's controlling will and Othello's chaos of body and mind (the fit comes on him as a kind of Dionysiac *sparagmos*). Shakespeare makes us see the power of the man without values over the man who is all values, and shows us how quickly one succumbs to the other. Here again is the thought we have been tracing from Agamemnon onwards: if man is a construct, then he can be deconstructed, and if his honour is central to the edifice, the loss of honour can bring it tumbling down. And here, too, is the clearest possible demonstration of the paradox by which, the more the male sees the female as unredeemably natural, the more unredeemably natural – bestial – he becomes himself. Othello, like Pentheus, pays the supreme price for focusing on Desdemona's relation to nature rather than his own.

Shakespeare's management of the emotions generated by Othello's collapse – a sight as embarrassing as it is terrifying, and daringly close to farce, the usual context of imaginary cuckolds – is so masterly that it seems grudging to notice that Acts IV and V have technical difficulties in common with *Hamlet*. The problem again is with the hero's *anagnorisis* and the concluding pile of corpses (admittedly less high in this case: only Desdemona's, Othello's and Emilia's). Othello is in a state of frenzy to the end of the play. He reintegrates himself sufficiently to comment on his own fate – 'An honourable murderer, if you will, / For naught I did in hate, but all in honour'; and 'one that loved not wisely but too well' (5.2.300–1, 353) – but this is still the baffled hero speaking, who cannot understand how his virtue turned to such bad uses. And the last interchange between him and Iago shows them still locked in perfect incomprehension:

> *Oth.*   Will you, I pray, demand that demi-devil
> Why he hath thus ensnared my soul and body?
> *Iago*   Demand me nothing. What you know, you know.
> From this time forth I never will speak word. (5.2.307–10)

The play itself does not get much beyond this, as witness the many critical attempts to understand Iago's motivation. What is lacking, as we noted above, is Shakespeare's preparedness to analyse the honour code itself, and to question the division inherent in the Christian definition of innocence, between bad people who think and have self-consciousness, like Iago, and good people who do not. An indication of how many difficulties are left unresolved by the plot is how little we might wish Othello to stay alive. For him as for Hamlet, death is the only answer to his predicament; and there is a kind of melancholy luxury about it, for him as for us: 'No way but this: / Killing myself, to die upon a kiss' (5.2.368–9). His death, and in its fantasy sacrifice style, Desdemona's too, are so genuinely satisfying that one is tempted to class them, not as actual deaths, but 'Renaissance' deaths which have less to do with terminal pain than with Christian notions of atonement. They affect us as being more right, as it were, than wrong; and the extent to which the stage conventions Shakespeare has inherited trade on the prestige of death, without analysing its causes, is a sharp reminder of how wisely the classical tradition kept death offstage, where its meaning could be analysed with no danger of overwhelming the audience.

For the implication in Othello's murder of Desdemona is that he is not really to blame. He was deluded and tricked; he committed the crime, but innocently ('all in honour'), and if he atones by suicide, he is in a sense a hero again. For a classical audience the mere fact of his suicide would hardly have sufficed. Why did he make a mistake, what did he learn, and what should the audience now understand? A pile of corpses brings a satisfaction of its own, but it does not answer these questions.

Hamlet and *Othello* have alerted us to two problems which seem impossible to avoid when writing tragedy in the Renaissance. One is the influence of Christian morality, which softens the connection between the doer and the deed. The doer's inner motivation is now stressed, rather than his defining act. This inevitably muffles the discussion of tragic responsibility: questions of 'who?' and 'what?' give way to 'why?' and 'how pardonably?' Another is the protective veil wrapped around female characters by the chivalric code. Looking at Ophelia and Desdemona, we are tempted to say that woman are a distinct species from men. Of course, Gertrude, Emilia and Bianca are there to show us that they are not: but the fact that women are so easily classified into camps, and that the dividing factor between them is sexual energy, suggests that Shakespeare's mind is no more free on this subject than any other mind of the period. This seesaw between idealization and demonization would be costly enough, if it were only a question of the characterization of women in the plays; but of course it has implications for the male characters too. For if sexual energy is part of 'fallen' nature, the drive towards maturity in both men and women is compromised. Girls in their shrouds (Ophelia, Desdemona) become more subtly commendable than women in their marital beds (Gertrude, in a second bed, is an object of outrage). And the men whose happiness might have come from reaching forward to confirm their adulthood in sexual mutuality, must mistrust any woman who responds to them.

Above all, the difficulty of associating heroines with sexual energy creates an odd silence in Shakespeare's plays about mothers and children, which only begins to be broken in *Macbeth*. Euripides takes for granted the power women derive from maternity, and carries on to ask what difference this makes to their lives as reasonable creatures. But there is no assumption that Ophelia, Desdemona (or, in our next play, Cordelia) will have anything to do with motherhood, and still less that they have to negotiate between nature and reason, just as men do. Shakespeare's idealism readily casts women in the mould of Mary (miraculously free of carnal knowledge, the pure intercessor) or the Magdalen (fallen into carnal sin), but not in the most obvious role of all, as mothers of children.

Perhaps what we are noticing is best summed up as the price of patriarchy. For, as is increasingly often remarked, the biological basis of the legal arrangements we call patriarchal is the need of a father to know that his offspring are his own. Although Shakespeare gives women no power in his plots as mothers (and in *King Lear*, he abolishes mothers altogether), he is hypersensitive to the issue of female chastity; and he shelters the heroines he creates from the remotest imputation against their purity. To modern eyes these heroines are wanting in human qualities, but it is very instructive to view them through the eyes of a reader to whom they made perfect sense, like Coleridge. The assumptions of patriarchy could not be more eloquently conveyed than in this enthusiastic nineteenth-century meditation on our heroines:

> But in Shak[e]speare all the elements of womanhood are holy, and there is the sweet, yet dignified feeling of all that *continuates* society, as sense of ancestry and of sex, with a purity unassailable by sophistry, because it rests not in the analytic processes, but in that sane equipoise of the faculties, during which the feelings are representatives of all past experience, – not of the individual only, but of all those by whom she has been educated, and their predecessors even up to the first mother that lived. Shakespeare saw that the want of prominence, which Pope notices for sarcasm ['Most Women have no Characters at all'] was the blessed beauty of the woman's character, and knew that it arose not from any deficiency, but from the more exquisite harmony of all the parts of the moral being constituting one living total of head and heart.[2]

If we apply Coleridge's remarks to Desdemona, her lack of a 'character' would stem from the fact that she is far above such a thing: what she has instead is an 'exquisite harmony of moral being', not produced (as it might be in a man) by 'analytic processes', but by conditioning. She is 'one living total of head and heart'; but it is a precondition of her state that she should not know how she got that way. And it is only if she remains such a moral sleepwalker that a man can have absolute security in the legitimacy of his offspring – because it is female fertility that, as Coleridge delicately puts it, '*continuates* society', and in which every male has a possessive self-interest.

If these are the incoherences that the patriarchal view of women and nature brings to *Othello*, what of our next play, where the hero is the patriarch of patriarchs and has three daughters?

King Lear (c.1605)

In the character of King Lear Shakespeare takes the astonishing risk of unmasking patriarchal power.[3] The ruler of a kingdom becomes a 'ruined piece of nature' (4.5.130), and the 'dragon' of Act I is so infantilized by the cruelty of two daughters that all the love of the third cannot restore him. How radically Shakespeare tears down in this play all the structures that patriarchy takes for

---

[2]   *Lectures 1808–1819 on Literature*, ed. R.A. Foakes, in *The Collected Works of Samuel Taylor Coleridge*, general ed. Kathleen Coburn, 5 (London: Routledge & Kegan Paul, and Princeton: Princeton University Press, 1987), pp. 269–70.

[3]   The dating of *Lear* is conjectural (it was first printed in 1608 as *The History of King Lear* and could therefore postdate *Macbeth*). The following argument shows the thematic grounds for the assumption that it predates *Macbeth*, which are also supported by metrical analysis. Shakespeare revised it to produce *The Tragedy of King Lear*, printed in the 1623 Folio, which is the version used here.

granted shows in the long history of its bowdlerization. From 1681, the play was only seen in the version of Nahum Tate, who marries Cordelia off to Edgar and keeps Gloucester and Lear alive to enjoy their retirement. It was not until this century, which is accustomed to the disappearance of value systems, that the play has been staged with enthusiastic frequency.

Shakespeare's tragedies seem follow the male through the roles he plays in a lifetime, and after considering the plight of a tragic son in *Hamlet*, and a tragic lover in *Othello*, Shakespeare now turns to the tragedy of a father. The intensity of his concentration on fatherhood shows in the total silence about mothers in the play; we may feel that no plot about families without mothers can be squarely based on reality, but it is clearly Shakespeare's decision (Gloucester's wife is as absent as Lear's). He posits, 'There was a man with three daughters; and there was a man with two sons' – and he develops their stories with the same unsparing attention to what is ugly and shameful in their predicaments that he brought to *Othello*.

Shakespeare's use of two stories, Lear's and Gloucester's, has an important resonance for the level of nihilism the play can reach. For in Gloucester's story he pays Aristotelian attention to the tragic sequence, and shows us a classic *hamartia* (mistaking Edgar's character), *peripeteia* (his blinding) and *anagnorisis* (full self-knowedge), to the point where Gloucester sounds like a character from a Greek play: 'I stumbled when I saw' (4.1.19). But in the Lear plot, to which this is only counterpoint, all sense of shape and sequence is defied. There is error, certainly, and reversal sends Lear out on to the heath. But he is too mad to recognize what his error was; and reversal is piled on reversal, so that he falls into Gloucester's loving care only to be forced to flee to Dover, and finds peace and security there with Cordelia, only to be caught and imprisoned. When we next see her in his arms she is dead and he is howling. Shakespeare alters his source play to make this possible (Cordelia originally won the war and lived to be queen), so we cannot doubt that he is deliberately twisting the knife: there may be impulses of love and creativity in the world he describes, but mad disorder is what finally prevails.

Whatever we say about Shakespeare's treatment, however, the subject of patriarchal succession is profoundly classical in itself. For succession is the key difficulty in securing patriarchal order. The power must not be divided, but at the moment of transition it is lodged between two bodies. One must therefore be deemed to be dead, if not actually so: 'Le roi est mort, vive le roi!' All patriarchal societies have veiled the awkwardness of this transition, and the brutal fact of the impotence of old age, with a passionate, compensatory reverence. Greek and Latin literature is full of such *pietas*, whether in the *Iliad* scene where Achilles awards Nestor a prize precisely because he is too old to compete in the funeral games, or in the *Aeneid*, where the helpless Priam's death at the hands of Pyrrhus is felt to be the ultimate horror of war. Shakespeare has already shown his alertness to these painful feelings surrounding old Priam: he makes his slaughter the part of the fictitious play that Hamlet and the Players recite to one another. In the Marlovian rhetoric, the mixture of horror and absurdity lurking in Priam's impotence shows through all the more strongly:

> With eyes like carbuncles the hellish Pyrrhus
> Old grandsire Priam seeks . . . Anon he finds him,
> Striking too short at Greeks. His antique sword,
> Rebellious to his arm, lies where it falls,
> Repugnant to command. Unequal match,
> Pyrrhus at Priam drives, in rage strikes wide;
> But with the whiff and wind of his fell sword
> Th'unnervèd father falls. Then senseless Ilium,
> Seeming to feel his blow, with flaming top
> Stoops to his base. (2.2.466–7, 471–9)

Priam is in Lear's condition, both king and 'old grandsire', still warrior enough to be fighting, but not strong enough to hit anyone ('striking too short at Greeks'). Indeed, he is so frail he is knocked over by the mere 'whiff and wind' of Pyrrhus' sword, but at the same time, his collapse is the collapse of Troy. In the grotesque discrepancy and interplay between these two truths lies the subject of Shakespeare's tragedy.

Before we look closely at the plot, however, we might pause to notice the sense in which the pathos surrounding Lear's fall is still deeper than Priam's. Because of the reverence for monarchical authority in this period, the figure of the king is lent emotions properly reserved for fathers, as we noted above. Playwrights often find themselves inside a childlike nexus of hope and admiration, which easily converts to disappointment, and a sense of being orphaned, when the king is revealed to be human at the last. Shakespeare's whole energy, of course, is devoted to showing that King Lear is cousin to Poor Tom, and 'robes and furred gowns hide all' (4.5.161) – but the length of time he devotes to the royal undoing, and the nervous horror expressed by watchers inside the play, suggest how great an effort it takes to see the man in the king. If we compare Lear with Oedipus in his old age, blind, tattered and accompanied only by Antigone, we see how much faster Sophocles can get through to the issue that concerns him, the value of Oedipus in death. The old Oedipus is embittered by his poverty and angry at his loss of status, of course; but after he, and we, have registered due shock, we get on to the real business of the play. The fact that kings are nonetheless men was only the starting point – and the one, indeed, on which tragedy depends.

Shakespeare not only takes longer, but swathes the king in a compensatory reverence beyond even Virgil's for Priam. The flood level of this tender unrealism is marked by Albany's returning of the kingdom to Lear, when he is only seconds from death and has no eyes for anything but Cordelia's corpse. 'For us,' says

Albany, 'we will resign / During the life of this old majesty, / To him our absolute power' (5.3.274–6). When the defeat of regality is denied as ardently as this, it is less surprising that Shakespeare pushes the Lear plot so vehemently towards nihilism. Only the collapse of poetic justice inside the play can convey the terror of the play's underlying thought: that if kings are not fathers on earth, God is not father in Heaven, and there is no such thing as justice.

The first scene opens up the nature of patriarchy at a stroke: an old king asks his three daughters, 'Which of you shall we say doth love us most?' (1.1.51). Here already is the audible counterpoint between the assumption of power (the royal 'we') and his advancing impotence (the reason he is asking the question). Here too is the interplay between the father's real claims, and his unblinking use of property for blackmail. (The division of the kingdom hangs on the daughters' answers: as he continues, 'That we our largest bounty may extend / Where nature doth with merit challenge', 52–3). The eldest daughters understand what lies beneath the words, submit to blackmail, and say what he hopes to hear, that they love him 'no less than life', 'as much as child e'er loved, or father found' (58, 59). But the youngest resists the charade and says she loves him 'according to [her] bond, no more nor less' (93) – at which point he thunders disinheritance and frenzied wrath, to the point of wishing her, not merely dead, but non-existent: 'Better thou / Hadst not been born than not t'have pleased me better' (233-4).

Clearly, something more is going on than Lear has openly declared; and we may suspect that it is something even more dangerous and alarming than the transition of power between the patriarch and his young successor: something that only goes on between fathers and daughters. The hidden element seems to be the father's secret hope of being totally supported by quasi-maternal care in the weakness of old age, as he was supported by maternal care in childhood. As Lear says, in broken-hearted disbelief, 'I loved her most, and thought to set my rest / On her kind nursery' (123–4). Cordelia's love was to have been his second cradle, and the only possible compensation for the bitterness of old age.

But if Shakespeare knows the treacherous hopes of paternal hearts, he also knows what daughters have to answer. Cordelia's speech is a version of Desdemona's to her father. She owes him all a filial daughter owes, but that is not undivided love:

> You have begot me, bred me, loved me.
> I return those duties back as are right fit –
> Obey you, love you, and most honour you.
> Why have my sisters husbands, if they say
> They love you all? Haply when I shall wed
> That lord whose hand must take my plight shall carry
> Half my love with him, half my care and duty.
> Sure, I shall never marry like my sisters,
> [To love my father all.] (1.1.96–103)[4]

---

4   Quarto line added (103).

To Lear's horror at an analysis 'so untender', she answers that it, and she, are 'true' (106–7). These are the facts that make ongoing life possible; and Cordelia might have added, as Desdemona did, that if her own mother had not similiarly withstood her father, Lear would have had no wife. She does not say so, of course, because such a reference would draw attention to the missing element of maternal power in the play, which Shakespeare does not want to include in the equation. But we may note in passing that the admirable realism of this exchange between Cordelia and Lear is not borne out by the play as a whole. The sense in which female sexual maturity is the guarantee of life's continuity is acknowledged here, only to disappear; and when Cordelia rejoins Lear, she does not love him 'according to her bond' after all, but far beyond it, just as he hoped. She loves him at the cost of her sexual maturity (she is a daughter again, not a wife), her marriage (France evaporates with a perfunctory excuse)[5] and finally, her life. The slippage between Shakespeare's opening clarity and the overwhelming emotionalism of his later treatment of Cordelia suggests that the truth she embodies, like Lear's own decline, is more than the play can contemplate.

We might also notice how quickly sexual maturity becomes a crime in Goneril and Regan. Their early treatment of Lear is only ambiguously evil, in that (as has often been noticed) their assessment of him is perfectly accurate: 'he hath ever but slenderly known himself', and they sensibly steel themselves for 'the unruly waywardness that infirm and choleric years bring with them' (1.1.292–8). One might take issue with the tone of this, but hardly the sentiments; and given that he has asked for the impossible, in wanting to retain 'the name, and all th' addition' of a king without the job itself, their impatience with the bargain is understandable. Lear takes his weak stand on blackmail, they on the underlying facts of life: 'I gave you all.' – 'And in good time you gave it' (2.2.423–4).

But whatever attention Shakespeare pays to the validity of their point of view is quickly lost in his pursuit of sympathy for Lear. Realism, it seems, is too close to Machiavellianism: daughters who can take such a tone are unnatural enough for anything. Goneril is a withered branch, a potentially deadly weapon, once the filial sap stops flowing. As Albany puts it in the Quarto *History*:

> That nature, which contemns it[s] origin
> Cannot be bordered certain in itself.
> She that herself will sliver and disbranch
> From her material sap perforce must wither,
> And come to deadly use. (Scene 16, 32–6)

After Goneril has barred her door to Lear, the 'deadly use' is quickly exemplified by her passionate contempt for her lawful husband, and lustful appetite for

---

5   'Something he left imperfect in the state / Which, since his coming forth, is thought of' (*The History of King Lear*, scene 17). There is no explanation given in the Folio version at all.

Edmund. She and Regan become mortal enemies in the contest, 'each jealous of the other, as the stung / Are of the adder', as Edmund observes (5.1.47–8). This sexual savagery is only a step away from savagery pure and simple, and Regan plays an exhilarated part in torturing Gloucester, while Goneril invites Edmund to deliver her from the 'loathed warmth' of her marital bed by killing Albany (4.5.265–7). Their end is of a piece: Goneril poisons Regan, only to commit suicide shortly after, when Edmund himself is dying. 'O indistinguished space of woman's will', marvels Edgar (4.5.271): female sexual appetite knows no limits.

The easy presumption here that one kind of evil leads to another, and from barring the door to Lear there is a rapid descent into the pit, should not prevent us from noting Shakespeare's particular logic. The pit is a sexual place – and it is the only location of sexual vitality in the play. There is otherwise no vitality of the sort that moves life forward: Cordelia, as we noted, talks of the necessity for it, but the plot shows her renouncing it in favour of protecting Lear. As the action pauses in Act III and we see the world through the whirling consciousness of fools and madmen, sexuality appears only in the grossest forms. Lear would 'strike flat the thick rotundity of the world' to crush its fertility and put an end to conception for good: 'all germens spill at once / That makes ingrateful man' (3.2.8–9) Poor Tom's excuse for his decay is that he 'served the lust of [his] mistress' heart, and did the act of darkness with her' (3.4.80–2). And Lear's disgust at the pretence of 'simp'ring dames' to chastity is so vociferous that we too might be grateful for something to sweeten our imaginations at the end of it:

> The fitchew nor the soilèd horse goes to't
> With a more riotous appetite. Down from the waist
> They're centaurs, though women all above.
> But to the girdle do the gods inherit;
> Beneath is all the fiend's. There's hell, there's darkness, there is the
> sulphurous pit, burning, scalding, stench, consumption. Fie, fie,
> fie; pah, pah! Give me an ounce of civet, good apothecary, sweeten
> my imagination. (4.5.120–7)

Lear, of course, is mad. But it cannot be accidental that this is what he most wants to say in his madness: that the gods have made woman as far as the waist, but 'beneath is all the fiend's'. And the seat of procreation is a dark and 'sulphurous' pit that 'burns' and 'scalds' – Hell in this world, rather than the next.

It is hard to avoid the conclusion that this hidden animus is part of Shakespeare's vision too, and that it helps give the plot its *Hamlet*-like distortions with respect to female sexuality. Virgins are sheltered from maturity, sexual activity is seen as bestial, and mothers are abolished – for they would make clear the desperate fallacy inherent in this state of recoil, that there is no life at all without the joining of male and female. But mad Lear, like Hamlet, is stranded outside time: and what he sees in his isolation is the unadulterated horror lurking in the natural sequence of things. What sexuality brings in its train is the maturity of daughters, the decay of fathers, and death. Thus women, with their infinitely alluring promise of total love and care, are godlike to the waist; but they are the devil's below, generating life and death in the same appalling act. This is where the stench comes from that Lear wipes off his hand, before he will let Gloucester kiss it – the 'smell of mortality' (4.5.129).

We must suppose that some such train of thought underlies the Lear plot because it is clear that the Gloucester plot is about the agony of fatherhood, too. But in the Gloucester plot we find the classical material about patriarchy we would have expected to find as the main plot: the emphasis on fathers and sons, not daughters, and the focus on the painful moment of transition where paternal authority is lost along with bodily strength. Edmund's letter purporting to come from Edgar expresses impatience with 'the oppression of aged tyranny, who sways not as it hath power but as it is suffered' (1.2.50–1). And he also relays as Edgar's the disobliging sentiment that, 'sons at perfect age, and fathers declined, the father should be as ward to the son, and the son manage his revenue' (74–6). Gloucester explodes with a similar wrath to Lear's: 'Abhorred villain, unnatural, detested, brutish villain – worse than brutish!' (78–9). Like Lear, he is much too quick to call attitudes 'unnatural' because they are 'abhorred' – they are, in fact, very natural, as Edmund knows – and, like Lear, he commits unnatural acts of his own, disinheriting Edgar and raising the hunt for him across the land. But all this material is subordinated to the Lear plot; and therefore we have to suppose that while Shakespeare is alive to the pain inherent in any patriarchal transition of power, he sees the pain of transition between fathers and sons as the lesser, if more obvious, case. The greater agony, beyond coherent expression – or the sufferer of it would not have to be a madman – is between fathers and daughters.

If we ask now what it is that makes this particular relationship so necessary that its disappointment reduces a king to madness, the answer may not only lie in Lear's hope of 'kind nursery' in his old age, important though that is. The imagery used to describe fathers and daughters suggests that they are one organism, bonded at the centre, in a way no father could suppose himself to be bonded with his sons. 'Filial ingratitude', cries Lear on the heath, between rage and tears. 'Is it not as this mouth should tear this hand / For lifting food to't?' (3.4.14–16). To him, Goneril and Regan are fangs rending the nurturing hand of their own organism: that is the measure of their unnaturalness. And similarly, in Albany's comparison of Goneril to a withered branch, the presumption is that the branches of a tree share its roots, and the same sap courses through their veins; though, if we probe the metaphor in a realistic spirit, we are bound to notice that most trees reproduce through seeds, and saplings may well quarrel with the parent tree for access to the light.

The last time we met this assumption of the organic unity of fathers and daughters was in *Oedipus at Colonus*, where Oedipus was shown leaning on his daughters as if they were his own legs and arms, and taking a melancholy satisfaction in the fact that no man would ever love them more than he had. The parallel may alert us to the peculiarity of the emotional subtext in both plays: in *Oedipus at Colonus* the reward of incestuous fatherhood is total care from daughters (though not from sons, of course, who are excoriated for their failure to 'nurse'). And in *King Lear*, the attempt of Cordelia to define a filial limit and claim a sexual destiny of her own, triggers such frenzied disappointment in her father that she must devote the rest of her life to making amends. Meanwhile, the sisters who took their sexual freedom without a backward glance die from excess of it.

We need to suppose some such underground presumption, at least, to explain the viciousness with which Lear curses his daughters for disappointing him. It feels very like the ferocity with which Oedipus curses his sons, willing them (successfully) to kill one another over their inheritance. Oedipus does not curse his daughters, of course; they do not have a wish that is not also his. Thanks to their incestuous origin their unity with him is perfect: they are, literally, branches of the same tree. But as Lear's daughters one by one display their distinctness from him, he strikes out at them with curses of quite startling savagery. With Cordelia he disclaims 'paternal care, / Propinquity, and property of blood' and makes a 'stranger' of her 'for ever' (1.1.113–16). Henceforth she is nothing to him. With Goneril he calls on the goddess Nature to 'convey sterility' into her womb: 'Dry up in her the organs of increase, / And from her derogate body never spring / A babe to honour her' (1.4.254–60). He would 'strike her young bones ... with lameness', blind her with 'nimble lightnings' and 'infect her beauty' with blisters (2.2.336–41). And when Regan joins forces with her, the weakness of his power to hurt them is no clearer than his titanic will to do so:

> No, you unnatural hags,
> I will have such revenges on you both
> That all the world shall – I will do such things –
> What they are, yet I know not; but they shall be
> The terrors of the earth. (2.2.452–6)

He begs the gods not to 'fool' him into bearing his maltreatment 'tamely': but there is no danger of his doing so. Insofar as his paternal curse remains a weapon, he uses it without scruple.

Another way of describing the underlying distortion of the plot would be to say that it makes an enemy of 'Nature'. It struggles to represent natural processes as unnatural – the freeing of daughters from the arms of their fathers, the need of sons to succeed to their patrimony – and generates enormous pathos in doing so, for the play also admits that the struggle is futile. Perhaps this analysis will seem unpleasantly close to Goneril's; but the case for saying that 'Nature' is the play's antagonist is supported by Edmund's invocation of her in his notorious soliloquy:

> Thou, nature, art my goddess. To thy law
> My services are bound. Wherefore should I
> Stand in the plague of custom and permit

> The curiosity of nations to deprive me
> For that I am some twelve or fourteen moonshines
> Lag of a brother? Why 'bastard'? Wherefore 'base',
> When my dimensions are as well compact,
> My mind as generous, and my shape as true,
> As honest madam's issue? Why brand they us
> With 'base', with 'baseness, bastardy – base, base' – [...]
> Well, my legitimate, if this letter speed
> And my invention thrive, Edmond the base
> Shall to[p] th' legitimate. I grow, I prosper.
> Now gods, stand up for bastards! (1.2.1–10, 19–22)

The moment we hear Edmund say that 'Nature' is his goddess, we know that he is irredeemably evil; and while we follow the logic of his argument against the law that bastardizes him with a certain exhilaration, we also feel that nothing he says can be right. It is a similar mixture of emotions to that generated by Machiavelli's ghost in *The Jew of Malta* ('admir'd I am of those that hate me most'). There is undoubtedly something alluring about Edmund's freedom of analysis, but in terms of the play, the level of realism at which he is working is self-evidently 'wicked'.

The oddity of associating an appeal to 'Nature' with evil in this way can best be felt by invoking a Greek comparison. If Hippolytus or Pentheus declared as firmly as Edmund that 'Thou, Nature, art my goddess' from their first entry, we would know that their tragedies could be averted. The supremacy of nature is exactly what their respective plays have to teach them: it is only because they are so resistant to the admission that they are torn apart so brutally at the end. The worship of nature in that context is a guarantee of sanity – not because Aphrodite and Dionysus are good, and deserving of worship, but because they they express the facts of nature as they are: that what lives, dies, and the only immortality available is by joining in sexual union with another.

But when Edmund says that 'Nature' is his goddess, we understand something else: that he is going to emulate nature in her lack of morality, and expose, or exploit, all the civilized structures that have been built to disguise her. Law will mean nothing to him, nor *pietas* towards old men; the only limits he acknowledges will be pragmatic – 'All with me's meet that I can fashion fit' (1.2.173). Nature here means, not the facts as they are, but unredeemed animality; and in the nihilistic view of the Lear plot, there is nothing to stop Edmund succeeding. He, Goneril and Regan between them reduce the kingdom to a 'state of nature', where humanity 'preys' on itself 'like monsters of the deep', as Albany says in the Quarto *History* (scene 16.48–9). Even Cordelia cannot restore the human order for long. She can comfort Lear, and even draw to herself Edmund's dying impulse to do 'some good . . . Despite of [his] own nature' (5.3.218–19) – but, in the bitterest dramatic irony of the play, the last-moment reprieve does not save her from being hanged.

What Shakespeare seems to be portraying is a world in which there is no possible accommodation with the facts of nature, but only an exhausted submission to them. And though this approach brings fathomless pathos in its train, and draws its audience deeper into the experience of suffering than any other of the tragedies, we have to doubt whether this is a plot that ends in wisdom, or simply an intense experience of empathy. We began by saying that Shakespeare takes the astonishing risk of unmasking patriarchy in this play; but what is also clear is that he is horrified by the weakness he uncovers. After Act I, the truth tellers among his characters are either vicious, or mad: and when Lear comes as close as he can to recognition of what he has done, it is not only Cordelia, but the play, that wraps him in loving sympathy:

> Lear   Be your tears wet? Yes, faith. I pray, weep not.
> If you have poison for me, I will drink it.
> I know you do not love me; for your sisters
> Have, as I do remember, done me wrong.
> You have some cause, they have not.
> Cor.   No cause, no cause. (4.6.64–9)

It is not true, but no one would want her to say anything else.

Perhaps the best indication of how reluctantly Shakespeare handles his material is his creation of Kent, the loyal follower who cannot be persuaded to leave his master. This gruff voice represents everything that was valuable in the system Edmund is demolishing. He is initially the one truth teller who is neither bad nor out of his wits; and he makes clear his definition of true loyalty in intervening with Lear as he turns against Cordelia: 'be Kent unmannerly / When Lear is mad' (1.1.145–6). But when Lear begins to suffer the consequences of his folly, Kent loyally returns, and from being the truth teller, becomes, like Cordelia, a loving liar – beginning with his solicitation to enter Lear's retinue:

> Lear   What wouldst thou?
> Kent   Service.
> Lear   Who wouldst thou serve?
> Kent   You.
> Lear   Dost thou know me, fellow?
> Kent   No, sir, but you have that in your countenance which I would fain
> call master.
> Lear   What's that?
> Kent   Authority. (1.4.22–30)

It cannot be true: regal authority is just what he has given away, and human authority has slipped through his hands like water since he cast off Cordelia. But that is all the more reason for Kent to accord it to him; and certainly, unless he does, Kent cannot enter into the relation he is so determinedly seeking, 'Service'. The servantless master and the masterless servant come together here like two magnetic poles, creating a world of feudal relatedness, in spite of the prevailing 'state of nature'. And since Kent has no other function in the play – for the space he occupies, he is quite uncharacterized – we must deduce that his role in the drama is as a chivalric bandage for Lear's sufferings. He cannot make a difference to the outcome, but he can be lovingly present till the end; where, to perfect his 'service', he can die: 'I have a journey, sir, shortly to go; / My master calls me; I must not say no' (5.3.297–8).

The collapse of poetic justice in this play, the way Shakespeare deliberately alters his sources so that Kent's honest service and Cordelia's selfless devotion make no difference to the outcome, has often been taken as a measure of the play's unsparing honesty. Shakespeare, it is felt, looks deeper and more steadily into the abyss here than anywhere else. But if it is true that the play takes nature as its antagonist, and recoils from the facts of life as if they should (somehow) be kinder – especially to fathers – our account of it would have to be more reserved. We would have to ask how much unresolved ambivalence lies in the Fool's jokes about making daughters into mothers, when Lear was indeed asking Cordelia for 'kind nursery'. And we might have to wonder why the play resists making a connection between Goneril's true perception that 'old fools are babes again', and Lear's titanic tantrums, in which he destroys what he has most need of. In the context of so much emotion, so unclearly focused, the collapse of poetic justice might seem less courageous than passionate – a passing on to the audience of Lear's own madness. Not only he, but we are forced to question the possibility of any justice, anywhere. The world becomes as disordered as the play; the view is admittedly a madman's, but no voice is heard contradicting:

> Thou hast seen a farmer's dog bark at a beggar? . . . An the creature
> run from the cur, there thou mightst behold the great image of
> authority. A dog's obeyed in office.
> Thou rascal beadle, hold thy bloody hand.
> Why dost thou lash that whore? Strip thy own back.
> Thou hotly lusts to use her in that kind
> For which thou whip'st her. The usurer hangs the cozener.
> Through tattered clothes great vices do appear;
> Robes and furred gowns hide all. Plate sin with gold,
> And the strong lance of justice hurtless breaks;
> Arm it in rags, a pygmy's straw does pierce it.
> None does offend, none, I say, none. (4.5.150–64)

'Reason in madness!' comments Edgar (171), as Lear pulls down the whole edifice of law by denying its all-important distinctions, between thoughts and deeds, and between the man and his office. 'None does offend' is his verdict, since all men are criminals of one kind or another, lust is universal, and furred gowns hide what tatters make plain.

But the law is a human construct, as the whole tradition of tragic plays affirms, and in its application, inevitably vulnerable to human weakness. It is built and rebuilt in every generation, however, because without it, it is still harder to be truly human; and Shakespeare's willingness to let a madman have the last word on the topic in this play may be a measure of the play's limitations as much as its insight.

Macbeth (*c.*1606)

We noted that the sequence *Hamlet, Othello, Lear*, takes Shakespeare through the key roles a man might play in a lifetime: son, lover and father. Looking at them through classical spectacles, we would have to call them partial, and therefore not quite the stuff of which classical drama is made. Although Greek heroes are sons, lovers and fathers, this is not all they are; but Shakespeare isolates these roles for scrutiny, and gives them a tragic importance in and of themselves. And they are parallelled by three female roles, the mother (Gertrude), beloved (Desdemona) and daughter (Cordelia, Goneril, Regan), which expose more clearly some of the Renaissance habits of mind Shakespeare cannot thus far shake off, and which give the plays their peculiar bias. Chief of these is the readiness to think of women as a different species, either much better, or much worse than men (or, centaur-like, better *and* worse) – but in any case too close to the radioactive centre of the plays to be calmly held in the same frame. And the tormenting issue that women are associated with is the indivisibility of sex and death: the terrible knowledge, as graffiti artists still phrase it, that 'life is a sexually transmitted disease'. Because these plays are in thrall to the terror they dramatize, they break off their analysis at the crucial moment, and do not analyse women's problems from their own point of view at all.

But one glance at *Macbeth* reassures us that this play is different. This hero is classically free-standing: he is mature, at the height of his physical and mental powers, and able to make and stand by his own decisions. Pathos, we sense, will not be a key effect in this play. Moreover, Macbeth belongs to that very species that has been hovering on the edge of Shakespeare's consciousness for so long, the Machiavel. The fact that the Machiavel has been brought into the centre of the play, and has been given imagination, ambition and dread to go with his cruelty and alienation, speaks volumes for Shakespeare's new conception. Indeed, Macbeth is not a Machiavel at all, if that means a character in whom the Renaissance expresses its horror of individuation, as we speculated above. Rather, he is Shakespeare's full portrait of what it might mean to be modern, and to break all the bonds of piety at a stroke.

For the first time, Shakespeare follows through the consequences of his own knowledge that a king, the 'Lord's anointed temple', is from another perspective only an old man with too much blood in him. Duncan may be wholly admirable of his kind; but there is nothing to stop him being murdered by a man who thinks he can live without bonds, if the opportunity arises. What is impressively calm in this conception is that, although punishment is certain, it is not overstated (as in the demons that carry Faustus off, or the fairytale combat with Edgar that ends Edmund's career). Shakespeare shows it to be nothing supernatural, but simply the consequences of Macbeth's own act. He gets what he wanted, and it is dust and ashes. And for good measure, Shakespeare will add a Machiavellian wife, not viewed (like Goneril and Regan) with the hostility that caricatures, but with the insight that sees how women make their decisions and live with them, just as men do.

The way the play is framed, then, already suggests that Shakespeare has reached a level of clarity he could not find before; and the pay-off is in the classical brevity and precision of the play as a whole (*Hamlet* and *Othello* are both half as long again). Readers who may still be resisting the analogy between classical and Renaissance drama, and who are unconvinced by my earlier promise to show Shakespeare gradually uncovering the same tragic subject we began with, may allow at least that this play has a number of familiar elements.

For instance, we are back in a world of oracles, though now given by witches rather than Apollo; and as with Oedipus, the drama turns on the misinterpretation of those oracles, even though they are true. Macbeth commits a classical *hamartia*, an intellectual mistake, as much as a Christian sin: he thinks he can help the oracles fulfil themselves by committing a crime, and that somehow the crime will be annulled by its alliance with Destiny. In terms of dramatic technique, Shakespeare gives us witches as supernatural agents who, like the Greek gods, suggest something about the inner life of the protagonist without taking over responsibility for it: they do not interfere with his autonomy, but they add greatly to the implications of what he does. And much of the play's imagery has a classical boldness, too: we hear continually of 'blood', 'milk' and 'gall', of breasts and daggers, sleep and dreams. Duncan's famous image for kingly responsibility, 'planting' ('I have begun to plant thee, and will labour / To make thee full of growing' 1.4.28–9) takes us all the way back to *Oedipus at Colonus*, where Oedipus reminded his sons of what they owed him for 'planting' them; and Macbeth's false security comes from an oracle that he has nothing to fear until 'planted' trees uproot themselves.

Whatever explanation we find for these parallels, it would be hard to deny that Shakespeare's imagination is working in the same area as his Athenian predecessors. He is trying to grasp how mankind fits into nature as a whole, and how far human bonds create a reality of their own. And the most striking parallel of all is the way he resolves his play with a stroke of 'unnaturalness' that takes us all the way back to the *Oresteia*. Macduff is invulnerable because he is 'not of woman born'. Macbeth can only be killed, and Scotland can only be restored to health, by a man who has bypassed birth, like the goddess Athena.

Perhaps the shortest way of suggesting the classical directness of this play, however, is to feel the force of its opening contrast between Duncan and Macbeth

– the one an old king, the other a warrior. A tremendous battle is in train, but Duncan does not fight; his part is to receive news, distribute care ('Go get him surgeons', 1.2.44) and express happy admiration for the feats being done in his name. The news he hears is that the hero who is winning the battle for him is Macbeth, who has just 'carved out his passage' to the chief rebel,

> Till he fac'd the slave,
> Which ne'er shook hands nor bade farewell to him
> Till he unseamed him from the nave to th' chops,
> And fixed his head upon our battlements. (1.2.20–3)

Duncan's heartfelt admiration overflows: 'O valiant cousin, worthy gentleman!' (24) and he lays the kingly plan to reward Macbeth with the title of Thane of Cawdor.

Already the play is outlining a problem even more radical than the crisis of patriarchy that opens *Lear*: the vulnerability of a king who is not strong, commanding a hero who is supremely so. (The sensitivity of this problem in Greek literature is evidenced by the collision between Achilles and Agamemnon in *Iliad I*. Agamemnon is the king, but Achilles is 'kingliest' in the primary sense of the 'strongest': a king among men, who can derail the whole campaign if he chooses.) Even Duncan's free and loving admiration of Macbeth is really testimony to the same thing – for the whole code of feudal mutuality, reward exchanged for protection, is built over the disobliging fact that without such a code, the strongest will always have power over the weak. Duncan's vocabulary of 'valour' and 'worthy gentleman' is in vulnerable contrast to the gross language of battle, which knows what happens when knife meets flesh. Bodies *can* be 'unseamed . . . from the nave to th' chops', and the fact that this normally only happens in a rebellion does not quite remove the shock of the reminder.

The way the plot then brings Duncan to stay under Macbeth's own roof gives another classical turn to the screw, for Macbeth becomes the host of this undefended piece of virtue:

> He's here in double trust:
> First, as I am his kinsman and his subject,
> Strong both against the deed; then, as his host,
> Who should against his murderer shut the door,
> Not bear the knife myself. (1.7.12–16)

The role of the host is to bar the door against harm to his guest, or there can be no social links at all, however fragile, in this primitive state of Scotland. By focusing on the sacredness of the trust invested in the host, Shakespeare takes his play into the area of difficulty so keenly felt in the *Oresteia*. It was a breach of hospitality that set going the Trojan War; and Zeus, we are told throughout the trilogy, is the great defender of the code between host and guest. The underlying reason seems to be the inherent vulnerability of all codes and promises: precisely because codes are only agreements, and promises are only breath, they need the greatest of all gods to protect them. They belong to the sphere we called masculine and transcendent, rather than the female realm of matter. There is no 'collateral' in nature for the mutual honour and forbearance of guest and host; just the opposite. Nature would prompt a shameless use of advantage, since the guest arrives alone, and disarms himself to sleep. But in every primitive society (indeed, most particularly in primitive societies), the cultural code insists on the guest's inviolability under a hospitable roof – or no man would be able to travel out of reach of his genetic security, his own clan or tribe. Macbeth knows as well as anyone what is meant by 'trust', and what bonds of sanctity bind him to Duncan, as kinsman, subject and host. But as Machiavel, he asks himself the terrifyingly modern question that the real Machiavelli asked: what collateral is there for these bonds? If force intervenes, what can prevent it?

We can see that Shakespeare wanted to pose this question in the plainest possible way from his avoidance of the opening his source in Holinshed gave him to contrast Duncan's laxness with Macbeth's severity. (Holinshed actually says that the people would have preferred a ruler halfway between them both).⁶ Shakespeare gives no hint that Duncan's way of ruling brought inevitable problems, and that it fell to Macbeth to solve them; he represents Duncan as irreproachable, so that Macbeth's crime can be of the purest kind, brought about simply by its possibility. Macbeth's own meditation on what his crime means becomes Shakespeare's directest attempt to state the reality we saw Marlowe flirting with in his *Jew of Malta* prologue: 'Might first made kings, and laws were then most sure / When, like the Draco's, they were writ in blood' (20–1). Macbeth is poised to show, like Machiavelli's ghost, that 'religion [is] but a childish toy' and it is mere 'foolery' to say that 'Birds of the air will tell of murders past' (14, 16).

But if this were all, Macbeth would only be a fuller portrait of Edmund, who was quite as successfully emancipated from bonds and sanctities. What makes this portrait more interesting, so centrally human, is that Macbeth testifies at every stage to the psychological experiment he is undergoing. He is fully equipped to comment on it, as critics have always noted: unlike his two-dimensional predecessors, for whom evil was a kind of frivolity, he uproots himself from the nexus of sanctities he lives in almost in agony, as a duty. His statement of why he should *not* do the deed, in the teeth of Lady Macbeth's taunts, could hardly be improved upon:

> *Macb.* We will proceed no further in this business.
> He hath honoured me of late, and I have bought

---

⁶ 'The beginning of Duncans reigne was verie quiet and peaceable . . . but after it was perceiued how negligent he was in punishing offendors, manie misruled persons took occasion thereof to trouble the peace and quiet state of the common-wealth, by seditious commotions.' *Chronicles of Scotland*, in *Macbeth*, ed. K. Muir (London and New York: Methuen, 1962, repr. 1986), p. 167.

Golden opinions from all sorts of people,
Which would be worn now in their newest gloss,
Not cast aside so soon.

Lady M.   Was the hope drunk
Wherein you dressed yourself? Hath it slept since?
And wakes it now to look so green and pale
At what it did so freely? From this time
Such I account thy love. Art thou afeard
To be the same in thine own act and valour
As thou art in desire? Wouldst thou have that
Which thou esteem'st the ornament of life,
And live a coward in thine own esteem,
Letting 'I dare not' wait upon 'I would',
Like the poor cat i'th' adage?

Macb.   Prithee, peace.
I dare do all that may become a man;
Who dares do more is none. (1.7.31–47)

Macbeth is pausing at the threshold of humanity. Beyond it, as he rightly says, is something else, for which Lady Macbeth gives him the name – 'What beast was't then?' He is as fortunate at this moment as he will ever be, and he knows what the elements of his happiness are: new 'honours' from Duncan, 'golden opinions' from 'all sorts of people' and the novel experience of adjusting to his elevated status, like bright new clothes 'which would be worn now in their newest gloss, / Not cast aside so soon.' This is the classic language of heroic *pietas*, by which the hero identifies with his public name: he has won it by valour, and the society he protected with his strong right arm has gratefully accorded it him.

The great taboo in this exchange is, of course, to snatch a status beyond what has been accorded, by force. This is why heroic literature is so rich in expressions of limit: for all warriors have a Tamburlaine-like appetite for the infinite, and unless they repeat to themselves very often 'who dares do more is none', they are very likely to trespass over the line that divides the strongest from the most powerful, the warrior from the king. (Banquo is there in the plot to show us a truer hero observing the line Macbeth crosses: 'So I lose none / In seeking to augment it' is his rebuff to an offer of 'honour' that he finds equivocal, 2.1.25–6.) But if this is the classic definition of the way in which a man becomes a beast, Shakespeare is also indebted in this portrait to his study of the Machiavel, with his notorious lack of 'integrity' (in the original sense of 'singleness' of self), and his unwillingness to be publicly known for what he is. Repeating 'who dares do more is none' will not be enough to save Macbeth, true as it is, and true as he knows it to be. He is already too self-conscious, too mentally mobile, to accept his definition of self from the public voice alone. Yesterday Macbeth was Thane of Glamis, today he is Thane of Cawdor; it is not a great leap to say that tomorrow he will be King – who, with the use of force, can coerce the public voice to agree with him.

While Duncan and Banquo both use the language of planting for the reciprocal bonds of love and service, Macbeth can only use the equivocal language of clothing, as if what is organic for them is only a matter of role-playing to him. 'Why do you dress me / In borrowed robes?' is his response to his first elevation, between horror and excitement (1.3.106–7). Lady Macbeth uses the same metaphor for the mental leap that first took him towards the murder: 'Was the hope drunk / Wherein you dressed yourself?' Perhaps role-playing is too simple a term for the moral giddiness that seizes Macbeth when he thinks about the difference between clothes and the man within, between inner truth and outer. What in the two-dimensional Machiavel is hypocrisy ('I am not what I am'), in him is a kind of vertigo. He looks over the bulwark erected by the honour code – the code which does so much to make inner and outer man one, creating the vulnerable but admirable unities we call Othello or Duncan – and he sees the abyss beneath: words separated from things, appearances from reality, deeds without names and events without record. It is perhaps because this is so genuinely horrifying, such an absolute test of manhood, that he can be roused by Lady Macbeth's contempt:

> What beast was't then
> That made you break this enterprise to me?
> When you durst do it, then you were a man;
> And to be more than what you were, you would
> Be so much more the man. Nor time nor place
> Did then adhere, and yet you would make both.
> They have made themselves, and that their fitness now
> Does unmake you. (1.7.47–54)

Lady Macbeth would redefine what it means to be a man. It is not the creature of limits, who dares what it 'becomes' a man to dare, and no more: it is the creature who can do whatever it can imagine, because it knows the truth – that there are no other obstacles at all. This mental courage would be real manhood; and it is perhaps because Macbeth is so genuinely appalled by the abyss, that he cannot resist her logic.

His other problem, of course, is with her feminine contempt. Lady Macbeth cannot bear the absurdity by which Macbeth is 'unmade' by the very luck that 'makes' the occasion so perfect – and it goads her to use a weapon never yet employed in the tragedies, her power as a mother:

> I have given suck, and know
> How tender 'tis to love the babe that milks me.
> I would, while it was smiling in my face,
> Have plucked my nipple from his boneless gums,
> And dashed the brains out, had I so sworn
> As you have done to this. (54–9)

The ferocity of this depends on the beauty of the phrasing 'how *tender* 'tis to *love* the babe that *milks me*'. It is only by describing what would have been the most abominable violation of her woman's 'honour' as a mother, the most atrocious breach of trust, that Lady Macbeth can convey her revulsion at Macbeth's failure to live up to *his* honour – defined, as above, as undertaking the hardest thing he can imagine.[7] This savage reproach pushes him over the threshold. From seeing the essential problem as a moral one ('this act would make a man a beast'), he accedes to her view that it is merely logistical ('this act takes hardihood and an alibi').

Macbeth's scruples collapse into mere seasickness – 'If we should fail?' – for which she has the medicine, a plan to drug the chamberlains:

> *Lady M.*   When in swinish sleep
>   Their drenchèd natures lies as in a death,
>   What cannot you and I perform upon
>   Th'unguarded Duncan? What not put upon
>   His spongy officers, who shall bear the guilt
>   Of our great quell?
> *Macb.*   Bring forth men-children only,
>   For thy undaunted mettle should compose
>   Nothing but males. Will it not be received,
>   When we have marked with blood those sleepy two
>   Of his own chamber and used their very daggers,
>   That they have done't? (67–77)

Behind Lady Macbeth's ready plotting, her deliberate matter-of-factness, we glimpse Clytaemnestra, the rational plotter whose only irrationality was supposing that her great act of revenge would have no consequences. Lady Macbeth has the same ability as that self-appointed Fury (and the Furies themselves) to think of bodies as mere bodies, and spilt blood as mere gilding – provided, of course, that it is not the blood of anyone she is related to. (Her famous pun on 'gilding' the grooms with 'guilt' admirably conveys how portable she takes guilt to be.) And as she infuses Macbeth with the same conviction, he feels he has been made 'male' in a new sense, emancipated into a fearlessness that is superhuman: 'Bring forth men-children only, / For thy undaunted mettle should compose / Nothing but males.'

Shakespeare's careful delineation of the steps by which Macbeth lobotomizes his moral nature suggests how superficially the plot is shaped as a standard tragedy of ambition. Macbeth himself describes 'vaulting ambition' as an ineffectual 'spur' when it comes to the push (1.7.25–7). What he finds so hard to

---

[7]   It is striking that Shakespeare needed classical precedents to create Lady Macbeth, which he found via Seneca: 'Lady Macbeth is modelled partly on Clytaemnestra, but her invocation of evil spirits, her wish to be unsexed, and her pretended willingness to dash out the brains of her infant are clearly influenced by Seneca's portrait of Medea' (*Macbeth*, ed. Muir, p. xlii).

get over are the difficulties in his own mind: his horror of the crime itself, and his fear of the consequences. It is the clarity of this that makes the play so classical, its emphasis on what happens in the mind rather than the heart, and on error rather than sin. And this focus is not unrelated to Shakespeare's use of an oracle to set the plot in train – for an oracle undid Oedipus too, wisest of men, and nothing could be more tempting to human arrogance than seeming foreknowledge.

Macbeth's problem again is not so much with the witches, who tell him the truth, but with his own mind. The contrast is enforced by the presence of Banquo, whose mind works quite differently:

First Witch	All hail, Macbeth! Hail to thee, Thane of Glamis.
Second Witch	All hail, Macbeth! Hail to thee, Thane of Cawdor.
Third Witch	All hail, Macbeth, that shalt be king hereafter!
Banq.	Good sir, why do you start, and seem to fear
	Things that do sound so fair? (*To the Witches*) I'th'name of truth,
	Are ye fantastical or that indeed
	Which outwardly ye show? My noble partner
	You greet with present grace and great prediction
	Of noble having and of royal hope,
	That he seems rapt withal. To me you speak not.
	If you can look into the seeds of time
	And say which grain will grow and which will not,
	Speak then to me, who neither beg nor fear
	Your favours nor your hate.
First Witch	Hail!
Second Witch	Hail!
Third Witch	Hail!
First Witch	Lesser than Macbeth, and greater.
Second Witch	Not so happy, yet much happier.
Third Witch	Thou shalt get kings, though thou be none.
	So all hail, Macbeth and Banquo! (1.3.46–66)

Macbeth 'starts' and seems to 'fear' the thrilling news, then falls 'rapt', too caught up in his own mental activity to speak. Banquo, by contrast, addresses the witches with precaution: he 'neither begs nor fears' their 'favour' or their 'hate'. (That is, he wants nothing specific from them, and reserves the right to think them malicious.) From one point of view, Macbeth's guilty 'start' only tells us that this prophecy chimes with a criminal thought he has already had, while Banquo's detachment shows how innocent he truly is. But if we probe deeper into the nature of the trap set by oracles, we can see a more general implication for human minds everywhere: even when the mind is given access to the truth, its understanding of it depends entirely on the context the mind itself supplies.

That is why Banquo is so truly wise to say that he does not care. If he does not care, he will not overinterpret what the witches say. He will allow them to 'look into the seeds of time / And say which grain will grow and which will not';

he understands that the harvest of a seed is the result of a natural process with which he has nothing to do. But Macbeth's mind supplies a context so coercive that the witches' truth operates as a kind of lie. It is true that he will be 'king hereafter'; but it is only in Macbeth's mind that that promise seems glorious, an assurance that he will be king in the same sense Duncan is king. The witches cannot be expected to add, 'the title will hang loose about you, like a giant's robe upon a dwarfish thief'; they do, however, say that Banquo will be 'lesser than Macbeth, and greater . . . not so happy, yet much happier.' But since Macbeth cannot imagine anything greater or happier than a king, he leaves this end of the prophecy uninterpreted.

As we watch Macbeth's mind coercing the truth into gratifying shapes and jumping unhindered from the present to the future, we can appreciate the full meaning of the Aristotelian term *hamartia* (often mistranslated as 'tragic flaw'). *Hamartanein* is a metaphor derived from archery, 'to err, to miss one's mark' – to aim for the target, but to misjudge it a little to one side or the other. Thus, tragic error in the Greek sense is endemic to the human mind in the act of thinking, as it aims for the appropriate goal but slightly misjudges its whereabouts. This is the sense in which Oedipus too commits *hamartia*: he hears a prophecy about the terrible things he will do to his parents, and runs directly away from them. But since he does not know who his parents are, or where they are living, he fulfils the prophecy with every step he takes.

In the same way, Macbeth creates his destiny by interpreting a truth he cannot leave alone – though he does recognize that the truth should need no assistance from him: 'If chance will have me king, why, chance may crown me, / Without my stir' (1.3.142–3). But thinking is a form of creativity that transports him, almost against his will, into the future:

> This supernatural soliciting
> Cannot be ill, cannot be good. If ill,
> Why hath it given me earnest of success
> Commencing in a truth? I am Thane of Cawdor.
> If good, why do I yield to that suggestion
> Whose horrid image doth unfix my hair
> And make my seated heart knock at my ribs
> Against the use of nature? Present fears
> Are less than horrible imaginings.
> My thought, whose murder yet is but fantastical,
> Shakes so my single state of man that function
> Is smother'd in surmise, and nothing is
> But what is not. (1.3.129–41)

Macbeth's hair is 'unfixed' and his 'seated' heart is 'knocking' because of the 'fantastical' murder in his mind; they are a foretaste of the terrible displacement he will experience after the murder when his 'single state of man' is divided against itself for good. Although what Macbeth is imagining is monstrous,

Shakespeare preserves our sympathy for him by suggesting he is in some way also a victim – of his own creative brain, which makes what does not yet exist so palpable to him. 'Present fears / Are less than horrible imaginings': Macbeth is steeled to the fears of the battlefield, but these terrors touch him in another place. Seized by his ghastly conception, he is immobilized ('function is smothered in surmise'); the future has displaced the present, and 'nothing is / But what is not.'

With Macbeth, Shakespeare seems to risk an inwardness, and even an identification with the Machiavel, that he did not attempt with Edmund in *Lear*. If the Machiavel has too much mental mobility, it does not only lead to crimes against others (though it does that too), but to suffering for himself. He faces a challenge that other characters in their 'single state of man' will never know: the endless negotiation between the real, and his mental conception of it. Macbeth is tempted by something that cannot tempt Banquo: a supernatural 'soliciting' of his imagination into hyperactivity, an irresistible desire to force the harvest of the 'seeds of time'. If they were growing anyway, in what sense is it a crime? Macbeth offers to force the future into the here-and-now, and his wife catches the impulse from him too. As she phrases it, when he reappears at his castle, 'Thy letters have transported me beyond / This ignorant present, and I feel now / The future in the instant' (1.5.55–7).

Because Machiavels are so mentally conscious, so aware of the power of consciousness to arrange and project reality, Macbeth and his wife both become stage managers in their plotting. It is only a matter of rearranging appearances ('dressing' the chamberlains in blood to evince their guilt, putting their daggers in place like props) and the future can be born. There is, of course, a black chasm to cross between: but they ask the night to supply a covering darkness, like the dimming of a stage between two scenes, when the knife will not see 'the wound it makes, / Nor heaven peep through the blanket of the dark / To cry, "Hold, hold!"' (1.5.51–3).

The speech Macbeth makes as he nerves himself to approach Duncan's chamber is borrowed from the worst Revenge tradition. But because we have been allowed so deep into his mental life we understand how coercive a 'screwing' of courage to the 'sticking-place' it takes to sound so dramatically evil. We recognize the inner dislocation it takes to make a man such an actor, even to his own eyes:

> Now o'er the one half-world
> Nature seems dead, and wicked dreams abuse
> The curtained sleep. Witchcraft celebrates
> Pale Hecate's offerings, and withered murder,
> Alarumed by his sentinel the wolf,
> Whose howl's his watch, thus with his stealthy pace,
> With Tarquin's ravishing strides, towards his design
> Moves like a ghost. Thou sure and firm-set earth,
> Hear not my steps which way they walk, for fear
> Thy very stones prate of my whereabout,

> And take the present horror from the time,
> Which now suits with it. Whiles I threat, he lives.
> Words to the heat of deeds too cold breath gives.
> *A bell rings*
> I go, and it is done. The bell invites me.
> Hear it not, Duncan; for it is a knell
> That summons thee to heaven or to hell. *Exit* (2.1.49–64)

Macbeth asks the earth not to hear his steps, not only to save him from discovery, but because it would interfere with the horror of the atmosphere 'which now suits with it'. This is the height of *grand guignol*, but Shakespeare preserves the true horror of the situation in the teeth of Macbeth's inauthenticity – because he shows the inauthenticity itself to be so ghastly. He has at last found the right dramatic context for the laboured self-consciousness of the two-dimensional Machiavel, which allows us to see how inner dislocation opens the gates to unnatural experiments. And one of the first symptoms is the arrogance that sees reality as something that can be stage-managed, and the self as an actor.

Lady Macbeth works as hard as her husband to live at this inauthentic level of detachment – 'The sleeping, and the dead / Are but as pictures' she says, when it is a matter of going back to the corpse – but Shakespeare shows with wonderful economy what fear still underlies this effort. She excuses herself: 'Had he not resembled / My father as he slept, I had done't' (2.2.12–13). Not even she, having 'stop[ped] up th'access and passage to remorse', could sustain the idea that Duncan was merely a superfluous actor in their drama when she saw him. Asleep, he was an old man like her father; and not even a Fury could raise her hand against the origin of her own life. When Macbeth returns with the simple statement that is classic in its self-definition, 'I have done the deed' (14), their staccato exchanges suggest a new experience of selfhood that they had not foreseen: selfhood dispersed, their senses untrustworthy, and fear running riot:

> *Macb.*   I have done the deed. Didst thou not hear a noise?
> *Lady M.* I heard the owl scream and the crickets cry.
>   Did you not speak?
> *Macb.*   When?
> *Lady M.*   Now.
> *Macb.*   As I descended?
> *Lady M.* Ay.
> *Macb.*   Hark! (2.2.14–17)

Above all, Macbeth has had his first taste of perfect alienation, in his inability to say 'Amen' to the prayer he heard the sons saying in their bedroom. He begins to recognize what else he murdered when he murdered Duncan:

> *Macb.*   Methought I heard a voice cry 'Sleep no more,
>   Macbeth does murder sleep' – the innocent sleep,

> Sleep that knits up the ravelled sleave of care,
> The death of each day's life, sore labour's bath,
> Balm of hurt minds, great nature's second course,
> Chief nourisher in life's feast –

Lady M.   What do you mean?
Macb.   Still it cried 'Sleep no more' to all the house,
         'Glamis hath murdered sleep, and therefore Cawdor
         Shall sleep no more, Macbeth shall sleep no more.' (2.2.33–41)

The powerful obliquity of a speech about sleep, not murder, allows Shakespeare to tell us truths about the consequences of evil we never learnt from Edmund, Goneril or Regan. The murderer who so dramatically uproots another life from its security, sleeping under a kinsman's hospitable roof, by the same act uproots his own. From this moment on, whoever else gets access to this glorious luxury, 'Macbeth shall sleep no more' – and what a luxury it is he only now understands, as we see from his torrent of imagery. But Macbeth will never sleep again, because he knows there are no sanctities on earth sufficiently powerful to restrain the man who wills himself to override them. And by what possible right would he, the outrager of the deepest sanctities, invoke any?

It is because Shakespeare pitches his account of evil at this level of psychological realism that he avoids anything strained in the manner of Macbeth's punishment. We watch instead Macbeth's increasingly frantic search for security ('To be thus is nothing / But to be safely thus') and the increasingly brutal murders he commits to assure it ('Our fears in Banquo / Stick deep', 3.1.49–51). We see him goaded from fear to fear ('O, full of scorpions is my mind, dear wife!' 3.2.37) and feeling even Duncan to be an object of envy:

> Better be with the dead,
> Whom we, to gain our peace have sent to peace,
> Than on the torture of the mind to lie
> In restless ecstasy. (21–4)

There could be no more fitting punishment for someone whose imagination defied reality than for him to suffer the riposte of the real world, as it refuses to respond to his stage-management any longer. Now his creative power of imagination becomes pure torment, as he finds himself prey to arrant superstition, and 'cabined, cribbed, confined, bound in / To saucy doubts and fears' (3.4.23–4). This is indeed what it is to have murdered security.

But Shakespeare suggests that he has murdered something else with Duncan, the connection between planting and harvest, and his own place in life's process. The deepest source of his torment becomes the evidence all around him that the process goes on, but only for others. Increasingly, the world is full of children – Malcolm, Donalbain, Fleance, Macduff's 'pretty chickens' – and though he lops off as many heads as he can reach, they spring up anew. The witches know that the perfect way to torture him is to show him Banquo's regal progeny 'stretch[ing] out to th' crack of doom' (4.1.133). Although he wears the crown and holds the sceptre now, the crown is 'fruitless' and the sceptre 'barren' to him. Their meaning should have derived from the way they were gained, and the way they could be passed on. But having been savagely stolen from Duncan, they will only briefly be held in Macbeth's grip, 'thence to be wrenched with an unlineal hand, / No son of [his] succeeding' (3.1.64–5). They have become mere baubles, a mockery of what he promised himself.

Shakespeare's effortless invocation of infertility here as Macbeth's profoundest punishment shows how far we are in this play from the nexus of terrors that so complicated the previous tragedies. There is no sexual revulsion in this play, no quarrel with nature; the interrelation of sexuality, generation and death is taken for granted, and it is shown as sufficient punishment for Macbeth's crime that nature and he can have nothing more to do with one another. 'He has no children', as Macduff piercingly observes; and when he has killed as many as he can, he will still not have any.

Shakespeare also suggests the underlying connection between Macbeth's sterility and his relation to time. He has always been hyperactive, forcing the future into the present, and attempting to 'trammel up the consequences' in the here-and-now. But in Act V he pays the full price of his coerciveness: the flow of time has collapsed into a staccato sequence of days, with no meaningful connection between them:

> Tomorrow, and tomorrow, and tomorrow
> Creeps in this petty pace from day to day
> To the last syllable of recorded time. (5.5.18–20)

There is no more distinction between such days than between beads on a string – nor between the human beings treading their way towards the same unmeaning conclusion: 'All our yesterdays have lighted fools / The way to dusty death' (21–2). And the dislocated Machiavel who stage-managed reality still sees himself as an actor, but no longer as Tarquin: he is a 'poor player' in a brief drama that has failed to deliver a meaning:

> Life's but a walking shadow, a poor player
> That struts and frets his hour upon the stage,
> And then is heard no more. It is a tale
> Told by an idiot, full of sound and fury,
> Signifying nothing. (23–7)

The Machiavellian intellect has met its ultimate rebuff: in its attempt to coerce life's meaning, it has prevented it from meaning anything at all.

Shakespeare's new clarity in *Macbeth* shows not only here, in how closely he scrutinizes crime and its consequences, but also in the level of realism he brings to his 'good' characters. Lady Macduff, for instance, is not swathed in the usual protective veil of female victims: she blames her husband for abandoning her

('He loves us not, / He wants the natural touch') and her clever son is testing her out on the subject of remarriage, moments before they are slaughtered (4.2.8–9, 40). It is noticeable, too, how little time anyone spends deploring Duncan's death. It is almost as if it had been expected: Malcolm responds to 'Your royal father's murdered' with 'O, by whom?', and Donalbain knows what to do, even before Lady Macbeth has fainted: 'Let's away. / Our tears are not yet brewed' (2.3.100, 123). The play works at something like the level of realism established by Macbeth himself: it has no illusion that innocence is its own preservative, and it wastes no energy deepening the pathos of injustice. Perhaps the only respect in which it oversteps the border of realism is in its 'supernatural' events – Duncan's horses that eat one another, and the unwillingness of the sun to rise, the day after the murder.

Otherwise, even what is 'supernatural' in the story turns out to be essentially realistic. When we first hear the prophecies that 'none of woman born / Shall harm Macbeth', and 'Macbeth shall never vanquished be until / Great Birnam Wood to high Dunsinane Hill / Shall come against him' (4.1.96–7, 108–10), we seem to be at the furthest reaches of gothic fantasy. Yet there is a daylight explanation for both impossibilities: Birnam Wood can walk, if branches are carried by individual soldiers; and Macduff is not of woman born, if he was 'from his mother's womb / Untimely ripped' (5.10.15–16). Viewed one way, these oracles can be seen as Nature's riposte to Macbeth, most 'unnatural' of men. But we may also note that they are in their own way unnatural phenomena: like himself, they are created by severance – hewn-off branches, a caesarean delivery.

Unlike Aeschylus, Shakespeare cannot draw on the wonderful suggestiveness of Greek theology to convey how Athena's birth through Zeus' forehead could be a paradigm for her citizens, a harbinger of a new way of living in the world. Nonetheless, Macduff's special origin does seem to carry a certain meaning for the play. Macbeth can only be overcome by someone as 'unnaturally' detached as himself: vengeance does not fall to Malcolm, son of Duncan, but to a hero who was cut away from his mother with a knife. At a symbolic level, we may say, Shakespeare is describing another Orestes, whose selfhood is built on the sharp severance of the female tie. But how that severance may not lead to frailty, but rather to a fuller and more masculine maturity, is suggested by the way that Macduff has shown himself to be the tenderest of husbands and fathers in the play, in a scene which offers a direct comment on Macbeth's definition of what 'becomes' a man:

> *Ross*   Your castle is surprised, your wife and babes
> Savagely slaughtered. To relate the manner
> Were on the quarry of these murdered deer
> To add the death of you. [. . .]
> *Macd.*   He has no children. All my pretty ones?
> Did you say all? O hell-kite! All?
> What, all my pretty chickens and their dam

         At one fell swoop?
Malc.   Dispute it like a man.
Macd.   I shall do so,
         But I must also feel it as a man.
         I cannot but remember such things were
         That were most precious to me. (4.3.205–8, 217–25)

If we take the whole play as, in a sense, a meditation on what makes a true man, we have our answer here: a man is not defined by what he dares, but by what he feels. Macbeth achieves his terrible level of individuation by cutting his tie to life itself, and his final, desperate daring is only another kind of insensibility. Macduff's superiority to Macbeth lies in the fullness of his bonds to his 'pretty chickens and their dam' – and his courage in not repressing, but giving free passage to his agony, when he has failed to protect the things 'that were most precious to [him]'. Shakespeare has found his way back to the classic question, 'what is a hero?'; and his answer has an Aeschylean ring to it – a fully individual male, detached from his mother, and able to love, procreate and attach himself unreservedly to others.

Coriolanus (c.1608)

Coriolanus is the last of Shakespeare's tragedies, and it has always been felt to be somehow distinct from them – perhaps only a 'Roman Play' in disguise. No one disputes the play's maturity and vigour, but its hero, with his narrow and undemocratic virtues, has never struck the tragic note for most audiences as convincingly as Macbeth, Othello and Lear. But at the end of this long journey from classical drama through the Renaissance we can perhaps see the play's distinctiveness in a clearer light. Does *Coriolanus* show, as was promised at the beginning, that Shakespeare has found his way through trial and error back to the archetypal tragic subject? If we analyse the content of the plot in the light of our discussion, is it familiar?

One thing we may notice is that, as with Macbeth, the hero is a classically free-standing figure who chooses and errs of his own free will. Shakespeare is no longer making a tragic situation out of those roles we called partial – son, lover, or father. Coriolanus is all three of these, of course, and the roles will turn out to be central to him, but what we see at the start of the play is the heroic warrior on whom wars and treaties depend. Others may have more power, but he is the strongest of them all: 'king among men' again in the primary sense. Something else we may notice, in which the historical story allows Shakespeare to go beyond even what he found in *Macbeth*: Coriolanus is rooted in a political community. He is the community's finest son, the embodiment of their *virtus*, and at different times he carries the community to the height of its power, and offers to destroy it. He cannot be usefully understood without his whole context, that of early republican Rome (c.490); so in this story Shakespeare has found his way back to the Greek issue, admirably conveyed by the Greek Plutarch in his *Lives*, of how a man's selfhood relates to his way of acting in his *polis*.

With this new complexity comes the possiblity of a new conflict, too: between the hero's primary debt to his family, and his military obligations. The plot, which climaxes in an interview between the hero and his mother with an army waiting by, is squarely based on the competing claims of blood and honour, the same opposition on which so many Greek plots depend. And the hero is faced with the classic choice between trampling on his mother's womb, and preserving his honour as a soldier. Here Shakespeare restores to the centre of tragedy what we said was so noticeably missing, the issue of maternal power. By the same token, he throws new emphasis on the fact that Coriolanus is male, a man 'born of woman'. While the definition of a man was, we said, central also to the plot of *Macbeth*, the emphasis was not as openly as here on the predicament of masculinity. For Coriolanus is entirely the son of his mother: as Plutarch puts it, 'being left an orphan by his father, [he] was brought up under his mother a widowe'.[8] (Shakespeare never mentions his father at all.) And she has trained him up in Roman *virtus* to the *n*th degree – that is, in a cultural frame designed to produce not merely men, but heroes.

The importance of *virtus* to the play has always been noticed. Plutarch himself comments on it: 'Now in those dayes, valliantnes was honoured in Rome above all other virtues: which they called *Virtus*, by the name of vertue selfe, as including in that generall name, all other speciall virtues besides.'[9] And the same assumption lies behind Cominius' praise of Coriolanus in the Senate:

> . . . It is held
> That valour is the chiefest virtue, and
> Most dignifies the haver. If it be,
> The man I speak of cannot in the world
> Be singly counterpoised. (2.2.83–7)

If Coriolanus embodies this *virtus* that makes Romans so Roman, Shakespeare has the opportunity to examine the whole honour code on which heroic masculinity is built: the pursuit of a 'name' at whatever price in blood, the deliberate transcendence of pain and fear, and the severance of primary ties that leaves a hero perfectly individuated.[10] This emancipation is Coriolanus' last promise to himself:

---

[8]   *Plutarch's Lives of the Noble Grecians and Romans, Englished by Sir Thomas North*, ed. W.E. Henley (London, David Nutt, 1895), vol. 2, p. 144.

[9]   Ibid.

[10]   Hence the importance of the way he is seen earning the name Coriolanus and rejecting his share of spoils: as he says in Plutarch, 'For I never had other benefit nor recompence, of all the true and paynefull service I have done, and the extreme daungers I have bene in, but this only surname' (ibid., p. 170).

> I'll never
> Be such a gosling to obey instinct, but stand
> As if a man were author of himself
> And knew no other kin. (5.3.34–7)

The ambivalent feelings aroused by Shakespeare's analysis of *virtus*, which in a sense is the construction of masculinity itself, are suggested by the strongly discrepant critical responses to the play, from Shaw's 'greatest of Shakespear's comedies' to T.S. Eliot's 'most assured artistic success', and by the description of Coriolanus as anything from a 'boy of tears' to 'a human war-machine'.11

There is universal agreement, however, about the play's political acumen. It opens by showing us the Roman 'mob' (in the strict sense of its derivation, *mobile vulgus*, the giddy multitude) and two patrician ways of handling it: that of Menenius, and that of Coriolanus. Menenius offers them a mollifying relation of goodfellowship ('What work's, my countrymen, in hand?' 1.1.53). Having discovered what he well knows, that the mob blames the patricians for witholding corn from them at a time of famine, Menenius tells them a fable that sounds like a much better answer than it is. 'There was a time when all the body's members, / Rebelled against the belly', accusing it of being 'idle and inactive' while hoarding all the body's food. But the belly has a perfectly good explanation to give to his 'incorporate friends': that he only receives the food first to distribute it to them:

> 'I send it through the rivers of your blood
> Even to the court, the heart, to th' seat o'th' brain;
> And through the cranks and offices of man
> The strongest nerves and small inferior veins
> From me receive that natural competency
> Whereby they live. And though ... all at once cannot
> See what I do deliver out to each,
> Yet I can make my audit up that all
> From me do back receive the flour of all
> And leave me but the bran.' (1.1.133–8, 140–4)

Menenius triumphantly applies this to his audience: 'The senators of Rome are this good belly', the source of all 'public benefit[s]'; and they are 'the mutinous members' which do not understand the degree of their dependency (146–52).

There are two fallacies at work here. The more open one is that, for all his heartiness, Menenius does not actually see himself as part of one body with these 'mutinous members'. He feels the same alarmed contempt for the unruly plebs that the other patricians feel, and in his direct exchange with the First Citizen his

---

11 G.B. Shaw, in *Shakespeare: A Bibliographical Guide*, ed. Stanley Wells (Oxford: Clarendon Press, 1990), p. 297; T.S. Eliot, in *Coriolanus*, ed. G.R. Hibbard (Harmondsworth: Penguin, 1967), p. 50; I.R. Browning ('*Coriolanus*: Boy of Tears'), ibid., p. 51; D.A Traversi, in *Shakespeare: A Bibliographical Guide*, p. 297.

metaphor is quite different: 'Rome and her rats are at the point of battle' (159–60). The less obvious fallacy is that the analogy of the body politic to a body cannot be pursued very far without breaking down: the belly's generosity to the rest of the body is entirely unconscious, because it and they are literally one organism. The body politic may be *like* an organism, but what it actually is is an assemblage of many separate human beings, each with a head, belly and limbs of its own.

Although these many organisms divide into classes with different functions, they are still far from being identified with that function alone, as evidenced by the different voices they speak with. (Shakespeare divides his citizens clearly, like his patricians, between those with more or less generosity, brains or herd instinct). If the various classes are to cooperate, then, it must be by conscious choice, an act of will on all sides. The relationship the plebs are seeking with the patricians is not that of limbs to belly, but of some kind of identification, whereby their hunger may be as real to the well-fed as it is to the sufferers. And their problem is that, for all the patricians' rhetoric, the well-fed feel nothing – except alarm at where such passions may lead. Coriolanus finds their complaints merely contemptible:

> They said they were an-hungry, sighed forth proverbs –
> That hunger broke stone walls, that dogs must eat,
> That meat was made for mouths, that the gods sent not
> Corn for the rich men only. With these shreds
> They vented their complainings. (1.1.203–7)

In this opening, we may say, Shakespeare puts the traditional view of the 'body politic' before us, only to strip it of its potent, quasi-religious appeal. Whatever this republic is, it is not a single organism in which the good of one is the good of all.

When Coriolanus first enters it is to show us a quite different way of relating to the plebs – by natural right of superiority:

> ... What's the matter, you dissentious rogues,
> That, rubbing the poor itch of your opinion,
> Make yourselves scabs? (1.1.162–4)

The energy displayed here is perhaps even more notable than the contempt. Coriolanus revels in the distinction between himself and the mob, with a Juvenalian scorn. The scornful tirade he unleashes allows us to see exactly what he takes the grounds of his superiority to be:

> He that will give good words to thee will flatter
> Beneath abhorring. What would you have, you curs
> That like nor peace nor war? The one affrights you,
> The other makes you proud. He that trusts to you,
> Where he should find you lions finds you hares,
> Where foxes, geese. (166–70)

The plebs are not truly men but a form of animal life (and servile, timid animals at that). Untrained and unprepared, they are incapable of answering for themselves: war frightens them, while peace makes them overconfident. It would be sickness to look for their good will, or indeed to rely on them in any way at all:

> . . . Who deserves greatness
> Deserves your hate, and your affections are
> A sick man's appetite, who desires most that
> Which would increase his evil. He that depends
> Upon your favours swims with fins of lead,
> And hews down oaks with rushes. Hang ye! Trust ye?
> With every minute you do change a mind
> And call him noble that was now your hate,
> Him vile that was your garland. What's the matter,
> That in these several places of the city
> You cry against the noble senate, who,
> Under the gods, keep you in awe, which else
> Would feed on one another? (*To Menenius*) What's their seeking?
> (174–86)

The noble man cannot rely on such creatures: they are the giddy vulgar, whose inherent disorder means that others must supply the order they lack: the gods above, and the noble Senate, whose role is to keep them 'in awe' and prevent them from 'feed[ing] on one another'. And with this evacuation of his superabundant contempt, Coriolanus then turns to one of his own class for explanation, as if the crowd could not be expected to talk: 'What's their seeking?'

Coriolanus' characterization of the mob helps justify the assumption we began with, that the analysis of *virtus* in this play is related to the definition of manhood itself. Coriolanus is implicitly denying that the mob, male though it be, is made up of men. In the sense he uses the term it is honorific: but the level of internal chaos he finds in the plebeians is so dishonourable he is reminded of animals – dogs, hares, geese – rather than anything human. The mob has appetite (they would 'feed on one another') but not self-consciousness ('with every minute [they] do change a mind'); to stoop to dealing with them is like dealing with those disqualified by nature from responding. It is absurd to ask such creatures for their 'vote'; hence the violent resistance of Coriolanus to the usual way of soliciting the Consulship. (One of his most poignant satirical strokes comes when he is hindered from assuming the new post: 'Have I had children's voices?' 3.1.32.)

But he is not always scolding the mob, and at other times we see what his way of relating to them can yield, as opposed to Menenius' methods: he can infuse them with his own *virtus*, and lend them the internal order they lack. When it is a matter of rallying exhausted troops and making them as passionate for honour as himself, Coriolanus is irreplaceable. The rabble hardens into a single fist, and he becomes the sword it wields, as outside Corioles:

> If any such be here –
> As it were sin to doubt – that love this painting
> Wherein you see me smeared; if any fear
> Lesser his person than an ill report;
> If any think brave death outweighs bad life
> And that his country's dearer than himself;
> Let him alone, or so many minded,
>   *He waves his sword*
> Wave thus to express his disposition,
> And follow Martius.
>   *They all shout and wave their swords, [then some] take him up*
>   *in their arms and they cast up their caps*
> O' me alone, make you a sword of me?
> If these shows be not outward, which of you
> But is four Volsces? (1.7.67–78)

This is the magic communication of *virtus* that makes Coriolanus the hero he is, and Rome so invincible.

But between whiles, as Shakespeare takes care to show us, Coriolanus' pursuit of honour runs quite counter to Rome's well-being (he is equally unmanageable to his friends as his enemies over the Consulship) and he is actively savage towards the plebeians in peace. It is as if his definition of Rome were so transcendent that the plebeians cannot belong to it. He can well imagine a Rome without them, and the concessions of the Senate anger him so much that in the opening scene he offers to create it:

> Would the nobility lay aside their ruth
> And let me use my sword, I'd make a quarry
> With thousands of these quartered slaves as high
> As I could pick my lance. (1.1.195–8)

Reluctant as we must be to agree with the mean-spirited Tribunes, they are quite accurate in their claim that he is the enemy of the people and has done everything he could to curtail their power.[12]

We began by noting that the play's political acumen has always been admired, and this analysis of Coriolanus' relationship with the mob in particular.[13] But after

---

[12]   The Elizabethan context of this political issue, why the 'servile' need nonetheless be accorded their 'voices', is given by Hooker in 1593: 'Because, although there be according to the opinion of some very great and judicious men, a kind of natural right in the noble, wise, and virtuous, to govern them which are of servile disposition; nevertheless for manifestation of this their right, and men's more peaceable contentment on both sides, the assent of them who are governed seemeth necessary.' *Of the Laws of Ecclesiastical Polity*, I.ix.12; quoted in *Coriolanus*, ed. Hibbard, p. 34.

[13]   See, for instance, A.C. Bradley, 'Coriolanus', in *Proceedings of the British Academy 1911–12* (London: Oxford University Press, 1914), pp. 461–5; and J.C.F. Littlewood, 'Coriolanus', *Cambridge Quarterly*, 2/4 (1967), 339–44.

our long journey from classical tragedy down to the Renaissance, we can perhaps restore to the term 'political' its original richness of meaning and grasp what it is that gives this play its close resemblance to Athenian drama. Coriolanus embodies the very best that Rome can be: he carries his *polis* to its most unhoped-for victories, and earns its gratitude in the form of a name that is meant to endure for ever (after Corioles, he is Caius Martius no longer). But he is also the injured hero who turns his back on his *polis*, refuses to answer to his name, and brings an enemy army to sack it, in pure revenge – thus embodying two of Aristotle's aphorisms in turn, 'man is a political animal', and 'the man without a *polis* is either a beast or a god'. And the cause of Coriolanus' madly erratic career is the mob, which he bitterly repudiates, but turns out to have more power over him than he ever supposed.

If we note the grounds of his horror of the Roman plebs, we may feel we have encountered this opposition before. His sense of their disorderly animality, their aptness for scourging, sounds not unlike Apollo's disgust at the Furies as 'a flock of goats without a herdsman'. Like the Furies they are 'rank-scented' (3.1.70), 'Hydra'-headed (96), or a contagion like 'measles' (82). There is no negotiating with such a pestilence. Like the Furies too, they live in the world of matter, not the world of honour: taken to the war, they drop their weapons to collect their spoils, and without Coriolanus to inspire them they would flee rather than fight. They do not have the Furies' connection with blood guilt and kinship, of course, but their whole way of being links them with what we have been calling the female realm. They too put bodies before values: their first cry is for food, and their second for safety, and they make a hero of Coriolanus, or expel him from Rome, according to how he affects their immediate well-being.

The closeness of this to the central debate of the *Oresteia* shows in the way both Coriolanus and the mob are shown as custodians of a vital truth, but unable to acknowledge each other's significance. Indeed, like Apollo and the Furies, they push each other into self-parody, in a frantic denial of the obvious fact that the Roman Republic has given birth to them both. Coriolanus' case has many of the advantages and defects of Apollo's case against the Furies: he is fully individuated, and so complete a hero that he will fight a whole city by himself if necessary; while the members of the mob are so weakly constructed that they behave like herd animals, running whichever way their leader runs. Coriolanus is self-constructed out of his own deeds and the name he has earned; the members of the mob have merely been born, and have no sense of honour by which to construct themselves as men, as opposed to males. Because Coriolanus has come so far from his birth, he increasingly seems to onlookers to be more than human, as if a god 'were slily crept into his human powers' says Brutus (2.1.217). And when he is poised to attack Rome, he seems still more wonderful. Menenius says,

> He no more remembers his mother now than an eight-year old horse . . .
> When he walks, he moves like an engine, and the ground shrinks before

his treading. He is able to pierce a corslet with his eye, talks like a knell, and his 'hmh!' is a battery . . . He wants nothing of a god but eternity and a heaven to throne in. (5.4.16–17, 18–21, 23–5)

Coriolanus' *virtus* sends even those who are about to be its victims into a kind of ecstasy: however terrifying he is, he embodies an irresistible hope of masculine emancipation.

But the defects of his virtues are equally obvious. His sense of individuality needs to be fed by antagonism: he feels rapture in expressing his contempt, and as one of the officers introducing the Capitol scene is made to say: 'He seeks [the people's] hate with greater devotion than they can render it him, and leaves nothing undone that may fully discover him their opposite' (2.2.18–21). The people are the whetstone of Coriolanus' self-esteem; and the gratification they obliquely give him seems more important than any of the usual rewards of the heroic life, to which he is surprisingly resistant. Not only does he refuse his proper share of the spoils (which he touchily resents as being too like 'a bribe to pay my sword', 1.10.38), but he will not even stay to hear himself praised in the Capitol:

> I had rather have one scratch my head i'th' sun
> When the alarum were struck than idly sit
> To hear my nothings monstered. [*Exit*] (2.2.75–7)

It is difficult to analyse the components of this resistance, but some part of it seems to be a fierce resentment of any other judgement, however positive – because it forces him to submit to another's (potentially limiting) definition, and he will only accept his own.

Other defects of his single-minded pursuit of honour have often been noted, like the almost comic 'Come I too late?' with which he rejoins Cominius outside Corioli, and his cross-questioning of him, on the very border of bad manners: 'Where is the enemy? Are you lords o'th' field? / If not, why cease you till you are so?' (1.7.27, 47–8). Cominius' reply is clearly intended to mark a difference: 'Martius, we have at disadvantage fought, / And did retire to win our purpose' (49–50). (He has earlier said, 'We are come off / Like Romans, neither foolish in our stands / Nor cowardly in retire', 1–3.) But Caius Martius is above good sense and the weighing of chances. His idiom is ecstatic (he embraces Cominius 'in heart / As merry as when our nuptial day was done', 30–1), he thinks the blood he is covered in is a 'painting' to be 'loved' (68), and the reality of the bodies dying on both sides of the struggle is lost to him, in this glorious opportunity to acquire more honour.

The point at which *virtus* can become dangerously transcendent has already been indicated by his admiring speech about Aufidius. The greatest honour in this game can only be acquired from the most deserving enemy; so that, as Coriolanus says of Aufidius in the very first scene,

> Were half to half the world by th' ears and he
> Upon my party, I'd revolt to make
> Only my wars with him. He is a lion
> That I am proud to hunt. (1.1.233–6)

At this point, the idea of turning against his own 'side' in pursuit of honour is hyperbolical, but what it reveals of Coriolanus' underlying logic is true enough. Honour is detachable from service to Rome; and one day Coriolanus will pursue it alone.

The clarity of Shakespeare's analysis of honour shows in how evenhandedly he conveys both the wonder of Coriolanus and his absurdity. The wonder is given full credence, but it does not merely alternate with absurdity: absurdity is an integral part of it. If individuation reaches the pitch where a single man can take on a whole city ('like an eagle in a dove-cote, I / Fluttered your Volscians in Corioles. / Alone I did it', 5.6.115–17), then it also allows a banished man to round on his *polis* and say, 'I banish you' (3.3.127). The hero's self-reliance is an astonishing achievement, but carried to this pitch it is a vice, cutting him brutally off from the living context that produced him. Sicinius is right to call him a 'viper / That would depopulate the city and / Be every man himself' (3.1.263–5); for Coriolanus cannot accept ways of being less individuated than his own. Even the standard Roman way, shown by Cominius, grates on him: anything short of being Coriolanus is insufficient.

This madness is grand, but it *is* madness, if we think back to the classic portraits of valour in the *Iliad*. There is a sense in which the heroism of Hector is an implicit criticism of Achilles', even though the Greek hero is stronger. Hector fights because his great strength obliges him to protect his city as long as he can, and he would feel shame before the citizens if he did less than he could. Achilles refuses to fight, to punish his own 'side' because he is stinted of honour; and the whole Greek army does not seem too great a sacrifice for his bottomless rage (he forgets for the moment, of course, that it includes Patroclus). Achilles is loyal to his code, but treacherous to his friends; and he comes to regret it as madness. Coriolanus, like Achilles, has built his whole life on the honour code; and the sense in which Shakespeare is uncovering the same tragic subject as the *Oresteia* shows in the Apollonian reliance Coriolanus puts on that code. He does not consider that it has the defects of all transcendent things: it only subsists by agreement, and if one party unilaterally alters the rules, it disappears.

Shakespeare indicates from Act I that Aufidius does not take the honour code in the same spirit as Coriolanus, so we know that any agreement between them will be vulnerable. Aufidius is tired of the code for the same reason that Coriolanus is not: he is invariably on the losing side, and resents the way his honour only augments his enemy's ('I would I were a Roman, for I cannot, / Being a Volsce, be that I am', 1.11.4–5). Since honour merely diminishes his sense of self, he will aggrandize it by whatever means become available:

> Mine emulation
> Hath not that honour in't it had, for where
> I thought to crush him in an equal force,
> True sword to sword, I'll potch at him some way
> Or wrath or craft may get him. (1.11.12–16)

We are aware for the rest of the play that Coriolanus is putting a literal-minded reliance on something that is a mere breath, an unspoken agreement. It carries him remarkably far: when he joins the Volscian camp, his power over the army he decimated in battle is felt as 'witchcraft', and Aufidius' first greeting of him is rapturous (4.5.102 ff.). But we know that the honour code that preserves his greatness and safety amongst these new allies will not stand very much strain.

Perhaps the best illustration of the vulnerability of the honour code, however, is the ambiguous sense in which Coriolanus' new allegiance can be said to be 'honourable' at all. Like Achilles, he considers himself emancipated from his former obligations by ingratitude. The dishonour heaped on him by the plebs, from which the patricians have not protected him, seems more than sufficient reason to change sides. As he goes, he promises proudly,

> While I remain above the ground you shall
> Hear from me still, and never of me aught
> But what is like me formerly. (4.1.52–4)

But what we see of him is quite *un*like him formerly: it is both painfully lower and uncomfortably higher. Much lower is his entry to Aufidius' house, muffled in disguise, hungrily sniffing the air ('the feast / Smells well', 4.5.5–6) and bandying insults with servants ('Go and batten on cold bits', 33). This is the Coriolanus who cannot announce his name, and cannot therefore be himself.[14]

But when he is known for who he is, he becomes, even more clearly than in Rome, a kind of god. Now that he is emancipated from all natural ties, he belongs to a new order of being, and the Volsces take strength from him as the plebs did formerly. As Cominius describes him,

> . . . He is their god. He leads them like a thing
> Made by some other deity than nature,
> That shapes man better; and they follow him
> Against us brats with no less confidence
> Than boys pursuing summer butterflies,
> Or butchers killing flies. (4.6.94–9)

Implicit in both the degraded, muffled Coriolanus and the superman, 'son and heir to Mars' (4.5.197), is the cost of breaking the ties that bound him to Rome.

---

[14]   It may also be true that Shakespeare finds it hard to imagine this fallen Coriolanus from the inside. This is the only time Coriolanus speaks a soliloquy and it is in an oddly sententious and external style: 'O world, thy slippery turns! . . . My birthplace hate I, and my love's upon / This enemy town' (4.4.12, 23–4).

When Coriolanus puts his individual honour above his former allegiance to the *polis*, he commits his *hamartia*, a profound error of understanding. His whole training has taught him to value transcendence – of bodily pain, of fear, of any lingering desire to put life above honour – to the point where he supposes no transcendence could be too great, even that of his own origins. But the reason why 'the man without a *polis* is either a beast or a god' is that he has come loose from the context that made him a man. He is either a beast whose concerns are mere food and shelter – the exiled and hungry Coriolanus; or a god who does not recognize himself in others – the Coriolanus who would massacre Rome 'in mere spite' (4.5.83). If Coriolanus is, technically, not dishonoured by taking sides with the Volsces, he is something yet more disturbing, disqualified from humanity.

This train of thought may help justify the claim that this play is political in the richest sense, and founded on the same opposition between Apollo and the Furies that made the *Eumenides* debate so resonant. For Coriolanus takes transcendence to the extreme; and in preparing to 'forge himself a name o'th' fire / Of burning Rome', he entirely represses the physical facts that will confront him like so many Furies in Act V: that his body was formed in his mother's, that he is bonded to his wife, and their love has issued in another life, his young boy, Martius. When Volumnia, Virgilia, Martius, and Valeria become his suppliants, they are not Furies in the literal sense, creatures for whom blood and kinship is the only reality – their arguments on this basis are mingled with more civilized considerations. But if we consider their final appeal, kneeling and mute, 'hold[ing] up hands for fellowship' (5.3.176), it is to the same truth of which the Furies are guardians: that bodies come before minds, and when lifeblood has been spilt, it cannot be restored.

If the suggestion that *Coriolanus* is Shakespeare's most Athenian drama carries conviction, it will be evident that this embassy scene, in which Coriolanus finally confronts his mother, is the most Greek of all. It has always been felt to be untypical, perhaps unhappily so: Bradley, for one, sees it 'more as a majestic picture of stationary figures than as the fateful climax of an action speeding to its close'.[15] But if Shakespeare is relying unusually heavily on long speeches and statuesque figures, we need to examine what this classical style makes possible. And in the light of our preceding analysis of tragic confrontations, we can see that Shakespeare is condensing in these figures a remarkably bold question. What is masculine *virtus* worth? What makes the male so strong, and at the same time, so fragile? Coriolanus and Volumnia, face to face as an army waits by, return us (as we noted earlier) to the primary confrontation of the *Oresteia*. How can a man live in the world of honour, when his body is rooted in the world of blood ties? In the journey from his mother towards the *polis*, why does his mother interpose her breasts; and what dangers does he run if he overrides the sancitities she represents – or submits to them?

---

[15]   Bradley, 'Coriolanus', p. 468.

Coriolanus shows us as lucidly as any Greek drama that masculinity is a construction, and that it is at its most vulnerable – but potentially at its greatest – when it confronts its origins in the body of a woman. In the course of this scene, and almost in silence, Coriolanus travels the whole distance back from godlike transcendence to humanity, from his resolution to stand 'as if a man were author of himself / And knew no other kin', to feeling 'a woman's tenderness' and having eyes that 'sweat compassion' (5.3.36–7, 130, 197). And by a profoundly tragic paradox, it is at the moment Coriolanus has proved himself most fully a man that he becomes vulnerable to the worst insult current in his world: 'Thou boy of tears!' (5.6.103). Although Coriolanus is at his greatest when he gives in to his mother's persuasion, he is also effectively ruined by it. He lacks, we may say, the heroic immunity given to Orestes by motherless Athena, or to Macduff, who was not 'of woman born'. The debate he is part of is conducted in terms of real people, not symbolic positions, and he will be murdered by Aufidius precisely *because* he gave in to his mother. He reneged on his masculinity, as the Volsces see it, which is a crime for which other men can show no mercy:

> Breaking his oath and resolution like
> A twist of rotten silk . . . at his nurse's tears
> He whined and roared away your victory,
> That pages blushed at him, and men of heart
> Looked wond'ring each at others. (5.6.97–8, 99–102)

Among all the other classical notes struck by this scene, it may seem too obvious for comment that it is the women who prevail successfully with Coriolanus: but it is clearly part of Shakespeare's vision of the climax that they can do what men cannot, and embody 'the bond and privilege of nature' Coriolanus was intending to break (5.3.25). In this, and in the long speeches in which Volumnia builds a rational plea on top of their mute appeal, we may be reminded of the role played by Athena in the *Eumenides*. The goddess of persuasion was effective precisely because she acknowledged both the truths protected by the Furies, and those advanced by Apollo. The embassy similarly comes to urge Coriolanus to acquire a different kind of honour as builder of an unhoped-for peace, as well as to restore him to the physical basis of life, the 'great nature' that made him a son, father and husband. By contrast, the appeals by Cominius and Menenius (which are Shakespeare's additions to Plutarch) rather help Coriolanus to be obstinate than prevent him. Cominius can only remind him of the Roman allegiance he has buried – and views him, in any case, as something more than man ('I tell you, he does sit in gold, his eye / Red as 'twould burn Rome', 5.1.63–4). Menenius, too, whose quasi-paternal appeal is expected to have more effect, merely gives Coriolanus a chance to display his intransigence in front of Aufidius with an abrupt: 'Away!' (5.2.80). Men act as a goad to Coriolanus' sense of honour; and they view him all too easily as a god themselves, someone who has gone beyond humanity to an exhilarating, as well as lethal, sphere of freedom.

But the women's appeal is a devastating mixture of elements, legitimate and illegitimate, to draw him down from his 'throne' and reunite him with what he has been, in the teeth of what he intends to be. We have the impression that in sustaining his rage, Coriolanus has simply forgotten the strength and reality of his other emotions. But they begin to overwhelm him at the very sight of the women ('I melt, and am not / Of stronger earth than others', 5.3.28–9), and a significant alteration Shakespeare makes to Plutarch is in the dignity and maturity of the feelings he displays towards them: he does not greet his mother first, but Virgilia, with a long kiss and a speech of tender adoration ('Best of my flesh . . .', 42). This, with his paternal rapture in Martius, and his great politeness to Valeria, are all Shakespeare's additions. If we had been supposing that Coriolanus was another Pentheus (whom in many ways he resembles), he is not unformed and boyish in his emotions. Nor is he unprepared for the dilemma the women are about to confront him with: he describes it with a Macbeth-like clarity:

> My wife comes foremost, then the honoured mould
> Wherein this trunk was framed, and in her hand
> The grandchild to her blood. But out, affection!
> All bond and privilege of nature, break;
> Let it be virtuous to be obstinate. (22–6)

Shakespeare emphasizes all the bonds inherent in this appeal, but the emphasis goes most strongly, as in Plutarch, on the bond with Volumnia – 'the honoured mould / Wherein this trunk was framed'. And Volumnia immediately plays on the filial gratitude that should flow from such a debt by scolding him, and inverting their roles with ferocious irony. There is a touch of Clytaemnestra in the way she gives him her maternal blessing as he kneels, then sardonically kneels to him, to show 'duty as mistaken all this while / Between the child and parent' (55–6). But this note of blackmail ('you are, and always will be, my son') is not her only weapon. What gives Volumnia her grandeur is her combination of male and female qualities, her investment not only in motherhood but honour, so that Coriolanus rights their inverted roles with fervid admiration:

> *Cor.*   What's this?
>   Your knees to me? To your corrected son?
>   [*He raises her*]
>   Then let the pebbles on the hungry beach
>   Fillip the stars; then let the mutinous winds
>   Strike the proud cedars 'gainst the fiery sun,
>   Murdering impossibility to make
>   What cannot be slight work.
> *Vol.*   Thou art my warrior;
>   I holp to frame thee. (56–63)

Volumnia enables Shakespeare to bring into this final confrontation not only the physical weight of Clytaemnestra (she assures her son very credibly that the first thing he will tread on as he marches into Rome will be his 'mother's womb / That brought [him] to the world,' 125–6) – but also some of the androgynous implications of martial Athena. For she passionately supports male honour and understands how it dignifies existence; she knows what sacrifices may be required to make a 'name'. (If Coriolanus had died young, in his first battle, she bravely says, 'his good report should have been my son. I therein would have found issue' 1.3.20–1.) But as a mother, a body that has been the 'mould' of another life, she knows that the self-construction of Coriolanus is a metaphor rather than a physical truth; and that in carrying it beyond the point where honour dignifies life Coriolanus is becoming a traitor, not only to Rome, but to his own best self.

Her arguments are designed to bring Coriolanus back to the world that formed him, and make him recognize that whatever victory he gained over Rome would be no victory; however he justifies himself, history will judge him for 'tearing / His country's bowels out' (103–4). (The metaphor of 'the body politic' here begins to carry its true weight.) Whatever name he thinks to earn, he will 'bear the palm for having bravely shed / [His] wife and children's blood' (118–19), and all his former fame will be lost in abhorrence. If he is noble, he should not brood on his wrongs; if he is a god, he should be like Jupiter, whose thunderbolts end with nothing worse than a split oak tree (150–4). Volumnia's confidence in the power of words shows at its most Athena-like in her vision of a mutually advantageous peace between the Romans and Volsces. She recognizes that Coriolanus cannot give way to her without 'poisoning' his honour, but she intends something much better:

> If it were so that our request did tend
> To save the Romans, thereby to destroy
> The Volsces whom you serve, you might condemn us
> As poisonous of your honour. No, our suit
> Is that you reconcile them: while the Volsces
> May say 'This mercy we have showed', the Romans
> 'This we received', and each in either side
> Give the all-hail to thee and cry 'Be blest
> For making up this peace!' (133–41)

It is a rare note of sweet reason in a world where fighters on both sides have been trained to 'run reeking o'er the lives of men as if / 'Twere a perpetual spoil' (2.2.119–20).

But the complexity of the emotions Shakespeare arouses at this climax shows in the way that we can feel the reasonableness of Volumnia's arguments while sensing that they are only half the point; and the other half lurks in the dreadful intimacy of her maternal reproaches:

> Thou hast never in thy life
> Showed thy dear mother any courtesy,

> When she, poor hen, fond of no second brood,
> Has clucked thee to the wars and safely home,
> Loaden with honour. Say my request's unjust
> And spurn me back. But if it be not so,
> Thou art not honest, and the gods will plague thee . . . (161–7)

The intermingling of love and blackmail, truth and coercion, is so complete that Coriolanus cannot initially speak at all (*'He holds her by the hand, silent'*). And when he does speak, it is with a much more complete *anagnorisis* than in Plutarch. Coriolanus is penetrated not only by a sense of what she has done, but what it will mean for him, and what it must look like from where the gods are sitting:

> O, mother, mother!
> What have you done? Behold, the heavens do ope,
> The gods look down, and this unnatural scene
> They laugh at. O my mother, mother, O!
> You have won a happy victory to Rome;
> But for your son, believe it, O believe it,
> Most dangerously you have with him prevailed,
> If not most mortal to him. But let it come. (183–90)

The tableau quality of the scene is at its intensest here, conceived by Coriolanus himself as a performance witnessed by laughing gods. But the stillness of it gives an opportunity to apprehend as fully as possible the significance of what Shakespeare is showing us: the tragic paradox by which Coriolanus becomes fully human only at the risk of his life – and the agent of his undoing is his mother. As we noted before, it is hardly surprising the play has triggered such powerful and disparate responses if it works in such a sensitive emotional area, and exposes the conflict thus openly. For if we ask, what does it say that *virtus* is worth, and why is the male at the same time so strong and so weak, the answer is clearly what it was in Athens: that masculinity must acknowledge its roots in the female, at the risk of self-transcendence so complete as to verge on parody. But when it comes down to earth, it must find something – be it law, marriage, or the *polis* – to protect it from the claim of the mother, or it cannot survive in maturity.

PART THREE

Modern Tragedy

Chapter 6

Ibsen and Strindberg

Is it straining a point, to pursue our enquiry beyond the Renaissance? Can modern tragedy have anything in common with Greek, or indeed with Shakespeare's? Two thoughts might justify the attempt at tracing a connection: one is that both Ibsen and Strindberg knew Greek plays and responded to them with plays of their own. The other is that, just as the *polis* seems to be the precipitating factor for Greek drama, and a new individualism for the Renaissance, so a case can be made for saying that women's emancipation is the social shock that sets tragic theatre going again, with the plays of Ibsen and Strindberg.[1] Gender issues come to life in Scandinavia with the suffragism of the 1880s: if women are joining men in the modern world of individuation and the vote, what role is left for the man to play?

Henrik Ibsen, *A Doll's House* (1879)

Something like this seems to have been Ibsen's motive for calling *A Doll's House* 'The Tragedy of Today',[2] though his handling of the theme is more satirical than that implies. (Modern audiences tend to applaud the ending without reservation: the break-up of families is no longer a tragic issue, and Ibsen does not stress what is lost rather than gained.) But it is striking how familiar is the account of gender roles even after such a lapse of time, and how precisely Ibsen demarcates the old battle lines: the family, and the law.

Nora is the chaste wife of patriarchal dreams: the loving mother of three chidren, sexually alluring to other men but only responsive to one, and innocently unaware of the rules that pertain beyond the threshold. The burden of financing and protecting her is happily borne by her husband Torvald, in the Apollonian capacity of barrister turned Bank Manager; and from their own point of view their marriage is an ideal union of female charm and male rationality. What it actually is is something more seamy, of course: an agreement between a doll and a doll's house owner to act out their unexamined roles for the approval of the world at

---

[1]   The physical terrain of Scandinavia retarded urbanization and left women's functions in an almost medieval mould until the nineteenth century (country women would have to supply their own families' needs from January to December, via the dairy, vegetable garden and brew house). The coming of railways and steamboats produced the first leisured generation of women in the mid-century, who condensed their rapid emancipation into the decades 1860–80 (see Brian W. Downs, *Ibsen: The Intellectual Background* (New York: Octagon Books, 1969), pp. 157–8).

[2]   This is how Ibsen referred to it in draft (*William Archer on Ibsen: The Major Essays, 1889–1919*, ed. Thomas Postlewait (Westport, Conn. and London: Greenwood Press, 1984), p. 205).

large. Ibsen takes sardonic pleasure in showing the level of inauthenticity between them, and the speed at which their lives disintegrate. In the first scene, however, Nora is Torvald's 'little squirrel frisking about',[3] eating macaroons and teasing her husband for more money, which he gives her with rueful indulgence ('it's incredible how expensive it is for a man to keep such a pet', p. 4). He thinks his greatest problem is with her spending and overlooks a much bigger area of misunderstanding, revealed in an exchange they have about the dangers of borrowing money. If they did, and he died in an accident, he asks, how would she ever pay it back? And Nora answers that if something so awful happened, she wouldn't care about debts, or the people whose money was lost. 'Who cares about them! They are only strangers!' (p. 2).

With this hint Ibsen opens up the issue that interests him: the difference between a woman's sense of realities and a man's, and consequently between her conscience and his. As he noted before writing the play,

> There are two kinds of spiritual laws, two kinds of conscience, one in men and a quite different one in women. They do not understand each other; but the woman is judged in practical life according to the man's law, as if she were not a woman but a man . . . A woman cannot be herself in the society of to-day, which is exclusively a masculine society, with laws written by men, and with accusers and judges who judge feminine conduct from the masculine standpoint.[4]

This crystallizes later in the classic exchange which reverberates all the way back to Clytaemnestra and Agamemnon: 'Nobody sacrifices his *honour* for the one he loves', says Torvald; and Nora replies, 'Hundreds and thousands of women have' (p. 84). Nora's understanding of honour is that love comes first (a love that does not, of course, embrace 'strangers'). When Torvald was ill and only the technical problem of a signature stood between her and the money she needed to take him abroad, she thought nothing of forging her father's signature to an IOU. She was saving Torvald's life in the teeth of his horror of debt, and saving her dying father the pain of knowing it; and she did it so naively that she dated the signature after her father's death. When she is told that she would be condemned for her act in a court of law because the law 'takes no account of motives', she answers, 'Then they must be very bad laws . . . I feel sure of one thing: it must say somewhere that things like this are allowed' (p. 29).

Although Ibsen is clearly sympathetic to Nora's case, he complicates our response by showing that it is not only in the public realm that she breaks the rules. In the realm of personal ties she creates some ugly tangles, too: she has long enjoyed the company of a gentleman admirer, Dr Rank, who allows her the same

---

    ³   Henrik Ibsen, *Four Major Plays: A Doll's House, Ghosts, Hedda Gabler, The Master Builder*, trans. James McFarland and Jens Arup (Oxford: Oxford University Press, 1981, repr. 1987), p. 2; all subsequent references are to this edition.
    ⁴   *William Archer on Ibsen*, pp. 205–6.

freedom from decorum she enjoyed with the maids when she was small ('for one thing they never preached at me. And they always talked about such exciting things', p. 50). She teases him with the silk stockings of her dance costume and distractedly wonders if she can ask him for a large loan, while he takes his last opportunity to make her aware that he is dying of syphilis. Her deafness to his appeal, and the cold disappointment she shows as he spoils her plan by making an open avowal of his feelings, are among the sharpest satirical effects in the play. If he loves her, she cannot ask him for money; and she reproaches him, not for what he feels, but for forcing their relationship out of its useful ambiguity. When he asks her whether she did not already know, she says, 'How can I tell whether I did or didn't. I simply can't tell you . . . Oh, how could you be so clumsy, Dr. Rank! When everything was so nice' (p. 49).

In Nora, Ibsen shows the price patriarchy pays for its insistence on female innocence. In practice, it means blankness. Having been treated as costume dolls, women have the moral grasp of costume dolls, and when Nora wakes up to her position, Ibsen does not underestimate the ferocity of her new feelings: 'For eight years [I've] been living with a stranger and [have] borne him three children . . . Oh, I can't bear to think about it! I could tear myself to shreds' (p. 85).

In Torvald, Ibsen gives a satirical insight into the kind of male who takes most advantage of the patriarchal bargain. Although Torvald has some admirable qualities – he was a scrupulous barrister who refused any case 'the least bit shady' (p. 9) and he fell ill from overwork in the effort to support Nora – his inadequacies are more striking than his virtues. (Indeed, one criticism of the play might be that it gives no weight to the idea that bank managers should be incorruptible; most people would prefer to bank their money with Torvald than with anyone else in the drama.) There are ominous tokens from the beginning that he is less strong than he appears. Nora has kept her secret so carefully because 'it would be terribly embarrassing and humiliating for him if he thought he owed anything to me' (p. 15). He is touchily sensitive with outsiders too: although he has a good public reason for dismissing a dubious employee, his private one is that the employee, Krogstad, knows him too well from their student days. And in relation to Nora, his sensuality and crude possessiveness are marked: within moments of realizing that Rank has left them to go home to die, he is trying to enjoy her: 'Well, perhaps it's all for the best. For him at any rate. [*Pauses.*] And maybe for us as well, Nora. Now there's just the two of us. [*Puts his arms round her.*]' (p. 74).

Most ominously, he has chivalric fantasies of heroism, which are ironically juxtaposed with his response at an actual crisis. 'Many's the time I wish you were threatened by some terrible danger so I could risk everything, body and soul, for your sake' (p. 74), he says, just before opening the blackmailing letter from Krogstad and rounding on Nora in furious disgust: 'This woman who was my pride and joy . . . a hypocrite, a liar, worse than that, a criminal! Oh, how utterly squalid it all is! Ugh! Ugh!' (p. 75). Self-pity, misogyny and vulgarity are all compounded in a flood of reproach: 'Now you have ruined my entire happiness . . . Here I am, at the mercy of a thoroughly unscrupulous person . . . [he can] order me about . . . I daren't even whimper . . . and it's all the fault of a feather-brained woman' (p. 76).

Ibsen deepens the satire by showing that when Krogstad miraculously withdraws his threat, Torvald reassembles himself just as fast. His forgiveness is as close to the surface as his revulsion, and it is made out of similarly patriarchal elements. He swathes Nora in reassuring protectiveness – 'like a hunted dove I have rescued unscathed from the cruel talons of a hawk' – in a speech of open dramatic irony. He thinks she is offstage undressing to sleep with him, while she is actually dressing to leave:

> You don't really imagine me ever thinking of turning you out, or even of reproaching you? Oh, a real man isn't made that way, you know, Nora. For a man, there's something indescribably moving and very satisfying in knowing that he has forgiven his wife – forgiven her, completely and genuinely, from the depths of his heart. It's as though it made her his property in a double sense: he has, as it were, given her a new life, and she becomes in a way both his wife and at the same time his child. That is how you will seem to me after today, helpless, perplexed little thing that you are. Don't you worry your pretty little head about anything, Nora. Just you be frank with me, and I'll take all the decisions for you . . . What's this? Not in bed? You've changed your things?
>
> Nora   [in her everyday dress]. Yes, Torvald, I've changed. (pp. 78–9)

As Ibsen neatly indicates, Nora has 'changed' in every sense, and Torvald is about to be startled out of his dream. But the preceding fantasy gives us an invaluable insight into the patriarchal contract. The more forgiveness Torvald can lavish on his erring partner, the more powerful he can feel; the sillier and more 'perplexed' she is, the more controlling he can be. ('I'll take all the decisions' translates literally as 'I will be both will and conscience to you.') She is already his 'property', but by bestowing 'new life' on her he makes her his property 'in a double sense'. The soaring possessiveness of the language is unmistakable, but the metaphor suggests something even more interesting: a jealous reappropriation of Nora's generative role, so that this mother of three will become not only his wife, but ('in a way', as Torvald modestly phrases it), 'his child'. He is about to crown his gratification by making love to this weak, passive entity that he owns twice over ('Not in bed?') when she calls a halt to the process in a voice he has never heard her use: 'sit down, Torvald. We two have a lot to talk about' (p. 79).

Nora's developing sense of morality not only prevents her from sleeping with a man she no longer feels she loves ('I can't spend the night in a strange man's room', p. 85), but from continuing to live out a role imposed on her without her consent. In her central exchange with her husband, Ibsen touches on the classic issue: how far a woman's life 'belongs' to society as a conduit for fertility, and how far to herself:

> *Tor.* This is outrageous! You are betraying your most sacred duty!
>
> *Nora* And what do you take to be my most sacred duty?
>
> *Tor.* Does it take me to tell you that? Isn't it your duty to your husband and your children?
>
> *Nora* I have another duty equally sacred.
>
> *Tor.* You have not. What duty might *that* be?
>
> *Nora* My duty to myself.
>
> *Tor.* First and foremost, you are a wife and mother.
>
> *Nora* That I don't believe any more. I believe that first and foremost I am an individual, just as much as you are – or at least, I'm going to try to be. I know most people agree with you, Torvald, and that's also what it says in books. But I'm not content any more with what most people say, or with what it says in books. I have to think things out for myself, and get things clear. (p. 82)

Ibsen is so enjoying Torvald's discomfiture, we may suspect, that he endows Nora with more clarity than she would be likely to have. (She casts her old life aside as neatly as a butterfly its chrysalis.) He also avoids another classic issue that rears its head awkwardly here: how much responsibility the individual may still carry for actions performed in ignorance. He plays down the reality of Nora's three children and her likely guilt at deserting them in favour of his main effect: that Nora has never been accorded human rights. '[Daddy] used to call me his baby doll,' she says, 'and he played with me as I used to play with my dolls':

> Our house has never been anything but a play-room. I have been your doll wife, just as at home I was Daddy's doll child. And the children in turn have been my dolls. I thought it was fun when you came and played with me, just as they thought it was fun when I went and played with them. That's been our marriage, Torvald. (p. 81)

Ibsen's last, and not least piercing irony, is that now Nora is refusing her former role Torvald must find a new one too:

> *Tor.* I still have it in me to change.
>
> *Nora* Perhaps . . . if you have your doll taken away.
>
> *Tor.* And be separated from you! No, no, Nora, the very thought of it is inconceivable.
>
> *Nora* [*goes into the room, right*]. All the more reason why it must be done. [*She comes back with her outdoor things.*] (p. 85)

Torvald makes facile promises, but Ibsen makes it clear that the prognosis is not good. His masculinity was always constructed out of contracts and bank stamps, and his instinct is to hold things together at any price. 'Couldn't we go on living here like brother and sister . . .?' he pleads; and Nora shows herself to be the only grown-up in this relationship when she answers, tying on her bonnet, 'You know very well that wouldn't last' (p. 85). She returns him his ring, and leaves the house in search of the experiences that will make her an adult capable of understanding the relation of morality to law; and the door bangs behind her.

Ghosts (1881)

The provocative quality of the writing in *A Doll's House* partly obscures the seriousness of the issues, it may be felt. Perhaps Ibsen came to the same conclusion, since in *Ghosts* he returned almost immediately to a more challenging variant of the plot. As has often been remarked, Mrs Alving is a Nora who did not leave but has continued to grow up in hiding. And the effect this kind of woman might have on her children, which is only notional in the earlier play, in this drama becomes the central theme. Ibsen noted in his preliminary jottings, 'These women of the modern age, mistreated as daughters, as sisters, as wives, not educated in accordance with their talents, debarred from following their real mission, deprived of their inheritance, embittered in mind – these are the ones who supply the mothers for the next generation. What will result from this?'[5] He is not only concerned with the injustice from the woman's point of view, but with something he did not fully acknowledge in relation to Nora: the dreadful mistakes a woman may make in her state of half-knowledge, and the power that may still lurk in apparent submission. Mrs Alving turns out to have had both power and freedom, of a kind; and it is her final recognition of what she did with them that gives the play its tragic gravity.

Not only is Ibsen unusually realistic about women's predicament in society, but he conveys the natural power inherent in motherhood with a directness we have rarely met since Euripides. Mrs Alving uses her leverage on her husband (he has got her servant pregnant) to send their son out of his reach at the tender age of seven; and even after his father's death, Oswald is allowed to inherit nothing from his father. Mrs Alving sinks her husband's money in the Orphanage project; 'anything my son gets is to come from me, and that's that', she says (p. 119). Mrs Alving, no less than Medea, feels that children belong to their mother; and Ibsen's most courageous dramatic stroke is to bring her to a position where she must choose between keeping Oswald to herself for ever, infantilized and helpless, or killing him in accordance with his own last wish. The boldness of this conception shows in the way that Ibsen violates the taboo against infanticide (even the idea of it) that the stage has maintained ever since *Medea*. It also shows in the reason why Oswald collapses into his mother's embrace. He has inherited syphilis from his father: the ultimate proof that a child receives its endowment from two parents, not one.

---

5   *Four Major Plays*, p. ix.

All this realism is embedded in a play with an interestingly classical structure. The very fact that Ibsen has seized on syphilis as an inheritance (rather than, say, haemophilia), suggests how well he has learnt his lesson from the Greeks. If 'life is a sexually transmitted disease' in the repressive moral climate of Norway, syphilis is the best expression of the spoilt life Captain Alving has lived for himself and bequeathed to his child.[6] The disease operates like a buried secret, showing that all actions have their consequences, however efficiently hidden, and that one generation lays traps for the next. As Oswald's doctor says, 'The sins of the fathers are visited upon the children' (p. 138) – for though each child is unique and a wholly new start, its uniqueness is made out of old and potentially contaminated materials. Even more classical is the interplay between the drama's many references to 'ghosts' and 'the sun': it is because 'we are all ghosts', says Mrs Alving, that 'we are, all of us, abysmally afraid of the light':

> It's not just what we inherit from our fathers and mothers that haunts us. It's all kinds of old defunct theories, all sorts of old defunct beliefs, and things like that. It's not that they actually *live* on in us; they are simply lodged there, and we cannot get rid of them. I've only to pick up a newspaper and I seem to see ghosts gliding between the lines. Over the whole country there must be ghosts, as numerous as the sands of the sea. (p. 126)

These myriad forms of half-life, stifling human vitality in guilt, repression and lies, suggest that Ibsen's 'ghosts' are his Scandinavian expression of the destructive effect of the Furies. 'Ghosts' – literally, 'spirits that return' – are perhaps what the Furies become if there is no Athenian wisdom in the culture to put them to good use. Instead of being firmly lodged underground, where fear can generate healthy awe and straighten the conscious lives of the citizens above, they glide unhappily amongst the living, creating nothing but inhibition and misery – the poisonous decay of unlived life. The chief carrier of this poison in the play is Pastor Manders, whose God is public opinion, and who ends up supporting a brothel instead of an orphanage in a muddle of hypocrisy and fear.

But there is a world of brilliant sunshine beyond dull Norway, where 'there isn't a glimpse of the sun all day' (p. 135). This is the world Oswald discovers when he goes to be an artist in Paris, and finds other young artists living a 'glorious, free life' of spontaneous loyalty to their partners, in unions unblessed by the church. Their 'joy of life' comes from their Dionysiac energy, their readiness to experience their emotions to the full; 'in other countries', he says, 'they think it's tremendous fun just to be alive at all' (p. 145). This realm of energy is also the proper subject of Apollonian art, for this experience is what Oswald has always tried to capture: 'Everything I've ever painted has turned on

---

6   It is fortunate that the medical knowledge of the period was sufficiently meagre to allow Ibsen to see syphilis as something bequeathed from father to son; in fact, almost everyone in the play could have been infected.

this joy of life . . . Light and sunshine and a holiday spirit . . . and radiantly happy faces' (p. 145). And under these circumstances work itself becomes a form of joy: 'they are the same thing, in fact. But people here don't know anything about that either' (p. 144). This is what Mrs Alving wanted for her son when she sent him away from the world of ghostly half-lives like her own and her syphilitic husband's, away from the 'poison' of 'this polluted house' (p. 118).

Mrs Alving has travelled farther than Nora: she has read 'advanced' books that have emancipated her from convention, and she sees her effort to sustain her husband's public dignity as 'a long, ghastly farce' (p. 120). But she is still child-like in her fantasy of making a clean break with the past: now that the Orphanage is complete and Oswald has come home she says, 'I shall feel as though that man had never lived in this house. There'll be nobody else here but my son and his mother' (p. 120). But life is a continuity, as tragic plots insist, and what Mrs Alving has prepared for herself with all her nineteen years of suppression – running her husband's estate, disguising his debaucheries and stifling the rumours – is only a series of more terrifying discoveries. Oswald has carried his father's inheritance inside him all along; and because he has been away so many years, he and she are essentially strangers. One last twist she could not foresee: because he does not know Regine is his half-sister, he plans to live with her.

Thus far, Ibsen is working on a favourite theme, the loss of long-cherished illusions. But the unusual seriousness of this play shows in the turn it takes when Oswald and Mrs Alving are finally left alone. Ibsen has already exploited the grotesque distance between those who cannot imagine death, and those who must expect it hourly, in the scenes between Nora and Dr Rank in *A Doll's House*. But the discrepancy is made more ghastly here by the fact that it is a mother and son who cannot grasp each other's realities, and because it is not death but infantilization that threatens. What Oswald must expect is a brainstroke that will leave him 'a helpless child again. To have to be fed, to have to be . . . Oh, it doesn't bear talking about!' (p. 160). The dilemma is exposed with a classic, almost Euripidean lucidity: when is a son not a son, but a man in need? When is a mother not a mother, but a friend? Oswald refuses to carry on living on such degrading terms, and needs a 'helping hand' to reach out to him when the final helplessness descends. His half-sister Regine would have done it, because she would have shared his horror and 'she was so marvellously light-hearted' (p. 162). Without her, he must look elsewhere:

> *Osw.* Well then, now you'll have to give me this helping hand, Mother.
> *Mrs. A.* [*with a scream*]. Me!
> *Osw.* There's nobody with a better right than you.
> *Mrs. A.* Me! Your mother!
> *Osw.* All the more reason.
> *Mrs. A.* Me! Who gave you life!
> *Osw.* I never asked you for life. And what sort of a life is this you've given me? I don't want it! Take it back! (p. 162)

Although, conventionally speaking, the tragedy here is Oswald's – he is the one facing death or humiliation – Ibsen's treatment makes it clear that the deeper dilemma is Mrs Alving's. She is being stretched on the Euripidean rack, between her role as a mother and her individuality as a woman. She gave Oswald life, a life he did not ask for. Having given it, she may equally take it away: 'there's nobody with a better right than you', as he says. But this is the child's point of view; as a mother, she has always nurtured his body and his spirit at the same time, and now she is being asked to choose between them. The poignancy of this choice rests on a familiar problem: both body and spirit are central to humanity, but bodies come first. In her generic role, as mother, there can be no value more important to Mrs Alving than life itself; and Oswald is asking her to annihilate it in him on the grounds that some kinds of life are not worth living. He is requiring her to be a friend to his spirit, not his body; and to kill not only him, but the mother in herself, in the name of something that transcends them both.

The excruciating request is made just at the moment Mrs Alving thought herself to be free – free of the need to placate convention, free of her husband and the past. But now she must fight clear of a desire much deeper than convention: to mother the son she was deprived of so long, and to confirm her motherhood, if she so chooses, in grotesque perpetuity. She has already shown herself a friend to Oswald's spirit in sending him away from home so early, at great cost to herself; and when Oswald begs for her promise now, she gives it – after a moment's silence: 'Here is my hand on it' (p. 163). But she does it to assuage his agony at the time; all her instincts pull in the opposite direction, as we see from the way she adds, 'if it becomes necessary. But it won't *be* necessary.' When the stroke almost immediately follows, Ibsen sums up the grounds of Oswald's appeal in the only syllables he can speak: 'The sun . . . The sun . . .'. And the play famously ends with Mrs Alving undecided, trapped between horror at him, and horror at herself: 'No, no, no! . . . Yes! . . . No, no! (p. 164).

In leaving the decision suspended, Ibsen essentially passes it over from Mrs Alving to the audience.[7] Rather than allowing us to blame her (which would probably be the result, whichever course she took), he leaves us with the dilemma she exposes. The power of the mother, which tragic plots so often view from the point of the son, is tragic for the mother too. What the hero sees as the hampering way she interposes her body between himself and his honour, from her point of view looks quite different. She is acting in the name of honour, too: but it is a woman's sense of honour, as Ibsen would describe it, which makes life itself the supreme value.

---

7   He was quite genuinely undecided. To William Archer's probing, he answered, 'I should never dream of answering such a difficult question.' When Archer speculated that Mrs Alving might hope that the illness was not incurable, Ibsen said: 'Probably that is the answer – that a mother would always postpone the helping hand with the idea that where there was life there was hope.' *Ghosts and Other Plays*, trans. Peter Watts (Harmondsworth: Penguin, 1964, repr. 1978), p. 294.

But Mrs Alving is not only a mother: she is an individual trying to live in the light, and she gave what Oswald asked her for, a binding promise. The precision of Ibsen's statement of her dilemma shows in the way it can still be described in Aeschylean terms, as the old argument between the Furies, Apollo and Athena. Oswald asks to be allowed to die in the name of transcendent values. His death would affirm what he affirmed in life, as an Apollonian artist: that creativity and the love of truth are what make us human, while the body is merely the physical vehicle, which decays and passes. All he can use to make his desire effective, however, is to ask for a promise, made of words; and after his stroke his body remains in the hands of his mother, for whom it is still the body she bore, and could care for for ever. If she takes on that role she will be what Oswald is most afraid of: a kind of Fury, for whom only the material realm of blood and bodies is real, and for whom a drooling, incontinent, overgrown baby is better than no baby at all. What he wants from her is a decision like Athena's: that she put minds before bodies, and however female in form, that she be male in outlook. Athena's casting vote for Orestes made it possible for Athenian sons to be Athenian citizens; and Oswald wants his citizen's rights, too, even from his mother. Athena, however, was born from Zeus' forehead. Mrs Alving is a human mother and whatever she does, the choice must split her apart.

The impact of Ibsen's analysis of these 'modern tragedies' across Europe was extraordinary: the controversy, venom and admiration they stirred showed how intimately he was diagnosing the audience's most intimate traumas. In literary terms, the importance of what he was uncovering is best attested by Strindberg, who wrote a short story in reply to *A Doll's House*, in which he shows the wife as balefully influenced by a feminist for a while, but happy to return to her husband's arms at the end. Not content with this, he went on to write a play, *Sir Bengt's Wife*, set in the sixteenth century: this also shows a wife rebelling against her husband, but the power of love preventing her from finally leaving (he actually sent this play to Ibsen, then in Rome). But these polemical revisions were written before the break-up of Strindberg's own marriage. After this, he expressed his feelings in a ferocious portrait of a marriage in which the wife far outdoes Nora or Mrs Alving in ignorance and destructiveness.

August Strindberg, *The Father* (1887)

In *The Father*, a wife compensates herself for her lack of power in law by monstrously abusing her power as a mother. She gets her husband certified as insane so that he has no rights over their daughter – and her weapon is the insinuation that he is not the daughter's father. It is impossible to view this play purely in terms of art: Strindberg himself said that 'as a creative writer I blend fiction with reality',[8] and the play is painfully autobiographical (at the time, he too was convinced that his ex-wife was trying to have him certified). It is deeply interesting, however, as a testimony to the feelings Ibsen's diagnosis aroused in a hypersensitive male. Strindberg felt Ibsen had abandoned the male cause and treacherously given the stage over to the wives:

> What would have happened to *A Doll's House* if Helmer had received a little justice? Or to *Ghosts* if Mr. Alving had been allowed to live and tell the audience that his wife was lying about him? No – just blame everything on them, blacken their names, tread them in the mud so that they haven't a square inch left clean – that makes for good theatre![9]

There is a larger idea than personal hostility behind the play, however. If the battle lines of the drama seem familiar, the power of mothers and the fragility of fatherhood, it is also because Strindberg has been fired by the *Oresteia* in the light of the new theory of matriarchy put forward by the historian Bachofen, 'Mother-right' (*Das Mutterrecht*, 1861). Bachofen suggested that the Greek drama reflected an actual historical event, a key moment in the establishment of civilization: the victory of patriarchy over an original matriarchy. This theory set off a Europe-wide discussion about the possibility that the emancipation of women could actually reverse this victory.[10] This makes it less surprising that Strindberg writes as openly as he does in this play about the sex 'war' in which 'one of us must go under' (p. 61) and pushes his characterization of both the Captain and his wife Laura to such extremes. There is also Social Darwinism at work: the Captain says, 'if it is true that we are descended from the ape, it must have been from two different species. We aren't of the same blood, are we?' (p. 61).

The husband Strindberg creates to carry the male side of the argument is an Apollonian male to the *n*th degree. He is a military man, and we first meet him booted and spurred in his study, with weapons on the wall and newspapers on his table. When not on the parade ground, he is making similarly important strides in science: he has discovered carbon in meteorites, we learn, and is about to astonish the scientific world with a paper. The Doctor says he has 'a powerful and lucid intelligence' (p. 37), and he epitomizes mental power and self-control. His only problem is with the women in his household: we learn that he lives not only with his wife and daughter, but his mother-in-law, his old nurse, and his daughter's

---

[8]   Michael Meyer, *Strindberg* (Oxford: Oxford University Press, 1987) [first publ. Secker & Warburg, 1985], p. 171.

[9]   Ibid. (letter to Edvard Brandes, 1887), intro., p. 16.

[10]   Bachofen's subtitle is 'an investigation of the religious and judicial character of matriarchy in the ancient world' and the theory is not hostile to women in itself (Simon Goldhill, *Reading Greek Tragedy* (Cambridge: Cambridge University Press, 1986, repr. 1992), p. 51). But the debate reached Strindberg from an 1886 article by Paul Lafargue, who speculated that 'a return to the matriarchal pattern would involve an equally long and bloody war' to the war that suppressed it (*The Father*, trans. Meyer, p. 14, n. 1).

governess, all of whom have different but equally impractical plans for the education of the daughter, Bertha. The Captain's rational plan is that she should train as a teacher. But he senses that the women are ganging up against him; and when his brother-in-law sympathizes ('you've too many women running your home'), the Captain answers, with a hint of Strindberg's own paranoia, 'You needn't tell me that. It's like a cage full of tigers – if I didn't keep a red-hot iron in front of their noses, they'd claw me to the ground the first chance they got' (p. 30).

If the women are strong, it is only by underhand means: 'between you and me, they're not fighting strictly according to the rules of chivalry', the Captain remarks (p. 32). All of them are associated with darkness in various ways (the mother-in-law does spirit-rapping, the nurse is a die-hard Baptist, the wife is an eavesdropper) and Bertha complains that 'everything's so gloomy, so horrible, like a winter night' in her home – though she obligingly adds, 'when you come, father, it's like throwing open the window on a spring morning!' (p. 43). In their obscurantism, ignorance and home-centred values these women are evidently a variant of the Furies at their worst; and chief amongst them is Laura, the wife, who is working in every way to undermine her husband. The plot blackens her to a point where she is less a character than a focal point for Strindberg's unmanageable feelings. Thus, she has not only intercepted the Captain's requests to his bookseller, so that his scientific discovery will probably be anticipated by someone else, but she has written to all his friends confiding her doubts about his mental stability. To make doubly sure, she has displaced their old doctor in favour of a new one, whom she has primed to see the Captain as a mental patient; and the climax of her plan is to send him mad by insinuating that his daughter is not his own. In this way, she can obtain legal control over her daughter, and settle the question of her future without reference to him: she thinks Bertha is a gifted painter, and wants her to train as an artist.

Strindberg's personal investment produces some confusion in the play on the subject of madness: he seems torn between implying that the Captain is as sane as anyone could be with such a wife, and insisting that no man can withstand the power of women. He also seems to have been impressed by the dialogue between Oswald and his mother about the progress of his softening of the brain, so that the Captain coolly predicts the onset of his own insanity, to odd effect: 'soon my judgment will be clouded and my thoughts begin to wander. This is the approaching dementia for which you have been waiting, and which may come at any time' (p. 56).

But despite the lack of credibility in the story, the grounds on which Strindberg alleges that women are the stronger sex are classically familiar. The issue of Bertha's education is central because the Captain feels 'it isn't enough for me to have given the child life. I want to give it my soul too' (p. 41). When he has to doubt whether he gave the child 'life' at all, he bursts out: 'To me this child was my life hereafter. She was my idea of immortality – perhaps the only one that has any roots in reality. Take her away and you cut short my life' (p. 58). What makes men critically weak in relation to women is that they cannot give birth.

The unfairness of nature's distribution of power shows in the following tirade, from a quarrel that ends with the Captain throwing a burning lamp at Laura. But that, Strindberg implies, is what happens when the Apollonian male is robbed of all he relies on: war, science, progeny, honour (there are overtones of 'Othello's occupation's gone'):

> *Capt.* You were always the one who had the upper hand . . . You could give me a raw potato and make me think it was a peach . . . For you lacked intelligence, and instead of following my advice you did as you wanted. But when, later, I awoke and looked about me and saw that my honour had been sullied, I wanted to wipe out the stain through a noble action, a brave deed, a discovery, or an honourable suicide. I wanted to go to war, but I couldn't. It was then that I turned to science. Now, when I should stretch out my hand to receive the fruits of my labour, you chop off my arm. Now I am without honour, and I cannot go on living, for a man cannot live without honour.
>
> *Laura* But a woman –
>
> *Capt.* She has her children, but he has none. (p. 61)

'A man cannot live without honour': in this context it becomes clearer than ever that the man's sense of himself is a construct, a 'name' made by any means available (brave deeds, scientific discoveries, even suicide if necessary). A woman, however simply *is*, as her children *are*. And the man's ultimate humiliation is that he will never know whether the children who bear his name are actually his. 'You can never be sure' (p. 28) is a point made in the second scene of the play, and reiterated four times.

Strindberg's lack of control in this area shows in the way the Captain's would-be nobility slides into pettishness: 'I wanted to go to war, but I couldn't. It was then that I turned to science. Now . . . you chop off my arm.' The imputation that Laura has witch-like powers ('you could give me a raw potato and make me think it was a peach') also belongs more to paranoia than to art: this is how Strindberg felt his wife dominated him in his own psychological collapse. But even if the testimony is involuntary, the seesaw between assertiveness and infantilism Strindberg portrays is striking, and not very far from Othello or Pentheus at their worst moments. The other side of aggressive misogyny is profound weakness.

When the end comes for the Captain, it does so in the form of his old Nurse with a straitjacket hidden behind her back. He and she have already had a premonitory exchange of impressive clarity:

> *Capt.* Can you explain to me how it is that you women can treat an old man as though he was a child?

> *Nurse* Don't ask me. I suppose it's because, whether you're little boys or
> grown men, you're all born of woman.
> *Capt.* But no woman is born of man. (p. 47)

And at the end of the play, it is she who wheedles him into the trap, by
reminiscing about the way she used to dress him in childhood:

> I had to coax you and say I'd give you a gold coat and dress you like a
> prince . . . [I] said: 'Put your arms in', and then I said: 'sit still, now, and
> be a good boy while I button up the back!' [*She has got the straitjacket on
> him.*] (p. 72)

Imprisoned by female treachery, and taunted in his helplessness by Laura ('Do
you think I am your enemy?'), the Captain is given a comprehensive speech of
denunciation by Strindberg, before he collapses into incoherence:

> I think you are all my enemies. My mother was my enemy. She didn't want
> to bring me into the world because my birth would cause her pain. She
> robbed my first embryo of its nourishment, so that I was born half-
> crippled. My sister was my enemy, when she taught me that I was her
> inferior. The first woman I kissed was my enemy – she gave me ten years
> of disease in return for the love I gave her. My daughter became my
> enemy, when you forced her to choose between you and me. And you, my
> wife, you were my mortal enemy, for you didn't let go of me until there
> was no life left in me. (p. 74)

The accusations that tumble out of the Captain's mouth are only astonishing in
their frankness. In more veiled guises, they are familiar: the grudging mother
('she robbed my embryo of its nourishment'), the dominating sister (it is for
brothers to assume superiority), the mistress who rewards a man's fidelity with
disease (women are poisoned bait, as in *Hamlet*), the daughter who must be all
her father's, or nothing (shades of *Lear*); and, finally, the wife who will stoop to
any low dealing to win the sex war, and does not seek power over her husband
but his annihilation (Clytaemnestra and Medea). If we stand back from this
barrage of charges for a moment, however, another pattern emerges: the
accusation that women are, always and everywhere, to blame, made with childish
fury. Viewed like this, the Captain's outpouring becomes an intelligible, if
paranoid, deduction from the stark fact that it is a mother who gives life, and
therefore is in some sense responsible for everything.

   In this light, the deep-seated ambivalence of the end of the play is easier to
understand. Laura can be left to carry the moral responsibility while the Captain's
sanity fades sadly away, in heroic raving: 'Ah, my brave lion's skin, that you
would take from me! Omphale! Omphale! . . . Awake, Hercules, before they take
your club from you!' (p. 75). His end is a variant of Oswald's terror in *Ghosts*, of
finishing up as an infantilized adult entirely dependent for bodily care on women.
But it is not as clear as in Ibsen that this conclusion is terrible; or rather, it is part
of its terror that it is also intensely desirable:

What kind of a pillow have you given me, Margaret? It's so hard and cold, so cold! Come and sit beside me here, on that chair. That's right. May I rest my head in your lap? So. That's warm! Bend over so that I can feel your breast. Oh, it is sweet to sleep at a woman's breast, whether a mother's or a mistress's, but sweetest at a mother's! (pp. 75–6)

We may think back to Pentheus, so fatally tempted by the 'cradle' of 'his mother's arms'. Death, under these circumstances, is a kind of luxury; among other things, it allows the Captain back into his Nurse's lap without reproach: 'I'm so tired, so tired. Good night, Margaret. Blessed be thou amongst women –' *He raises himself, but falls with a cry in the NURSE's lap.* (p. 76).

Ibsen acknowledged being 'gripped' by Strindberg's 'violent strength', though he drily noted, 'Strindberg's observations and experiences in the sphere of which *The Father* principally treats do not accord with my own.'[11] To judge from *The Master Builder* (1892), *Little Eyolf* (1894), *John Gabriel Borkman* (1896) and *When We Dead Awaken* (1900), the power of women was of much less concern to him for the rest of his career than the destructiveness of men. The polarity between men's needs and women's is relentlessly exposed in these plots, where the men are full of guilt and the women of bitterness, and the men's fulfilment (save in the case of Allmers in *Little Eyolf*) is always bought at the price of the women's creativity. Aline Solness had a gift 'for building up children's souls'[12] but all the nurseries in her house are empty; Ella Rentheim has been 'cheated . . . of a mother's joy and happiness in life'[13] by Borkman's career, and Irena, the artist's Muse, violently reproaches Rubek: 'I should have brought children into the world, many children . . . That should have been my vocation; I should never have served you, you poet!'[14] Again and again the women reproach the men with a 'sin that there's no forgiveness for . . . the sin of killing love in a human creature' (Ella to Borkman, p. 331). And with Irena the bitterness finally takes the form of 'thin sharp knife' she draws from her breast, as she asks, like another Clytaemnestra: 'Arnold – have you done some harm to our child?' (p. 268). This 'child' is the only thing he allowed her to give birth to, the cold stone sculpture for which she modelled.

But the men in these later plays of Ibsen serve the powers that they hear calling to them, with a perturbation not unlike Strindberg's: Solness talks to God from church spires, Borkman hears metals singing to him in the mines and calling for their freedom, and Rubek serves his art so perfectly it annihilates his ability to live. And Ibsen's handling of these heroes is a mixture of denigration and awe.

---

[11] Meyer, *Strindberg*, p. 186.
[12] Henrik Ibsen, *The Master Builder and Other Plays* [*Rosmersholm, Little Eyolf, John Gabriel Borkman*], trans. Una Ellis-Fermor (Harmondsworth: Penguin, 1958), p. 172.
[13] Ibid., p. 334.
[14] Ibsen, *Ghosts and Other Plays*, trans. Watts, p. 271.

Their faults and absurdities are unsparingly observed, but the imperatives that drive them, and their submission to the 'troll' within, he cannot satirize: they stand, we must suspect, for what he knew about himself and the way the impersonal service of art cut across the demands of ordinary life in his own marriage.

In each play Ibsen imagines a 'pagan' character who might be blessedly immune to guilt, like Hilde in *The Master Builder* or the lustful bear-hunter in *When We Dead Awaken*; but his real concern is with the guilt-laden victims at the centre of the plays, who receive messages from another world which cause nothing but destruction in this one. John Gabriel Borkman ruins his bank by wild speculation, but the play allows him to describe his dream with the utmost seriousness. It was worth sacrificing his marriage to Ella for the sake of advancement at the bank, says Borkman, because 'if it comes to that, then one woman can be replaced by another'; but his work at the bank could not be postponed. He wanted to 'waken all the slumbering spirits of the gold' in Norway:

> All the sources of power in this land – I wanted to make them subject to me. Everything that earth and fell and wood and sea contained and all their riches – I wanted to subdue it all and create a kingdom for myself and through it the well-being of many, many thousands of others. (p. 332)

The faint echo here of the Jew of Malta's vision of the earth's bounty, and of the poetry inherent in commerce and wealth, is reminiscent of Marlowe's ambivalent empathy with his overreachers. Is Ibsen's seesaw of guilt and aspiration in these late, repetitive plays perhaps a modern variant of Marlowe's? Certainly he shares Marlowe's problem that his defiance of Christianity absorbs his best energy, and while deriding the ethic of duty ('that horrid, ugly word . . . so cold and sharp' as Hilde puts it, p. 164), he still retains the habit of thinking in terms of sacrificial death. All his heroic sinners end the plays by climbing to their last fall, Solness from his tower, Borkman high on the mountainside, and Rubek on an even higher peak, swept away by an avalanche. And an Athenian would be surprised to learn that 'pagans' without guilt are exempt from other problems: Ibsen's assumption that outside Christianity there are no gods to struggle with, is nothing if not wishful.

It is only in *Little Eyolf* that Ibsen manages to analyse the competing claims of men and women in any sustained way, and where the ambiguity of the hero's aspirations is not swept away by a cathartic death. Allmers is still alive at the end of the play, and still confronting an agonizing choice between his instincts as a male and the expectations of his wife. Although this makes the play less dramatically satisfying, it has other satisfactions missing from the more conclusive plots above: bold analysis of the sexual dynamic of Allmers' marriage, for instance, and a conscious treatment of incest – a subject which Ibsen has often touched on (*Ghosts, Rosmersholm*) but never before allowed into the centre of a play. *Little Eyolf* is a drama full of hesitations and unfinished suggestions; but that may be because the truths it is trying to tell are such painful ones.

Little Eyolf (1894)

As a hero, Allmers has none of the magnetism of Solness or Borkman, and no radiant vision to confide to us. Ibsen has the courage to make him unprepossessing: 'a thin, slightly built man, about thirty-six or thirty-seven years old, mild-eyed, and with thin brown hair and beard' (stage direction, p. 218). He is a bookish former tutor, living on his wife's money, who has come down from his vacation in the mountains having decided not to write his long-awaited masterwork, a tome on 'Human Responsibility'. He is devoting himself instead to a human responsibility nearer hand, his crippled son, Little Eyolf:

> I'm going to try and bring light to all the rich potentialities that are dawning in his child's mind. All the seeds of nobility in him, I want to make them shoot up – to flower and come to fruition . . . Eyolf shall be the crowning achievement of our family. And I will find my new life-work in making him that consummation. (p. 230)

This commitment to a real, earthbound responsibility, promising as it sounds, is shot through with irony in the context. This vision of his new obligations has come to Allmers after he has plagued the child for years with laborious lessons, and he was stargazing in the mountains when he made his decision ('almost in communion with them', p. 231). Even when Allmers intends to be as creative as a mother, Ibsen implies, he does so as a male, for whom the world of the real can only be approached by way of transcendence; and the level of coercion lurking in his vision shows in the way he phrases himself, '*making* him that consummation.'

The Apollonian hero in this play, then, has none of the natural advantages of Solness and John Gabriel Borkman, magnetic and persuasive as they are. What he has, rather, are the manifest limitations of Apollo in the *Eumenides*, deracination and a nervous self-consciousness that is not the same thing as self-knowedge. But because Allmers is so lacking in charm, Ibsen can tell truths about him that he tells nowhere else: for instance, that his response to his wife's sexual needs is deep fear, and his most heartfelt attachment in the play is an incestuous one, to his half-sister Asta (although the play will reveal that she is not related to him after all). On the subject of the Allmers' marriage, Ibsen is notably direct: Rita tries to seduce her husband by loosening her hair, lighting rose-pink lamps, and putting champagne on the table; to all of which, Alfred asks about Little Eyolf's digestion and goes to bed (p. 238). Driven to more and more open demands, Rita seems more and more voracious. But Ibsen shows that it is the desperate evasiveness of Allmers that is making her so: 'I *must* share myself between Eyolf and you', he says, with pretend rationality, when Rita demands that he be all hers (p. 236). But when Rita finally asks, 'What did you feel for me, then, at the very beginning?', Alfred is cornered, and he answers in one shocking word: *skrekk*, 'dread' (p. 261).[15]

---

[15]   Northam comments, 'There is no English word that I can think of capable of applying the whiplash of the Norwegian 'skrekk'. Alfred's single word needs to be felt

It is another token of the honesty of the play that Little Eyolf's lameness is not for the sake of pathos, but has a secret history like the syphilis in *Ghosts*. He was not born lame, but became so from a fall as a baby, when Rita and Alfred left him to sleep among pillows on a table while they made love. This alone would justify their corroding guilt, as parents caught between the child's rights and their own, and unable to repair in a lifetime the inattention of a minute; but the occasion was still more significant. At the 'irresistibly beautiful moment' (p. 262), swept away by Rita's passion, Alfred confided to her a secret which gives us a clue to the deeper cause of the lameness of Little Eyolf: that Asta would have been called Eyolf if she had been a boy, and this was his pet name for her when they were small. With this we can tie together all the other hints about Alfred and Asta's relationship: their special intimacy when left as orphans, her pleasure in wearing his cast-off boy's clothes, and his deep protectiveness towards her, which made marrying a rich wife the best solution to their joint poverty. The feelings between Alfred and Rita are as hopelessly crippled as Eyolf.

Ibsen is acute about the pathology of incest: it goes along with a deep need to return to the past and block out the forces that make for change. Alfred is shown yearning for his innocent childhood with Asta, after what seems to him the profound contamination of marriage. His religious reverence for their old life when even their sexual difference was disguised, reverberates back to Hippolytus' reverent comradeship with Artemis in the 'inviolate meadow' of chastity. And his deep desire to remain Asta's brother for ever may remind us of Antigone's conviction that brothers are more serious, and longer-lasting, than husbands:

> *Allm.* I'll come to you – my dear, dear sister. I *must* come back to you. Home to you, to be purified and restored after my life with –
>
> *Asta* [*shocked*] Alfred, that's a sin against Rita!
>
> *Allm.* I have sinned against her. But not in this. Oh, just think of it, Asta! What was our life like together, yours and mine? Wasn't it like one long, high holy day from first to last?
>
> *Asta* Yes, it was, Alfred. But a time like that can't be lived over again.
>
> *Allm.* [*bitterly*] Do you mean that marriage has ruined me so completely?
>
> *Asta* [*peaceably*] No, I don't mean that.
>
> *Allm.* Well, then, we two will live our old life over again.
>
> *Asta* [*decidedly*] We can't do that, Alfred.
>
> *Allm.* Yes, we can. A brother's and a sister's love –
>
> *Asta* [*breathless*] Yes, What?
>
> *Allm.* That relation is the only one that's not subject to the law of change.
> (p. 264)

---

almost as a physical blow because the revelation is so vital for all its brevity . . . we have suddenly revealed to us a marriage entered into in terror by the husband; terror mitigated for a while by physical infatuation, and subdued by something quite different, the need to provide for Asta.' John Northam, *Ibsen, a Critical Study* (Cambridge: Cambridge University Press, 1973), pp. 201–2.

Asta has just discovered from reading her mother's old letters that she is not Alfred's half-sister as they always supposed, so it is at this point she must reveal to him the disappointing truth: their relationship is subject to the 'law of change' after all. Ibsen shrewdly shows Alfred trying to cling on to Asta anyway – their relationship will be 'just as sacred for all that' he assures her (p. 264) – but Asta knows better. She tears herself away from the passion between them, which has lost its protective barrier, and leaves reluctantly with one of Ibsen's happy pagans, the road-builder Borghejm. 'It is a flight', she admits, 'from you – and from myself' (p. 273).

It is perhaps because he tells such deep if unwelcome truths about Alfred's Apollonian rationality – its boggy foundations, which make his ambitions so transcendent, and about the interplay between fine words and crippled feelings – that Ibsen's imagination is able to generate such an extraordinary expression of the forces Alfred is struggling with in the shape of the Rat Wife. This openly symbolic character is so unexpected, and so full of vitality, that the one scene in which she appears almost derails the realism of the rest. But if we attend to the details of her presentation, and to her oddly tender speeches about vermin, we can see that Ibsen is doing something parallel here to his creation of the 'ghosts': finding a Scandinavian equivalent to the Furies.

The Rat Wife is a 'little, thin, shrivelled' (p. 222) old maid in black, with a lively black dog, much like the 'aged maidens' who snuffed out Orestes in Delphi. Like them, she is confident in her wisdom, but connected with sources of horror that no one wants to be reminded of; after she leaves the house, Rita rushes out for air. Her language about the rats deliberately reminds us of the 'gnawing' of bad conscience, and her opening line is precision itself: 'Have the master and mistress got anything that gnaws (or 'torments', *gnager*) here in the house?' Allmers denies that they have – 'We? No, I don't think so' – but she is echoing the word he has just used of Eyolf's lameness – 'how this gnaws [*nager*] at my heart, all this'.[16] When rodents flourish they destroy all the sustenance around them. The Rat Wife has just been dealing with a plague on the islands where 'it swarmed and teemed with them'; and as she gleefully says, 'up on the beds they scribbled and scrabbled the whole night long' (the location, we might feel, is not accidental). However reluctantly, the islanders were forced to send for her – 'because they'd nothing left to live on' (p. 223).

The Rat Wife's unexpected warmth of feeling for the rats allows us into an interesting area of ambivalence. She does not poison them or treat them as genuine vermin: she charms them into the water by playing her pipes, and they drown themselves like the rats of Hamlin. The watery depths are 'as quiet and nice and dark for them as ever they can want', she says; 'they sleep down there, such a long, sweet sleep. All of them, that human beings hate and persecute' (p. 225). Her partiality to the rats and her sense that they deserve kindness for being

---

16   Northam, *Ibsen*, p. 189 (translations his).

(with a biblical echo) 'hated and persecuted so bitterly' (p. 222), takes us oddly close to Athena's judgement on the seemingly hateful Furies: 'Yet these, too, have their work. We cannot brush them aside' (*Eum.* 476).

Athena's tolerance was, of course, in deliberate contrast to Apollo's detestation: 'They hold the evil darkness of the Pit below / Earth, loathed alike by men and by the heavenly gods' (*Eum.* 72–3). The Rat Wife's curious protectiveness towards her vermin, and the shuddering revulsion that she evokes in Rita's sitting-room, re-establishes something of that Aeschylean contrast. Civilized people only send for her when they are driven to it; and though she evidently expects to have work to do in this house, no one admits to knowing what she has come for, least of all Alfred. There is also an Aeschylean irony lurking in her function, which is simply to drown the vermin because people find them hateful, just as Apollo wanted to scourge the Furies out of his temple. This is not the same thing as finding the right place for the insistent reminders of a bad conscience; but it does put a stop to the 'gnawing.'

Some such explanation is required, if we are to follow the nightmare logic of the plot after the Rat Wife's disappearance. For she does succeed in drowning something from the house: she drowns Little Eyolf, who follows her, entranced, to the end of the jetty and falls in. Little Eyolf was the most tormenting of all the rats in this home; and Ibsen shows what a level of honesty he intends to maintain in this play by not making his death the dramatic climax (we are only at the end of Act I), but a radical way of exposing the Allmers' marriage. Eyolf's underwater corpse converts, by familiar Greek logic, into another tormenting Fury. Their son was seen 'lying on his back. And with wide open eyes . . . Day and night he will be before me', wails Rita (p. 254).

She and Alfred now turn against one other, launching their accusations with intimate cruelty. Alfred sees Eyolf's death as what Rita most wanted, because Asta had intercepted the child's love after the accident. She furiously assents: 'Exactly! I can't bear to share a thing with anyone else! Not when it's love!' But her charge against Alfred is still more accurate: although he intended to 'make a wonder-child' of Eyolf, he has 'never had any real love for him either, not really'. When Alfred protests that he only wanted to make the child happy, she says: 'But not for love of him. Look into yourself . . . and examine all that lies beneath it – and behind.' They bitterly conclude that 'we two have never really possessed our own child'; yet 'here we are, grieving like this, over a strange little boy' (pp. 256–7).

Now the child is dead, Alfred is driven to still more desperate strategies to fend off Rita's sexuality. They will never be wholly free from Eyolf's presence again, he says, with the child between them:

> Allm. [*slowly, looking sternly at her*] There must always be a barrier
>   between us two in future.
> Rita   Why must there – ?

Allm.	Who knows whether the wide open eyes of a child aren't watching us night and day?
Rita	[*low, shuddering*] Alfred – that's a terrible thought to have!
Allm.	Our love has been like a consuming fire. Now it must be quenched –
Rita	[*going towards him*] Quenched!
Allm.	[*in a hard voice*] It is quenched – in one of us. (p. 260)

In drawing the battle lines between husband and wife, Ibsen shows a classic firmness: on the woman's side a frantic hunger for the realities of bodies and sexual passion, and on the man's, a defensive transcendence, a drive towards any pseudo-abstraction that evades the life of the body:

Rita	[*as if turned to stone*] And you dare say that to me!
Allm.	[*more gently*] It's dead, Rita. But in what I feel for you now, in our common guilt and longing to atone – in that I think I see a kind of resurrection –
Rita	[*violently*] Oh, I'm not interested in resurrections!
Allm.	Rita!
Rita	I'm a warm-blooded human animal, myself! I don't go round drowsing – with fish-blood in my veins. [*Wringing her hands.*] And to be shut in for a life-time – in remorse and misery! Shut in with someone who's no longer mine, mine, mine. (pp. 260–1)

It is in this context that we learn that Allmers married Rita in a state of 'dread'. This brutal honesty leads us on to the history of Eyolf's lameness, and the telling detail about Asta-Eyolf which makes it clear why this marriage has been crippled from the first.

Alfred ends Act II with no defences left. He has neither his dream of self-fulfilment by means of Little Eyolf, nor his secret reliance on 'Big Eyolf', Asta. Rita, for her part, no longer seems to have a husband. Ibsen's late plays are full of desolate marriages, but this is the one in which he best conveys the staleness of marital stalemate. But as he lingers on the emptiness, he also indicates the potential for growth in this marriage if each partner can meet the other half-way. The end of the play shows Rita and Allmers feeling their way towards a reconciliation; and at the last moment they achieve a hand-clasp – not very much in itself, but a great deal in the context.

Their dialogue centres on the classic question of what place transcendence has in human life, and what are the necessary claims of the real world. Rita shows the first sign of growth, in saying that she would be willing to share Alfred with his book, if he would return to work; 'I'm more easily satisfied now,' she says (p. 276). Alfred, however, is still yearning for the mountains, which for him are synonymous with 'the peace and well-being of the presence of death' – and being grounded for him is something to deplore: 'We're so earthbound, Rita, both of us' (p. 278). But they are interrupted by something more obviously earthy, the screaming and yelling from the fishermen's shacks on the beach below, as the drunken fathers come home and set upon their children. Alfred is disgusted: the hovels should be swept away, he says, and the people dispersed (like vermin, we are tempted to add). But the intrusion sets off a new train of thought in Rita: she speaks in a warmer, more positive voice of a plan that is coming to her, to fill up her life when Alfred has gone back to his mountains:

> As soon as you've left me, I shall go down to the shore and bring all those poor, outcast children up here with me to our place. All the wretched little boys . . . I will make them my own . . . They shall have Eyolf's rooms to live in. They shall have his books to read. His toys to play with. They shall take turns at sitting in his chair at table. (p. 280)

Alfred is incredulous: 'I don't know a person in the world less fitted for a thing like that than you' (p. 280). But Rita is not to be shaken: she replies, like a graver Nora, 'Then I must educate myself for it. Teach myself. Train myself.' All these verbs in the Norwegian have the prefix '*opp-*', meaning 'up' or 'upwards'; this is her version of transcendence, which becomes truly valuable at last when attached to the real.[17] It turns out that all Alfred's talk about 'human responsibility' in preparation for his unwritten book has not been wasted. This is Rita's understanding of it; and in spite of himself, Alfred is moved to a new unselfishness. It is true that they have never shared their wealth: 'Perhaps I could join you? And help you, Rita?'

The rightness of Rita's instincts shows in her ready acknowledgement that she does not expect to love the boys ('at least, not yet'), but 'to make [her] peace . . . with the wide open eyes'. Little Eyolf will cease to be a Fury to them; and they will find a repose that is not the drowsy underwater kind: 'You'll see – the peace of the sabbath will rest upon us from time to time', she promises Allmers (p. 282). And to complete the Aeschylean train of thought about the conversion of guilt to creative uses, Ibsen shows them imagining how the transcendent peace of the mountains may come to them in life, not death. Eyolf and Asta may covert to their good spirits, to Scandinavian Eumenides. 'We shall know then, perhaps, that the spirits are with us . . . those whom we have lost', say Allmers:

> Rita   [*nodding slowly*] Our Little Eyolf. And your big Eyolf, too.
> Allm. [*gazing ahead*] It may be that, once or twice on life's way, we shall see a glimpse of them.
> Rita   Where shall we look, Alfred – ?
> Allm. [*fastening his eyes on her*] Up.
> Rita   [*nodding her agreement*] Yes, yes. Up.
> Allm. Up, – to the mountain-tops. To the stars. And to the great stillness.
> Rita   [*holding out her hand to him*] Thanks. (pp. 282–3)

The play ends on this small gesture. But we have seen so much backsliding, regression and inauthenticity on the way, that we can value the mutuality of this

---

[17] Northam, *Ibsen*, p. 213.

broken dialogue for what it is worth. And its inevitable load of symbolism compresses thoughts Ibsen has given full embodiment to in the play – in Alfred's fascination with the mountains, and the wastefulness of his impulse to *be* 'up' rather than look 'up', as here. The fact that, as we began by saying, he is left alive at the end, 'earthbound' at the foot of all his original visions, is as agonizingly uncomfortable for the audience as for him. But Ibsen's willingness to imagine him growing there, and even turning back towards his wife, tells us more about the interrelation of male and female strengths than the climactic atonements of more dazzling heroes, who fall from their towers of aspiration. Ibsen's ability to see guilt, not as something ineradicably fixed, but as something capable of change and creative application, builds on his central perception in *Ghosts*, that it is the way that guilt is repressed that makes it a plague; and in both plays the vitality and imaginative authority of his symbolism suggest that he has found his way back to the underlying truths of the *Oresteia*.

Chapter 7

Lorca

Can we trace our tragic subject any farther than *Little Eyolf*? In this chapter I shall suggest that we can, in Spain under its brief Republican government of the 1930s. Lorca wrote three 'rural tragedies' before the outbreak of the Spanish Civil War, *Blood Wedding*, *Yerma* and *The House of Bernarda Alba*, all of which are quite spectacularly expressive of the issue, 'what shall we do with the Furies?' And if it took such a deep political and social emergency to produce this sudden flowering of tragic theatre, Lorca's achievement may help us guess at the reasons why other twentieth-century writers, for all the sincerity of their efforts, have only succeeded in alluding to tragedy rather than creating it.

It cannot be irrelevant that Federico García Lorca (1898–1936) was born into a Spain still in the birth-pangs of modernity, where the Church was still attempting to wield a Counter-Reformation authority (it taught that voting for a liberal candidate was 'a mortal sin').[1] The country's violent swings between Fascism and Republicanism in Lorca's lifetime opened up the same central question as the Athenian *polis*, how to exchange outer discipline for inner discipline without lapsing into chaos. And the Andalusian culture of Lorca's childhood (he was born near Granada) gave him a still deeper insight into the paradoxical relations of passion and restraint, in its obsession with honour. No European country defined 'manhood' more anxiously than Spain, or showed itself more alive to the connection between passion and death.

Another suggestive fact about Lorca is that he was born on the land, but educated in the liberal circle in Madrid that included Manuel de Falla, Buñuel and Dalí. He thus leaped several centuries in his own lifetime, from the village world where his father was the largest landowner and he had more than 40 cousins, to the self-conscious modernity of Madrid. Because of his upbringing his ears were full of Andalusian folk-song and flamenco, and his first career was as a guitarist under Manuel de Falla. It was only by degrees that he became a lyric poet, and then a playwright, the latter as much in response to the public need as to his own development. The Republic of 1931 financed a touring company of students, La Barraca, to take Lope de Vega and Calderón to the rural population, most of whom had never seen a play and a third of whom were still illiterate. Lorca was charged with training the students, adapting the plays, and arranging the lighting and music; and, as a reporter described an open-air performance of *Life is a Dream*, he was rewarded with 'row upon row of peasant faces, smiling, in ecstasy, above all expectant, fearing and desiring what was going to happen next on the stage. And suddenly the expectation was relieved in a burst of laughter and

---

[1]   J.B. Trend, *The Origins of Modern Spain*, quoted in Ian Gibson, *The Death of Lorca* (St Albans: Paladin, 1974), p. 30.

applause.'[2] His practical training came as close as any modern writer's could to Shakespeare's, reviving the classics, acting one day and writing the next, and making theatrical magic for the semi-literate out of costumes, music and gloriously expressive language.

His world, like that of seventeenth-century London, was craving a forum for the discussion of the intimate trauma of the clash between time-honoured pieties and the freedoms of modernity, and Lorca saw the theatre as that forum: 'an open tribunal where the people can introduce old and mistaken mores as evidence and can use living examples to explain eternal norms of the heart'.[3] As the seriousness of the dramatist's role was borne in on him, his plays modulated from puppet dramas and farces into the 'rural tragedies' of the 1930s, where we can see him touching the key notes of classical tragedy with deep understanding.

Blood Wedding (1933)

The opening of Blood Wedding is ostensibly a dialogue between a mother and her son, just leaving for the vineyard. But the son is on the point of marriage (Lorca calls him Novio, 'the Bridegroom'), his mother has lost her husband and another son in a feud, and the son has asked her for a knife to cut the vines:

Mother   (muttering and looking for it). The knife, the knife . . . Damn all of them and the scoundrel who invented them.
Bridegr. Let's change the subject.
Mother   And shotguns . . . and pistols . . . even the tiniest knife . . . and mattocks and pitchforks . . .
Bridegr. Alright.
Mother   Everything that can cut a man's body. A beautiful man, tasting the fullness of life, who goes out to the vineyards or tends to his olives, because they are his, inherited . . .
Bridegr. (lowering his head). Be quiet.
Mother   . . . and that man doesn't come back. Or if he does come back it's to put a palm-leaf on him or a plateful of coarse salt to stop him swelling. I don't know how you dare carry a knife on your body, nor how I can leave the serpent inside the chest.[4]

The simple act of the son's departure uncovers potentially tragic tensions: life beginning (the son has just acquired the vineyard, which is why he can marry)

2   Ian Gibson, Federico García Lorca: A Life (London and Boston: Faber & Faber, 1989), p. 332.
3   Federico García Lorca, Three Plays, trans. Michael Dewell and Carmen Zapata (Harmondsworth: Penguin Books, 1992), introduction, p. xii.
4   Federico García Lorca, Plays: One [Blood Wedding, Doña Rosita the Spinster, Yerma] trans. Gwynne Edwards and Peter Luke (London: Methuen, 1987, repr. 1994), pp. 33–4. All references are to this edition unless otherwise stated.

juxtaposed with a memory of life ending (his father's and brother's corpses); and a sense of the beauty and vitality of the human body ('a beautiful man, tasting the fullness of life', *con su flor en la boca*)[5] and the smallness of the knife, like the bite of a 'serpent', which is all it takes to turn it into putrefying flesh. The play's paradoxical title, *Blood Wedding*, will be justified: new life will be extinguished in blood at the very moment of inception.

The world of the play is profoundly familiar too: it is one in which the circularity of the blood feud has never been arrested, and no one wants anything better. It is the world of the *Oresteia* without Athena; or perhaps more precisely, the world of Sophocles' *Electra*, where submission to the revenge ethic produces strange excitements and peculiar satisfactions. The Greek note is struck both in the fanatical adherence to 'honour' in the play, which makes the death of the two male protagonists inevitable from the start, and in the unnaturally submissive role allotted to women. Their part is simply to bear sons, to mourn them in silence, and wear black, in Electra-like loyalty to the past. The Bridegroom's mother has mourned her menfolk indoors as village propriety demands; she says, 'It's twenty years since I went to the top of the street' (p. 37) and she is half-maddened from stifling the 'scream' inside her: 'I have to force it down again and hide it in these shawls' (p. 65).

The world Lorca is describing is one where, for lack of Athena and the *polis*, both Apollo and the Furies are flourishing in their worst aspects – and the brunt of the damage is borne by women. What he brings before the 'open tribunal' in this play is the waste and squalor of a moral code in which honour takes precedence over any claim life can make. Not even the women can admit to any allegiance to Dionysus, the love of life for its own sake: the cult of masculine honour has been forced on them so brutally that they have internalized it as much as the men, and it is the Bridegroom's mother herself who sends him off to vengeance or death at the climax of the play, striking a note indistinguishable from a weary satisfaction: 'The hour of blood has come again' (p. 73, *Ha llegado otra vez la hora de la sangre*).

But since life is something that must be tossed away when honour requires, the Furies claim their own satisfactions by underhand means. They lurk in the Mother's ferocious attachment to her own blood, to the red liquid itself:

> It takes a long time [to bear a son]. That's why it's so terrible to see your blood spilt on the ground. A fountain that spurts for a minute and has cost us years. When I reached my son, he was lying in the middle of the road. I wet my hands with his blood and I licked them with my tongue. Because it was mine. You don't know what that means. I'd put the earth soaked by it in a monstrance of glass and topaz. (p. 65)

---

    5   Federico García Lorca, *Bodas de sangre*, ed. H. Ramsden (Manchester: Manchester University Press, 1980, repr. 1990), p. 4.

The nakedness of this emotion takes us all the way back to the Furies' reverential excitement over Orestes' blood, the 'bitter-swallowed drench' they anticipated with such rapture (*Eum.* 266). Blood, divorced from full humanity, becomes a value in itself – the 'materiality' of the Furies seen at its worst in a loving mother.

As the play becomes more dream-like and moves on to an openly symbolic plane in Act III, Lorca expresses the peculiar exhilaration of blood-thinking in a dialogue between the Moon and Death. The Bride has run away from her own wedding, with the son of the family that killed the Bridegroom's father and brother. The Moon is supplying the treacherous moonlight the pursuers need, and Death, in the shape of an old beggar woman, will point the way. Both of them are impatient, sensing the pleasure to come:

> *Moon*   Now they come near.
>   Some through the ravine, others by the river.
>   I shall light up the stones. What do you need?
> *Beggar Wo.* Nothing.
> *Moon*   The wind is starting to blow hard, and double-edged.
> *Beggar Wo.* Light up the waistcoat, open the buttons,
>   For then the knives will know their path.
> *Moon*   But let them die slowly. And let the blood
>   Place between my fingers its soft whistle.
>   See how my ashen valleys are awakening
>   With longing for this fountain and its trembling rush. (p. 78)

In this lascivious exchange, Lorca hints at the subterranean connections between barrenness and bloodthirstiness, sensuality and pain. The moon's 'ashen valleys' long for the rush of blood as an orgasmic irrigation; the fingers take terrible pleasure in the blood's 'soft whistle' (*su delicado silbo*). The note of intimacy with death is compellingly caught in the Beggar Woman's focus on waistcoat buttons: once they shine, the knives themselves will know their way (*las navajas ya saben el camino*). Although, at the level of the dialogue, no one has wanted this disaster, and even the errant lovers resisted their flight to the last, the play enforces the feeling that no other end was desired or desirable, and the Moon and Death have appetites in which everyone shared.

We sense the Furies of unfulfilled passion, too, in the little that gets said about the lovers' feelings. As the loveless arranged marriage approached, Leonardo, the cast-off lover, felt the 'silver wedding-pins / Turned [his] red blood black' and his flesh filled 'with poisonous weeds' (p. 82). The Bride felt her heart has 'putrified from holding out' (*podrido de aguantar*). Repression has only made everything worse:

> *Leon.* To keep quiet and burn is the greatest punishment we can heap upon ourselves. What use was pride to me and not seeing you and leaving you awake night after night? No use! It only brought the fire down on top of me! You think that time heals and walls conceal, and it's not true, not true! When the roots of things go deep, no one can pull them up!

> *Bride* (*trembling*) I can't hear you. I can't hear your voice. It's as if I'd
> drunk a bottle of anise and fallen asleep on a bedspread of roses.
> And it drags me along, and I know that I'm drowning, but I still go
> on. (p. 57)

It is in this sleepwalking mode that the lovers leave the wedding, compelled by a passion neither can analyse or name. Leonardo asks, 'Which hands / Strapped the spurs to my boots?' and the Bride simply answers, 'These hands, that are yours' (p. 81). In emphasizing the involuntariness of their motions, Lorca recreates something like the atmosphere of the end of the *Bacchae*, and perhaps for the same reasons. When passion has been repressed as ferociously as here, it returns as an irresistible, nameless power that destroys what, under different circumstances, it would have fertilized. The Bride can only say to the Bridegroom's Mother that she did want to marry her son, as desperately as a woman on fire from sores, inside and out, craves a little water (*un poquito de agua*). But – 'The other one's arm dragged me like a wave from the sea, like the butt of a mule, and would always have dragged me, always, always, even if I'd been an old woman and all the sons of your son had tried to hold me down by my hair!' (p. 90). This is not so much passion as possession, Pentheus-like, by Dionysus.

After the 'two long, piercing screams' that mark the mutual slaughter of the Bridegroom and Leonardo, the plot springs one last surprise. Even though the First Woodcutter spoke so confidently of what would be happening while the hunters searched – 'They'll have mixed their blood by then' (p. 75) – and even though our last glimpse of the Bride and Leonardo is of their perfect unity – 'Nails of moonlight join us, / My waist and your hips . . . If they separate us it will be / Because I am dead' (p. 84), nonetheless, what the Bride says in her terrible last confrontation with the Mother is that her honour is still intact: 'I want her to know that I'm clean (*limpia*), that even though I'm mad (*loca*), they can bury me and not a single man will have looked at himself in the whiteness of my breasts' (p. 90). The moment seems bizarrely Spanish: so much drama about a code that is not, finally, broken, is potentially an anti-climax. But if it is not Lorca's ultimate concession to the prejudices of his audience, the insistence that two men have died for something that did not happen may be the sharpest of all his effects in the play. For the honour code, at its worst, is merely about appearances: and the Mother who sent her only son unhesitatingly in pursuit of the family honour, is left to grieve over the meaninglessness left behind by such over-insistence on a code. She cannot even cut the Bride's throat, though the Bride offers it to her (it would be 'less effort than cutting a dahlia in your garden'): 'What does your honour matter to me? What does your death matter to me? What does anything matter to me? Blessed be the wheat, for my sons lie beneath it. Blessed be the rain, for it washes the faces of the dead. Blessed be God, for He lays us side by side so we can rest' (p. 91).

In the light of this barren ending we can better understand the puzzling lullaby that Leonardo's young wife and mother-in-law sing in Act I. Its central motif is of a great stallion standing by water that it refuses to drink. The horse is exhausted, its hooves are bleeding, but its resistance to the water is still stronger:

> Horsey will not touch the bank,
> Even though the bank is wet,
> Even though his mouth is hot,
> Streaming tiny drops of sweat.
>
> To the mountains cold and hard,
> He could only call and neigh,
> Horsey's throat is hot and parched,
> And the river bed is dry . . . (p. 40)

It is something in the stallion itself that prevents it from slaking its thirst in the water, and the river seems to stop flowing in sympathy. The blocking of the fertility that water connotes in a hot, dry country, and the blocked sexual energy it connotes by extension, could not be more powerfully expressed.[6] There will be no truly human satisfactions in this play, only the satisfactions familiar to Apollo and the Furies at their worst: the remote and abstract one, for Apollo, of knowing that the Bridegroom's family honour was saved; and for the Furies, the perverted fusion of pain and bodily ecstasy that lurks in the knife's entry into human flesh. Lorca ends the play with an intimate meditation on knives and bodies, as he began it:

> *Mother* Neighbours: with a knife,
>   With a small knife (*cuchillito*),
>   On a day appointed, between two and three,
>   The two men killed each other for love.
>   With a knife,
>   With a small knife
>   That barely fits the hand,
>   But that slides in clean
>   Through startled flesh (*las carnes asombradas*)
>   And stops at the place
>   Where trembles, enmeshed,
>   The dark root of a scream (*la oscura raíz del grito*). (p. 92)

In the wasteland of infertility described by the play, watered only by blood, it is not surprising that only the knife knows the pleasure of entering another body; or that all it quickens in the body's deepest recess is 'the dark root of a scream'.

---

6   The song is an adaptation of an Andalusian lullaby: *A la nana, nana, nana, / a la nanita de aquel / que llevó el caballo al agua / y lo dejó sin beber*. Lorca referred to six versions he knew in a lecture on lullabies, and commented on the 'mysterious, strange anguish' (*una rara angustia misteriosa*) of its central motif, the horse that is taken to the water but not allowed to drink. As he adapts it, the restraint is inside the stallion himself. (Ramsden, *Bodas de sangre*, pp. 76–7.)

Yerma (1934)

In this play, a year later, Lorca was quite consciously retreading classic terrain, and feeling now that his subject was best expressed in the figure of a woman: '*Yerma* will be the tragedy of the barren woman. The theme, as you know, is a classical one. But I want to develop it in a new way. A tragedy with four main characters and a chorus, as tragedies should be. It is necessary to return to tragedy. The tradition of our theatre compels us to do so.'[7]

Seneca's *Medea* and Sophocles' *Electra* were revived in Spain in the same year, and it cannot be coincidental that the play unites themes from both: the power of a maddened woman over an unwitting husband, and the living death of sterility in a patriarchal culture. Lorca finds in the despair of his female figure the ultimate logic of the code of his culture: when the law of absolute honour, which Yerma entirely respects, meets head-on with the equally imperious demands of nature, it perverts a loving, creative woman into pure destructiveness. And the confidence of his treatment shows in the new name he gives her, which is not a name at all, but the word for land that is unsown, untilled, waste: *tierras yermas*.

Yerma's suffering enables Lorca to pose the question perhaps only Euripides has framed so clearly before, though so many tragic plots take it for granted: the question, 'Why are the Furies female?' And Lorca's implicit answer is much the same as Euripides' – that women stand in a different relation to nature from men. This may be why, in spite of the *Medea* and *Electra* parallels, the boldest effects in *Yerma* are more reminiscent of the *Bacchae* than any other play. Lorca leads us from a village world in which Pentheus apparently reigns supreme – Yerma is confined to the *oikos* under 24-hour supervision, while Juan, her husband, goes about his manly business out of doors – to a shrine high in the mountain, a Spanish Mount Cithaeron. Here, a living folk custom, the pilgrimage barren women make to a saint to plead for children, is revealed as a Dionysiac outburst of the kind Pentheus was most afraid of, with masked dancing, wine, bawdy songs and bands of single men roaming by night to give religion their assistance:

> If you come to the Romeria
> To pray for a filled-out belly
> Don't come to it dressed for a funeral
> But put on your best Sunday blouse.
> Come along by the path near the wall
> To where the fig-trees grow thickest
> And I'll furrow you into the ground
> Till the cocks shout break of day. (p. 201)

---

    7   From an interview given in 1934 (Gwynne Edwards, *Dramatists in Perspective: Spanish Theatre in the Twentieth Century* (Cardiff: University of Wales Press, 1985), p. 103).

Yerma is offered a new, fertile husband there by a Pagan Crone (*Vieja Pagana*),[8] the last and most convincing of our pagan revivals in tragedy; and Yerma refuses, bearing out what was said of Dionysus in Euripides – that 'even in the rites of Dionysus, / The chaste woman will not be corrupted' (*Bacch.* 317–18). But the price of so much restraint is fearsomely high. And when it breaks down, as it finally does (Juan has followed Yerma to the mountain, and she fights him off as he attempts to make love to her), the strength of a bacchant arm, which can uproot pine trees, is also the terrible strength of Yerma as she throttles her husband.

Lorca follows Euripides, we see, in making Yerma an unwilling Bacchant: she is married modesty incarnate, and her prayer at the shrine is reverentially Catholic: 'Listen to the prayer of this penitent / on your holy pilgrimage. / Open your rose within my body / Though it be covered with a thousand thorns' (p. 199). She begs the old woman to explain to her why she is still childless after so much effort:

> *Pagan Wo.* What can I tell you? I just lay flat on my back, started to sing, and kids came like water. You've got a lovely body. Why don't you do something about it? There are plenty of stallions kicking at the stable door . . . Men like to pleasure us, girl. They like to undo our plaits and give us water to drink from their own mouths. That's what makes the world go round.
>
> *Yerma* Yours perhaps; not mine. It's my mind goes round and round and all I feel and all I think about is where is my son? When I give myself to my husband it's just for that. Not for pleasure – never for pleasure.
>
> *Pagan Wo.* (*Patting Yerma's stomach*). No wonder that's still empty.
> (pp. 168–9)

In her own chaste and docile way, Yerma is denying the godhead of Dionysus as much as Agave. The Pagan Woman's phrase 'the children came like water' is the clue to her plight: fertility flows of its own accord, and the free exchange of pleasure is its conduit. It cannot be made a means to an end, any more than water can; the Dionysiac flow of life, the *hygra phusis*, is its own value.

There is one character in the play, Victor, in whose presence Yerma feels these things (significantly enough, he has a beautiful singing voice that 'flows . . . like a fountain', p. 173). But Juan was her father's choice for a husband, and she submitted to patriarchal authority:

> *Yerma* My father found him for me and I took him. Happily. And that's the honest truth. Then from the moment we were engaged I had no thought but – children. When I looked at him, I could see myself reflected in his eyes, very small, very docile, as if I were my own child. (pp. 168–9)

---

[8]   Spanish quotations from *Yerma*, ed. Robin Warner (Manchester and New York: Manchester University Press, 1994), p. 86.

'Perhaps that's why you haven't got kids yet', comments the Pagan Woman. Lorca could not convey more ironically than through such candid testimony as Yerma's the diminution of passion implicit in these patriarchal arrangements. She sees herself as reflected in her husband's eyes, so very small and manageable (*muy chica, muy manejable*) that she could be her own child – another Nora. He also conveys the contempt for Dionysus implicit in the religious dogma that marriage is for the bearing of children only, in which Yerma so ardently believes. Saner women in the play can say that there are other things to live for ('we are all here for a reason', says Maria, *cada criatura tiene su razón*), but Yerma knows only children.

The intensity of Lorca's concentration on her as a figure is remarkable; here he dramatizes the conflict between 'old and mistaken mores' and the 'eternal norms of the heart' just as he promises. On the one side are the obsession with male honour which confines women to the *oikos* – one husband, one set of walls – and the Catholic teaching which tolerates sexuality only as a means to an end. And on the other is Yerma's hunger to be a mother, to be a conduit for life itself: the deep, unassuageable passion to bring new life out of her body and into the world. Masculine restraint and female creativity meet in her person, and torture her. Although she ends the play as a murderer, it is clear that she herself is dying by inches, much as Euripides' Phaedra is dying in the *Hippolytus*. We noted of Phaedra that her body and her honourable will are at variance, so that she consents to sin merely by staying alive; and Lorca achieves a similar conundrum in Yerma, who, once she has internalized masculine values, finds that her own body is her enemy.

Because Yerma is a sympathetic figure, Lorca can delve deeper into the mystery of how creativity becomes perverted than writers who take the femaleness of the Furies for granted. In Yerma's rapturous dreams of giving birth, he evokes the miraculous power of female fertility in language that returns us to the miracle on Cithaeron, where the earth nourished the women, and the women nourished the earth's creatures. The ground spurted milk and honey for the Bacchants, and new mothers suckled baby animals at their full breasts:

> Yerma   Just pick up the babies and wash them in fresh water! Animals lick them, don't they? With my own child, that wouldn't disgust me. I have the notion that women who have just given birth are glowing inside, and that their babies sleep on top of them for hours and hours, listening to the stream of warm milk that goes on filling their breasts so they can suckle, so they can play until they don't want any more, until they pull their heads away. 'Just a little bit more, my child . . .' And their faces and chests are covered with white drops![9]

---

[9]   *Yerma*, in *Three Plays*, trans. Dewell and Zapata, pp. 99–100.

The reverent sense of fertility here, of the unbidden power of the female body, and the utter relief, physical and metaphysical, of giving birth, means that Lorca can pass to the description of the torment inherent in barrenness with no explanation. Simply to be denied the hope of this relief is agony enough: 'Every woman has blood enough for four or five sons. But if you don't have them your blood turns to poison', says Yerma (pp. 164–5). It 'pricks my belly / As though it were swarmed by wasps! . . . A childless woman is like a bunch of thistles – something fit for God's rubbish heap' (p. 185). The more years go by in her barren marriage, the more Yerma feels herself being turned into the same kind of thwarted, black-clad creature as her warders, her husband's unmarried sisters, whom the neighbours compare to the flourishing plants that sprout up on graves (*esas hojas grandes que nacen de pronto sobre los sepulchros*).

The way 'red' blood turns 'black' and the flesh itself can fill with 'poisonous weeds' was shown in *Blood Wedding*, too. But now Lorca gives it a classic context: not merely human passion, but the profoundest of all passions, life's passion to renew itself. The centrality of his vision shows in how readily Yerma's predicament could be expressed in terms of the relation of the Furies to the Eumenides. For the Furies' frenzied, swarming, plague-bringing intensity is only the perversion of their other powers as well-wishers, *eu-menides*: to bring fertility to Athens, fattening the cattle, ripening the crops, and marrying men to women in happy fruition. It is only because her body cannot be claimed by fertility that Yerma becomes destructive – because the flow of life goes round her, not through her:

> I'm sick and weary. Weary of being a woman not put to proper use. I'm hurt, hurt and humbled beyond endurance watching the crops springing up, the fountains flowing, the ewes bearing lambs and bitches their litters of pups, until it seems the whole countryside is teeming with mothers nursing their sleeping young. And here I am with two hammers beating at my breasts where my baby's mouth should be. (p. 186)

And in her mounting despair she expresses the dream that Hippolytus and Jason dreamt before her, when they too were baffled by the terms of human existence: 'I know a child's born of man and woman. Oh, if only I could have one by myself!' (p. 193).

Lorca's treatment of her husband Juan, the physical reason for Yerma's barrenness, may also remind us of Euripides. Like Jason, Juan sees 'the outline of things, but not the details indicative of their nature' – so that his first account of their marriage is quite cheerful: 'The farm's doing well, and no children costing us money' (p. 160). Like Pentheus, he also receives many warnings about the minefield through which he is striding – and does not recognize them until Yerma's powerful hands are on his throat. We are told that his family have had trouble producing children for generations: 'a miracle that any one of them put a girl in the family way. They've nothing but gobs of spit between the lot of them', says the old woman (p. 203). But more than that, he does not actively want children. He would sooner work his fields than lie with Yerma; indeed, there is a shade of Allmers in the way he fends off the sexual reality of marriage: 'I've got to irrigate the fruit trees all night . . . You go to bed and get some sleep' (p. 174). As in Ibsen, his fundamental argument with his wife is about what reality actually is. Juan's values are attached to trees, flocks and land – so that Yerma's hunger for what is missing seems quite mad:

> *Juan*   Once and for all stop crying for the moon, for things that are only in the air and in the darkness of your mind – things that have nothing to do with real life.
>
> *Yerma* (*with dramatic surprise*) With real life? That have nothing to do with real life!
>
> *Juan*   Yes. We can't control things that haven't happened.
>
> *Yerma* (*violently*). Go on! Go on!
>
> *Juan*   This thing means nothing to me, d'you understand! Absolutely nothing! There! It's time I said it. What matters to me is what I can hold in the palm of my hand and see with my own two eyes. (. . .)
>
> *Yerma* And do you never think how much it means to me?
>
> *Juan*   Never. (pp. 204–5)

Here again is an expression of that male rationality, like Helmer's or Jason's, which makes rationality a vice: sensible as Juan's attitude is, it does not encounter the greater realities above and beyond it, like the necessity for life to reproduce itself, and Yerma's need to be part of that process. And as with Jason, Juan's 'firmness' is actually *hubris* asking for its *nemesis*. It will be returned to him by Yerma with interest, as the power born of despair in her two strong hands.

This dialogue is the one that leads to the murder, and it is an impressive last twist of the plot that makes Juan here, for the first time, reach out physically to Yerma. Against the Dionysiac background of the Romeria, by moonlight, and with masked dancers acting out songs like these, he feels something quite new to him:

> *Female Masker* Ah, how love garlands the secret places
>   And pierces them with thrusts of molten gold.
>
> *Male Masker*   Seven times she groaned
>   Nine times she rose,
>   And fifteen times they coupled
>   Under the jasmine in the orange grove.
>
> *Third Man*   Now give it the horn!
>
> *Second Man*   No rose without a thorn! (p. 201)

The maskers move offstage, and it is against the background of '*a great chorus of song*' in the distance (p. 204) that Juan asks Yerma to accept that there will be no child, and at the same time, that he can still be her lover:

> *Yerma* You won't ever change?
>
> *Juan* Never. Accept it.

Yerma Childless.
Juan   Peaceful. You and me together in peace and happiness. Hold me!
         (*He holds her*)
Yerma What do you want?
Juan   I want you. In the moonlight you look so beautiful.
Yerma That look in your eyes – hungry for flesh but not for me.
Juan   Kiss me . . . like this . . . and like this.
Yerma That, never . . . never like that.
         Yerma gives a shriek and seizes Juan by the throat. She forces him
         backwards and slowly she strangles the life out of him. Again the
         singing is heard from the Romeria. (pp. 205–6)

If Juan's Dionysiac impulse is the last drop in Yerma's cup of bitterness, it is
because it is a hunger 'for flesh but not for me'. (Literally: 'like a dove you want
to devour', *comer una paloma*.) It is still not an act of communion that could give
birth to a child, but a gross parody of it – a hunger for what he can see with his
eyes and hold in his hand. What kills Juan, and Yerma too, in every sense that
matters, is the classic issue she has already articulated: that it takes a man and a
woman to bear a child. And the play ends with desolate clarity on her recognition
that now she has killed whatever chance she had of having one. As people start
to gather round, she cries, 'What do you want to know, that I've killed him? Yes,
I've killed him. I've killed my son' (p. 206, *¡Yo misma he matado a mi hijo!*).

The House of Bernarda Alba (1936)

In this play written two years later, on the brink of war, Lorca's concentration on
women reaches its climax: there are no male roles in the play at all. The entire
cast is Bernarda's female household (*la casa*) – five unmarried daughters, a
grandmother, and the servants. Men are only offstage, being buried (the play
opens with the funeral of Bernarda's husband), telling lewd stories on the patio,
singing on the way to harvesting, or riding under girls' windows; the potent figure
of Pepe el Romano, who dominates the girls' imaginations, is never actually seen.
But the stagecraft is expressive of Bernarda's whole frame of mind: all outsiders
are unwelcome but men are the supreme enemy, and she protects the honour of
her *casa* with ferocious vigilance. The play is subtitled 'A Drama of Women in
the Villages of Spain' (*Drama de Mujeres en los Pueblos de España*), with the
pointed rider, 'these three acts are intended as a photographic documentary' (*un
documental fotográfico*).[10] Lorca is bringing to the 'public tribunal' something he
has seen for himself in Andalusia, and indeed grew up with: 'In the house
immediately next to ours lived "Doña Bernarda", a very old widow who kept over

---

[10]   English quotations from *Three Plays*, trans. Dewell and Zapata; Spanish
quotations from *La casa de Bernarda Alba*, ed. Allen Josephs and Juan Caballero (Madrid:
Catedra, 1996).

her spinster daughters an inexorable and tyrannical watch. They were prisoners deprived of all freedom of choice and I never spoke with them; but I saw them pass like shadows, always silent and always dressed in black.'[11]

At the same time, however, Lorca's determined exposure of Spanish village life sends resonances out to Greek drama: for *casa* is an excellent translation of *oikos*, in terms of the family's public honour, and also in terms of the power of the mother over her children before they cross the threshold. What Lorca reconstructs in his darkly glittering, Goyaesque portrait of Bernarda Alba, is the apogee of maternal power. But Bernarda, like Yerma, has also internalized the masculine code of honour, for which she will sacrifice anything – not excluding her children's lives. Once again, in this play, we see the fearful cost of control which refuses to compromise with life itself. And beyond the drama of Bernarda's family, we see foreshadowed the fate of the whole of Spain, embarking in this same year on a civil war that will terminate in ferocious Fascist control, and require the silencing of all its major artists. Lorca himself was shot without trial soon after he had put the finishing touches to this play.[12] The centrality of Aeschylus' question, how can the Furies and Apollo be reconciled to one another before they annihilate Athens? – could not be more painfully shown than by *The House of Bernarda Alba*.

The precision of Lorca's framing of the play in terms of one *casa* in one *pueblo* shows in the implicit commentary on the nature of village life. Villages are inhabited by families, not citizens, and they settle their own problems by 'wild justice' because they cannot imagine any higher courts of appeal. Thus Lorca evokes with unsentimental clarity the settled hatreds that dwell behind each front door, and the sense in which each *oikos* is enduringly at war with its neighbours. It is a world of secrecy and slander, hypocrisy and ineradicable mistrust. It has modernized to the extent that brides now wear white veils 'like in the big cities' and wine is drunk bottled – 'But inside we rot away (*pudrimos*) over what people will say', says one of the daughters (p. 131). Even a servant of 30 years is felt as an outsider to the 'family circle' (p. 149) and Bernarda expresses her deep resentment at having to invite her neighbours into the house after the funeral by immediately having the floor scrubbed: 'You would think a herd of goats had walked on it!' (p. 126). She talks with hatred of the *pueblo* as a place with no river, only wells 'where you always drink the water fearing that it's poisoned' (p. 125). And while it is true that her guests were muttering 'Dried-up old lizard!' as they drank her lemonade (*¡Vieja lagarta recocida!* p. 124), it is also

---

[11] In conversation with Carlos Morla Lynch (Gwynne Edwards, *Dramatists in Perspective*, p. 116). More precisely, it was at his cousin's house he saw this family, and he used their real name, 'Alba' (Gibson, *Federico García Lorca*, p. 436).

[12] Lorca was taken out of hiding and shot by the Nationalists on 18/19 August 1936. His crime was his liberal politics, but undoubtedly his homosexuality was an additional motive, as a classic threat to Spanish masculinity (revealed in the testimony of one of the men involved); see Gibson, *Lorca*, pp. 464–8.

true that she is a great poisoner of the public wells herself, worming out old secrets and using them to keep others in her power.

Lorca also touches on another key element of village life in making Bernarda so powerful over her family. In her role as a mother she is another Fury, combining the fundamental power of fertility with psychological terrorism. Her hold over her *casa* extends to her telling her daughters what they have seen, when what they saw displeases her, or regulating what can be thought in her presence: 'There are things we cannot and should not *think*! I give orders' (p. 149). She has seen two husbands into the grave – it is not accidental that the play begins with her burying the only alternative source of authority in the family – and the rampant nature of female power has rarely been so credibly expressed since Clytaemnestra. She even has the source of strength Sophocles noted of Clytaemnestra in *Electra*, that she colonizes her daughters mentally, and fills them with a cruelty like her own: it is her voice that they use to hurt one another. Men may rule the world beyond the threshold, where they pay whores for their pleasure, and marry coolly for land and oxen; but Bernarda's matriarchal power is primary, and she can prevent her daughters getting access to husbands as long as she wishes. As Lorca makes the youngest daughter say, echoing Medea, 'To be born a woman is the worst punishment' (p. 144).

But as with *Yerma*, part of Lorca's theme is the deadly effect of adding masculine values to female power. Spain has not evolved an Athenian way of harmonizing the two, so that neither gets a chance to display its vices. On the contrary, each is provoking the other to do its worst – so that Bernarda is the vehicle both of rampant, blind maternity and extreme authoritarianism, in the relation of her *casa* to the outside world. She brings to the job of containing female disorder a heavy literalism, more characteristic of the Furies than Apollo. She is fascist in a quite literal sense – she carries a cane and beats her daughters with it – and like Pentheus, she is driven to talk of chains and imprisonment: 'I have five chains for you, and this house my father built' (p. 149). She reminds herself of the necessity of keeping order with a kind of passionate self-pity: 'I must use a firm hand with them. Bernarda, remember: this is your duty!' (p. 149, *Bernarda: acuérdate que esta es tu obligación*). But no matter how vigilant she is, her daughters are at the windows, peeping out of doors, making assignations, and dreaming over stolen pictures. She cries, 'how one must suffer and struggle to get people to behave decently and not like savages!' (p. 129, *no tiren al monte demasiado*)[13] – with a despairing aversion like that of Pentheus or Hippolytus, contemplating the disorderly mass of womankind.

The struggle is so demanding that she cannot take cognizance, any more than Pentheus, of the fact that their behaviour is being provoked by the extremity of

---

[13] The metaphor is from goat-herding, 'breaking loose' in a proverbial spirit the Greeks would have understood: *la cabra siempre tira al monte*, the goat always runs back up the hill.

her restraint. She only knows that what she is doing is right, and the one way of keeping the family beyond public reproach. But we may suspect deeper motives, for which propriety offers the excuse: the jealous rancour of old age, the hatred of infertility for fertility, and the pleasure of doing to others as she has been done by. These motives can be discerned in the way she clamps her daughters into far deeper than obligatory mourning, just as it was in her own generation. And she anticipates the darkness and stagnation of her *casa* with a true Fury's satisfaction:

> During our eight years of mourning, no wind from the street will enter this house! Pretend we have sealed up the doors and windows with bricks. That's how it was in my father's house, and in my grandfather's house. In the meantime you can begin to embroider your trousseaus. I have twenty bolts of linen in the chest from which you can cut sheets. Magdalena can embroider them. (p. 126)

The only one of her five daughters who will be allowed to contemplate marriage during these eight years is Angustias, the eldest, who has a sufficient dowry and has been asked for by Pepe el Romano. But the engagement is cynical on his side: Angustias is old and frail, and he loves Adela, the youngest and most beautiful, the only daughter who dares defy Bernarda. Meanwhile, Martirio is hungering for Pepe, too. The knowing old servant, Poncia, tries to tell Bernarda what passions are building up inside her *casa* – but Bernarda's rage and arrogance prevent her from hearing, in an exchange of Pentheus-like *hubris*:

> Poncia   For Pepe to be with Angustias seems wrong – to me, and to other people, and even to the air. Who knows if they'll get their way!
> Bernar. Here we go again! You go out of your way to give me bad dreams. And I don't want to listen to you, because if things turn out the way you say, I will have to claw you to pieces! (*te tendria que arañar*).
> Poncia   The blood wouldn't get as far as the river!
> Bernar. Fortunately, my daughters respect me and have never gone against my will.
> Poncia   That's true. But as soon as you turn them loose, they'll be up on the roof.
> Bernar. I will bring them down soon enough, by throwing stones at them!
> Poncia   Of course you are the strongest!
> Bernar. I've always been able to hold my own. (*¡Siempre gasté sabrosa pimienta!*)[14] (pp. 151–2)

It is striking how naturally Spanish village life yields Lorca the same motifs Athenians might recognize: the mayhem implicit in women climbing out of the *oikos* to be publicly visible on the roof, the necessity of 'stoning' them into decency, and the revelation that parental authority may come down to being the

---

[14]   Literally, 'I've always used strong pepper!'

'strongest' (*la más valiente*). And even more classical is the violence of the explosion, when it comes.

There is a premonitory first explosion outside the house at the end of Act II, which operates as a kind of commentary on the dialogue above. Something has brought a 'big crowd' into the street and 'all the neighbours are at their doors!' as the maid excitedly says (p. 153). An unnamed young woman – typically, she is only called 'Librada's daughter, the one who's not married' – is being dragged down the street, and Poncia comes rushing in with the news. The girl has given birth to an illegitimate baby:

> Poncia   And to hide her shame, she killed it and put it under some rocks. But some dogs, with more feelings than many creatures, pulled it out, and as if led by the hand of God, they put it on her doorstep. Now they want to kill her. They're dragging her down the street, and the men are running down the paths and out of the olive groves, shouting so loud the fields are trembling (*estremecen los campos*).
>
> Bernar.   Yes! Let them all bring whips made from olive branches and the handles of their hoes! Let them all come to kill her!
>
> Adela   No. No! Not to kill her!
>
> Martirio   Yes, let's go out there, too!
>
> Bernar.   Any woman who tramples on decency (*pisotea la decencia*) should pay for it!
>
> [*Outside, a woman screams, and there is a great uproar.*]
>
> Adela   They should let her go! Don't go out there!
>
> Martirio   [*looking at Adela*] She should pay for what she did.
>
> Bernar.   [*in the archway*] Finish her off before the police get here! Burning coals in the place where she sinned! (*¡Carbón ardiendo en el sitio de su pecado!*)
>
> Adela   [*clutching her womb*] No! No!
>
> Bernar.   Kill her! Kill her!
>
> CURTAIN (p. 154)

Lorca ties together a number of effects with this climax. At the level of plot we now know that Adela identifies with Librada's daughter, and her sister Martirio understands why she is clutching her womb, though Bernarda is still blind to it. But Lorca also throws into dramatic relief the repulsive mixture of emotions with which the community responds to the sexual transgressor. She is their legitimate prey, to be dragged, whipped and trampled upon as she trampled upon the community's code. There is joy in finally having an appropriate outlet for their envy and self-suppression: fertility has got loose and it must be annihilated before it spreads (not for nothing is she *Librada*'s daughter). Bernarda is the chief Fury, in calling for her to be burnt alive in the very location of her pleasure and fruitfulness: 'Burning coals in the place where she sinned!' She shows herself contemptuous of the public law that would spoil their revenge ('before the police get here!'), and for the sake of urging the crowd to such an orgy of cruelty, she breaks her iron law against being seen out of doors – she stands in the archway of the house. But the other Furies are not far behind. Martirio wants to 'go out there, too!', for some savage compensation for her own way of life, 'martyred', sanctimonious, and bitterly envious of her younger sister. And the men pour excitedly out of the olive groves, shouting loud enough to make the ground tremble: Lorca could not convey more economically the interplay of sexual repression and sadism in the revenge code (the same interplay he showed in *Blood Wedding*, but now expressed in human figures), or the sense in which the appetites represented by the Aeschylean Furies never go away.

It is an associated idea, as in *Yerma*, that when fertility is not allowed natural expression it cannot be held 'on ice', but festers, and emerges in squalid forms: the murdered baby under the rock, or the intimate sadism of Bernarda behind the mask of decency. The whole culture, those within the code as much as those outside it, is paying the price for failing to negotiate any better relation between law and fertility, or admit any other solution than repression, and more repression. Lorca ironically indicates the fatuity of putting Dionysus in chains by the tremendous thuds that are heard through the wall at the beginning of the last act. Bernarda has a large herd of horses and is about to put a magnificent stallion out to breed with her new mares. He kicks so furiously against confinement she is forced to let him out 'before he kicks down the walls' (p. 156); and her pride in the stallion's virility ('He must be hot', she whispers, *debe tener calor*, p. 155) and her willingness to admit that he is beyond her mastery, contrast pointedly with her presumption that she can master Dionysus in every other form. The coming explosion is the direct result of her arrogance.

In fact, Adela has been meeting Pepe el Romano every night. 'He takes me into the reeds at the edge of the river!' she proudly asserts to her jealous sister, and no punishment will ever make her repent:

> I can't stand the horror of this house any more, not after knowing the taste of his mouth! (*el sabor de su boca*) I will be what he wants me to be. With the whole town against me, branding me with their fiery fingers, persecuted by people who claim to be decent, and right in front of them I will put on a crown of thorns, like any mistress of a married man! (p. 166)

Knowing how deeply encoded in Lorca's symbolism is the impossibility of ever reaching the water – the water the stallion does not drink, the water no man gives Yerma from his mouth – we can appreciate the depth of resonance he intends to give the lovers' meeting place, 'the reeds at the edge of the river'. Adela, among all her tortured, starved and baffled sisters, and unlike Yerma, claims her share in the fullness of life. And she invokes the holiest symbol of Christian suffering, the 'crown of thorns', for her pagan right. In Spain, Christ has no monopoly on the bitter dignity of withstanding the sadistic crowd – so must 'any mistress of a married man!' Adela is the first heroine in these plays whose Bacchic energy finds an outlet – 'I could bring a wild stallion to his knees with the strength in my little finger!' (p. 166) – and who chooses in full awareness of what she is doing: 'I saw death under this roof, and I went out to look for what is mine, for what belongs to me!' (p. 165).

It only takes a whistle from the corral to bring the denouement about: Pepe is waiting in the dark for Adela, and her jealous sister, Martirio, alarms the sleeping household. Lorca crowds an impressive number of effects into a mere two pages of dialogue. The different reactions of the sisters to the scandal, and Bernarda's wrath, are only part of them; the sisters divide between wanting to turn Adela out and insisting she stay. Angustias, as Pepe's fiancée, says 'You're not leaving here – you and your triumphant body! (*tu cuerpo en triunfo*) Thief!' (p. 167). The high moment of liberation is when Bernarda lifts her avenging cane for the last time and Adela seizes and breaks it in two: 'this is what I do with the tyrant's rod! Don't take one step more' (p. 167). We also see Adela's triumphant reliance on Pepe's male strength and authority: after all the false control of Bernarda, the true master of the *casa* is acknowledged at last. This is the final threat that goads Bernarda beyond herself:

Adela No-one gives me orders but Pepe . . . I am his woman. [*To* Angustias] Get that into your head – and go out to the corral and tell him. He will be master of this entire house! He's out there, breathing like a lion!
Angus. My God!
Bernar. The gun! Where is the gun?
[*Bernarda runs out.*] (p. 167)

While the sisters wrestle with one another, there is the sound of a shot, and Bernarda comes back to say with fierce satisfaction, 'I dare you to find him now!' She has only succeeded in scaring Pepe el Romano off her land, but the jealous Martirio uses the occasion to twist the knife: 'That's the end of Pepe el Romano!' And this is enough to bring the catastrophe about: for Adela, who was strong enough to live, is strong enough to die, and the next thing we hear after she runs wildly out calling 'Pepe! My God! Pepe!' is a 'heavy thud' as she hangs herself in the next room.

When Bernarda sees the body from the threshold she screams. But she does not run to take it down. That would be tantamount to an admission – and her immediate response is to deny what has happened and rearrange reality, at whatever price. The gargantuan effrontery of Adela and Pepe can, and must be resisted. And standing at the edge of chaos, she re-establishes order in two merciless speeches, by which Lorca sounds all the keynotes of the play with brilliant economy. She closes the lid on the family sarcophagus, and we hear the dull thud:

Bernar. Pepe, you may go running off alive, through the shadows of the poplars, but one day you will fall. Cut her down. My daughter has died a virgin (*ha muerto virgen*). Carry her to her room and dress her in white. No one is to say a thing. She died a virgin. Send word for the bells to toll twice at dawn.

Martirio She was fortunate a thousand times over – she had him.

Bernar. I want no weeping. We must look death in the face. Silence! [*To another daughter*] Be quiet, I said! [*To another daughter*] Tears, when you're alone. We will all drown ourselves in a sea of mourning (*un mar de luto*). The youngest daughter of Bernarda Alba has died a virgin. Did you hear me? Silence! Silence, I said! Silence!

Curtain (pp. 168–9)

Bernarda is not a monster – 'we will all drown ourselves in a sea of mourning', and some of the tears will be hers – but we recognize now that every decision she is making guarantees the prolongation of the sickness, in and out of the *casa*. Even the 'sea' of mourning will doubtless become an aspect of the general perversion; and for the sake of the neighbours, there will neither be truth ('My daughter has died a virgin') nor audible grief ('silence!'). Inside they may 'rot away over what people will say'; but iron control is the only method Bernarda knows. Lorca lets a note of triumph be heard, however, even through Martirio's jealousy: 'she was fortunate a thousand times over – she had him'.

PART FOUR

Conclusion

Chapter 8

Tragedy and the Historical Moment

The familiar account of the history of tragedy takes it for granted that modernity brings it to a halt. Hence, presumably, the nostalgia that tinges our admiration for the genre: these works are great, but we have lost the secret of producing them. As George Steiner puts it in *The Death of Tragedy*, 'The decline of tragedy is inseparably related to the decline of the organic world view and of its attendant context of mythological, symbolic, and ritual reference.'[1]

The argument of this book is different, however. While fully-fledged modernity is clearly incompatible with the genre, the transition to modernity, with its attendant shocks and discoveries, is of its essence; and this transition is always going on somewhere in the world, as it did in Spain in the 1930s. Countries with violently disjunctive histories are particularly fertile in tragic insight (South Africa would be a contemporary example); but if this insight is to eventuate in tragic plays rather than, say, novels, something more is required. Drama depends on the existence of an established theatrical space and an audience, and great drama depends on all these coinciding with a great writer. Perhaps this makes it easier to understand why tragedy is written so rarely, and why, since the Renaissance, it has not been written in English. The conditions for tragedy are only likely to occur once in the development of any culture (though it could be argued that, thanks to the Counter-Reformation, they did recur in Spain). And in this light it may be easier to understand why tragic plots should have so much in common, if they essentially record the same transition: the movement from blood-thinking to thinking, and from family bonds to citizenship, in the evolution of human equality before the law.

These propositions cannot be proved in any straightforward sense. The argument of this book rests only on the extent of overlapping concerns in tragic plots, as we have traced them, and the reader's sense of the plausibility of the explanation given. But although the theory cannot be proved with any rigour, we might usefully look for corroboration from the opposite direction, and consider under what circumstances tragedy does *not* get written. At the beginning of the last chapter it was suggested that 'Lorca's achievement may help us guess at the reasons why other twentieth-century writers, for all the sincerity of their efforts, have only succeeded in alluding to tragedy rather than creating it' – and the reader who found this more provocative than helpful deserves a fuller explanation here.

---

[1] George Steiner, *The Death of Tragedy* (London: Faber, 1961, repr. 1963), p. 292.

Tragedy, as this book began by saying, depends on a theatre and an audience – more precisely, on a representative theatre and a deeply involved audience, along Athenian lines. In a sense, as we have seen, the *Oresteia* was a collaboration between Aeschylus and his newly enfranchised audience, which could not have been written without them or at any other time; when the disadvantages of democracy became more evident, Athens got the plays of Euripides instead. In the same way, Lorca responded to the Spanish emergency with *The House of Bernarda Alba* rather than the provocative play he had been planning, which would have had to remain a private satisfaction: *The Drama of Lot's Daughters*, about the superiority of sodomy to incest.[2] The greatness of *Yerma*, too, seems to stem from the way that Lorca can express his private torment about the forbidden status of his homosexuality and his blocked fertility through a female predicament of the widest public resonance.

This obvious point about the mutual dependence of writer and audience helps us understand the fact that the figure in English culture who most resembles Lorca, D.H. Lawrence, also wrote plays at the start of his career, but stopped when he did not find the theatre capable of being the 'public tribunal' he needed for his art. All Lawrence's serious work is in novels; a form in which, unlike the theatre, his art could weather the extreme hostility (and active censorship) it provoked. These novels are squarely on the tragic issues we have been uncovering, but they have the anti-tragic tendency of their genre, which is to demonstrate that life goes on. In *Sons and Lovers* (1913), Lawrence handles with passionate assurance the Oedipal theme he knows to be central to his upbringing: 'It is a great tragedy, and I tell you I've written a great book. It's the tragedy of thousands of young men in England.'[3] But the story ends with the natural death of the mother and the young artist-Lawrence struggling loose from her deep, Fury-like hold. He sets his face towards the Apollonian city, which will support him in his new way of being: 'His fists were shut, his mouth set fast. He would not take that direction, to the darkness, to follow her. He walked towards the faintly humming, glowing town, quickly.'[4]

In *The Rainbow* (1915) Lawrence maps the tragic terrain even more boldly: like Lorca, he sees that the issue of modernity is most poignantly focused in women. If the keynote of modernity is a new self-consciousness, the most dramatic form it can take is in newly emancipated womanhood; and he shows how such a consciousness evolves in his heroine from its roots two generations back, in an inarticulate farmer's marriage to a 'lady'. The journey from wordlessness to language, from the village farm to teacher training college, is assessed by Lawrence with energetic justice. Physical richness is exchanged for

---

[2]   Gibson, *Federico García Lorca*, p. 396.

[3]   Letter to Garnett, 1912, in John Worthen, *D.H. Lawrence: The Early Years, 1885–1912* (Cambridge: Cambridge University Press, 1992), p. 456.

[4]   D.H. Lawrence, *Sons and Lovers* (Harmondsworth: Penguin Books, 1962), p. 511.

mental clarity, and security without questions, for insecurity amidst many questions; but Lawrence knows it cannot be otherwise, for himself or his heroine, and he leaves her heroically unsupported at the end of the novel, seeing a rainbow form itself as the promise of a better future, still undefined.

If this is tragic material, then, it is tragedy as it appears in novels: caught in the ongoing flow of time, and rendered through concentration on the individual, without the crowding together of generations which gives tragic drama its potency. It is significant that babies are not an issue for Lawrentian heroines, and neither are their obligations to parents or the outside world; in *Women in Love* (1921) the bonds with wider society cease to be felt at all. Without regretting Lawrence's unwritten plays, we can perhaps conclude that what energizes tragic drama, unlike fiction, is its brevity. It needs to represent a human conundrum in the length of time for which an audience can seriously pay attention – two or three hours; and so it clings to the central and obvious human predicaments because eccentricity is, literally, a waste of time.

Lawrence was not setting out to write stage tragedy, but what can we say of those who consciously did, like T.S. Eliot, Yeats and Synge?

T.S. Eliot, *The Family Reunion* (1939)

If we set *The Family Reunion* beside the *Oresteia* on which it is based, or indeed Lorca, the distance between tragedy and would-be tragedy is clear. It is not enough to appropriate such a public form for private purposes, as Eliot seems to be doing, in positing a tragic hero who may have murdered his tormenting and unstable wife. Though we feel the playwright's deep identification with the guilt at the centre of the drama, the play shows all the signs of immersion in the same guilt: obliquity, vagueness, and a tone that swings wildly from facetiousness to pain. The list of *dramatis personae* tells us in what a state of defensive inauthenticity Eliot set out. It combines such Agatha Christie propositions as 'Amy, Dowager Lady Monchensey' and 'Sergeant Winchell', with – 'the Eumenides', taken straight and unadapted from Aeschylus. And the hero, Harry, is conceived as having a 'sensibility and intelligence' above the rest, and addressing his problems to only the 'most sensitive and intelligent' in the audience; the other 'material, literal-minded and visionless' characters are expected to occupy the attention of the groundlings.[5] Eliot's Apollonian elitism towards his audience reveals a chasm of misunderstanding: he has not begun to consider why tragic consciousness should ever have to come to terms with the world of matter or, fundamentally, why heroes must have wives.

---

[5]   This is his account of his intention in *Sweeney Agonistes*, but it also fits *The Family Reunion*, as A.D. Moody notes, in *Thomas Stearns Eliot, Poet* (Cambridge: Cambridge University Press, 1979, repr. 1980), p. 173.

This blank spot also shows in his metaphysics. The play is full of animus against women; drunken wives, coercive mothers and female academics are all treated with distaste (Agatha the don has had 'thirty years of solitude, in a women's college, / Trying not to dislike women').[6] But there is no attempt to explain why, in that case, the Eumenides are female, and what in the context of this play has converted them from Furies into the 'bright angels' that Harry must follow, to convert his guilt to good purposes. If the play reminds us of anything, it is not Aeschylus but rather *Little Eyolf*. It turns on the same nexus of male agony, that mixture of sexual horror, passionate abstraction and obliquity that made Allmers so fascinatingly embarrassing. But Eliot is not diagnosing the problem, he is suffering it: and so the play tapers off into vagueness, leaving us unclear whether Harry ever committed the crime he fled from (pushing his drunken wife overboard) or where exactly he is going when he follows the Eumenides (though there is an implication that he is not long for this world – just the sort of comfort Allmers would have clung to).

Eliot is not a playwright, and the decorous London audience of the 1930s cannot make him one. Not even the public crisis of 1939 can contribute a sense of the relation of private destinies to politics: this is a play of private emotions and talking heads, in which the characters speak the idiom of *The Four Quartets* plus water: '. . . It is love and terror / Of what waits and wants me, and will not let me fall / Let the cricket chirp' (p. 115). Eliot's lack of a sense of an audience allows the verse to bury itself at times in the dictionary: 'Where the dead stone is seen to be batrachian, / The aphyllous branch ophidian' (p. 56) is only the most startling example (it translates as 'where the dead stone is seen to be a toad and the leafless branch a snake'). And the only admission of sexual passion in the play takes the form of a reluctant allusion to fire:

> There are hours when there seems to be no past or future,
> Only a present moment of pointed light
> When you want to burn. When you stretch out your hand
> To the flames. They only come once,
> Thank God, that kind. (pp. 102–3)

The play undoubtedly has a tragic subject, in the response of Harry's superfine consciousness to guilt, and the way guilt detaches him from the reality of the external world. But the subject is not examined, it is merely 'given'; and we only glimpse the Hamlet-like malice and energy Eliot might have shown if he had had the courage to excavate his own emotions – as when Harry comments, of his duller brother's accidental concussion, that it 'cannot make very much difference to John . . . If he was ever really conscious, / I should be glad for him to have a breathing spell' (p. 87).

---

6 T.S. Eliot, *The Family Reunion* (London: Faber, 1939, repr. 1962), p. 116.

W.B. Yeats, *Cathleen ni Houlihan* (1902)

If Eliot's play shows that it is actually counter-productive to invoke mythology without re-creating it (he later admitted that on stage, the Eumenides looked like 'uninvited guests who had strayed in from a fancy dress ball'),[7] Yeats's intensely mythic drama reveals another problem: that the value of any mythology depends, not on its antiquity, but on the quality of thought that has gone into it. For Yeats the 'old stories' are so beguiling, and his mission to bring them to his audience so urgent, that he has no energy left for examining the implications, political or human, of what they embody. Thus in *Cathleen ni Houlihan*, wronged Ireland becomes an old crone who visits a peasant cottage and speaks mysteriously of her griefs: 'Too many strangers in the house', 'My land that was taken from me . . . my four beautiful green fields.'[8] A French force is landing on the nearby beach, and the young man of the cottage, who was about to marry, tears himself away to join it. The crone mutters with alarming complacency, 'It is a hard service they take that help me . . . They that had red cheeks will have pale cheeks for my sake; and for all that they will think they are well paid' (p. 11). And as she goes out, singing 'They shall be remembered for ever; / They shall be alive for ever', the old woman is seen in her 'true' nature: as 'a young girl [with] the walk of a queen' (pp.11, 13).

The groundwork of this play may remind us of *Blood Wedding*, in the way a marriage is intercepted by the ancestral call to blood, but Yeats sees only the glamour of the Fury's point of view – of unswerving loyalty to the past, and the romance of blood sacrifice. Unlike Lorca, he does not recognize what terrible pleasures can be found in the spilling of blood, and how quickly red blood turns black and festers. Also unlike Lorca, he was unlikely to be killed himself for writing as he did, though he had to ask himself later how many other men were: 'Did that play of mine send out / Certain men the English shot?'[9] Yeats's 'queenly' old woman is part of his own private revolutionary mythology, and too sanitized a character to reach through to tragic issues. We may smell more of the authentic Fury in Joyce's memorable characterization of Mother Ireland – as 'the old sow that eats her farrow'.

---

[7]   His later opinion was that 'their failure is merely a symptom of the failure to adjust the ancient with the modern' in the play as a whole. ('Poetry and Drama' in *On Poetry and Poets* (London: Faber & Faber, 1957), p. 84).

[8]   W.B. Yeats, *Selected Plays*, ed. A. Norman Jeffares (Dublin: Gill & Macmillan, 1974, repr. 1991), p. 8.

[9]   W.B. Yeats, 'The Man and the Echo' ll. 11–12, *The Collected Poems of W.B.Yeats* (London and Basingstoke: Macmillan, 1933, repr. 1977).

J.M. Synge, *Riders to the Sea* (1903)

Synge is generally acknowledged to have a better claim to be the tragedian of the Irish revival, and it is striking that he returns to realism from Yeats's bardic world of Crones and Blind Men, Warriors and Warrior Queens. In *Riders to the Sea*, peasants wear flannel and burn peat, and old mothers lose their sons to a credible enemy, the sea. Lorca himself was impressed by this play (translated into Spanish in 1920), which locates tragic issues among the hard facts of peasant life and uses their own Anglo-Irish idiom.[10] And the plight of mothers was central to Synge's interest in the Aran Islands:

> The maternal feeling is so powerful on these islands that it gives a life of torment to the women. Their sons grow up to be banished as soon as they are of age, or to live here in continual danger on the sea; their daughters go away also, or are worn out in their youth with bearing children that grow up to harass them in their own turn a little later.[11]

If Synge's realism comes as a relief, however, we also have to notice that Synge himself was not part of the world he describes. He visited the islands to learn Gaelic from their residual Gaelic speakers, along with numerous other philologists from the Continent, and his worst exposure to the elements they lived with came in ferry boats and curraghs. He views the islanders with sympathy rather than identification and, unlike Lorca, he cannot see their lives as exposing the underlying truths of his own, much as he values the primitive experiences they give him access to. He tells, for instance, of a burial at which the bereaved mother found the skull of her own mother had been thrown up by the gravediggers, and 'keening and shrieking over it with the wildest lamentation', beat on the coffin of her drowned son, holding her mother's skull in the other hand (p. 355). His representation of island life has a Wordsworthian touch of distance (the women at the burial 'beat with *magnificent* gestures on the boards of the coffin', my emphasis), and the peasant idiom of his plays has the careful rightness of a reproduction. Synge knows how much Gaelic grammar underlies the islanders' English, as we hear in Maurya's grieving over the family dead:

> There was Sheamus and his father, and his own father again, were lost in a dark night, and not a stick or sign was seen of them when the sun went up. There was Patch after was drowned out of a curragh that turned over. I was sitting here with Bartley, and he a baby lying on my two knees, and I seen two women, and three women, and four women coming in, and they crossing themselves and not saying a word. I looked out then, and there were men coming after them, and they holding a thing in the half of a red

---

[10] The Mother's lament for her last son in *Blood Wedding* is in fact an adaptation of Maurya's climactic speech (Gibson, *Federico García Lorca*, p. 340).

[11] J.M. Synge, *The Aran Islands* (1907), in *Collected Plays and Poems and The Aran Islands* (London: Everyman, 1992, repr. 1996), p. 308.

sail, and water dripping out of it – it was a dry day, Nora – and leaving a track to the door. (p. 23)

When Lorca writes in folk idiom he is constantly surprising, and he creates 'sayings' which sound as though they have always been current; Synge sounds too much as though he is consulting his notes, and would sacrifice the pace of a speech for its linguistic accuracy.

Another sign that Synge is taking the islanders seriously in one sense but not in another, is that the only 'action' in the play is the mother's glimpse of her dead son's ghost, riding behind his brother on a grey pony. It is the pony that knocks the living son into the sea: and Synge is content to leave the mystery there, with its folklore implications that the dead are envious of the living, and that a mother has the power of second sight. Picturesque as this is, it is not altogether unlike Eliot's use of the Eumenides in the way it leaves the connection between human action and tragic consequences uninterrogated, and shelters behind someone else's mythology. Bartley does nothing to invite his destiny, save decide to take his horse to market – the kind of decision a peasant must make on the islands, if economic life is to go on at all. And Synge does nothing to show us what the envy of the dead towards the living might mean in actual experience.

If he had been more determined to tell the truth about peasant life, he would have had to think harder about something that struck both him and Yeats as appealingly subversive: the deep contempt of the islanders for the law. On the islands, the passions that caused crime were seen to make the law futile, and Synge quotes approvingly the local saying, 'Would anyone kill his father if he was able to help it?' (p. 298). He would also have had to admit how hostile the islanders were to his own solitary, intellectual way of being, particularly the women. When Mauryas are not mourning their sons, their female power has menace in it. Synge tells in *The Aran Islands* of a moment when the women's low view of him was borne in on him alarmingly, and he glimpsed (we might say) why the Furies are so immovably contemptuous of Apollo.

The confrontation took place against a madly Dionysiac background, when the islanders' pigs were being tied up for transport to the mainland. The shrieking of the apprehensive animals drove the islanders 'wild with excitement', and the pigs 'foamed at the mouth and tore each other with their teeth'. The men sailed off with their cargo and Synge was left on the slipway with a band of women and children:

> The women were over-excited, and when I tried to talk to them they crowded round me and began jeering and shrieking at me because I am not married. A dozen screamed at a time, and so rapidly that I could not understand all they were saying, yet I was able to make out that they were taking advantage of the absence of their husbands to give me the full volume of their contempt. Some little boys who were listening threw themselves down, writhing with laughter among the seaweed, and the young girls grew red with embarrassment and stared down into the surf.

> For a moment I was in confusion. I tried to speak to them, but I could
> not make myself heard, so I sat down on the slip and drew out my wallet
> of photographs. In an instant I had the whole band clambering round me,
> in their ordinary mood. (p. 334)

In this confrontation between the women's massed and contemptuous fertility,
and the celibate, self-conscious male with nothing but photographs to protect
himself with, lies the potential for a more powerful tragic plot than Synge ever
actually put in a play.

The value of Eliot, Yeats and Synge to our general argument, then, would be
that by comparison with Lorca's their tragic plots are frail, and their investment
as playwrights lacking in courage. They expect mythology to work its magic
purely by being mythical, and they fail to locate the tragic subject in themselves
before locating it in their characters. Even at the most formal level, the reason
why their plays are not current in the modern repertoire is easy enough to see:
these works are undeveloped, and have so little action that they are really better
understood as animated tableaux. *Cathleen ni Houlihan* and *Riders to the Sea* are
no more than ten pages long; even *The Family Reunion*, which has two acts,
barely amounts to a theatrical evening. The theatre is highly valued for itself, but
there is not enough sense of what to use it for, or of how to meet the audience's
deeper needs. Historically speaking, the Irish public was surely crying out for a
dramatist who would tell the truth about the Furies; but Yeats was not that man,
and the nervous gentility of the Dublin audience set the tone. (It was as much as
Synge could do to protect his plays from bowdlerization by his own actors: the
audience famously rioted at the mention of 'an essential item of female attire
which the lady would probably never utter in ordinary circumstances even to
herself' – 'shift' – in *Playboy of the Western World*.)[12]

If we look for writers who did hold the stage in a professional way, we must
look to America, where Eugene O'Neill and Arthur Miller wrestled with the same
problems but came up with bolder solutions. Eliot later remarked of *The Family
Reunion*, 'I should either have stuck closer to Aeschylus or else taken a great deal
more liberty with his myth.'[13] And in this context O'Neill is interesting, since he
tried both methods: *Mourning Becomes Electra* attempts to recast the whole
Oresteia in a Civil War setting, while *Long Day's Journey into Night* is a family
tragedy of destructive guilt, based on O'Neill's understanding of his own.

Eugene O'Neill, *Mourning Becomes Electra* (1931)

This trilogy is both more naive and more stageworthy than anything Eliot could
have done with Greek tragedy. It comprises three short plays full of action, each

---

[12]   *J.M. Synge: Interviews and Recollections*, ed. E.H. Mikhail (London:
Macmillan, 1977), p. 51.

[13]   T.S. Eliot, *On Poetry and Poets*, p. 84.

with its own climax, and with an obvious forward movement ('Homecoming', 'The Hunted', 'The Haunted'). But it is naive in its assessment of what was worth retaining from the original: O'Neill insists on his characters' 'mask-like' faces ('That's the Mannon look. They all has it. They grow it on their wives'),[14] the set is a New England house 'of the Greek temple style' (p. 9), the chorus is a gossipy group of townsfolk, and the hero's name, Ezra Mannon, is clearly meant to chime with 'Agamemnon'.

Taken as a whole, the trilogy is a terrible warning against offering to wield the club of Hercules. The more O'Neill invokes the *Oresteia*, the more frail and parasitic his own construction seems; but we may also note that his instinct took him to a credibly Aeschylean parallel, in making him set the play in the home of a victorious Brigadier-General returning from the war (the action takes place in 1865). The Civil War is indeed the watershed of American modernity; and the freeing of the slaves, if O'Neill had confronted it, could have brought out the profoundest tragic issues in the country's structure. The promising start he made in *All God's Chillun Got Wings* (1924), where a black–white marriage is destroyed by the whole legacy of the past, would have translated very aptly into the concluding debate of the *Eumenides*: 'What shall we do with the Furies?'

But O'Neill's interest in the *Oresteia* is not in its political wisdom: he views it, rather, through Freudian spectacles, and the places where he most vigorously modernizes the trilogy are in the marriage of Ezra Mannon and Christine (Clytaemnestra), and the psychology of their children Orin (Orestes) and Lavinia (Electra), each of whom has the appropriate Freudian complex. O'Neill shows some consciousness of the tragic conundrum of gender, in the way Ezra returns from the battlefield a 'hero', yet bound by a code of masculine rigidity he hates ('sitting numb in my own heart – like a statue of a dead man in a town square', p. 94). But this martial construct is very soft inside, and speaks the bathetic idiom Hollywood was to make famous, as he appeals to his chilly wife:

> Mannon (*drawing himself up with a stern pride and dignity and surrendering himself like a commander against hopeless odds*).
> All right, then. I came home to surrender to you – what's inside me. I love you. I loved you then, and all the years between, and I love you now. (p. 94)

The vacancy of this is not Mannon's but O'Neill's, and the play's sentimentality shows in the way all the characters dream of escaping the repressive culture of New England for warm South Sea islands. Mannon's hope for his marriage is to go off on a voyage together to 'some island where we could be alone a while. You'll find I have changed, Christine' (p. 95). The cure for their various unhappinesses is simply to be released from sexual inhibition, as Lavinia is, on a brief holiday before the last play:

---

[14] Eugene O'Neill, *Mourning Becomes Electra* (London: Jonathan Cape, 1966, repr. 1989), p. 21.

> I loved those Islands . . . there was something there mysterious and beautiful – a good spirit – of love – coming out of the land and sea. It made me forget death. There was no hereafter. There was only this world – the warm earth in the moonlight, the trade wind in the cocoa palms – the surf on the reef – the fires at night and the drum throbbing in my ear – the natives dancing naked and innocent – without knowledge of sin! (p. 238)

If this is the underlying structure of the play (a travel agent's version, we may say, of Ibsen's paganism), the surface action is still more unrecognizably Aeschylean: Christine kills Ezra by administering the wrong angina pills, Orin shoots her lover on board his ship in Oedipal envy, Christine shoots herself in romantic despair, and the children waste away in guilt and self-reproach. Orin finally commits suicide, too, and Lavinia ends the trilogy by incarcerating herself in the house with the family ghosts, an Electra who knows just what the role involves: 'I'll live alone with the dead, and keep their secrets, and let them hound me, until the curse is paid out and the last Mannon is let die! . . . You go now and close the shutters and nail them tight . . . And tell Hannah to throw out all the flowers.' (pp. 287–8).

Long Day's Journey into Night (1956)

O'Neill is so hampered by his classical parallels that we may feel a play in which he forswears them altogether can only be the better for it. In *Long Day's Journey into Night* there is no classicism at all, save the Aristotelian adherence to the experience of one day implicit in the title. But a determined modernity brings a familiar problem in its wake – the necessity to provide a plot, with conflict and development, and here O'Neill has little advantage over Yeats and Eliot. The play is another 'family reunion', in that the sons have returned home after failing to make a success of their lives outside; and O'Neill fills up four acts, from 8.30 a.m. to midnight, simply by showing that whatever was bad at the start of the day gets worse. The main 'action' is that the drug-taking mother, who has been in remission, starts taking drugs again, and the artistic younger son is diagnosed as having TB. But O'Neill's mind is clearly elsewhere, on the intimate psychology of family life: each character has strength and charm, but these are made inoperative by some disastrous weakness, and much as they love each other they sabotage themselves and their loved ones with equal determination.

There is some awareness in the play of the need for a critique of the Irish peasant past, in the presentation of the father as wrecked by sentimentality and the bottle, and twisted by his harsh experience as an immigrant. For all his charm (he is a decaying popular actor with a real love of Shakespeare), he is a miser who anxiously switches off light bulbs, and will send his dying son to the cheapest sanatorium while recklessly buying up land, the only form of security he knows.

His long day's journey is really a slow slide down a drunken slope to depression – where he is joined by his sons, who are as whisky-soaked as he is; and all this is counterpointed with their bitter reproaches to the mother, for her disappearance in a haze of morphine.

The play's essential collaboration with this haziness shows in its failure to suggest what any of the Tyrones could have done about their fate: the father is the prisoner of his impoverished childhood, his wife is the prisoner of her quack doctor's prescription, the elder son is the prisoner of envy of his brother and hatred of his father, and the younger brother is dying, as artists will. 'None of us can help the things life has done to us',[15] says the mother, and mournful sirens hoot offstage to suggest the deepening fog. The only alternative vision O'Neill gives us is the artistic son's Dionysiac raptures from his time as a sailor:

> When I was swimming far out, or lying alone on a beach, I have had the same experience. Became the sun, the hot sand, green seaweed anchored to a rock, swaying in the tide. Like a saint's vision of beatitude. Like the veil of things as they seem drawn back by an unseen hand. For a second you see – and seeing the secret, are the secret. For a second there is meaning! Then the hand lets the veil fall and you are alone, lost in the fog again, and you stumble forward nowhere, for no good reason! (*He grins wryly.*) It was a great mistake, my being born a man, I would have been much more successful as a sea-gull or a fish. (pp. 134–5)

For all the would-be resonance of this, the artist is clearly still caught up in a maudlin self-consciousness that makes death the more attractive option. There is a distinctly Strindbergian note to his conclusion (Strindberg was one of O'Neill's heroes): 'As it is, I will always be a stranger who never feels at home, who does not really want and is not really wanted, who can never belong, who must always be a little in love with death!' (p. 135).

Perhaps the clearest indication that O'Neill has not thought through his family history with complete honesty is that it would be impossible to deduce from his play how such a family produced Eugene O'Neill. Insofar as he appears, it is as the little baby Eugene who died long ago of the measles, and of course, as the poetical Edmund, who is dying too. We may suspect that the 'deep pity and understanding and forgiveness for *all* the four haunted Tyrones' (dedication, p. 5) which O'Neill felt he had put into the play, was more easily come by than sharp analysis – and that in his scheme of things, what makes tragedy romantic is failure.

Arthur Miller is not exempt from romanticizing failure, too: *Death of a Salesman* (1949) is an egregious example. As he later admitted himself, 'My weakness is that I can create pathos at will. It is one of the easiest things to do. I feel that Willie Loman lacks sufficient insight into his situation which would have

---

¹⁵ Eugene O'Neill, *Long Day's Journey into Night* (London: Jonathan Cape, 1966, repr. 1979), p. 53.

made him a greater, more significant figure.'[16] But two of his plays have interesting resonances for our argument. *All My Sons* and *A View from the Bridge* both turn on the experience of being an immigrant – not viewed purely in terms of psychology, as with Tyrone, but as a syndrome with tragic repercussions for the hero's attitude towards the law and his own family. At his best, Miller dares to complete the thought that Synge left unfinished about peasant contempt for the law; and he finds his way back to genuinely classical terrain by focusing on the class of Americans for whom modernization has happened brutally fast – the immigrants from the Old World to the New.

Arthur Miller, *All My Sons* (1947)

The hero of this play is an equivocal type: the self-made businessman. But Miller, who had Jewish immigrant factory owners on both sides of the family, sees the heroic potential of the life of economic self-reliance amidst precision machinery:

> *KELLER is nearing sixty. A heavy man of stolid mind and build, a businessman these many years, but with the imprint of the machine-shop worker and boss still upon him. When he reads, when he speaks, when he listens, it is with the terrible concentration of the uneducated man for whom there is still wonder in many commonly known things, a man whose judgments must be dredged out of experience and a peasant-like common sense. A man among men.*[17]

Keller's ethnic background is not specified, though we are free to assume he is Jewish: what matters is that he has the immigrant's sense of the roots of things – and also of the danger of a world in which financial ruin was as close as financial success. When the play opens he is apparently safely established, rich, loving (the warmth of his family ties is much emphasized) and looking forward to passing on his self-made business to his one surviving son. But the nastiness that emerges from the 'cellar' of the Keller family is that this structure is built on a buried crime: his supplying to the Air Force cylinder heads that he knew to be cracked, and which led to the death of 21 pilots and the suicide of his younger son. The whole play turns on his refusal of responsibility for this crime, and the climax is the moment of self-knowledge when he says of the dead pilots, 'they were all my sons' (p. 170), and shoots himself offstage.

It has always been recognized how much this play owes to Ibsen, in Miller's exploitation of a long-buried secret, but we may notice something more, in the interplay between the loving father's sense of duty to his family, and his lack of

---

[16] Harold Bloom (ed.), *Arthur Miller* (New York and Philadelphia: Chelsea House Publishers, 1987), p. 43.

[17] Arthur Miller, *A View From the Bridge and All My Sons* (Harmondsworth: Penguin Books, 1961), pp. 89–90.

it towards outsiders. As someone clawing for a livelihood in a new country he is somewhat in the lawless position of Nora, who did not extend financial probity to people who were 'only strangers'. Businessmen too may be 'idiotic' under pressure, and Miller captures very well the self-made man's terror of slipping backwards, in the wartime panic that made equivocation easy. ('Every half hour the Major callin' for cylinder heads, they were whippin' us with the telephone. The trucks were hauling them away hot, damn near', p. 118.) Keller relives it all with myopic frenzy:

> I'm in business, a man is in business; a hundred and twenty cracked, you're out of business; you got a process, the process don't work you're out of business; you don't know how to operate, they tear up your contracts, what the hell's it to them? You lay forty years into a business and they knock you out in five minutes, what could I do, let them take forty years, let them take my life away? [*His voice cracking*] I never thought they'd install them. I swear to God. I thought they'd stop 'em before anybody took off. (p. 157)

Although the comparison with Ibsen also points up the poverty of Miller's dramatic method (there is no possibility of an electrifying entrance by the Rat Wife in this style of drama, and Miller's best effort at symbolism is the tree that blows over at the start of the action), still the old debate between family feeling and the law is well caught. Keller's mistake is a *hamartia*: he did not feel his obligations to other people's sons as he did to his own, and the price he pays is that his own son (who was also a pilot in the war) cannot bear to acknowledge him. When Keller says, 'Chris, I did it for you', his son's fury is a classic analysis of the limits of the *oikos*:

> Where do you live, where have you come from? For me! – I was dying every day and you were killing my boys and you did it for me? What the hell do you think I was thinking of, the goddam business? Is that as far as your mind can see, the business? What is that, the world – the business? What the hell do you mean, you did it for me? Don't you have a country? Don't you live in the world? What the hell are you? You're not even an animal, no animal kills his own, what are you? What must I do to you? I ought to tear the tongue out of your mouth, what must I do? [*With his fist he pounds down upon his father's shoulder. He stumbles away, covering his face as he weeps.*] What must I do, Jesus God, what must I do? (p. 158)

In this context, Keller's admission that the pilots were 'all his sons' is powerful, trite as it sounds: he is using the language of family beyond the family, and the whole play tells us how long a journey it was to make.

A View from the Bridge (1955)

Miller puts the immigrant mentality to still more pointed use in *A View from the Bridge*, where the protagonists are Italian longshoremen in New York and the illegal immigrants to whom they give a temporary home. The play is framed, somewhat archly, by the testimony of a lawyer, who deliberately points up the anomaly of his position among the immigrants: behind the 'suspicious little nod' with which they acknowledge him, he says, 'lie three thousand years of distrust. A lawyer means the law, and in Sicily, from where their fathers came, the law has not been a friendly idea since the Greeks were beaten' (pp. 11–12). Miller wants a classical resonance for his play, we note, but it is not merely a matter of decor. His tragic hero has an Italian capacity for passion, but his passions are rank and destructive (incest and homosexuality bring this play to a new level of frankness), and when the knives are finally out, in defence of the hero's 'name', the blood spilt is not armchair gore.

The ambiguous hero in this play is a longshoreman, Eddy Carbone. Like Keller, he is attractively warm and direct, but he is nursing a disastrous passion of which only his wife is aware – an incestuous love for his niece, whom he has raised from childhood. Miller notes the tokens of his obsession and his stratagems for keeping it out of conscious view: he fusses over everything to do with her, from the length of her skirts to her taking a job, and the fineness of the line between his old-world paternalism and possessive jealousy is well marked. Miller also indicates the way the girl herself collaborates, enjoying both his admiration and her prolonged dependence ('like you sit on the edge of the bathtub talkin' to him when he's shavin' in his underwear', as the wife points out, struggling not to be jealous, p. 43). This triangle is upset by the visit of two of the wife's cousins as illegal immigrants. Marco has a hungry wife and children in Italy to support, but his brother Rodolpho is single, and intends to stay in America. Rodolpho and the niece fall in love, and he becomes the focus of Eddie's violent hate.

With Rodolpho, Miller takes the plot into a surprisingly dangerous area, that of Pentheus' confused fascination with Dionysus in the *Bacchae*. Rodolpho is bizarrely blond, with a high operatic tenor and unexpected gifts for dress-making and cookery. Cutting out a dress 'he looks like an angel', says Eddie, uncomfortably – 'you could kiss him he was so sweet' (p. 47). He has easy access to femininity without being effeminate – he also covets a large blue motorbike – but Eddie masks his jealousy from himself as horror that Catherine has fallen for a 'punk', and enters into an aggressive relation with Rodolpho that has half-erotic undertones. The end of Act I finds him making an excuse to box with him in a manner partly cruel, partly excited; and in the next act he forces himself drunkenly between the lovers to part them for good – by kissing Catherine on the mouth, to mark his possession of her; and then pinning Rodolpho's arms and unexpectedly kissing him, too. He does it, he says, to show Catherine what

Rodolpho is made of, but the moment opens vertiginous perspectives on Eddie himself.

Eddie's only way of removing Rodolpho, when Catherine still takes his side, is to denounce him to the Immigration Bureau. To 'shop' illegal immigrants is the ultimate crime in Eddie's Italian world, and he commits it at the price of isolating himself from his whole community, and uncovering three other illegal immigrants as well – including Rodolpho's brother Marco, who spits on him publicly: 'That one! He killed my children! That one stole the food from my children!' (p. 77). The lovers avoid Rodolpho's extradition by marrying, and the climax of the play is Eddie's demand for Marco's apology on the brink of the wedding: 'I want my name, Marco' (p. 84). 'Anima-a-al!' is the only name Marco will give him, as they fight to the death, and the unarmed Marco turns Eddie's own knife against him.

What is impressive about this plot is the number of classical issues it manages to reanimate – incest, the price of masculinity, the revenge ethic, the 'name' – while keeping a sober sense of the real. Miller tells the truth about the peasant poverty that produces emigration: when Catherine wants to go to Italy, Rodolpho tells her 'in two years you would have an old, hungry face. When my brother's babies cry they give them water, water that boiled a bone' (p. 60). He also sees that the closeness of the immigrant community is the other side of its capacity for incest – as Eddie says, truly enough, of his welcome for his wife's relatives, 'I give them the blankets off my bed. Six months I kept them like my own brothers!' (p. 77). Miller manages, we may say, to combine two things which are always falling apart in twentieth-century tragedy, the normal and the grand-scale. And he does it, interestingly enough, because he has come to a conclusion about Greek drama which chimes closely with the argument of this book. He noted, in preparation for this play,

> The secret of the Greek drama is the vendetta, the family ties incomprehensible to Englishmen and Americans. But not to Jews. Much that has been interpreted in lofty terms, fate, religion, etc., is only blood and the tribal survival within the family. Red Hook [the immigrant slum where the play is set] is full of Greek tragedies.[18]

It is because of this vision that Eddie's seemingly ugly life takes on such dramatic resonance.

Miller's ambitions for this play show in the fact that he wrote the first version in verse, the only mode he thought adequate to its importance. The 'choric' lawyer originally ended the play with these lines, which show both the value of Miller's conception and the terrible difficulty of realizing it in the language available:

---

18   Bloom, *Arthur Miller*, p. 109.

> Most of the time we settle for half,
> And I like it better.
> And yet, when the tide is right
> And the green smell of the sea
> Floats in through my window,
> The waves of this bay
> Are the waves against Siracusa.
> And I see a face that suddenly seems carved;
> The eyes look like tunnels
> Leading back toward some ancestral beach
> Where all of us once lived.
> And I wonder at those times
> How much of all of us
> Really lives there yet,
> And when we will truly have moved on,
> On and away from that dark place,
> That world that has fallen to stones?[19]

The perception is serious (and 'how much of all of us / Really lives there yet' is a key question) but the loose movement and lapses into bathos show how hopeless was Miller's ambition to hold the American stage with dramatic poetry. The second version of the play was in prose, and Miller had to content himself with the resonance that could be got from Italian-American street slang.

If Miller cannot be compared with Lorca, then, it is perhaps for different reasons than O'Neill. With O'Neill, it is the attempt to find tragic issues inside individual psychology that seems self-defeating. Miller is more certain that the Greek insistence on dramatizing the private life along with its social context gives the truer perspective: 'For when the Greek thought of the right way to live it was a whole concept, it meant a way to live that would create citizens who were brave in war, had a sense of responsibility to the polis in peace, and were also developed as individual personalities.'[20]

From here, it was easier for him to see that tragic tension arose at the threshold between the home and the *polis*, between 'belonging' and standing alone as an individual, and ultimately in the risk of public judgement. Even when he manages to embody this vision in his plots, however, he remains the victim of his use of language: Miller is not a poet, as Lorca is, and he cannot make his language memorable. It cannot hint at the world of the invisible behind the visible, or evoke the living connections between man and nature which make *The House of Bernarda Alba* so unselfconsciously potent (as when Adela says 'He takes me into the reeds at the edge of the river!', Bernarda craves a 'bolt of lightning between her fingers' to blast her with, or Martirio's breast bursts with envy like a

---

[19] Quoted in Neil Carson, *Arthur Miller* (London: Macmillan, 1982), pp. 83–4.
[20] 'On Social Plays', quoted by Carson, *Arthur Miller*, p. 85.

'bitter pomegranate').[21] Even if Miller had been a poet, we may guess that the language itself would remain a problem. It is too modern – too clean, too stripped of organic connection, too Apollonian – to do the work of Lorca's language; which is, of course, one of the things modernity means. Abstraction is always a sacrifice of weight, and here is another proof of it, operating on the playwright himself. Miller can go to the streets for the language of colour and force – Italian-American, Yiddish-American, and all the other accents he employs – but none of them is as potent as the language of the homeland. When Marco cries 'Anima-a-al!', we hear what Miller means; but it is not the same as '*Animale!*'

If we say, then, that tragedy depends on the historical moment, we are perhaps saying several associated things at once. The state of the language itself is part of what makes tragedy possible: it needs to be able to face backwards to the peasant past, and forwards to the urban future; it needs rootedness and self-consciousness, two things no language holds together for very long. And it is a related thought that a culture in which the language is looking both ways is likely to be a culture in painful transition, where the social and political order are being radically rearranged. This is the historical moment which gives the tragedian his chance: it reveals to him the hidden structures of civilization (the Furies nesting under Athens, the rats under Scandinavian floorboards) and at the same time delivers him a needy, passionate audience. Because of their own inner disorder, and the external disorder of the times, the members of this audience can tolerate truths normally too painful to be told; they welcome the profound truth of what they see. And the tragedian who is most likely to be able to meet this public emergency with the requisite courage is the one on whom the strains of the time press most deeply. He will not be a Yeats or an Eliot, who (by class, wealth or temperament) has been settled on the far side of the common danger for too long to remember how it feels, but someone who has made the perilous journey in his own lifetime: an Ibsen, Lorca or indeed a Shakespeare, who has left the village of his childhood for the city of his maturity, and for whom the work of what the world calls 'Emancipation', 'Republicanism' or 'Reformation' is an inner battle that is never completed.

Our argument has left out of account one of the undisputed giants of modern drama, however, who may be an important witness on the subject of public and private emergencies: Anton Chekhov. Unlike the other authors we have been considering, Chekhov did not set out to write tragedies: he saw his plays, like his stories, as part of his comic vision of Russian life, and it was his audiences and directors who interpreted them tragically. But Chekhov wrote on the brink of a revolution and civil war just as Lorca did, and would seem to have had the 'historical moment' for tragedy *par excellence*. What should we understand by his insistence that comedy was the fitting response?

---

[21]   *The House of Bernarda Alba*, trans. Dewell and Zapata, pp. 165–7.

Anton Chekhov, *The Cherry Orchard* (1904)

Chekhov described this play while he was writing it as 'not a drama but a comedy: in places almost a farce'.[22] We know from his letters that this description genuinely described the play, in origin at least: the first version was a farce in four acts, and included a comic role for his wife ('a stupid woman', perhaps Varya), another for Stanislavsky (Lopakhin) and a one-armed billiards-player (the role that presumably metamorphosed into Gayev). Chekhov retained the definition 'a comedy', too, in the subtitle of the finished drama; but the English stage, no less than the Russian, has found it impossible to exclude an elegiac note from a play so clearly about the end of the old order: the axing of the cherry orchard, and the slow death of everything associated with it.

Nostalgia for picturesquely feudal ways of life and fecklessly charming aristocrats, however, comes easily after they are safely defunct; if we want to understand the grounds of Chekhov's reluctance to take the purely tragic view of this social transition, we need to remind ourselves that he himself was the grandson of a serf, and that the year after the play, 1905, saw the first outbreak of revolution in the wake of Russia's defeat by Japan. If we assume that Chekhov is analysing a social breakdown at its eleventh hour, a breakdown of which he has been the beneficiary, it is easier to notice the farcical sub-structures in the apparently realistic plot: that the estate owner Lyuba Ranevskaya runs away from her lover in Paris to Russia, and then back to him in Paris; that although everyone expects to be devastated by the loss of the estate, it actually makes them feel much better; and that 87-year-old Firs, the reluctantly emancipated house serf for whom everyone intended to do their best, is accidentally locked into the house and left alone to die.

The death of Firs gives an edge to another aspect of the play that is easily sentimentalized: the quasi-familial relations of the *oikos*-like estate, where old retainers like the nanny are never dismissed, where Firs chases his middle-aged master across the stage with his overcoat and scolds him for wearing the wrong trousers, and Lyuba's entourage includes all kinds of superfluous characters from the past, who consume what little she has left (including Simeonov-Pishchik, an even more penniless landowner than herself). On closer examination, these interrelations reveal something less picturesque: the human muddle left over from the Emancipation of the serfs in 1861. As Firs puts it, 'Those were the days. The serfs had their masters and the masters had their serfs, but now everything's at sixes and sevens and you can't make head or tail of it.'[23] What the Emancipation

---

[22] Letter to M.P. Alekseyeva, 15 Sept. 1903 (*The Oxford Chekhov*, vol. 3, trans. and ed. Ronald Hingley (London, New York and Toronto: Oxford University Press, 1968–75), app. IV, p. 319.

[23] Anton Chekhov, *Five Plays*, trans. Ronald Hingley (Oxford: Oxford University Press 1980), p. 264.

revealed was a world in which feudal relatedness had enabled each class to specialize in some human capacities and delegate the rest to someone else – and much of Chekhov's satirical effect depends on how they are now revealed as incapable of living by themselves.

As Firs phrases it in the original, 'now everything's *vrazdrob* [in bits and pieces], and *nie poimyosh nichevo* [you can't understand anything]'.[24] Everyone in the play holds some vital part of the jigsaw – but not more than a part, hence, Chekhov implies, the comedy. Lyuba and Gayev have powerful, deep-seated emotions, but they lavish them on a cherry orchard or the furniture (Gayev makes a speech to his 100-year-old bookcase), and they completely fail to learn where money comes from: 'Yesterday I had lots of money but I've hardly any left today' is a typical observation of Lyuba's, made just as she drops her purse (p. 261). Her adopted daughter, Varya, knows how to manage money and feeds the estate on milk soups, but she cannot manage personal emotions, and her dream for herself is the old Russian Orthodox one, of becoming a wandering pilgrim. The tutor, Trofimov, talks about the importance of work but remains an 'eternal student', immature and puritanical. Meanwhile, the servants divide between those who have 'forgotten their place' like the valet and maid, who have lost their morals and developed a taste for champagne, or Firs, who carries the responsibility for his master's physical needs to the bitter end. 'Mr. Leonid hasn't put his fur coat on, I'll be bound', is his last audible anxiety (p. 294).

In all this, the character who has managed to assemble most of the working parts of a complete human being is Lopakhin. He is rich and generous, feeling and practical; to Gayev he is only a *kulak* ('a lout of a peasant out for what I can get', p. 248), but he still reveres Lyuba for wiping his bloody nose when he was beaten by his father as a boy, and he spends most of the play trying to save her estate for her. If he does not succeed, it is because she barely hears what he is saying. The idea of chopping down the orchard for middle-class *dachas* is too vulgar to be entertained, though to Lopakhin's thinking, it is only another way of making the orchard bloom ('so far your holidaymaker only has his tea on the balcony, but he may very well start growing things on his bit of land and then this cherry orchard will become a happy, rich, prosperous place', p. 250). This is not our cue to suppose him a philistine; Trofimov comments on his deep feelings and 'sensitive fingers like an artist's' (p. 286), and this, combined with his passion for work ('I can't stand not working – look, I don't know what to do with my arms', p. 285) makes him sound very like the hero of the play.[25]

---

[24]   A.P. Chekhov, *Izbrannie proizvedenia v trech tomach* [*Collected Works in Three Volumes*] (Moscow: Khudozhestvennaia Literatura, 1971), vol. 3, p. 562.

[25]   Chekhov wanted Stanislavsky to play this role – but he, son of a textile manufacturer, preferred to play Gayev (Laurence Senelick, *Anton Chekhov* (Basingstoke and London: Macmillan, 1985), p. 120).

But the comedy of the plot is how ineffectual all his good intentions are in mending the social fabric. Nothing he says makes any difference, and he is left bidding for the cherry orchard at auction himself, in a way that reveals the underlying guilt that is pulling this society apart. If it is too soon for Lopakhin to be a 'gentleman', if he cannot help but crow his triumph, it is because of the terrible past:

> Great God in heaven, the cherry orchard's mine. Tell me I'm drunk or crazy, say it's all a dream. [*Stamps his feet.*] Don't laugh at me. If my father and grandfather could only rise from their graves and see what happened, see how their Yermolay – Yermolay who was always being beaten, who could hardly write his name and ran round barefoot in winter – how this same Yermolay bought this estate, the most beautiful place in the world. I've bought the estate where my father and grandfather were slaves, where they weren't even allowed inside the kitchen. I must be dreaming, I must be imagining it all. It can't be true. (p. 282)

If the reasons for Lopakhin's giddy feelings here could be acknowledged, the society of which he is the most hopeful growing point might begin to knit itself together. But Lyuba only collapses, weeping, and Varya angrily throws him the estate keys from her belt. Whatever future Lopakhin is ushering in, they want no part of it.

Chekhov's sense that he was writing at a historical turning point is clear from the number of new characters in this play. Lopakhin the rising businessman is only one example; Trofimov the student revolutionary is another, and so too are the rootless characters inside and outside the family, like the governess Charlotte who has no identity papers, and the menacing beggar who appears unexpectedly on the edge of the estate. In Act II Chekhov orchestrates their voices together with wonderful economy, and conveys at the same time the atmosphere of post-prandial quiet, and the rumble of approaching revolution. In its own way, this act is as politically diagnostic as *The House of Bernarda Alba* – but with characters whose unwillingness to inhabit their own fate means that the 'historical moment' is not tragic at all.

The act is set, significantly, just beyond the estate, in the outside world. The neighbouring town is dimly visible, and a road leading to the new railway. All the characters strike the note of disorder and fragmentation in their own key: Charlotte meditates on her utter solitude in the world and eats a gherkin ('I'm longing for someone to talk to, but there isn't anyone', p. 258), while the conceited valet enjoys his conquest over the fluttery maid, whom he clearly expects to abandon. When the main characters enter, they are in a state of unfocused distraction. Gayev and Lyuba have enjoyed a good meal in town ('how handy it is now they've built the railway', says Gayev, p. 260 – he appreciates modernity without grasping its implications) and they cannot hear Lopakhin's last-ditch attempt to get them to assent to his plan for leasing the cherry orchard, though he asks them three times in rising desperation, 'Yes or no. Just one single word' (p. 260). Gayev is distracted by embarrassing memories of talking too much to the waiters, and continually plays an imaginary game of billiards, while Lyuba is puzzled by the sudden emptiness of her purse ('I go round simply squandering money, I can't think why', p. 261). When Lopakhin does finally get their attention, it is because he gives up and decides to leave:

Lopakhin   I'm going to burst into tears or scream or faint. This is too much, I've had about all I can stand! [*To* Gayev] You're an old woman.
Gayev   What's that?
Lopakhin   I say you're an old woman. [*Makes to leave.*]
Mrs. Ranev.[*terrified*] No, don't go away, my dear man. Stay with us, I implore you. Perhaps we'll think of something.
Lopakhin   'Think'? This isn't a question of thinking.
Mrs. Ranev.Don't go away, I beg you. Besides, it's more amusing with you around. [*Pause.*] I keep expecting something awful to happen, as if the house was going to collapse around our ears.
Gayev   [*deep in thought*] Off the cushion into the corner. Across into the middle. (p. 262)

As Chekhov implies, it is not that Lyuba and Gayev do not know what is happening: in some part of herself Lyuba realizes that their house is 'collapsing around [their] ears'. The reason they have no energy to respond to Lopakhin's straightforward request is that they are so bound up in denying what they know – in keeping Gayev's billiard-game going, and pretending that 'something' may be thought of. The remoteness of their relation to their own disaster is what goads Lopakhin to call Gayev an old woman, *baba* – female 'idiocy' could go no farther. And if, finally, Lyuba is desperate to keep Lopakhin with them, it is only for his basic warmth, not his intelligence – 'it's more amusing (*veseleye*, cheerful) with you around.'

The sub-tragic quality of all this shows in her next sighing remark, 'I suppose we've committed so many sins . . . ', which, like everything she says, is both true and not true enough. She reminisces about her follies in love, the worthless man she followed to Paris, but this is not the heart of the matter. The long-standing crime to which she is an accessory lurks in the beautiful cherry orchard, as the tutor describes it to her daughter Anya at the end of this act:

Don't you see that from every cherry-tree . . . men and women are gazing at you? . . . Owning living souls, that's what's changed you all so completely, those who went before and those alive today, so that your mother, you yourself, your uncle – you don't realize that you're actually living on credit. You're living on other people, the very people you won't even let inside your own front door. We're at least a couple of hundred years behind the times. (p. 269)

The accuracy of this is shown by how deliberately vague these aristocrats are about the nature of money, about where it came from in the past and where it might come from in the future. And the price they pay for symbiosis with slavery is the loss of their instinct for independence, so that they wince away from any decision that would make them stand forth in the world as authors, rather than sufferers, of their destiny.

The symbolic reach of Chekhov's realism shows in the economical way he indicates the state of this society with a reference to the sunset, and the noise of something breaking apart in the distance. The comic elements in this dialogue are brilliantly interwoven with messages about the guilt-ridden past and the revolutionary future:

Gayev	The sun has set, my friends.
Trofimov	Yes.
Gayev	[*in a quiet voice, as if giving a recitation*] Nature, glorious Nature, glowing with everlasting radiance, so beautiful, so cold – you, whom men call mother, in whom the living and the dead are joined together, you who give life and take it away –
Varya	[*imploring him*] Uncle dear!
Anya	Uncle, you're off again.
Trofimov	You'd far better pot the red in the middle.
Gayev	I am silent. Silent.
	[*Everyone sits deep in thought. It is very quiet. All that can be heard is Firs's low muttering. Suddenly a distant sound is heard. It seems to come from the sky and is the sound of a breaking string. It dies away sadly.*]
Mrs. Ranev.	What was that?
Lopakhin	I don't know. A cable must have broken somewhere away in the mines. But it must be a long, long way off.
Gayev	Or perhaps it was a bird, a heron or something.
Trofimov	Or an owl.
Mrs. Ranev.	[*shudders*]. There was something disagreeable about it. [*Pause.*]
Firs	The same thing happened before the troubles, the owl hooting and the samovar humming all the time.
Gayev	What 'troubles' were those?
Firs	When the serfs were given their freedom. [*Pause.*] (p. 267)

The symbolic reach of this dialogue shows in the way Chekhov manages to locate the social disaster in its real context – the natural world, 'so beautiful, so cold', where the 'living and dead are joined together' and where even the Revolution will eventually be buried. But this truth is enunciated by Gayev, in whose mouth it is rhetoric, a defence against experience; and so, like all the other sustaining truths in this play, it appears only to disappear again. The mysterious sound which 'dies away sadly' is a unique touch of the supernatural in Chekhov, and feels like nature's own voice made audible (it makes Lyuba shudder and brings tears to

Anya's eyes without her knowing why). But he immediately naturalizes it by showing how differently each character hears it: for Lopakhin, who knows about mining, it could be a breaking cable, for Trofimov, an owl, and to Firs, in a stroke of mournful comedy, it is a reminder of the portents heralding the worst thing that ever happened in his world, 'when the serfs were given their freedom'. Firs is the perfection of the old social system, the man who has internalized slavery till he is a kind of human dog, and he will resist becoming more till the day he dies.

Firs' addiction to slavery is frightening enough, but it is not as openly menacing as the sudden appearance of a drunken stranger. The scene has taken place near the road to town; and the stage direction makes it clear that this tramp is part of the enormous landless proletariat created by the Emancipation:

Mrs. Ranev.	Come, let's go in, everyone. It's getting late. [*To* Anya.] You've tears in your eyes. What is it, child? [*Embraces her.*]
Anya	It's nothing, Mother. I'm all right.
Trofimov	There's somebody coming. [*The Passer-by appears. He wears a shabby, white peaked cap and an overcoat. He is slightly drunk.*]
Passer-by	Excuse me asking, but am I right for the station this way?
Gayev	Yes. Follow that road.
Passer-by	I'm uncommonly obliged to you. [*With a cough.*] Splendid weather, this. [*Declaiming.*] 'Brother, my suffering brother!' 'Come out to the Volga, you whose groans – .' [*To* Varya.] Miss, could you spare a few copecks for a starving Russian? [*Varya takes fright and shrieks.*]
Lopakhin	[*angrily*]: Even where you come from there's such a thing as being polite.
Mrs. Ranev.	[*flustered*]: Here, have this. [*Looks in her purse.*] I've no silver. Never mind, here's some gold.
Passer-by	I'm uncommonly obliged to you. [*Goes off.*] [*Everyone laughs.*] (pp. 267–8)

The alarm this tramp arouses, and Lyuba's readiness to bribe him to go away, suggest the depth of meaning he carries with him, like the Rat Wife – or rather, one of the rats themselves, gnawing away at everyone's subconscious. In his tipsy rootlessness ('am I right for the station?'), his ill-health ('*with a cough*') and fluent rhetoric of brotherhood and suffering, he is in every detail the proletarian who will be manning the barricades in 1917. The guilt and fear connected with him show in the discrepancy between his actual demand ('a few copecks') and Varya's wild shriek; and when Lyuba cannot find any silver in her purse, a gold coin does not seem too much to secure his disappearance, even if it is all the money she has. The social fabric is patched together a little longer – and everyone laughs with relief.

We know how little Chekhov intended such scenes to draw tears from his antagonism to their contemporary staging. As he said to one admirer,

> You say that you have wept over my plays. Yes, and not you alone. But I
> did not write them for that; it is Alexeyev [Stanislavsky] who has made
> such cry-babies of my characters. I wanted something else. I wanted to tell
> people honestly: 'Look at yourselves. See how badly you live and how
> tiresome you are!' . . . Is that what makes them weep?[26]

The lachrymose view of his audience is the very attitude he is putting satirically
before them: the preference for tears over action, and regression over self-
definition. 'All the inhabitants of *The Cherry Orchard* are children and their
behaviour is childish',[27] was the more bracing post-revolutionary view. But even
this, we may note, is not quite adequate to the complexity Chekhov presents. The
characters are childish but not children: they are adults without enough adult
characteristics to justify their status. The work they would have to do to make
themselves adequate characters for tragedy, as with Ibsen's Nora, would be
enormous. Leaving the house (as with Nora) would be the obvious pre-condition;
and this is presumably why Chekhov makes the play turn on the sale of the estate,
and why the characters themselves are so unexpectedly relieved by it, in spite of
their foreboding. But to be helplessly ejected from an estate is not as positive an
achievement as deciding to leave it; and hearing Lopakhin put the axe to the
cherry orchard is not the same thing as putting the axe to it oneself. In all this, the
characters are revealing themselves to be as enslaved by the past as Firs, if in a
more elegant manner.

Perhaps the stringency of Chekhov's criticism, and its profoundly serious
implications, for all the farcicality of the mode, is only understandable in the light
of our supposition above – that the greatest tragic dramatist is someone on whom
the strains of the time press most deeply, and who has made the journey of
emancipation in his own lifetime. Chekhov is the son of a man who was born into
serfdom (his grandfather bought his family's freedom just before the
Emancipation) and therefore he knows at first hand what even Lorca or Ibsen
could not know: the mental deformities slave status brings with it and the
unremitting struggle to purge them, which a single generation can barely achieve.
When he writes about his own youth (in the following oblique description to an
early patron) he describes a journey that perhaps only an emancipated slave in the
ancient world would recognize:

> What aristocratic writers take from nature gratis the less privileged must
> pay for with their youth. Try to write a story about a young man – the son
> of a serf, a former grocer, choirboy, schoolboy and university student,
> raised on respect for rank, kissing the priests' hands, worshipping the ideas
> of others and giving thanks for every piece of bread, receiving frequent
> whippings, making the rounds as a tutor without galoshes, brawling,
> torturing animals, enjoying dinners at the houses of rich relatives,

[26]   To A.N. Tikhonov, in Maurice Valency, *The Breaking String: The Plays of
Anton Chekhov* (New York: Oxford University Press, 1966), pp. 298–9.
[27]   A.R. Kugel, in Senelick, *Anton Chekhov*, p. 122.

needlessly hypocritical before God and man merely to acknowledge his own insignificance – write about this young man who squeezes the slave out of himself, drop by drop, and who, one fine morning, finds that the blood coursing through his veins is no longer the blood of a slave but that of a real human being.[28]

It is because Chekhov knows in every fibre of himself what unremitting effort it takes to become 'a real human being', and how sweetly seductive are all the excuses the habit of slavery makes, that his analysis of the Russian muddle is so lucid. He has made the journey inch by inch, and so his account in this play of what it is to be humanly 'unfinished'[29] is unsparing. Unlike other Russian writers, he has no programmatic solution for the social disaster in preparation; but he will not lie by pretending that any of the 'victims' had no choice: 'I hate lying and violence, whatever form they may take . . . [and] I regard trade-marks and labels as prejudicial. My holy of holies is the human body, health, intelligence, talent, inspiration, love and absolute freedom – freedom from force and falsehood.'[30] If the characters in his plays do not live in this vigorously Athenian atmosphere, the price they pay is clear enough, and articulated by Firs in his bewilderment as he dies: 'Life's slipped by just as if I'd never lived at all' (p. 294).

If Chekhov could not bear to call his plays anything but comedies, then, and his audience have almost always felt them to be tragedies, there is perhaps no real disagreement. The same phenomena are under discussion – but Chekhov is viewing them from an upright position, and through the severest humanist spectacles. It is his privilege to have arrived in the twentieth century from a depth of degradation unknown in the rest of Europe, in a culture so fossilized in religious myticism and autocracy that its Reformation and regicide are still pending (as he makes Trofimov say, 'we're at least a couple of hundred years behind the times'). What from one point of view is a social disaster, is from another a unique opportunity for an artist to recapitulate and analyse the stages in the development of a human being. And the country estates on which Chekhov sets his plays are perhaps the ultimate incarnation of the power of the family as we have defined it, of clan organization untouched by public law. A Russian estate is, like the original Athenian *oikos*, an undifferentiated unity of property and persons, animals and slaves, men and women; and as Chekhov analyses the slow-motion dissolution of this hydra-headed organism, he also indicates with fierce clarity the point at which tragic responsibility might be possible for its human members. One day; if they do the work.

---

[28]   Letter to Suvorin, in V.S. Pritchett, *Chekhov: A Spirit Set Free* (London: Hodder & Stoughton, 1988), p. 36.

[29]   Chekhov coined what seems to be a nonce-word for 'unfinished, half-baked' in *nedotyopa*, which Firs uses grumpily throughout the play. More precisely it means 'half-chopped-down', which gives extra resonance to the last line, spoken by Firs to himself as the axe sounds offstage, 'Ah, you're *nedotyopa*' (Senelick, *Anton Chekhov*, p. 133).

[30]   To Pleshcheyev, in Pritchett, *Chekhov*, p. 46.

Bibliography

Aeschylus, *The Oresteia*, trans. Robert Fagles (Harmondsworth: Penguin Books, 1985).
——, *The Oresteia*, trans. Richmond Lattimore (Chicago: University of Chicago Press, 1953).
——, *Aeschylus*, trans. H.W. Smyth (Cambridge, Mass.: Harvard University Press, 1926), vol. 2.
Archer, William, *William Archer on Ibsen: The Major Essays, 1889–1919*, ed. Thomas Postlewait (Westport, Conn. and London: Greenwood Press, 1984).
Aristotle, *The Complete Works of Aristotle*, trans. Jonathan Barnes (Princeton: Princeton University Press, 1984).
Arnold, Matthew, *The Poetical Works of Matthew Arnold* (London: Oxford University Press, 1942).
Bacon, Francis, *The Essays of Francis Bacon*, ed. Samuel Harvey Reynolds (Oxford: Clarendon Press, 1890).
Benveniste, Emile, *Indo-European Language and Society*, trans. Elizabeth Palmer (London: Faber, 1973).
Bloom, Harold (ed.), *Arthur Miller* (New York and Philadelphia: Chelsea House Publishers, 1987).
Boswell, James, *Boswell's Life of Doctor Johnson*, ed. G.B. Hill (Oxford: Clarendon Press, 1887).
Bradley, A.C., 'Coriolanus', *Proceedings of the British Academy 1911–12* (London: Oxford University Press, 1914).
Carson, Neil, *Arthur Miller* (London: Macmillan, 1982).
Chekhov, Anton, *Five Plays*, trans. Ronald Hingley (Oxford: Oxford University Press, 1980).
——, *Izbrannie proizvedenia v trech tomach* (Moscow: Khudozhestvennaya Literatura, 1971).
——, *The Oxford Chekhov*, trans. and ed. Ronald Hingley (London: Oxford University Press, 1968–75).
Coleridge, Samuel Taylor, *Lectures 1808–1819 on Literature*, ed. R.A. Foakes, in *The Collected Works of Samuel Taylor Coleridge*, general ed. Kathleen Coburn, 5 (London: Routledge & Kegan Paul, and Princeton: Princeton University Press, 1987).
Donne, John, *The Epithalamions, Anniversaries and Epicedes*, ed. W. Milgate (Oxford: Clarendon Press, 1978).
Downs, Brian W., *Ibsen: The Intellectual Background* (New York: Octagon Books, 1969).
Edwards, Gwynne, *Dramatists in Perspective: Spanish Theatre in the Twentieth Century* (Cardiff: University of Wales Press, 1985).
Eliot, T.S., *The Family Reunion* (London: Faber & Faber, 1939, repr. 1962).
——, 'Hamlet and His Problems', in *Hamlet*, ed. C. Hoy (New York and London: Norton, 1963).
——, *On Poetry and Poets* (London: Faber & Faber, 1957).
Empson, William, 'Up-dating Revenge Tragedy', in *Hamlet*, ed. C. Hoy (New York and London: Norton, 1963).
Euripides, *Bacchae*, ed. E.R. Dodds (Oxford: Oxford University Press, 1944, repr. 1960).
——, *The Bacchae*, trans. William Arrowsmith, in Euripides, *Complete Greek Tragedies*, ed. David Grene and Richmond Lattimore, 5 (Chicago: University of Chicago Press, 1959, repr. 1975).

——, *Electra*, trans. Emily Townsend Vermeule, in Euripides, *The Complete Greek Tragedies*, ed. David Grene and Richmond Lattimore, 5 (Chicago: University of Chicago Press (1959)).

——, *Hippolytus*, trans. David Grene, in Euripides, *The Complete Greek Tragedies*, ed. David Grene and Richmond Lattimore, 1 (Chicago: University of Chicago Press, 1955, repr. 1967).

——, *Medea*, ed. D.L. Page (Oxford: Clarendon Press, 1938).

——, *Medea*, trans. Rex Warner, in Euripides, *The Complete Greek Tragedies*, ed. David Grene and Richmond Lattimore, 1 (Chicago: University of Chicago Press, 1955, repr. 1967).

——, *Orestes and Other Plays*, trans. Philip Vellacott (Harmondsworth: Penguin, 1972).

Freud, Sigmund (1970), *Introductory Lectures on Psychoanalysis*, trans. Joan Rivière (London: George Allen & Unwin, 1970).

García Lorca, Federico, *Bodas de sangre*, ed. H. Ramsden (Manchester: Manchester University Press, 1980, repr. 1990).

——, *La casa de Bernarda Alba*, ed. Allen Josephs and Juan Caballero (Madrid: Catedra, 1996).

——, *Plays: One*, trans. Gwynne Edwards and Peter Luke (London: Methuen, 1987, repr. 1994).

——, *Three Plays*, trans. Michael Dewell and Carmen Zapata (Harmondsworth: Penguin Books, 1992).

——, *Yerma*, ed. Robin Warner (Manchester and New York: Manchester University Press, 1994).

Gibson, Ian, *The Death of Lorca* (St Albans: Paladin, 1974).

——, *Federico García Lorca: A Life* (London and Boston: Faber & Faber, 1989).

Gill, Christopher, 'The Articulation of the Self in the *Hippolytus*', in *Euripides, Women, and Sexuality*, ed. Anton Powell (London and New York: Routledge, 1990).

Goldhill, Simon, *Reading Greek Tragedy* (Cambridge: Cambridge University Press, 1986, repr. 1992).

Greville, Fulke, *Selected Writings of Fulke Greville*, ed. Joan Rees (London: Athlone Press, 1973).

Hegel, G.W.F., *Aesthetics*, trans. T.M. Knox (Oxford: Clarendon Press, 1975).

Homer, *The Odyssey*, trans. Robert Fitzgerald (New York: Doubleday, 1961, repr. 1963).

Ibsen, Henrik, *Four Major Plays: A Doll's House, Ghosts, Hedda Gabler, The Master Builder*, trans. James MacFarland and Jens Arup (Oxford: Oxford University Press, 1981, repr. 1987).

——, *Ghosts and Other Plays*, trans. Peter Watts (Harmondsworth: Penguin, 1964, repr. 1978).

——, *The Master Builder and Other Plays*, trans. Una Ellis-Fermor (Harmondsworth: Penguin, 1958).

Kyd, Thomas, *The Spanish Tragedy*, ed. J.R. Mulryne (London: A. & C. Black, 1989).

Lawrence, D.H., *Sons and Lovers* (Harmondsworth: Penguin Books, 1962).

Levin, Harry, *The Overreacher: A Study of Christopher Marlowe* (Cambridge, Mass.: Harvard University Press, 1952, repr. 1964).

Littlewood, J.C.F., 'Coriolanus', *Cambridge Quarterly*, 2 (1967), 339–44.

Machiavelli, Niccolò, *The Prince*, trans. Robert M. Adams (2nd edn, New York and London: Norton, 1992).

Marlowe, Christopher, *Complete Plays and Poems of Christopher Marlowe*, ed. E.D. Pendry (London and Rutland, Vt.: Dent, 1976).

——, *Doctor Faustus*, ed. Roma Gill (London: Ernest Benn Ltd., 1968; repr. London: A. & C. Black, and New York: Norton, 1989, 1991).

Meier, Christian, *The Political Art of Greek Tragedy*, trans. Andrew Webber (Cambridge: Polity Press, 1993).

Meyer, Michael, *Strindberg* (Oxford: Oxford University Press, 1987).

Miller, Arthur, *A View From the Bridge and All My Sons* (Harmondsworth: Penguin Books, 1961).

Moody, A.D., *Thomas Stearns Eliot, Poet* (Cambridge: Cambridge University Press, 1979, repr. 1980).

Northam, John, *Ibsen, a Critical Study* (Cambridge: Cambridge University Press, 1973).

O'Neill, Eugene, *Long Day's Journey into Night* (London: Jonathan Cape, 1966, repr. 1979).

——, *Mourning Becomes Electra* (London: Jonathan Cape, 1966, repr. 1989).

Padel, Ruth, *In and Out of the Mind* (Princeton and Oxford: Princeton University Press, 1992).

Plato, *The Laws*, trans. A.E. Taylor (London: Dent, 1934).

Plutarch, *Plutarch's Lives of the Noble Grecians and Romans, Englished by Sir Thomas North*, ed. W.E. Henley, vol. 2 (London: David Nutt, 1895).

Pritchett, V.S., *Chekhov: A Spirit Set Free* (London: Hodder & Stoughton, 1988).

Segal, C.P., *Tragedy and Civilization: An Interpretation of Sophocles* (Cambridge, Mass.: Harvard University Press, 1981).

Seneca, *Tragedies* (Loeb text), trans. Frank Justus Miller (London and New York: Heinemann and G.P. Putnam, 1917).

Senelick, Laurence, *Anton Chekhov* (Basingstoke and London: Macmillan, 1985).

Shakespeare, William, *The Complete Works*, ed. Stanley Wells and Gary Taylor (Oxford: Clarendon Press, 1988).

——, *Coriolanus*, ed. G.R. Hibbard (Harmondsworth: Penguin, 1967).

——, *Hamlet*, ed. C. Hoy (New York and London: W.W. Norton, 1963).

——, *Hamlet*, ed. G.R. Hibbard (Oxford and New York: Oxford University Press, 1987).

——, *Macbeth*, ed. K. Muir (London and New York: Methuen, 1962, repr. 1986).

Shakespeare: A Bibliographical Guide, ed. Stanley Wells (Oxford: Clarendon Press, 1990).

Sophocles, *Antigone*, ed. R.C. Jebb (Cambridge: Cambridge University Press, 1888).

——, *The Electra of Sophocles*, ed. R.C. Jebb (Cambridge: Cambridge University Press, 1908).

——, *Oedipus Coloneus*, ed. R.C. Jebb (Cambridge: Cambridge University Press, 1990).

——, *The Oedipus Cycle*, trans. Dudley Fitts and Robert Fitzgerald (New York: Harcourt, Brace & World, 1939, repr. 1971).

——, *Oedipus Tyrannus*, ed. R.C. Jebb (Cambridge (Cambridge University Press, 1902).

——, *Three Tragedies [Antigone, Oedipus the King, Electra]*, trans. H.D.F. Kitto (Oxford: Oxford University Press, 1962).

Steiner, George, *The Death of Tragedy* (London: Faber, 1961, repr. 1963).

Strindberg, August, *The Father, Miss Julie and the Ghost Sonata*, trans. Michael Meyer (London: Methuen, 1976).

Synge, J.M., *Collected Plays and Poems and The Aran Islands* (London: Everyman, 1992, repr. 1996).

——, *J.M. Synge: Interviews and Recollections*, ed. E.H. Mikhail (London: Macmillan, 1977).

Thomson, George, *Aeschylus and Athens: A Study in the Social Origins of Drama* (London: Lawrence & Wishart, 1973).

Valency, Maurice, *The Breaking String: The Plays of Anton Chekhov* (New York: Oxford University Press, 1966).

Vernant, J.-P., *Myth and Thought among the Greeks* (London: Routledge & Kegan Paul, 1983).

Vickers, Brian, *Towards Greek Tragedy: Drama, Myth, Society* (London and New York: Longman, 1973, corr. edn 1979).

Webster, T.B.L., *The Tragedies of Euripides* (London: Methuen, 1967).

West, Rebecca, *Black Lamb and Grey Falcon* (New York: Viking Press, 1941).

Winnington-Ingram, R.P., *Sophocles: An Interpretation* (Cambridge: Cambridge University Press, 1980).

Worthen, John, *D.H. Lawrence: The Early Years, 1885–1912* (Cambridge: Cambridge University Press, 1992).

Yeats, W.B., *The Collected Poems of W.B. Yeats* (London and Basingstoke: Macmillan, 1933, repr. 1977).

——, *Selected Plays*, ed. A. Norman Jeffares (Dublin: Gill & Macmillan, 1991).

Index

Aeneid 100, 132
Aeschylus 10, 37
    male-female conflict in 12, 18, 21–2
    on marriage 16–17, 21, 30
    Oresteia 3, 4, 10–31, 32, 33, 37, 39,
        45, 46, 48, 52–3, 54, 55, 57, 60,
        70, 78, 93, 113, 114, 123, 143, 144,
        162, 164, 166, 168, 174, 182, 183,
        186, 189, 194, 195, 198, 199, 208,
        212, 219, 224, 225, 226
    conversion of Furies 28–30, 48, 51,
        194
    see also Apollo; Athena; Furies
anagnorisis 93
Aristotle 71, 162
Arnold, Matthew 1
Apollo 2, 11, 22, 25, 37, 43, 45, 46, 54,
    162, 179, 182, 189, 191, 198, 201, 223
    antagonism to Furies 23, 27, 29
Athena 24, 25, 28, 37, 143, 169, 192
    gives birth to citizens 27, 155, 182
    'magic words' of persuasion 22–3,
        29, 40
Athens
    anthropomorphic religion 11
    staging of tragedy 9–11
    at war 54

Bachofen, J. J. 183
Bacon, Francis 99
Benveniste, Emile 52

Chekhov, Anton 233, 240–1
    Cherry Orchard 234–41
    non-tragic vision 233, 234, 240
Coleridge, Samuel Taylor 130–1

Dionysus 2–3, 80–94, 122, 139, 179, 198,
    203, 212, 230
    ecstasy of belonging 81–2
    hygra phusis 81, 83, 86, 90, 203
    'terrible and gentle' 85, 88, 127
Donne, John 116

Eliot, T. S. 116, 226, 233
    Family Reunion 219–20, 221, 223, 224
Euripides 10, 54, 125, 205
    Bacchae 65, 80–94, 122, 168, 185,
        187, 200, 202–4, 209, 230
    commentary on Sophocles 55–7
    critique of rationality 61, 69–70,
        83–4
    Electra 10, 55–8, 60, 64
    Hippolytus 65, 70, 72–80, 97, 190,
        204, 205, 209
    hostility to Apollo 54, 61, 64
    and the irrational 54, 65
    on marriage 66–8, 76
    Medea 65–72, 74, 80, 124, 178, 186,
        205, 206, 209
    Orestes 58–65
    parallels with Aeschylus 93
    preoccupation with outlaws 59, 62, 68
    on women 65–8, 74–5, 78–9, 87, 90;
        and infanticide 65, 70–2, 80, 90,
        92–3; and nature 74, 80, 85–7, 93,
        202

Freud, Sigmund 42
Furies 11, 21, 27, 33, 37, 40, 45, 49, 58,
    93, 162, 166, 182, 184, 191, 192, 196,
    198, 199, 201, 204, 209, 221, 225, 233
    avenge matricide 24
    contemptuous of Apollo 223
    convert to Eumenides 29–30, 194,
        205, 220
    missing from Sophocles 33, 36, 45
    see also tragic heroine

Garcia Lorca, Federico196–7, 217, 218,
    219, 221, 222, 223, 232–3, 240
    Blood Wedding 196–201, 205, 212,
        221
    concentration on women 202, 207
    Drama of Lot's Daughters 218
    Greek parallels in 198–200, 202–7,
        208–12
    House of Bernarda Alba 196,
        207–14, 218, 232, 236

infertility in 202, 205, 210
theatre as 'tribunal' 197, 204, 207
Yerma 196, 202–7, 208, 209, 212, 218
Greville, Fulke 3

hamartia 143, 150, 166, 229
Hegel, G. W. F. 32
hero *see* tragic hero
honour *see* tragic hero; tragic heroine

Ibsen, Henrik 173, 183, 187–8, 228, 229,
    233, 240
    Doll's House 173–8, 180, 183, 194,
        204, 206, 240
    critique of patriarchy 175
    women and law 174
    Ghosts 3, 178–82, 183, 184, 186, 195
        infanticide 178, 181–2
    Greek parallels in 179, 182, 190–5
    guilt in 187–8, 195
    John Gabriel Borkman 187
    Little Eyolf 187–95, 206, 220, 239
        incest in 188, 190–1
    Master Builder 187
    paganism in 188, 191, 226
    Scandinavian Furies in 179, 191–2,
        194, 233
    When We Dead Awaken 187
Iliad 132, 144, 164
individuation 3–5, 30, 41, 115–16, 162
    see also Macbeth; Machiavel;
        Machiavelli

Johnson, Samuel 4, 30

Kyd, Thomas
    Spanish Tragedy 99–101, 102, 112–13

law
    anti-female 30–31
    human construct 141
    misapplied to women 174
    peasant contempt for 223, 228
    'sense of law' 27, 31
Lawrence, D. H. 218–19
    'kick at misery' 2

tragic issues in 218
Life is a Dream (Calderón) 196

Machiavel 99, 102–4, 108, 116, 122, 125,
    139, 142, 145, 146, 151, 152, 154
Machiavelli, Niccolò 102, 104, 105, 145
Marlowe, Christopher 104, 188
    blasphemy in 105, 109
    Doctor Faustus 108–12
    Jew of Malta 104–8, 111, 139, 145,
        188
    Tamburlaine 104, 108, 111
Miller, Arthur 224
    All My Sons 228–9
    Death of a Salesman 227
    immigration and tragedy 228, 230,
        231
    View from the Bridge 228, 230–33

Odyssey 10, 12
O'Neill, Eugene 224
    All God's Chillun 225
    Long Day's Journey 224, 226–7
    Mourning Becomes Electra 224–6

Plato 97, 98
Plutarch 157

Seneca 97–8, 202
Shakespeare, William 112, 173, 197, 233
    Coriolanus 120, 156–70
        archetypal plot 156–7, 162, 166
    Greek parallels in 113–14, 116, 118,
        120, 122, 124, 127–9, 130, 131–42,
        143, 144, 149, 155, 156, 162,
        166–7, 169–70
    Hamlet 3, 11, 59, 112–19, 120, 129,
        130, 132, 133, 136, 142, 143, 186
        not tragic 117
    King Lear 120, 130, 131–42, 144,
        151, 186
        antagonistic to Nature 138–9
        fathers and daughters in 134–5,
            137
        patriarchy in 131–4, 137, 140
        sexual recoil in 136

Shakespeare, William (cont'd)
  Macbeth 120, 130, 142–56
    infertility in 154
    hero as Machiavel 142–3, 145,
      151, 154
  Merchant of Venice 107
    monarchy in 103
    mothers in 117, 130, 132, 135,
      147–8, 157, 166–70
  Othello 120–31, 132, 143, 185
    women in 114, 125–6, 130–31, 143,
      154
    and sexuality 117–18, 121, 127,
      130, 135–7, 138
Socrates 54, 73, 77
Sophocles 10, 32–3
  antagonist of Aeschylus 33, 45, 46,
    48, 51–3
  Antigone 33, 36–40, 43, 45, 49, 190
  attitude to gods 32, 51–2
  Electra 10, 19, 33–6, 39, 45, 198,
    202, 209
  and Furies' world view 38–40, 48
  and incest 41–2, 46–7, 50
  Oedipus 3, 4, 40–47, 50, 118
  Oedipus at Colonus 47, 48–53, 133,
    137, 138, 143
  an 'unpersuaded Fury' 48
Steiner, George 217
Strindberg, August 4, 182–3, 227
  The Father 182–7
  Greek parallels 182–5
  'no woman born of man' 4, 186
  sex 'war' 183, 185–6
  Sir Bengt's Wife 182
Synge, J. M. 219, 228
  Aran Islands 223–4
  Riders to the Sea 222–4

tragedy
  archetypal plot 3–5, 12, 121, 156
  central conflicts of
    Apollo and Dionysus 2–3, 5, 93,
      118–19, 162, 198
    blood and law 31, 217
    family and state 32, 37, 157, 166,
      229, 232

reason and passion 3
and Christianity 101–3, 107, 110–11,
  130, 188, 203, 204, 212
collaboration with audience 1, 6, 218,
  233
death of, 217
depends on consciousness 93
historical moment for 5–6, 121, 173,
  196, 208, 217–18, 224, 225, 233,
  241
journey from blood bonds 30, 120
language of 232–3
lex talionis in 19, 22, 35
modern paganism in 188, 203, 226
monarchy in 103, 133
not ambivalent 2
'purely paternal heredity' in 24, 70
'Renaissance' deaths in 129
response to democracy 9–11, 98, 218
Revenge in 99–101, 112–14, 121, 151
transitory phenomenon 97, 217
tragic hero
  confronts maternal breast 20–21, 57,
    60, 166–7
  fears regression 42, 90, 92, 182, 186
  freestanding 5, 19–20, 142, 156
  honour of 17–18, 123, 128, 146,
    163–6, 174, 185, 198
  'male lunacy' of 14, 17–18, 22
  in political community 156–7, 162
tragic heroine
  attitude to law 174, 229
  'female idiocy' of 14–15, 17–18, 22,
    237
  as Fury 16, 68, 148, 182, 184, 199,
    209, 210, 211
  honour of 17, 169, 174, 181, 200,
    204, 208
tragic heroine (cont'd)
  and infanticide 65, 70–2, 93, 181,
    207, 208

West, Rebecca 14

Yeats, W. B. 219, 222, 223, 226, 233
  Cathleen ni Houlihan 221, 224

DATE DUE
